THE SHAKESPEARE HANDBOOK

THE
SHAKESPEARE
HANDBOOK

LEVI FOX

The Bodley Head
London

THE SHAKESPEARE
HANDBOOK

A MOBIUS
INTERNATIONAL BOOK

The Shakespeare Handbook was
conceived, designed, and edited
by Mobius International Ltd, 197
Queens Gate, London SW7 5EU

Copyright © 1987 Mobius
International Ltd, London

A CIP catalogue record
for this book is available
from the British Library

ISBN 0 370 31273 2 (hardback)
ISBN 0 370 31274 0 (paperback)

Published in the United States
in 1987 by G.K. Hall and Company
First published in
Great Britain in 1988

Printed in Italy for
The Bodley Head Ltd
32 Bedford Square
London WC1B 3EL
by Mondadori

CONTENTS

INTRODUCTION

I have often said that if, by some stroke of magic, William Shakespeare could come back next week he would be admitted instantly to any country of the world without a passport, though if he needed one, the endorsement of Stratford-upon-Avon would be sufficient. This assertion is based on my experience as Director of the Shakespeare Birthplace Trust, which has given me the opportunity of witnessing at first hand evidence of the unique appreciation and appeal of William Shakespeare, poet and playwright of Stratford.

There is no other writer, poet, dramatist, scholar, artist, or man of the theater who enjoys such universal veneration and popularity. Admiration for Shakespeare unites all peoples, irrespective of language, politics, or religion. There is not a single civilized nation that does not read, translate, study, perform, and enjoy the plays of Shakespeare. Right from the beginning, his achievement, both as poet and dramatist, has been recognized as having something prodigious about it, something which, in its general acceptability and in its universal appeal, has set him apart, the greatest genius of the English-speaking world.

It is therefore not surprising that the output of published papers and books dealing with every conceivable aspect of Shakespearean subject matter is formidable, and that the student, not to mention the interested layman, finds the problem of selection very difficult. *The Shakespeare Handbook* has been specifically planned to assist in this situation, by providing within the covers of one book a convenient companion reference source for students, librarians, and Shakespeare enthusiasts in general.

The team of author contributors is impressive. Some are distinguished scholars with international reputations, while others, younger and not yet so well known, have produced work which in their presentation of facts and interpretation promises to equal the quality of that of their senior colleagues. It is not easy to achieve a unity of theme and treatment in a compendium of this kind, but in my opinion *The Shakespeare Handbook* succeeds admirably in doing so.

The scope of the treatment is comprehensive. Against the background of the Elizabethan world and the Stratford-upon-Avon and London which provided the setting for Shakespeare's life and work, there follows a detailed examination of the Elizabethan and Jacobean theater and of the plays for which Shakespeare was responsible. The treatment is centered around the sources and the traditional groupings, not forgetting the text itself. Shakespeare himself was pre-eminently a man of the theater, so not the least valuable part of the *Handbook* deals with Shakespeare in performance, music and song, as well as Shakespeare on film. It follows that this is an extremely handy book for the playgoer to have around.

Illustrations always add attraction and usefulness to a companion volume of this kind. These form a special feature of it, not to mention the detailed index.

The Shakespeare Center,
Stratford-upon-Avon

LEVI FOX

CHRONOLOGY

1564 William Shakespeare born. Christopher Marlowe born. Plague rife in the summer months. John Hawkins began second voyage to the New World.

1565 Mary Queen of Scots married Henry Stuart, Lord Darnley. John Hawkins introduced sweet potatoes and tobacco to England. *Gorboduc* published.

1566 John Shakespeare became an alderman. Gilbert Shakespeare born. Edward Alleyn, Robert Devereaux (Earl of Essex), and the future King James I born. David Rizzio murdered.

1567 Thomas Campion, Thomas Nashe and Richard Burbage born. Lord Darnley murdered. Mary Stuart married the Earl of Bothwell and was forced to abdicate from the throne of Scotland. John Hawkins and Francis Drake sailed to the West Indies.

1568 John Shakespeare appointed bailiff. Mary Queen of Scots took refuge in England. Bishop's Bible published.

1569 Joan Shakespeare born. The Queen's Interluders visited Stratford.

1570 Thomas Middleton born.

1571 Anne Shakespeare born. John Shakespeare appointed Chief Alderman. Warrant issued for the arrest of John Shakespeare for the nonpayment of £30 debt.

1572 St Bartholomew's Day massacre. Thomas Dekker, Ben Jonson, and John Donne born. Francis Drake attacked Spanish harbors in America.

1573 Thomas Heywood and Inigo Jones born.

1574 Richard Shakespeare born. Elizabeth I granted license to Leicester's Men. Burbage obtained license to open a London theater.

1575 John Shakespeare bought two houses in Henley Street. John Marston and Cyril Tourneur born. Queen Elizabeth I visited Kenilworth on a royal progress.

1576 John Shakespeare applied for grant of coat-of-arms. The Theatre and The Curtain built.

1577 John Shakespeare ceased to attend Council meetings. First edition of Holinshed's *Chronicles* published. Francis Drake began circumnavigation in the 'Golden Hind'.

1578 John Shakespeare mortgaged the Arden property at Wilmcote, sold his wife's inherited share of the Snitterfield estate, and was excused the levy for poor relief. Mary Fitton born. James VI became King of Scotland. *Euphues* published.

1579 Anne Shakespeare died. John Fletcher born. Francis Drake annexed New Albion, California. *School of Abuse*, and *The Shephearde's Calendar* published.

1580 John Shakespeare fined £40 for failing to appear before the Queen's Bench. Edmund Shakespeare born. John Webster born. Francis Drake returned from circumnavigation. Earthquake in London recorded.

1581 Francis Drake knighted.

1582 William Shakespeare married Anne Hathaway. *Divers Voyages Touching the Discovery of America* published.

1583 Susanna Shakespeare born. Philip Massinger born. Queen's Men established. *Anatomy of Abuses* published.

1584 Francis Beaumont born. Walter Raleigh annexed Virginia and was knighted.

1585 Hamnet and Judith Shakespeare born. Expeditionary force sent to the Netherlands.

1586 John Ford born. Sir Philip Sydney died.

1587 Mary Queen of Scots executed. Thomas Nashe born. The Rose built. Second edition of Holinshed's *Chronicles* published. *The Tragical History of Romeus and Juliet* reprinted. First performance (?) *Tamburlaine* (1).

1588 Robert Armin and Richard Tarlton born. Robert Dudley, Earl of Leicester died. Spanish Armada defeated. First performance (?) *Tamburlaine* (2) and *Dr Faustus*.

1589 Duc de Guise and Henri III murdered. Civil war in France. James VI of Scotland married Anne of Denmark. First performance (?) *The Spanish Tragedy*, *The Jew of Malta*, and *Friar Bacon*.

1590 *The Faerie Queene* (1-3), and *Rosalynde: Euphues Golden Legacy* published.

1591 Robert Herrick and Christopher Wren born. *Astrophel and Stella* published. First performance (?) *Orlando Furioso*.

1592 John Shakespeare listed as recusant. Robert Greene died. Edward Alleyn married Joan Woodward, Philip Henslowe's step-daughter. *Groatsworth of Wit* and *Kind-Harts Dreame* published. Philip Henslowe began his diary; on 3 March, he recorded a performance of *Harey the vj* by Strange's Men. First performance (?) *Ed-*

ward II, *King Henry VI* (1, 2 and 3), *King Richard III*, and *Titus Andronicus*. Theaters intermittently closed because of the plague from June onward.

1593 Christopher Marlowe killed. George Herbert born. Plague closed the theaters (11,000 deaths). *Venus and Adonis* published. First performance (?) *The Massacre at Paris*, *The Taming of the Shrew*, *The Comedy of Errors*, *Two Gentlemen of Verona*, and *Love's Labour's Lost*.

1594 Thomas Kyd died. The theaters reopened in May. *The Rape of Lucrece* published. First performance (?) *Romeo and Juliet*. *King Leir* registered. Performances of *Titus Andronicus* and *The Taming of the Shrew* recorded by Philip Henslowe at Newington Butts (5 and 12 June). *The Comedy of Errors* performed at Gray's Inn (28 December).

1595 William Shakespeare mentioned among players paid £20 in total for plays presented before the Queen. The Swan built. *Defence of Poesie* published. First performance (?) *A Midsummer Night's Dream*, and *King Richard II*.

1596 Hamnet Shakespeare died. William Shakespeare granted arms. Writ of attach-

ment issued to Sheriff of Surrey to enforce William Shakespeare and three others to keep the peace. Blackfriars Theater opened. Sir Francis Drake and George Peele died. Calais captured by the Spaniards. *The Faerie Queene* (4-6) published. First performance (?) *King John* and *The Merchant of Venice*.

1597 William Shakespeare bought New Place, two cottages and two barns in Stratford. The tax collector of St Helen's, Bishopsgate reported nonpayment of five shillings tax by William Shakespeare. A Privy Council order limited London companies. Bacon's *Essays* and James VI's *Daemonologie* published. First performance (?) *The Isle of Dogs* and *King Henry IV* (1).

1598 William Shakespeare listed as tax defaulter. Irish rebellion. Lord Burghley and Philip II of Spain died. Elizabeth I boxed the Earl of Essex's ears. The Theatre demolished and the Globe built. First performance (?) *Every Man in his Humour*, *King Henry IV* (2), and *Much Ado About Nothing*.

1599 William Shakespeare named as shareholder in the land for the Globe, and recorded as owing taxes. Edmund Spenser died. Invasion scare. Earl of Essex disgraced after failure of Irish campaign. The Fortune built. *The Passionate Pilgrim* published by William Jaggard. First performance (?) *The Shoemaker's Holiday*, *Every Man Out of his Humour*, *Sir John Oldcastle* (1), *Histriomastix*, *King Henry V*, *As You Like It*, and *Julius Cæsar*.

1600 William Shakespeare recorded as owing 13 shillings and fourpence tax in Sussex. The future King Charles I born. First performance (?) *The Merry Wives of Windsor* and *Troilus and Cressida*.

1601 John Shakespeare died. Thomas Nashe died. The Earl of Essex executed following rebellion. The Earl of Southampton tried and reprieved. Spanish expedition landed in Ireland. *The Phœnix and the Turtle* published. First performance (?) *Cynthia's Revels, The Poetaster, Satiromastix, What You Will*, and *Hamlet*.

1602 William Shakespeare bought 107 acres of farmland in Old Stratford and a cottage in Chapel Lane. Tyrone defeated in Ireland. Spaniards surrendered. First performance (?) *Gentleman Usher, Sir Thomas Wyatt*, and *Twelfth Night*.

1603 Last record of William Shakespeare's acting in public theater (*Sejanus*). Queen Elizabeth I died. Accession of James I. Sir Walter Raleigh imprisoned in the Tower. The Chamberlain's Men became the King's Men. Severe plague (30,000 deaths) closed theaters from March. Philip Henslowe ended his diary. *A Midsummer Night's Dream* performed at Hampton Court (1 January). First performance (?) *A Woman Killed with Kindness, Hoffman*, and *Sejanus*.

1604 William Shakespeare mentioned in the accounts of the Master of the Great Wardrobe as appearing at the coronation of King James I with the King's Men. The Earl of Oxford died. *Counterblast to Tobacco* published. The theaters reopened in the spring. *Othello* performed at Whitehall (1

November). *The Merry Wives of Windsor* (4 November) and *Measure for Measure* (26 December) performed at Court. First performance (?) *The Dutch Courtesan, All Fools, The Malcontent, The Honest Whore* (1 and 2), *Westward Hoe, All's Well that Ends Well, Measure for Measure*, and *Othello*.

1605 William Shakespeare left 30 shillings in gold by Augustine Phillips, fellow actor and musician. Gunpowder plot. The Red Bull built. *Advancement of Learning* published. *Love's Labour's Lost* (January), *King Henry V* (7 January), and *The Merchant of Venice* (10 and 12 February) performed at Court. First performance (?) *Eastward Hoe, Northward Hoe, If You Know Not Me, You Know Nobody*, and *Trick to Catch the Old One*.

1606 Susanna Shakespeare listed as recusant. William Davenant born. John Lyly died. *King Lear* (5 May) performed at Whitehall. First performance (?) *Sophonisba, Volpone, Rape of Lucrece* (Thomas Heywood), *The Woman Hater, Macbeth*, and *King Lear*.

1607 Edmund Shakespeare died. Susanna Shakespeare married John Hall. Virginia colonized. *Hamlet* performed on the 'Dragon' in Sierra Leone. First performance (?) *Knight of the Burning Pestle, Humour Out of Breath, Antony and Cleopatra, Coriolanus*, and *Timon of Athens*.

1608 Elizabeth Hall born. Mary Arden Shakespeare died. John Milton born. Children at Blackfriars Theater disbanded. King's Men took over the private theater at Blackfriars. First performance (?) *Philaster,*

The Maid's Tragedy, and *Pericles*.

1609 Plague (4,000 died) intermittently closed the theaters. Truce in the Netherlands. *Sonnets published*. First performance (?) *Epicoene* and *Bonduca*.

1610 First performance (?) *The Alchemist* and *Cymbeline*.

1611 Authorized version of the Bible published. First performance (?) *Catiline, Amends for Ladies, The Woman's Prize or The Tamer Tamed, The Winter's Tale*, and *The Tempest*.

1612 Gilbert Shakespeare died. *Apology for Actors* published. First performance (?) *The White Devil*.

1613 Richard Shakespeare died. Susanna Hall sued John Lane for defamation. William Shakespeare bought the Blackfriars Gatehouse. The Globe burnt. The Hope built. Princess Elizabeth married Frederick V of Bohemia (20 performances of the King's Men during the celebrations). First performance (?) *The Duchess of Malfi, The Two Noble Kinsmen*, and *King Henry VIII*.

1614 First performance *Bartholomew Fair*.

1615 William Shakespeare involved in a law suit with Matthew Bacon concerning Blackfriars property.

1616 Judith Shakespeare married Thomas Quiney, and both were excommunicated. Francis Beaumont and Philip Henslowe died. William Shakespeare signed his will 25 March. He died and was buried on 25 April.

CHAPTER 1

THE ELIZABETHAN WORLD

Traveling times in Shakespeare's England were much greater than today, emphasizing the dominance of local society and the regional distinctions in the country.

The danger in asking what England was like when William Shakespeare was alive, is its apparent familiarity: its towns (Stratford-upon-Avon, London, Canterbury, York, Norwich); its countryside; its institutions (parliament, the Church of England, the monarchy); its society (Queen, lords, knights, gentlemen and the rest); above all its language – on the page and on the stage we hear the voices of Shakespearean England. Or, rather, we think we hear them, just as we imagine that we know its towns and countryside, or we assume that we can recognize its structures and its society. We hear, we imagine, we assume, and again and again we find ourselves misled.

The England of Shakespeare's day was many times larger than it is now. Perhaps this is a quixotic way of putting it, but it does jolt us with the reality of what traveling times then meant. In the late 16th century, a good pace for a single horseman was 40 miles a day.

We can see a more usual pace by examining the route from Stratford-upon-Avon to London which Shakespeare must have taken many times. Stratford is some 95 miles from the capital. An early start would have enabled the dramatist to spend his first night in Oxford, followed by a second at, say, Uxbridge in Middlesex, so allowing him to reach the theater on London's Bankside, mid-morning the following day. When Shakespeare traveled with a theatrical company, probably on foot and laden with the costumes and props, 12 miles would be a good day's journey.

*When carefull man hath carked all the yeare
And sees how god hath prospered his encrease
He kills his swyne And minds to make good cheare
To passe the tyme while winters rage doth cease*

December
Capricornus

Farming dominated the community and was the occupation of the majority of people.

The much greater impact of the distances Shakespeare was familiar with introduces us to the first important point which we need to notice about the England of his day – the country was very diverse. This was true of the people; the distances and the difficulty of communication meant that there were marked regional distinctions – in dialect, customs, social structure, and wealth. Of course, historians today can see that there were signs in the country of a move toward greater integration, but there was a long way to go and the pull of local society was still dominant.

REGIONAL VARIATION

The self-contained nature of English regional societies was reinforced by the absence of a national economy. Trade which was centralized on London, such as cloth export or the supply of food to the City itself, was still the exception. A steady growth of internal trade was taking place, but this was on the basis of an increasing interchange between specialized regions whose individual economy reflected factors such as the nature of the soil, geographical location, and not least the prevailing climate. Trade expressed diversity, not unity.

HIGHLAND AND LOWLAND POPULATIONS

Over and above these regional variations, there was the major division in the country between the highland zone – roughly the north and west of England, which was predominantly a pastoral area – and the lowlands of the south and east which practised mixed farming. Once again the division can be seen in social terms, for there was more than merely distance and altitude between the upland shepherd and the living-in farm servant in an open field village of the lowlands. It was also a matter of relative wealth. A county in the southeast, such as Kent, was expected and able to pay ten times the tax per acre of upland Derbyshire, for example.

The highland/lowland division was reflected also in the distribution of the population. The highest density of settlement – 100 people per square mile or more – was found in central and east Somerset, south Devon, Middlesex, and the area around Norwich, and 50 to 100 was usual in the southwest, East Anglia, and the east Midlands as a whole. In the highland zone, by contrast, 50 was a maximum, and the greater part was at or below 20 per square mile. The towns were equally unfairly shared between north and west and the south and east. As late as 1669, when Shakespeare's granddaughter wrote her will, out of the ten leading towns, only two were in the north.

'Towns' is, perhaps, a misnomer; only London, which by 1600 had perhaps 200,000 inhabitants, was much of an urban community, either by our reckoning or by contemporary European standards. Perhaps a dozen other places reached 10,000; the rest in our terms were villages. That description would include many of the important county centers which were focuses for local government, and 'village' would still be true even where, as many such towns did, they also accommodated a cathedral and a diocesan administration. Shakespeare's county town, Warwick, had a population of under 2,000; Worcester, also a county town and the cathedral center where he had to make his marriage arrangements, had about 5,000, while Stratford itself was a mere 1,200 or so.

THE ELIZABETHAN ECONOMY

Much diversity, therefore, but two developments affected the whole of the English economy over the century, and especially during Elizabeth I's reign: a rise in population and a surge in prices. The first was certainly one of the key experiences of the English people of Shakespeare's generation. When he was born the country's population was of the order of 3.1 million. Already that was a third greater than when his father had been born, even though a few years before William's birth a series of disasters had, as we shall see, killed one in 20 of the population. Shakespeare, indeed, was one of a renewed boom in babies, and this boom continued for the rest of his life, by which time the English nation had grown by a further 50 per cent.

POVERTY

The consequence of all this was poverty. Poverty had been endemic in medieval times, of course, but much of it had been seasonal, rural, and settled. In the 16th century another sort of poverty became dominant – chronic and mobile, with the search for work leading to the appearance of a serious problem of vagrancy. A minority of 'sturdy beggars' gave the migrants a bad name by cheating or threatening respectable folk (and in so doing gave rise to an early fashion for 'crime' literature). These were reinforced from time to time by discharged soldiers and sailors desperate for support. Understandably, therefore, the laws against vagrancy were severe, something which traveling actors escaped only by being licensed by a prominent nobleman.

The evidence suggests that the mobile poor would have done better to stay at home where communal feeling would at least have guaranteed bare subsistence. But how bare that could be, Shakespeare himself knew from close acquaintance. In the Forest of Arden in the last years of his life, conditions were so bad that in 1613-14 the children of the poor began to die in dozens; in 1615 and 1616 many women ceased to ovulate and when they began to conceive again in 1617-19, they all too often miscarried.

So it is no surprise that people chose to move in search of work or charity or both. The best opportunity of either seemed to be London, where industrial expansion and new building promised jobs, and where the scale of poverty had led the authorities to set up a sophisticated system of relief. The poor therefore crowded into the slums of both the eastern and the western suburbs to fight a losing battle against disease.

INFLATION

Poverty was made worse by inflation, decisively worse. To observers of 20th-century increases, this may seem an exaggerated way to describe a price rise of only

The wool trade was profoundly important in 16th-century England, and Cotswold sheep were the best in the country.

95 per cent over the 44 years of Elizabeth's reign. Yet that increase followed a period of static or declining values; it was neither steady nor uniform, and there was almost nothing that any government could do to soften the harsh impact of economic reality. Above all the phenomenon was appreciated by only a few experts; popular explanations were in terms of the sin of greed.

One factor outside government control was the gentle but relentless pressure on prices of the rise in population we have already observed. This was not there at the start of the reign because a famine in 1555-57, followed by an influenza epidemic in 1557-59, produced an actual reduction in the nation's numbers – the last time this was ever to occur. It took a decade or longer before more mouths began to put up prices again, but then the rise was a sudden 20 per cent as other factors came into play as well – the collapse of silver in the European trade system (of which England was a part) under the influence of imports from South America, and the capture of bullion from the Spaniards directly, culminating in Drake's return to England in 1580 with upward of half-a-million in treasure on board the 'Golden Hind'.

Through all these years Elizabeth was fortunate in having to face very few poor harvests – unlike the 1550s when the crops failed four times in seven years – but in the 1590s four bad seasons in a row and the demands of the war against Philip of Spain, fought in Ireland, France, the Low Countries, and on the high seas, forced prices to catastrophic heights. By 1597 the pound would buy only one half the food it had bought in 1590, and in isolated regions, people died of starvation.

FINANCIAL OPPORTUNITY

Inflation, on the other hand, is never uniformly disastrous, and against the picture of grinding misery for some must be set opportunity for others. The burgeoning of the Elizabethan theater is a case in point. More theaters vied for custom in Shakespeare's London than in today's city 20 times larger – with space for audiences of up to 3,000 in some houses. The key factor was the spending power of the metropolis. A minimum admission charge of only one penny (when a common laborer in London

For some, inflation offered opportunity. By the end of Elizabeth's reign, all but the poorest were more richly dressed and lived in better furnished houses than they had at the beginning.

WILL SHAKESPERE GENT.

Social mobility was, of course, totally at variance with the official view of Elizabethan society. This envisaged society as a hierarchy, with a place for everyone, and everyone staying in that place. It emphasized birth and lineage, coats-of-arms, forms of dress and behavior appropriate to rank, and the way in which all this reflected the greater order built into the universe by God. But for a price, a pedigree could be invented, a coat-of-arms granted, and dress and behavior would do the rest. As it was said, 'who can live idly and without manual labor, and will bear the port, charge and countenance of a gentlemen, he shall be called master and taken for a gentleman'. Of all this the copybook example is again William Shakespeare, with his new coat-of-arms, his style of 'gentleman' and the

deference of the Stratford townsfolk to 'Master Shakespeare'.

then earned perhaps ninepence a day) meant that there was money in entertainment. And it was Shakespeare who made it. His entrepreneurial flair led him to profit from every level of theatrical activity. He was the resident playwright of the Lord Chamberlain's Men; he acted with the company; he was a 'housekeeper', that is a shareholder earning a dividend on performing profits; finally, he invested in theatrical property, putting up 10 per cent of the capital to build the Globe, followed by 14 per cent to purchase the lease of the Blackfriars theater.

Unlike the long-lost playhouses, plenty of building survives today to show that Shakespeare was not alone in his increasing wealth. The day was almost over of the great feudal magnate with his retinue of gentleman servants; Lear's daughters were right to see their father's social ideas as anachronistic. Now the peers led a homogeneous élite and one which was in general doing very well. The evidence is not only in great mansions like Longleat or Burghley (which survive from those created by Elizabeth's courtiers), but in numerous substantial manor houses in almost every county in the land. The number of gentry was rising, perhaps half as fast again as the rest of the population. They were biologically more successful than the lower orders and they were recruiting from below.

GOODS AND CHATTELS

Yet it was not only the élite of Elizabethan England who were prospering. The yeomen, wealthy peasants, and prosperous townsmen were equally able to provide themselves with larger, lighter, and warmer houses. And everywhere homes were more comfortably furnished. Traditionally there were plenty of fabrics even in a modest English house: sheets, blankets, and cloth woven by the family. Now tapestry and carpets are found, and an upsurge in embroidery which was henceforth devoted to secular instead of ecclesiastical purposes. Tableware improved, again at all social levels, with better glazed earthenware and pewter, or with glass and silver for the well-to-do. Furniture advanced in quantity, in quality, and in elaboration. Clothing for the rich was enhanced by finer and lighter cloths introduced by refugees from religious persecution in Flanders, while to judge by the complaints of moralists (and by surviving fragments), the dress of all but the poorest improved too. England in 1603 was far wealthier than in 1558.

SEE ALSO: Ch 1 14-5, Ch 2 28-30, 37, 47, 48, 50-2, Ch 3 56-7, 64-5, 70-2, 80

RELIGION

Population growth and inflation, poverty and rising standards, these helped to shape the Elizabethan world. Other experiences were equally or more formative. It was under Elizabeth that individual conviction began to matter on a large scale. Prior to the Reformation, religious truth had been on a par with the sunrise and the sunset — objectively true. Individuals would vary in the seriousness of their personal response, anticlericalism might flourish, and there perhaps was a good deal of scepticism about the pious details – Chaucer's Wife of Bath certainly read St Paul's epistles in a highly personal manner!

> For hadde God comanded maydenhede,
> Than hadde he dampned weddyng with the
> dede.
> And certes, if ther were no seed ysowe,
> Virginitee, than wherof sholde it growe?
> Poul dorste nat comanden, atte leeste,
> A thyng of which his maister yaf noon
> heeste.

Yet all this was within a factual acceptance of existing religion which never entertained the possibility of an alternative. Only heretics believed differently — and they were deluded by the Devil!

The Reformation, however, raised the possibility that there *were* alternatives, and by so doing it smashed for ever the mold of ideological unity. Men now had to choose between one belief and another, and from that moment they became divided into the ideologically acceptable and the outsiders. Under Henry VIII this had been realized only by a few of the most perceptive; even in the more radical religious changes under Edward VI, Englishmen were still expected to attend the same parish church and hear the same priest that they had always done. It was Mary's Catholic restoration which ended this passivity, and when in 1559 Elizabeth set out to reassert through parliament the supremacy of the crown over the English church, the higher clergy and an important minority of laymen resisted, first in the House of Lords and after defeat there, in the security of their own homes. For the first time there was within the English community a significant group which was alienated from the majority on ideological grounds. Pluralism had entered English life.

PROTESTANT PLURALISM
Pluralism emerged also in the Protestant camp. In 1559, convinced Protestants were agreed that the church settlement of that year which married reformed doctrine to a traditional system of church government and liturgy could only be an interim. They were mistaken, and eventually a small minority, principally clerics with strong links with Calvinist churches abroad, began a vociferous campaign for alternative presbyterian forms of government and worship or, what was more shocking to an age which believed in 'one church – one state', spread notions of a 'gathered church' of true believers alone, separated entirely from the (to them) corrupt Church of England. Historians are wrong to assume that these were what contemporaries principally meant by the term 'puritan', and they were never more than a small pressure group. Yet their noise made it worth Shakespeare creating the character of Malvolio in *Twelfth Night*, and was a considerable nuisance to a state determined to preserve the 1559 church settlement. Eventually there were prisoners and martyrs on the Protestant as well as the Catholic side. There were 'outsiders' now at both extremes of English religious opinion.

CATHOLICISM
This is not, of course, to deny that for much of Elizabeth's reign the country was above all confused about religion. General adoption of the 1559 Prayer Book certainly did not mean enthusiasm, a reaction one could hardly expect for the fifth major ecclesiastical change in ten years. It took a decade for even the most convinced Catholics to realize that their faith was now incompatible with attendance at the parish church where they and generations of their forefathers had always worshipped.

Next, as it became increasingly difficult for Catholics to believe that the religious tide would soon turn again in their favor – 'waiting for a day' they had called it – they were faced with a revolutionary requirement to establish as a minority sect what for centuries had been the public faith of the whole nation. Clergy surviving from the reign of Mary managed to keep Catholicism alive, but not until a new generation of priests could be produced in seminaries set up abroad did it have a future.

The first of these younger reinforcements arrived in England in 1574, but they have always suffered by comparison with a small number of Jesuit missionaries who arrived later. These came with a quite different vision – of a great campaign to return England to the Catholic faith and allegiance to the Pope in Rome – and it met with little welcome among the recusant community. After all, the main effect of the Jesuit challenge was to call down upon Catholics the full weight of religious discrimination and bloody persecution: the only possible response the state could make to men who were attempting to persuade Englishmen who recognized Elizabeth as head of the church, to accept the Pope's authority instead. Catholic life survived because, unlike the Jesuits, seminary priests were prepared to adhere to the discretion desired by gentry families, wealthy and prominent enough to protect them and to defy (in decent secrecy) the royal proscription of Catholic rites.

A NATION OF PROTESTANTS

As the years passed, however, the Elizabethan religious settlement gradually began to inspire loyalty and support. The explicit Calvinism of its principal doctrines and its most influential clergy was seen to put the country within the security of the main European Protestant camp. There was widespread support for its dominant ethos which was in the correct sense 'puritan', that is concerned for a greater purity, ideally in church ritual but far more important, in the spiritual and moral character of the nation. Even the survival in the Anglican church of traditional forms of government and liturgy was increasingly seen to have advantages, supporting the forces of continuity and stability in national life. What was more, the authority of the laity over the church, through parliament and through a substantial control of church appointments, kept

the clergy in the subordinate place which most Englishmen thought was proper. More and more the English changed from being 'a Protestant nation' because of parliamentary enactment, to 'a nation of Protestants' by choice.

SEE ALSO: Ch 1 13-5, 16, Ch 2 37-8, 43, Ch 3 63, 68-9

The title page of a catechism by Alexander Nowell (1573), a Dean of St Paul's, London, written for boys beginning to study Latin (providing both religion and grammar). It shows an Elizabethan schoolroom.

THE INTERNATIONAL SCENE

Ideological pluralism and an established Erastian church remain living realities in 20th-century England; the same is true of the consequences of another central experience of Shakespeare and his contemporaries – overseas expansion. Early European colonization had seen the English to the fore, but this had not continued. Only in 1551, with the decline of their traditional market at Antwerp, did English merchants and seamen seriously turn their minds elsewhere. Under Elizabeth this produced a flowering of enterprise and imagination which united the great of the land with the financial expertise of the City of London and the pig-headed obstinacy of English seamen to create a legend.

What it is salutary to remember is the amount that the legend of Elizabethan seafaring owes first to clever publicity (supremely Richard Hakluyt's *Principall navigations, voiages and discoveries of the English nation*, whose work inspired Shakespeare's *The Tempest*), then to the innate glamor of adventure, and finally to the self-image of Englishmen as all seadogs at heart. The reality was different. When Elizabeth died, England possessed not one foot of land in either the New World or the East. Even when Shakespeare died, the English had only a toehold in Virginia and it was to be four more years before the shaky start of the New England colony.

It was not, then, the practical results of Elizabethan overseas exploration which mattered – except in so far, and the point is a serious one, that it was an outlet for the unemployed, and especially for the more unruly. What did matter was the impact of the knowledge of the wider world which the expeditions brought back. Naturally, we must not exaggerate.

But granted that there was for the Elizabethans at large no immediate 'culture-shock', there can be no doubt that the educated came to realize for the first time how different the world outside Europe was:

LITERATURE AND THE WIDER WORLD

Awareness of the wider world began to influence literature. Maria in *Twelfth Night* alludes to the novel map projection of Gerardus Mercator, given popular currency in the enlarged 1599 edition of Hakluyt. *He does smile his face into more lines than is in the new map with the augmentation of the Indies.* (*Twelfth Night* III ii 75).

Some poets and writers actually went on expeditions – George Turbeville, Thomas Lodge, John Donne – while Walter Raleigh was a principal entrepreneur of colonies and exploration. It was two members of a Raleigh expedition of 1585-86 who perhaps demonstrate the impact of the New World at its most intense. Thomas Hariot, a brilliant mathematician, wrote the enthusiastic and perceptive *Briefe and true report of the new found land of Virginia* (1588), while John White produced maps and exquisite watercolors of American fauna and flora, and 21 illustrations of Indian ways and people which still vibrate with life after 400 years.

Philip II of Spain responded to Elizabeth's support for Dutch resistance by attacking England in 1588, but his massive Armada was defeated.

still seen as inferior, but new in kind, in a way that would one day raise questions which would not go away.

One distraction from the New World was privateering and piracy. In unsettled times men were looking, not for strange sights or long-term investments, but for a profitable alternative to peace-time trade. Commerce-raiding, which brought in between £100,000 and £200,000 a year, meant that English efforts were concentrated on the shipping lanes of the European coastline and not on the New World.

FOREIGN POWERS

The experience of foreign danger was, in one way, the *leitmotif* of Elizabeth's whole reign. Her title to the throne was suspect in Europe, but neither Spain (whose dominions also included the Low Countries) nor France was in a position to object in 1558 since each was bankrupt. Nor, in view of their mutual antipathy, was it safe for either to do so because England, though militarily weak, was a potential threat to both. Thus although Spanish control of England would complete a Habsburg encirclement of France, any such possibility would bring France to England's immediate aid. In the same way, any French threats would have provoked an Anglo-Spanish alliance.

Elizabeth's answer to the foreign menace was diplomacy. The strongest card which she had to play was her marriage, and initially the Queen seemed fully to expect that she would marry; as for her subjects, they were totally convinced that she must do so, and quickly, to give England a king and an heir to make it safe. Elizabeth's options were, however, severely limited. The recent example of her sister ruled out for the time being any foreign prince, while marriage to Robert Dudley, later Earl of Leicester, the Englishman Elizabeth found most attractive, would never have been acceptable to the rest of aristocracy.

However, Elizabeth's instinctive feeling

that now was not the time to marry, gradually became a suspicion that marriage itself might not be desirable or necessary. Should she not gamble on her own survival, keep rivals quietly hopeful by not producing a child of her own and at the same time gain the maximum diplomatic advantage from the possibility that she *might* marry?

ENGLAND AND SPAIN

In the end it was the problem of the Low Countries which brought the war Elizabeth had striven so long to avoid. Any strengthening of Spanish power there threatened both England and France. Elizabeth was forced to respond herself to the success of the Duke of Parma, Philip's governor in the Low Countries. Limited though the English effort had to be, it was sufficient to block Parma. If Spain was to assert its control over the Netherlands, England had to be conquered first.

Early in 1587 the English became convinced that an Armada was being prepared. Mary Queen of Scots (of no further value as a hostage) was executed to remove a focus for Catholic treachery, and a preemptive strike – 'the singeing of the king of Spain's beard' – delayed invasion for a year. When the Armada did come in 1588 the English, Catholic and Protestant alike, supported Elizabeth to a man, and the navy and its auxiliaries was strong enough to deny Philip success.

However, 1588 was not the end of the danger. Invasion scares continued, and in 1601 the Spaniards succeeded in putting 4,000 men ashore in Ireland. Gradually, too, the economic dangers of war became clear. The Queen sold land, raised taxes, and in order to equip troops and to supply ships, the counties had to levy as much again on the rates. Economics alone made nonsense of the hawks who wished to carry war to Spain itself, to say nothing of the organizational immaturity which made such ideas quite unrealistic.

SEE ALSO: Ch 2 40, 57, 60, Ch 4 88, 134-5

MARY QUEEN OF SCOTS

The strategic dilemma of the great powers certainly helped in the immediate dangers following Elizabeth's accession, when the Dauphin's wife (and from 1559 Queen of France) was her Catholic cousin and rival claimant to the English crown, Mary the Queen of Scotland. Confident that Spain had to stay neutral and aided by growing religious dissension in France, Elizabeth was able to force the French out of Scotland without a continental war. When in 1561 the widowed, but still pro-French Mary returned to her northern kingdom, neither great power showed much inclination to support her English title, and certainly not when Mary was forced to abdicate in favor of her infant son, James, and in 1568 take refuge in England, where she spent the rest of her life in protective custody. There she was a constant focus and instigator of Catholic plots against Elizabeth, but she was also a hostage, tying the hands of Philip II.

For Protestant Englishmen, nevertheless, the Queen of Scots and her scheming became the symbol of all they feared. After the reign of Mary I, whose marriage to Philip II had made England a Spanish satellite and caused her to lose Calais, Elizabeth had appeared the last salvation from foreigners. Now as plot followed rumor and rumor followed plot, as popish priests smuggled in their treason, as abroad Catholicism seemed everywhere on the march, English xenophobia became fixed in a violent hostility to Spain and Catholicism.

THE POWER OF THE MONARCH

For Englishmen to be in a position and a mood to fantasize about a victory over Spain, the superpower of the day, was a measure of the success Elizabeth had achieved by the end of her reign. Certainly at its start in 1558, few could have expected either the young Queen, or English independence to survive, still less that by 1603 England would be poised to go ahead over the next 100 years to become a world power. To have kept out invaders, escaped religious war, and avoided bankruptcy, civil commotion, social unrest, and economic collapse was a record unique in Europe. How was it achieved?

Part of the answer is the innate strength of the Tudor crown. It is easy to stress continental doubts about Elizabeth's right to rule. What must equally be stressed is that the English respect for the rights to property, which had in 1553 foiled the plans of the Duke of Northumberland to keep Mary I from the throne, guaranteed in 1558 overwhelming support for the rights of her sister. Similarly, it is easy to stress that the troubles of recent reigns had left the legacy of monetary, social, religious, and international problems we have already noticed, and forget the other side. The significance of the crisis period between 1540 and 1558 is that the work of Henry VII and Henry VIII and his great ministers, Wolsey and Cromwell, had stood up to challenge. There was no administrative breakdown, no civil war, and the enhanced prestige of the crown was never at risk.

CONSENSUS

Systems, however, are no stronger than the individuals who run them, and Elizabeth herself made a quite vital contribution to the survival and successes of Elizabethan England. Royal power in England was still highly personal. It is a situation which Shakespeare shows us time and again on stage, supremely, perhaps, in *King Lear* and

Elizabeth ruled as well as reigned, and one of her main achievements was to express a consensus which united the great mass of the political nation.

in *The Winter's Tale*. Decision-making and responsibility belonged to the monarch immediately. Admittedly, like Lear and Leontes, the Queen could on occasion be impossible to work with; she made mistakes; she could be ruled by prejudice; she was temperamentally averse to taking decisions. Yet Elizabeth was in charge; as she said, there was one mistress and no master in England. And it was to her credit that she had selected such a remarkable team of able and energetic servants.

Responsibility within and for the state was, thus, more personal to Elizabeth and more absolute than is often realized. Her power, however, was limited by political realities, as power must always be. With the royal income inadequate to finance either an efficient staff of administrators or the military force to compel obedience, effective authority arose within the social hierarchy – from the dependence of tenants on landlords and the deference of the many to the great and wealthy few. For example, although the crown might nominate justices of the peace, if those appointed did not already enjoy a recognized local authority

ELIZABETH AND PARLIAMENT

Consensus lay at the heart of the Elizabethan parliament: Queen, Lords and Commons united to seek a common mind and the common good. The famous squabbles of crown and parliament are often examples of this very agreement, with parliament going beyond the accepted limits of behavior on, for example, the need for the Queen to marry, in order to ensure that the common good as they saw it *was* taken notice of. As for the remaining disputes, these arose from attempts by zealots to advance their own religious emphases. For example, Peter Wentworth's famous plea in 1576 for free speech arose from the failure of puritan activists to force through additional church reform, and the reaction of the Commons reveals clearly the unsympathetic attitude of the majority. Wentworth was stopped in mid-flight, interrogated and imprisoned, and accepted back when his temper had been cooled. The episode was certainly not the major crisis historians have made it out to be; it came before the House on only three days in a session of five weeks.

A Procession of Queen Elizabeth I, attributed to Robert Peake the Elder. The picture is a visual mystery, and for centuries scholars have tried to penetrate its secret.

and status, their statutory powers meant little. For the Queen to govern, therefore, it was vital that she recruit and keep the support of those with real power. And here we have the final, indeed the ultimate reason for English survival and success in the later 16th century – Elizabeth I's ability to unite the mass of the political nation.

The word consensus is modern, but not the concept; the socio-political system of Elizabethan England was intended to comprehend within it as wide a range of difference as possible. Religion is an obvious example. The 1559 church settlement was not designed to achieve a grudging minimum of acceptance; still less a middle way between Catholicism and Protestantism. It tried, instead, to avoid too much definition. The successful recipe was quietness and loyalty within a generous construction of the rules.

THE CULT OF GLORIANA

Consensus, therefore, depended on persuasion as well as comprehension in policy and in patronage. The key to persuasion was the royal image. In order to make herself the focus of loyalty, Elizabeth exploited all the disadvantages of being a woman in a man's world to create the myth of 'Gloriana'. It was no mere vanity which led her to show off her skill on the virginals or in dancing, or encouraged her ostentation in jewels and dresses. And a goddess had to have worshippers, which is where the royal court came in. Since the court was the source of promotion, the social center of the land, and the focus of politics and power, anyone who expected to matter in the Elizabethan world had to make some appearance there. In doing so, he or she automatically exalted the sovereign on whom great and small alike attended. Even those who kept court appearance to a minimum relied on relatives and friends to make sure that the Queen was reminded of them and remembered they were loyal.

At court, a round of activity encouraged conspicuous display in the service of the monarch. Indoors there were religious ceremonies, masques, dancing, and, of course, plays. No royal Christmas was complete without the actors; Elizabeth had her own company in the 1580s and in later years the Lord Chamberlain's Men (no doubt with Shakespeare) were often at court. Outdoors there was hunting and above all tilting.

The cult of Gloriana enabled Elizabeth and her courtiers to sublimate the reality of an aging female ruler into fervent adulation of monarchy itself. The temptation is to dismiss it as trivial and artificial, but given Elizabethan education and thought forms, it was a language of great subtlety. The mythology and images of Gloriana resembled nothing so much as a series of Russian dolls, each opening to reveal another within, and the Queen was mistress of them all. Her portraits are heavy with allegory and symbolism and had much of the character of the sacred icons which the Reformation had banished from England. To possess Elizabeth's picture was as much a statement of faith as a statue or medallion of the Virgin Mary had ever been. Elizabeth was divine majesty.

TILTING

The tiltyard was a standard feature in all of Elizabeth's main palaces, but the activity there was more a combined pageant and literary game than a mock combat. The intending warrior would appear in allegorical costume with his servants to present to Elizabeth a symbolic *impresa*, or painted device, accompanied by some graceful speech which allowed the jouster to display his 'wit'. The *imprese* were later hung in the Shield Gallery at Whitehall, and the whole business had its deadly serious side. A courtier could do himself a great deal of good or harm and needed the best advice he could get; in the next reign, the Earl of Rutland engaged Shakespeare to design and Richard Burbage to make an *impresa* for him at the enormous cost of £4 8s. – equivalent today, to engaging the leading Hollywood scriptwriter and the top man in Broadway production jointly to design a greetings card!

THE QUEEN AND THE PEOPLE

Projecting the royal image was, also, more than a private in-game between the ruler and the élite. Elizabeth was concerned to reach out to the nation at large. Thus the public were regularly admitted to the tiltyard to watch 'the great' disporting themselves to the glory of their sovereign, otherwise the performance lost half its point! In fact, the court was much less closed than we might expect. Any respectable person might watch the Queen process to chapel of a Sunday and present a petition if he would. Charles Blount was first noticed by Elizabeth when he went to Whitehall to see her dine.

Elizabeth was also regularly about in the neighborhood of her various residences. The future Bishop Goodman remembered how, in the November of Armada year, the news went round, 'if you will see the Queen, you must come quickly'. He was taken to Somerset House; after an hour and a half, Elizabeth came out.

THE ROYAL PROGRESS

Goodman lived at Westminster and must have had similar opportunities later, but for most Englishmen the chance to see their sovereign was the royal progress. This took place in the summer every two or three years, especially in the 1570s and the 1590s, lasted a couple of months, and covered 200 miles or so. Courtiers loathed them; the gentry whose homes Elizabeth commandeered found royal attention a mixed blessing; corporations exerted themselves to please; clerics polished their Latin, and ordinary people cheered all the way.

Some of the very great put on elaborate and expensive shows to greet the Queen, especially if they had a favor they wanted. For example, when Elizabeth visited the Earl of Leicester at Kenilworth in 1575, she was subjected to a barrage of complex mythology which proclaimed the necessity for her to marry him. But even so, Elizabeth was ready to break off to attend a country wedding and called the Coventry townsmen back a second time to perform a play.

Elizabeth knew that monarchy was a matter of communication, with commoners as much as courtiers. Progresses were worth every rainstorm and jolt of her coach.

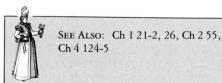

SEE ALSO: Ch 1 21-2, 26, Ch 2 55, Ch 4 124-5

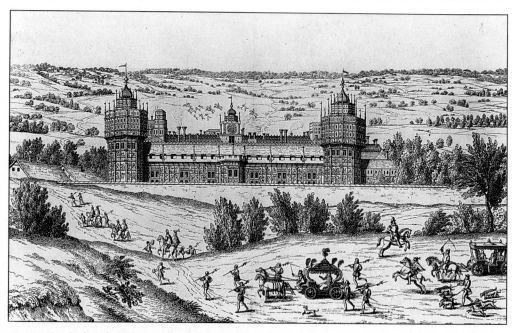

Queen Elizabeth on her Way to Nonsuch by Hoefnaegel.

THE ACCESSION OF JAMES I

In 1603 Elizabeth was succeeded by James VI of Scotland, and the competition was on to stand well with the new monarch. Cecil (who had secretly arranged the succession of James) came out on top; Raleigh lost out and was convicted of treason for alleged involvement in a Catholic plot. Unlike Elizabeth, James believed that a king ought to be generous to those surrounding him. The resulting bonanza soon threatened financial disaster, but it was popular. One small indication of the buoyant mood was James's take-over of Shakespeare's company as 'His Majesty's Servants'. The new King was by no means the ineffective figure created by later, politically unsympathetic writers, and public enthusiasm was intense.

THE GUNPOWDER PLOT

The omens were also good for religious consensus in England. This was true negatively, because (except in the popular imagination) Catholicism was no longer a danger. Initially, of course, there was the disastrous 'Bye Plot' of 1604 and the 'Powder Treason' of 1605, when bitter disappointment that James had not, despite early rumors, relaxed Elizabeth's penal laws, led a tiny minority of Catholics into violence. The 1605 episode was one on which Shakespeare may have been more informed than most, for his company was regularly at court, and Warwickshire was the provincial base of the conspiracy.

The plots produced the inevitable outburst of anticatholicism and the most stringent penal laws ever. The government, however, knew that the political loyalty of the main recusant community was never in doubt, and realized that its own long-term advantage lay in exacerbating the divisions within the recusant community so as to isolate the Jesuits and their supporters. The majority of England's Catholics, in their turn, recognized that the future lay in

At the beginning of James I's reign in 1603, there was little nostalgia for Good Queen Bess. Public enthusiasm for the new king was intense, but disillusion followed increasing corruption.

separate development, and began to erect a screen of discreet apartheid.

At the opposite pole of opinion, moderate puritans continued to be comprehended within the established church, even positively encouraged. The King agreed with many of the criticisms they made of the church at the Hampton Court Conference (1604) and with the call for a new translation of the Bible ('the Authorized Version' published in 1611). When the bishops tightened discipline after the Conference, James ensured that only a handful of the most recalcitrant puritans suffered. Radicals and extremists acepted defeat in England, and began to look to the freedom of Holland or the New World.

POLITICAL CORRUPTION

The reign of James I, therefore, did not see any immediate crumbling of the Elizabethan consensus. But all was not well. Political corruption was on the increase, fed

by James's own lavish ways, by the pressure of inflation, and also by a slackening of the monarch's personal supervision of patronage. Despite the King's introduction of numerous Scots into the English court, Cecil (soon created Earl of Salisbury) maintained the dominance over royal favor which he had established in the last months of Elizabeth's life, carefully freezing out potential rivals. That James I tolerated this, and did nothing to create alternative routes to royal favor for men of ability, contradicted the idea of political comprehension and threatened to undermine the Elizabethan legacy of consensus between the monarch and the political nation.

The threat became a reality when James allowed a monopoly of patronage to continue after Salisbury's death, first in the hands of the young Scottish courtier, Robert Carr, later Earl of Somerset, and then in those of the magnificent but incompetent George Villiers, later Duke of Buckingham. The frustration which this caused among the political élite explains much of the trouble the King finally had to face in parliament.

GOOD QUEEN BESS

In religion too, changes began to come, though after Shakespeare's death. Then, the growth of the new fashion for 'Arminian'

A minority of Catholics, disappointed that King James had not relaxed Elizabeth's penal laws, plotted treason, but were caught and executed.

opinions and 'High Church' practices began to threaten the protestantism of the church from within. In particular, tolerance by James I of clerics holding these new opinions allowed the movement to become established and paved the way, unintentionally, for that reversal by which his son Charles I would identify puritanism as sedition and Arminianism as the true faith.

And as the waning glamor of the new dynasty revealed these cracks in the English consensus, so the Elizabethan world appeared in a new light. 'When we had experience of a Scottish government,' Bishop Goodman wrote, 'the Queen did seem to revive; then was her memory much magnified'. Englishmen began once again to celebrate the anniversary of her accession, and her reign became synonymous with 'the good old days'. Given the problems and dangers Elizabeth had faced, the legend was hardly good history, but it was powerful politics. James I's son went to the block in 1649, in part because of his own foolishness. But he also died because he had turned his back on his great predecessor, he had failed to follow the ways of 'Queen Elizabeth of happy memory'.

CHAPTER 2

SHAKESPEARE'S LIFE

The birth of Shakespeare celebrated by George Cruikshank.

William Shakespeare was born in April 1564, almost certainly in the house in Henley Street in Stratford-upon-Avon which is so much honored today.

The Stratford parish register has an entry for 26 April 1564, noting the christening of 'Gulielmus, filius Johannes Shakspere' (William, son of John Shakspere). It has sometimes been though that in Elizabethan England a christening would be arranged three days after a birth, and a tradition dating from the 18th century has it that England's greatest poet (some people would have said England's greatest son) was born on the ancient feast day of England's patron saint, St George: 23 April. We know from his tomb that Shakespeare died on 23 April 1616 aged 52, which restricts the choice of birthday, of which we have no record at all. Three days seems a reasonable interval between a birth and a christening. So there is general agreement that he was born on 23 April 1564.

SHAKESPEARE'S FAMILY

His father, John Shakespeare, was a glover and wittawer (that is, he dressed soft white leather) in Stratford, where he also traded in barley, timber, and wool. The glovers had an honorable craft with good trade. When his first son, William, was born, John Shakespeare, a farmer's son who had moved in from the country, was becoming prosperous and could look confidently to the future. He already held office in the town. Two daughters had died in infancy: he was to have eight children in all – three more sons and two more daughters. Only five survived: William, the eldest, Gilbert, Joan, Richard, and Edmund. The latter, 16 years younger than William, died in 1607, at 27. He was described as 'a player' and was buried in St Saviour's, Southwark, not far from the Globe Theater, four months after his own bastard infant Edward had been buried at St Giles's Cripplegate. (That intriguing information is virtually all we know of him).

Their mother, John Shakespeare's wife Mary, was the daughter of Robert Arden, a substantial gentleman-farmer in the village of Wilmcote, four miles northwest of Stratford. Mary Arden, after her father's death, brought to her marriage a more than adequate portion. So when William was born, the Shakespeares would be not at all without means, and hope.

THE SHAKESPEARES

John Shakespeare's father, Richard, had probably farmed land around the village of Snitterfield, three miles north of Stratford, and six miles from Warwick. Here were two farms, one of 100 acres with a house and a cottage, the other of 60 acres with a house. From 1528 to 1560, it seems, Richard Shakespeare was tenant of the smaller one. The owner of both farms was Robert Arden, whose own father had bought the estate in 1501. Other Shakespeares are known to have lived in Snitterfield.

Richard is identifiable from legal records. In October 1535 he was fined for keeping too many cattle on the common pasture; and in October 1560, every tenant was ordered to 'make his hedges and ditches betwixt the end of the lane of Richard Shakespere and the hedge called Dawkins' hedge'. There are other records: we hear of him as a juryman, and as a man of

The house in Henley Street, Stratford-upon-Avon, where Shakespeare was born and grew up.

[A facsimile of a handwritten parish register is shown, with entries including the date 1564.]

WHAT'S IN A NAME?

John Shakespeare carried an ancient, and rather complicated, name. The 18th-century scholar Edmond Malone wrote, *Whatever may have been the origin of the name, the family of Shakespeare is of great antiquity in the county of Warwick.* Later research has shown Shakespeares in the Stratford area as far back as the mid-13th century. By 1500 the name had become fairly widespread in central England, and known from Cumberland to Kent, and even into Ireland.

The great Shakespearean Sir Edmund Chambers in 1930 quoted 83 different spellings of the name, from Chacsper, via Sadspere and Shaxbee, to Shaksbye: that of the poet's father, John, is spelled 20 different ways. John himself signed documents with a mark, so that we are unable to fix a definitive spelling through his signature.

We are on firmer ground with his playwright son, having three signatures on his will and three on other documents; but we still find variation. He signs himself Shakspere, Shakspeare, Shaksp, Shakspē. This does not matter very much. Spellings of all kinds were variable up to quite recent times. What is significant is the clear indication that the first syllable is more often short, so that locally in Stratford the family name was pronounced something more like 'Shaxpere'. It is almost certain that this was how the poet named himself.

authority, held in respect. His pleasant, lightly-wooded farmland is today still much as it was, the fields dominated by the fine parish church, in which his children would have been christened.

On Richard's death in 1561, his son John, the poet's father, was granted the administration of his estate. But by that time John had made the important move from village to town. He had his good house in Henley Street certainly by April 1552, when he first – ignominiously – appears in the town records: he and two other men were fined quite severely for not using the 'common muckhill' at the end of the street away from the town; John Shakespeare and the others had created a *sterquinarium* (midden or dunghill) in Henley Street itself. Some time later, in about 1557, this elder son of Richard Shakespeare the tenant farmer of Snitterfield, and the youngest child, Mary, of Robert Arden the owner, were married.

THE ARDENS

The Ardens came from Wilmcote, where Robert farmed his own freehold land. He belonged to a grander line than the Shakespeares. Probable ancestors had been sheriffs of Warwickshire, and the clan name goes back to before the Norman Conquest in 1066. Some Ardens had been very

---

The bedroom in which Shakespeare probably was born, furnished in 16th-century style, with a half-headed bed and a baby's rocking cradle.

wealthy. Though Robert's family was humbler, there was money enough. A tradition dating from the late 18th century identifies as his the ample farmhouse now known as 'Mary Arden's House'. It still gives a good idea of how such a comfortably-off family would live. Robert had eight daughters.

In his will dated 24 November 1556 he left most of his property to his youngest daughter, Mary, who became quite well provided for. It is estimated that she could have been ten years younger than her husband; though we do not know how old she was when her father died, it is possible

The forest of Arden supplied timber for houses in the nearby villages, and less prosaically, was an inspiration for the setting of As You Like It.

that she was still young. Even so, she was one of the two executors, and the inventory of the farmhouse at her father's death indicates the prosperity of the Wilmcote branch of the Ardens.

SEE ALSO: Ch 1 11-2, 14, Ch 2 31-2, 47, 48-52, 64-5, Ch 4 132-3

STRATFORD-UPON-AVON

The Stratford in which the newly-married set up house was, as it still is, a pleasant, small English Midlands town. It had a very ancient history as a settlement on slightly-rising ground alongside the point where a major thoroughfare, or *straet*, could ford the river Avon. It is in William the Conqueror's 11th-century Doomsday Book of course, but there was apparently a monastery in Anglo-Saxon times, and there is evidence of a Roman settlement.

By Tudor times the development of agriculture had made Stratford into the thriving market town it remains today. King John in 1196 had granted it a market; one of the two weekly markets is still for cattle, and *rother*, the Old English word for an ox or cow, has given its name to one of the principal thoroughfares. Stratford was granted a charter under Edward VI, and continued to thrive. Great fairs made it a center of attraction. A development of one of them, Stratford Mop Fair (12 October), still survives. The town was a craft and trading center of importance, widely known. It was on the itinerary of provincial tours of various traveling companies of players from London.

To be an alderman of such a town, as John Shakespeare was, and then Bailiff (mayor), and Chief Alderman, and Justice of the Peace, was to be a man of more than local distinction. Perhaps we can catch a glimpse of such life seen from home in the moments in his son's play, *Much Ado About Nothing* (III v), where Dogberry and Verges try to tell something of urgent significance to Leonato, the most important man in the town, when he is busy and distracted on the morning of his only child's wedding and when his patience with his 'tedious neighbors' is understandably limited.

When William Shakespeare was growing up, Stratford was a leafy, riverside town formed on a medieval grid of wide streets, three parallel to the river and three at right-angles. Just to the north was the Forest of Arden – not a forest in the sense of being dense with great trees, but a broad, pastoral, open land, quite well-wooded in

A long-established settlement, Stratford remains today a pleasant Midlands town.

THE CLOPTON FAMILY

The bridge was the benefaction of Sir Hugh Clopton, a local man who had gone to London and become in succession alderman, sheriff, and Lord Mayor, of London. He used his great wealth in ways that benefited his home town, in the construction of the bridge, and in other things. He built for himself 'a pretty house of brick and timber' (as the antiquary John Leland described it in about 1540) at the corner of Chapel Street and Chapel Lane. A good dwelling, it will feature again in this story, when as 'New Place' it is the house that Shakespeare will buy with his own London-acquired wealth, and retire to live in with his family. Sir Hugh Clopton also organized the improvements to the chapel of the Guild of the Holy Cross, just across Chapel Lane from his house. In the century before Shakespeare was born, this chapel (to this day rightly admired) had had a school house added to it: and that and the adjoining almshouses, also attached to the Guild, make an attractive group.

places, where Rosalind and Celia could buy *the cottage, pasture, and the flock* (*As You Like It* II iv 87).

Communications with the town to the south and east, and thus to London, had been much strengthened by the replacement of the old wooden bridge across the Avon. At the end of the previous century, a superb stone bridge of 14 arches, with a long stone causeway at the town end and walls on each side, had been built. This fine structure, known as Clopton Bridge, to this day brings in all the traffic from the south and east, however heavy.

The Clopton family tombs and memorials fill the small chapel at the end of the north aisle of Holy Trinity, Stratford's impressive parish church. The chapel was built by Sir Hugh Clopton as a family mausoleum. Holy Trinity stands to the south of the town by the banks of the Avon, its nave, tower, and spire rising high above the trees. Some of it dates from the early 13th century, and most of it was completed before 1520. In 1763, the stone spire replaced the smaller wooden one. The font where Shakespeare and his family were baptized was broken by puritans in the 17th century. Otherwise, that beautiful church is still more or less as William Shakespeare knew it.

So the Stratford of the young Shakespeare was a pleasant, thriving, prosperous town with good buildings, and even touches of something finer, in Holy Trinity and Clopton Bridge, a famous center for trade and crafts.

It is important to emphasize this. One of the curiosities of Shakespeareana is that peculiar popular myth, now at last disappearing, that Shakespeare was not, so to speak, Shakespeare, but someone else altogether, such as Bacon or the Earl of Oxford. This has been a curiously tenacious myth which still, from time to time, is put forward with much enthusiasm, but little scholarship. This strange notion was nourished by the conviction that Stratford in the 16th century was a dirty and insignificant huddle of squalid dwellings. The argument, in part, ran that the extraordinary knowledge shown by Shakespeare could only have come from someone socially elevated – in London and at court, preferably. Thus was snobbery wedded, as always, to ignorance.

SEE ALSO: Ch 1 11, 13-5, Ch 2 33-6, 37-8, 39-42, 48-9, 50-2, Ch 4 130-1

EDUCATION

Young William Shakespeare went to Stratford's Grammar School, and received there as good an education as any Grammar School boy in England, which is saying a good deal. He was taught by well-paid Oxford men, and in that fact was better educated than his peers at Eton. He was the beneficiary of a process of educational reform which can be traced in the foundation of so many excellent Grammar Schools in the 16th century in towns and cities throughout the land.

SMALL LATINE, LESSE GREEKE

It is unmistakable that Shakespeare not only never lost the Latin texts he learned, but also that they fired his imagination. In the school in Stratford, he made for himself a solid and deeply-dug foundation on which his later growth could so confidently rise. That self-appointed classical elitist Ben Jonson seems to be condescending to Shakespeare when he says in the prefatory poem to the first Folio that Shakespeare had 'small *Latine*, and lesse *Greeke*'. But Ben Jonson's standards were impossibly high, and modern evidence shows that Shakespeare left school with better Latin than, it is said, a student who has just taken a Classics degree at a modern university.

All learning includes drudgery. After 'petty school', started at five years old, where the schoolboy would learn to read and write, he would move, at about the age of eight, to the Grammar School next door. There he would begin to learn Latin, starting by memorizing the grammar by rote. No doubt, sitting at the heavy wooden desks in the Stratford schoolroom from six or seven in the morning to eleven, and from one in the afternoon to five or six in the evening, each working day throughout the year, could oppress the fieriest spirit. But on the open page were passages of Ovid, Virgil, Horace, and Juvenal – never to be forgotten by William Shakespeare.

Far from being a rural clod, Shakespeare benefited from an excellent education.

POETRY

Juvenal is Hamlet's 'satirical rogue'. Virgil governs the First Player's long solo in *Hamlet* Act II ii. Every play yields its full crop of classical reference and allusion, often unexpected. Rosalind quotes Julius Cæsar's terse message to Rome on his victory at Zela (*As You Like It* V ii 28). Tennyson once noted how odd it was for an ancient Scottish thane to refer so familiarly to detail in the inner life of Mark Antony.

But Ovid was the clear favorite, in schools, and for him. His first published work, the long poem *Venus and Adonis*, was taken from Ovid's *Metamorphoses*, and his second, *The Rape of Lucrece*, from the *Fasti*. The *Metamorphoses* had been translated into somewhat curious English verse by Arthur Golding in 1567, and Shakespeare certainly knew that book, which is not unjustifiably marketed today as 'Shakespeare's Ovid'. But there was no English version of the *Fasti*, and the Bodleian Library in Oxford has a Latin copy of Ovid's *Metamorphoses* with the signature 'W^m Sh^r' on the title page.

Shakespeare's plays, especially in the first decade of his writing career, from about 1590, teem with Ovidian references and effects. The two scenes that since the 18th century have been called the 'Induction' to *The Taming of the Shrew* (possibly the first dramatic scenes we have from his pen) establish a world of color, movement, sensuality, classical allusion, and pleasure which is Ovid-in-English, further developed in the play that follows.

The first note that we have of Shakespeare's public reputation, made in 1598 by the schoolmaster Thomas Meres in a book, *Palladis Tamia*, (about philosophy and the arts) is to the fact that *the sweete wittie soule of Ovid lives in mellifluous and honey-tongued Shakespeare*. Though in that remark he is referring specifically to Shakespeare's poems, including the as-yet-unpublished sonnets, Meres goes on at once to refer to Shakespeare as *the most excellent* for comedy and tragedy.

COMEDY

Erasmus's educational principles also included the study of Latin comedies in the original, as a means both of learning the Latin that was spoken on the streets of Rome, and as a means of acquiring the health-giving qualities that good comedy can suggest, including the value of good behavior. So, from the Roman comedies of Plautus and Terence, William Shakespeare would learn to work with, and probably act from time to time, the witty dialogue. He would take in dramatic shape, too, especially the classical five-act form.

RHETORIC AND LOGIC

The Elizabethan school curriculum has itself been exhaustively studied. Latin grammar and texts are what we should expect to find there, but what seems alien to us is the emphasis on rhetoric and logic, and in particular the formal exercises to manufacture tropes and figures of speech for use in

---

ADULT RECOLLECTION

Some characters and situations in Shakespeare's plays mock the idea of schooldays: Jaques has

> . . . the whining school-boy, with his satchel
> And shining morning face, creeping like snail
> Unwillingly to school.
>
> (*As You Like It* II vii 145-7)

This may be Jaques's characteristic, and rather insufferable, loftiness, as well as being part of a well-known literary tradition of the time. The schoolmaster Holofernes in *Love's Labour's Lost* is ridiculed for his pedantry: but he is not unbelievable, and many of us have met him. Moreover, he is given a moment of true moral courage when he rebukes his

supposed betters for their bullying, protesting firmly to the lordly gentlemen, *This is not generous, not gentle, not humble* (V ii 621). The jokes in *The Merry Wives of Windsor* Act IV i are more at the expense of the interfering Mistress Quickly than the Welsh schoolmaster, Sir Hugh Evans.

In other words, it is possible to make too much of a fanciful picture of Elizabethan Grammar School days as an insufferable, or risible, grind. Some comment has no doubt been more influenced by Victorian portraits like Dickens's Doctor Blimber, at whose academy Paul Dombey's spirit was crushed, than a true understanding of what Erasmus had set in train 300 years before.

The brilliance and imagination of classical writers, first encountered in the schoolroom, influenced Shakespeare throughout his life.

writing. Following closely the Romans Cicero and Quintilian, and Erasmus himself, the pupils would learn to write formal letters, and then essays, and then orations for speaking, all in prose, before being allowed to study Latin poets in order to imitate them.

In all this work they made use of the arts of *elocutio*. Elizabethan theorists distinguished the two main methods of varying plain speech: by the use of tropes and by the use of figures. Tropes (or 'turns') transfer meaning from the literal to the imaginative, as in metaphor; some of these tropes are still familiar to us as devices like allegory, irony, litotes, and hyperbole. Figures, of which Cicero listed about a hundred, deal more with the nuts and bolts of a sentence, the arrangement of the words. To modern generations who can take fright at the terms 'noun' and 'verb', most of these look like fearsome monsters. Indeed, some of the figures which the Elizabethans elaborated from Cicero have been known to agitate even our modern scholarly specialists, hard put to it to distinguish between *Hypozeuxis* and *Hypozeugma*, though such people can take *polyptoton, epanorthosis*, and even *bdelygmia* or *onedismus* in their stride.

But, whatever alien creatures they appear to us, they were not for every pupil dry, dusty, or barren. Some, and possibly most, Elizabethan schoolboys, in working from Cicero's apparently mechanical lists, clearly relished that combination of technicality and potential for invention which schoolboys in any age can love. More recently, it has shown itself in the dedicated enthusiasm with which boys would make intricate scale drawings and models of the workings of complex engines – and today master the technicalities of computers like ducks entering water. The evidence for this is overwhelming. It lies in that outpouring of wonderful prose and poetry, in which the English language first established itself as equal to, and better than, Latin. This happened later in the reign of Elizabeth and under James, where for two dozen years it seemed that no-one could write badly, and most wrote with brilliance.

THE EDUCATIONAL LEGACY
The point I am making is that we often get Elizabethan education wrong. When his schooldays were behind him, Shakespeare

*Games
and sports
featured in the
young Shakespeare's
life as in that of any boy.*

was very far from being the broken relic of an educational tyranny, like Toots in Dickens's *Dombey and Son*. Nor was he soon burnt out from the competitive need to achieve, as can easily happen to modern young people. Shakespeare went on to grow, year by year, in a quite astonishing development of ideas and flowering of language. His feeling for words and what they can do grew so fast, for example, that in one play alone, *Hamlet*, he made up 600 new words. Such coinages are frequent everywhere, and speak of great linguistic confidence.

His skill with tropes and figures, too, is beyond modern belief – and not only his, of course: Lyly, Nashe, Sidney, Spenser, Marlowe, Ben Jonson, Drayton, Daniel, Middleton – the list can go on and on.

William Shakespeare was exceptional, true (not least, in not having followed school with university, as so many of the writers of the time had done): but he was not, as his admirers in the 18th and 19th centuries tended to think, a rural clod animated by a single divine bolt of lightning. He was the product of a remarkable and widespread educational method. What he learned in that upstairs room at Stratford had organic life. That we are writing this book is an indication of the power of that life.

SEE ALSO: Ch 3 81-4, Ch 4 87-9, 96-7, 132-3, 158-9, 164-5, Ch 6 214-6, 217-8

RELIGION

As a Grammar School boy, William Shakespeare also learned some Greek, with some of the Greek New Testament as a set text. At the beginning of the century, Erasmus had provided Europe with a printed New Testament in Greek (its original language), and that document, translated for the first time into English by William Tyndale in the 1520s and 1530s, became the spiritual driving force of the English Reformation.

The religion of Shakespeare's school at Stratford was, as of all English schools of the time, the Church of England – a national, English, reformed, Protestant church. Whatever else may be claimed from time to time about members of Shakespeare's family; or about people he knew, or might have known; or about his 'lost years' between Stratford and London; or on the basis of single words uttered about him long after his death by people far from Stratford, there is no evidence that he was anything but as solid a member of the Church of England as almost everyone else in Stratford and London. The Church of England was a *via media* between the old Roman Catholic church and the newer, and sometimes wilder, Protestant sects.

In modern times, both sides try to stake a claim for the world's most famous poet and playwright: Roman Catholics and, to a lesser extent, evangelicals, appear in scholarly journals, or in books, bagging the Bard. The matter is contentious, and the conduct of the debate not particularly happy.

Unmistakably, he was baptized into the Church of England; brought up in its doctrines as a boy; married and was buried according to its rites; and brought his children up 'C. of E.' In his plays and poems he can refer with equal ease, and comparable inventiveness, to Protestant, Catholic, Jew, classical pagan, animist, or whatever.

'THE SHAKESPEARE TESTAMENT'

It is just faintly possible that some unhappiness which, the evidence could suggest, might have overtaken the family home in Henley Street, may have some slight Roman Catholic connection. That handsome house, traditionally known as Shakespeare's birthplace, and at that time two houses made into one, was only part of his father's estate. He had other property, and had owned since 1556 a house in Greenhill Street. In William Shakespeare's earliest boyhood his father John must have stood in his son's eyes for prosperity and honor. John Shakespeare moved upward in civic dignity, to become, after alderman, High Bailiff (or mayor) of Stratford in 1568. He applied for a grant of arms, though nothing came of it. (His son was to make a successful application in adulthood.)

But, from the time when William Shakespeare was about ten years old, we can watch his father's fortunes begin to suffer. The records tell of litigations and debt. His name was removed from the list of aldermen because he had stopped attending meetings. He had to use some of his wife's inheritance, and sell the Greenhill Street house. (Fortunately, his son's attendance at Stratford Grammar School was free). The cause of this extended crisis – for which there is ample evidence – is not known. The records can, however, be made to yield an over-colored picture. This coloring, again, has itself been used to suggest curious religious goings-on, whether Puritan or Catholic.

One exotic item in such display is the claim that workmen in April 1757 found a six-leaved manuscript notebook in the roof of the since-demolished half of the then double Henley Street house. Eighteenth-century commentators reported that it was a Catholic confession of faith in 14 articles. The story raises insistent doubts at every point. Soon after the discovery, the first page of the notebook went mysteriously missing, just before the manuscript was to be printed. Then it reappeared, in not very trustworthy hands, with John Shakespeare's name incorporated into the text ('I, John Shakespeare, an unworthy member of the holy Catholic religion . . .'). The notebook itself has disappeared. Yet it has been dignified by the name of 'John Shakespeare's Spiritual Testament'. Certainly, we know that such pamphlets circulated throughout Europe, many of them printed in France. *The Testament of the Soule* is known to have been printed in English. Yet scepticism has to remain the most active ingredient in this mix of tale, supposition, invention and imposture.

Did John Shakespeare die a 'papist', as an Oxford cleric in about 1700 noted of his celebrated son? The issue is unknowable. When Susanna Shakespeare, John's granddaughter, William's elder daughter, was 22, she was listed, with 20 others, as not having attended Easter communion. There could have been many reasons for this, and her case was dismissed. Some of the 20 were Catholics. Some others are said to have had Catholic connections. Much has sometimes been made of this. Unfortunately, many claims about William Shakespeare's father's and daughter's 'secret religion' are hindered by some very shaky scholarship. Susanna, we know, soon married, in Holy Trinity, a man (John Hall) who was, as S. Schoenbaum puts it, 'impeccably Protestant'.

SCRIPTURAL REFERENCES

The Bible is Shakespeare's biggest source. Those parts of his works in which no Biblical reference is discernible, like the last two acts of *Julius Cæsar*, are rare indeed. The full extent of Bible influence is only now beginning to be grasped. From home,

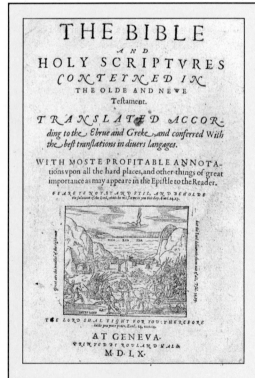

THE GENEVA BIBLE

What is far beyond dispute is that at a Protestant school, and at home, Shakespeare would have got to know the Bible very well indeed; the New Testament to some extent in Greek at school, but the whole Bible in the much-used translation into English which came out of Geneva in 1560. The New Testament had been revised by a Fellow of Magdalen College Oxford, Laurence Tomson, in 1576. This Geneva Bible, often now unjustly condemned either as violently Calvinist, or as being of only piffling significance ('The Breeches Bible'), deserves neither fate, as is now increasingly understood. Encyclopedic, massively helpful in annotation, illustrated, lucid, its Old Testament translations into English the most accurate of the century, its New Testament properly dependent on Tyndale, it was a *locus* of Renaissance and Reformation scholarship, and simply the Bible in English, used by Christians of every persuasion.

Because copies are now hard to find, many statements about it are made by people who have not read it. It is very far from being objectionably Calvinist – and the handful of specifically Calvinist annotations it does contain amid the hundreds of thousands of marginal notes, chapter-heads, introductions, glossing, concordances, and so on would have appeared unremarkable in most parts of Elizabeth's church. This Geneva Bible, in its Tomson revision, was Shakespeare's Bible.

He also knew the Bishops' Bible, published in 1568 by the conservative Bishops of the Church of England to bring the Bible in English closer to what they considered the 'original' Latin version, though of course that Latin translation was originally made several centuries after the Hebrew and Greek originals. (It should not need spelling out that Shakespeare had nothing whatever to do with King James's 'Authorized Version' of 1611. I am still surprised to be told that Shakespeare was brought in by King James to 'put the poetry into the King James Version'.)

or church, or school, he received a familiarity with Scripture which would put most modern Bible readers to shame. That familiarity probably came from all three, with his own reading as well. The Geneva Bible was specifically printed for the home reader – by the fireside, round the table, on the road, in the fields. The Bishops' Bible, in opposition, was a lavish lectern Bible, without annotations, made to be read aloud from the front of stone churches to the populace assembled below.

Shakespeare's plays with most Biblical references, it seems, are, in order of composition, – and the method of reference changes notably as his artistry matures – *King Richard III*, *King Richard II*, *Love's Labour's Lost*, *The Merchant of Venice*, *Hamlet*, *Measure for Measure*, *King Lear*, and *The Winter's Tale*. Though few pass unmentioned, the books of the Bible most often quoted are Genesis, Job, Psalms, Matthew, Luke, and Revelation. He makes use of the whole Bible, including the Apocrypha ('a Daniel come to judgement' *The Merchant of Venice* IV i 218, 328, 335).

Knowing one's way round the Bible in the vernacular (a Northern European attribute, incidentally) was as automatic in Shakespeare's boyhood and manhood as knowing one's way round the highways is today. But for Shakespeare, such knowledge was as fertile as his understanding of Ovid or Plutarch, and bore fruit in characters and dramatic situations. To take an example from my own recent research on the 'Nazarite' crux at *The Merchant of Venice* I iii 30, there are a group of gospel incidents between Matthew 8.23 and 10.1 which, including Geneva-Tomson's copious notes, associate swine, a ship in difficulties, drowning, my daughter, synagogue, publican, mercy, marriage, not taking revenge, injury, mixed beasts, and wolves – all part of the constellation of ideas in that play. Some of the key elements are on the same Bible openings.

SEE ALSO: Ch 4 100-1, 112-3, 128-9, 152-3, 158-9, 162-3, 166-7, 140-1, 172-3

MARRIAGE AND ADULTHOOD

On 28 November 1582 the Bishop of Worcester authorized the marriage of 'William Shagspere' and 'Anne Hathwey of Stratford'. The groom was 18. The bride was 26, and pregnant. An entry in the register of Holy Trinity records the baptism of Susanna, daughter to William Shakespeare, on 26 May 1583.

Those are the bare facts. All the rest that has been written on the subject – and it is massive – has to be speculation, or myth, or legend, or invention. The bride was probably the eldest daughter of a family living at Shottery, a hamlet a short walk from Stratford. A thatched farmhouse there is now labeled 'Anne Hathaway's Cottage', and Shottery is full of coaches.

Who Anne was, whether William loved her, or she him, whether they were happy, where she lived at first while he was in

Anne Hathaway lived at Shottery, an easy walk from Stratford for a young and very eager suitor.

Oil painting of Stratford in the 18th century. Probably little had changed since Shakespeare's time, although the church had a new spire.

London, and much, much else is not known. That unfortunate gap in our knowledge has not prevented romancers in their hundreds from rushing in. For our purposes, sober fact must do. When Susanna was 18 months old, Anne bore William twins, Hamnet and Judith, named at the christening on 5 February 1585, also in Holy Trinity, after family friends.

THE 'LOST' YEARS

From the date of the twins' christening until his emergence in London seven years later as the target of an attack by a fellow-writer, Robert Greene, the records of Shakespeare are blank. Again, myths, legends, and fanciful speculations fill libraries: but the rest is silence.

Romancers are, however, given tantalizing grains of sand to hold in the palm of the hand. The Bishop of Worcester's clerk, entering the names of the bride and groom in the Register the day before the authorization, on 27 November 1582, made a mistake, and wrote down the bride as 'Anne Whateley of Temple Grafton'. There is a small flourishing, Shakespeare's 'other-Anne' faction.

A much more vigorous sect maintains as gospel those later stories, the subject of gossip from the late 17th and the 18th centuries, about young William being in so much trouble for deer-stealing from the park at Charlecote, home of the Lucy family, that he had to leave Stratford and hide in London. Another company follows John Aubrey at the end of the 17th century, recording in his *Brief Lives* that Shakespeare 'had been in his younger yeares a Schoolmaster in the Countrey'. The Roman Catholic cause and speculation about these 'lost years' come together in suggestions that he was an assistant teacher to a Lancashire Catholic household. Like so much else that has been put forward, the idea does not stand up to rigorous examination.

Yet in its way, this tantalizing seven-year gap is rather attractive, allowing everyone to construct an apprenticeship to his or her own mind, unfettered by the inconvenience of recorded fact. So Shakespeare, on the evidence of his apparently extraordinary inside knowledge, has been in the army, a lawyer's office, at sea, and so on. In the glass of those 'lost years' you see what you want to see: no bad way to approach so universal an artist. Some have him, attractively, in northern Italy (of which he has, of course, extraordinary inside knowledge – extraordinary, in fact, in that it is so often wrong) and my own favorite, frankly imaginative, has him roaming Italy as an impressionable young man trying to get on with writing the epic he knows he was born to write, but for ever distracted, not least by a company of *commedia dell' arte* players . . .

STRATFORD TO LONDON

Shakespeare's route from Stratford to London, where he appears in 1592, would take him through the sheep-filled, rolling hills of the Cotswolds, which look to the cathedral towns of Gloucester and Oxford for their centers. Some of Shakespeare's most powerfully-communicated sense of place is associated with that route southeast from Warwickshire. When properly played, the loving scenes of ancient and autumnal calm in Justice Shallow's orchard in *King Henry IV* Part 2, so broken in upon by Falstaff and his corrupt recruiting methods, still make a line of feeling to that world of farming and good country living.

From Stratford to London he could have taken several routes, until he reached the Thames valley. A playwright of the mid-17th century, Sir William Davenant, was later said by John Aubrey to have had a personal interest in claiming that Shakespeare took the route through Oxford. Aubrey reported that Davenant liked to boast in his cups that he was the natural son of William Shakespeare, born of an affair between Shakespeare and the beautiful wife of the innkeeper of the Crown Tavern in the Cornmarket in Oxford. No doubt Davenant was boosting the genes that gave him what genius he felt he had. There is no evidence that this was more than fantasy.

PLAYER AND PLAYWRIGHT

Shakespeare may have settled in London before he was 21 and already with a wife and three children. When exactly he arrived, and what he did when he first got there, are unknown. The myths and legends have him holding horses, or being a not very good actor. Even what plays he wrote first, and when he wrote them, and how they were received, we do not know. The procedure of dating the works is always made to appear a little more confident than it can truly be. We lack hard evidence of dating for many of

The Thames was a main thoroughfare in 16th-century London, the streets of which were crowded, dirty, and often dangerous.

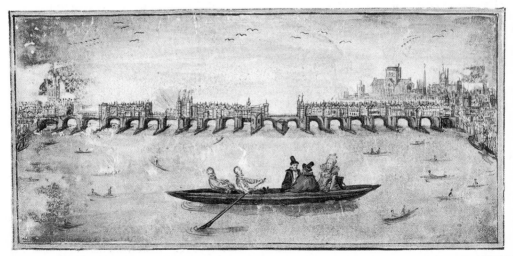

the plays. We neither know which of half-a-dozen came first, nor what the date of that composition was.

What is certain is that he brought with him to London a countryman's love and acutely observed knowledge of that landscape he knew best, around Stratford and through the Cotswolds, and its wildlife. This is visible throughout his career, of course, but can be seen very strikingly in his early long poems as well as the early plays. It is now no longer quite so fashionable as it was to write books demonstrating Shakespeare's remarkable knowledge of the life of the country, from local names for wild-flowers to the animal life in the hedgerows, from the ways of birds of all kinds to the observed movement of the weather and the seasons.

But those older books do tell a significant story. And the editor of the recent Arden edition of *The Taming of the Shrew*, Brian Morris, goes out of his way to note Shakespeare's refusal to have any truck with the fabulous and inaccurate picture of what that little animal the shrew was and did, as declared by contemporary natural historians. Instead Shakespeare went for his own quite detailed observations, matching his young woman as 'shrew' to a quite new and refreshing reality (in which, for example, strong hunger is important), as well as doing something unexpectedly different, under that title, from the painful 'wife-taming' sources and analogues.

The plays and poems give far too many instances of special observation for proper recording here. One will have to do. The poem *Venus and Adonis* contains a moving account of where Shakespeare's sympathies lay in the sport of hare-coursing. After three stanzas describing the hare's desperate running, and the tactics he employs to try to baffle his pursuers' scent of him, Shakespeare writes,

'By this, poor Wat, far off upon a hill,
Stands on his hinder legs with list'ning ear,
To hearken if his foes pursue him still;
Anon their loud alarums he doth hear;
 And now his grief may be compared well
 To one sore sick that hears the passing-bell.

'Then shalt thou see the dew-bedabbled wretch
Turn and return, indenting with the way;
Each envious briar his weary legs do scratch,
Each shadow makes him stop, each murmur stay;
 For misery is trodden on by many,
 And being low never reliev'd by any.

(697-708)

Part of one of the famous Sheldon tapestries (woven on looms at Barcheston Manor – Shakespeare's 'Barson') depicting a somewhat romanticized, and certainly non-Shakespearean view, of hare-coursing.

SEE ALSO: Ch 2 37-8, 44-5, Ch 4 96-7,118-21, Ch 5 186, Ch 6 214-5

LONDON

The London to which Shakespeare came – which has to be distinguished from Westminster, where the court was, up-river to the west – was a crowded city of just under a quarter of a million inhabitants, all crammed north of the Thames inside the wall which ran in a rough semicircle from Fleet Ditch in the west (by Fleet Street) to the Tower in the east. The medieval cathedral of St Paul's stood on the highest point. The only bridge over the Thames was London Bridge, with its 20 arches, and houses on it. South of the river was Southwark, dominated by the church of St Mary Overy (now Southwark Cathedral). Below its high elegant tower lay the Bankside attractions, well outside the City jurisdiction, of gardens, brothels, bear-baiting, and theaters.

Contemporary maps of London, usually 'views' from south of the river, are often conventional in detail of ordinary housing, but try to get the major public and private buildings right. They give an impression of a densely-built city with many noble build-ings round the skirts of St Paul's. Shakespeare's London, as he came to it, was an unhealthy but nevertheless thriving place of merchants and craftsmen. Not long after

he probably arrived, it was cruelly visited by plague, in 1592-94, and again in 1603. Norden's maps of 1590 and 1600 first show theaters on Bankside. Later, better-known panoramas, like those of Visscher, about 1616, and Hollar, whose 'Long View' was published in 1647 in Amsterdam, show details of various theaters, not always helpfully (Hollar reversed the names of the New Beargarden and the Globe).

Eighteenth-century tales of young Shakespeare founding a thriving horse-holding business, and so coming to the notice of the players, smack more of prejudice about rural clods than of truth. Since some London acting companies in-cluded Stratford in their provincial tours in Shakespeare's boyhood, it is perhaps a reasonable speculation that in his early days in London he was attached to one of them, as actor or writer or both. Which company, in which month of which year, it is impossible to say. Moreover, the acting companies appear, disappear, meld, split, travel, collapse, and re-emerge under a different name, in a way as difficult to follow as the genealogies of modern pop groups, which in some ways they resemble.

A contemporary view of Shakespeare's London: the Bankside theaters, the churches, and the mass of buildings clustered on London Bridge.

THE EARLY PLAYS

The only assured information we have about Shakespeare and the theaters in the 1590s, and our first sighting of him in London, as it were, comes from the pen of an apparent enemy, Robert Greene, in his pamphlet *Greene's Groatsworth of Wit*. Greene, who liked to style himself 'Master of Arts of both Universities', was a not-unsuccessful member of the loose group of 'University Wits': playwrights like John Lyly, Thomas Nashe, George Peele, and Christopher Marlowe.

Lyly, Nashe, and Peele carried the mixed traditions of English comedy from aristocratic private performances to the new London public theaters, often writing with a brilliant, if rather shallow, charm. From such plays as Lyly's *Endymion* or Greene's *Friar Bacon and Friar Bungay* comes the richness of Elizabethan comedy as Shakespeare in particular made it his own. Greene wrote vivid pamphlets describing the ways of the London underworld, and had a true understanding of Romance.

But for all his lively and attractive writing, Greene was a difficult, quarrel-some, reprobate man, quick to take offence and attack supposed enemies. Shortly before his death, in squalor, he published his *Groatsworth of Wit*, in which he referred to, *. . . an upstart Crow, beautified with our feathers, that with his* Tygers hart wrapt in a Players hyde*, supposes he is as well able to bombast out a blank verse as the best of you; and beeing an absolute* Iohannes fac totum*, is in his own conceit the onely Shake-scene in a countrey.* This is, all scholars agree, a clear reference to Shakespeare, not least in its parody of a famous and cruel line from Shakespeare's *King Henry VI Part 3*. From this we can tell that Shakespeare was already in 1592 successful enough as a playwright to have upset Greene: and, moreover, that Shakespeare, a mere actor, had the nerve to consider himself a universal genius.

According to the conjectural datings by many scholars, by 1592 Shakespeare had written the three *King Henry VI* plays and possibly *King Richard III*, and *The Taming of the Shrew*, *The Comedy of Errors*, *The Two Gentlemen of Verona*, and possibly *Titus Andronicus*; eight plays, putting him already on a level with, or ahead of, University men like Marlowe, in output. Our first record of Shakespeare in London, for all its malice, does imply impressive achievement.

THE POET

The following year, 1593, Shakespeare first appeared in print. His fellow-Stratfordian, the printer Richard Field, now in London, and a few years older than Shakespeare, published his slim volume, the poem *Venus and Adonis*. Though not much to modern taste, Shakespeare would live to see this 'first heir of my invention' eight times reprinted (there were 16 editions in all before 1640). It was dedicated to the 19-year-old Earl of Southampton, in a rather distant manner.

Shakespeare's second long poem, a far more somber work, *The Rape of Lucrece*, came out the following year, 1594, again from Richard Field: there were eight editions of this up to 1640. This time the dedication to Southampton is warmer. There is no account, however, of any connection between the two men, beyond those two dedications.

THE RETORT COURTEOUS

There is more to the story of Greene's *Groatsworth*, which was edited for the printer by his fellow-playwright Henry Chettle, whom Francis Meres also praises as one of the best for comedy. Chettle wrote, or helped with, 48 plays for Philip Henslowe and his Admiral's company, the principal rival to Shakespeare's. In his own pamphlet, *Kind-Hart's Dream*, also of 1592, he apologizes for the part he played in publishing Greene's attack on Shakespeare: *I am as sorry as if the originall fault had been my fault, because my selfe haue seene his* [Shakespeare's] *demeanor no less ciuill than he exelent in the qualities he professes: Besides, diuers of worship haue reported, his vprightnes of dealing, which argues his honesty, and his facetious grace in writting, that aprooves his Art.*

Here we have a strongly attractive picture of Shakespeare the man and artist ('facetious grace' means something more like 'polished grace'). There is no means of knowing which gentlemen sprang to Shakespeare's defense, though speculation has rushed in to close the gap.

PUBLICATION

Shakespeare's first play to see print in the form we know it had been *Titus Andronicus* in 1594, another slim volume, paperback as they all were, in Quarto size – about half the dimensions of a modern magazine. *King Richard III* followed in 1597. From then until his death in 1616, nearly half of Shakespeare's 38 plays appeared in this Quarto form, some, like *King Richard II* or *King Henry IV* Part 1, as many as five times. These single-play Quarto volumes are of great importance in giving us an account of what his Elizabethan and Jacobean audiences could read of him at the time.

The great first Folio of 1623, our prime source for the texts of the plays, was itself dependent, of course, on most of these Quartos. Some, like the earlier printings of the second and third *King Henry VI* plays, or *The Taming of A Shrew* (as opposed to *The Taming of The Shrew*), were what have been dubbed 'Bad Quartos', which means that the text printed is found to be in some way seriously defective, compared to what we have in the first Folio, or in another Quarto.

Celebrated Bad Quartos are of *King Henry V*, *The Merry Wives of Windsor*, and the first Quartos of *Romeo and Juliet*, and *Hamlet*. Perusal of the latter produces incredulity in modern readers: how could anyone have bought a text that had half missing, called Polonius 'Corambis', and so garbled the lines as to produce:

To be, or not to be, I there's the point,
To Die, to sleepe, is that all? I all:
No, to sleepe, to dreame, I mary there it goes

Yet there is often something more to these Bad Quartos than meets the untrained eye. They can be useful tools, in knowing hands, in establishing what Shakespeare probably wrote, as sometimes opposed to what could appear in even the best contemporary printed texts.

Shakespeare first appeared in print in 1593, when Venus and Adonis *was published.*

This lack of fact has, again, not prevented invention – indeed, some of the wildest myth-making in all the Shakespeare story, almost all of it the product of the late 20th century. Such wild arabesques of invention suggest, in their milder form, that Southampton was the 'Fair Youth' in Shakespeare's sonnets: as if such fictions as the Elizabethan sonnet-sequences present had to have, by some perversion of art, reference to 'real', rather than artistic, fact. (One may as well try to seek out the 'original' of Beatrice in *Much Ado About Nothing*.) The second element in these modern Southampton myths, which, I must

be at pains to stress, has also no evidence whatever to support it, is that William Shakespeare and the Earl of Southampton were homosexual lovers.

The dates of the two long poems support the idea that Shakespeare had withdrawn from London while the theaters were closed on account of the plague. He seems to have been back in London and writing for the theater by 1595. This was a particularly fruitful return. Four plays apparently all belong to the same year, and they all share an intense, and new – even for Shakespeare – power of lyricism. They are *King Richard II*, which is a long dramatic poem, containing no prose; *Love's Labour's Lost*, which plays aristocratic games with courtly language, and studies the quest for defeating death through poetry; *Romeo and Juliet*, Shakespeare's most lyrical 'tragedy', and the amazing *A Midsummer Night's Dream*, which does more with the idea of comedy, structurally, thematically, and imaginatively, than ever before.

SEE ALSO: Ch 3 56-66, 81-5, Ch 4 87-105, 108-13, 118-21, 176-9, Ch 6 214-8

CONSOLIDATION AND SUCCESS

By the end of 1598, an important year for Shakespeare, he had probably written 16 plays, including establishing himself firmly in the genre of plays on English history, a form he seems pretty well to have invented, and having traveled far down the road of his own kind of romantic comedy of love leading to marriage. In tragedy, his first brilliant essay in the full Aristotelian sense was still three years off, in the infinitely powerful *Hamlet*. His first two tragedies, *Titus Andronicus* and *Romeo and Juliet*, had been in styles he did not follow.

THE SONNETS

By the end of 1598, many scholars think, he had written many, if not all, of his 154 Sonnets, which circulated mainly in manuscript until 1609, when they were printed by George Eld for Thomas Thorpe. Their famous, and less than lucid, dedication, has set off yet more fantasias of speculation as to who the 'Mr. W. H.' there mentioned 'as the onlie begetter of these insuing sonnets' could have been. Like the significance of the dimensions of the Great Pyramid in Egypt, or the location of the lost land of Atlantis, or the meaning of the smile of the Mona Lisa, the dedication and printing of Shakespeare's sonnets has been made into a Great Mystery. Thus have been attracted all kinds of folly, from sheer piffle (some) to gross misunderstanding of the nature of Elizabethan sonnet-sequences (more).

That matter is of only faint significance. Of supreme importance is the stature of these sonnets, which hold their own with the greatest of the time, like Sir Philip Sidney's *Astrophel and Stella*, and even out-top them. They are highly, individually, Shakespearean, and wander across the emotional territory of various (but not all) kinds of love. They do this by means of a number of *personæ*, who, to some extent already part of the convention, allow the poet the freedom to explore. To attend to anything else but this is to stray; and that way madness lies.

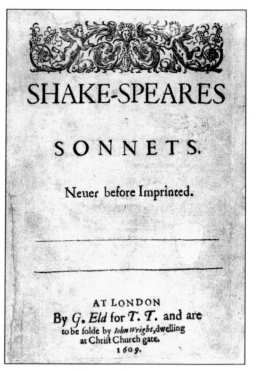

SHAKE-SPEARES

SONNETS.

Neuer before Imprinted.

AT LONDON
By *G. Eld* for *T. T.* and are
to be folde by *Iohn Wright*, dwelling
at Chrift Church gate.
1609.

Shakespeare's Sonnets were probably completed by the end of 1598. They were printed in 1609 by George Eld for Thomas Thorpe.

OTHER POEMS

Other poems generally appear in Complete Shakespeares. The short, strange, metaphysical, untitled poem, beginning *Let the bird of loudest lay*, and usually called *The Phœnix and Turtle*, Shakespeare contributed to a collection of poems called *Love's Martyr* (1601) to celebrate the love of Sir John Salisbury and his wife, symbolized through the collection by the love of the Turtledove (Constancy) and the Phœnix (Love). *A Lover's Complaint* is doubtfully ascribed to Shakespeare: it was printed by Thomas Thorpe at the end of the Sonnets volume. *The Passionate Pilgrim* of 1599 is a miscellany of poems by various writers, including five by Shakespeare, though the earlier editions ascribe the whole book to him on the title page.

SEE ALSO: Ch 4 90-1, 178-80, Ch 6 214-8

THE ACTORS

In 1598, we know that Shakespeare acted in Ben Jonson's *Every Man In His Humour*: Jonson, in his 1616 Folio edition of his plays, graciously, and most helpfully, listed the actors who first presented them. In spite of some later rather derogatory gossip, we can safely assume that Shakespeare was a more than competent actor. Later remarks tell of him playing Adam in *As You Like It* and the Ghost in *Hamlet*.

The company he was with, in 1598, was the Lord Chamberlain's Men, the best in London. Their only real rivals, Philip Henslowe's Admiral's Men, played at the Rose on Bankside, with Edward Alleyn as their star, and presently moved to the Fortune north of the City. Alleyn, who had married his proprietor's stepdaughter, had first presented Marlowe's tragic heroes, and was known for a kind of ranting style. The Lord Chamberlain's Men had Richard Burbage, the son of the builder of the Theatre, north of the City, and the owner of the Blackfriars Theater. Burbage seems to have had the edge on Alleyn as the greatest actor of the age. For him, Shakespeare wrote the parts of Hamlet, Othello, King Lear, Antony, Coriolanus, and others.

THE GLOBE

But also in 1598, the Lord Chamberlain's Men pulled down their northern Theatre, and carried the timbers across the Thames to build on Bankside a new theater, the Globe. The management of this was in the hands of what were called 'sharers', of whom Shakespeare was one.

For the opening of the Globe, in May 1599, we may reasonably speculate, Shakespeare wrote (as he certainly did at this time) *King Henry V* and *Julius Cæsar*. Indeed, the opening lines of the latter play have added force if they were the first words spoken on that great platform stage, addressed to an audience containing apprentices who should have been at work (a source of grievance to the City fathers):

Hence! home, you idle creatures, get you home,
Is this a holiday?

(The references in *King Henry V* to the 'wooden O' could, however, suggest a real rather than imaginative inadequacy, and may point elsewhere.) For the next dozen years we must imagine Shakespeare writing for that purpose-built, acoustic box, open to the weather, holding 3,000 people, with the actors using the large space of the 40-foot square wooden promontory of a stage thrusting out into the yard.

These were the years of Shakespeare's very great success. In 1603, on the death of Queen Elizabeth and the accession of King James, the Lord Chamberlain's Men became by royal patent the King's Men, with Shakespeare's name near the head of the list. He then led the list of nine players appointed grooms of the king's chamber for the coronation procession, and awarded new liveries. He was managing, and acting in, and writing for, a great company.

The Chamberlain's Men demolished the Theatre in 1598, and used the timbers for the Globe.

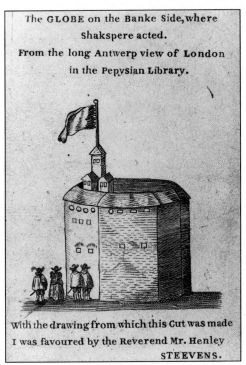

The GLOBE on the Banke Side, where shakspere acted.

From the long Antwerp view of London in the Pepysian Library.

with the drawing from which this Cut was made I was favoured by the Reverend Mr. Henley
STEEVENS.

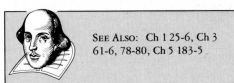

SEE ALSO: Ch 1 25-6, Ch 3 61-6, 78-80, Ch 5 183-5

A WORTHY GENTLEMAN

Shakespeare had not forgotten Stratford. Indeed, he had probably instigated the grant of arms conferred in 1596 on his father, John Shakespeare, whereby he acquired the status of gentleman. Though he, William Shakespeare, lived in London, first at Bishopsgate, to the north, close to the Theatre, and then on Bankside, close to the Globe, he was, from 1597, consolidating his own position in his native town.

He bought the great house of New Place, the second largest dwelling in Stratford, and apparently moved his family into it in 1597. Documents show him buying land at Shottery and north of the town. In 1602 he bought a cottage close to New Place, and he made investments in local commodities in 1605. He was much more than comfortably off. (His house, New Place, was pulled down by its vexatious owner in 1759. Today we see the house next door, Nash House, the home of Thomas Nash, the first husband of Shakespeare's granddaughter Elizabeth Hall, and the extensive gardens and the foundations of New Place itself, adjoining.) He was wealthy, the most admired playwright on

The grant of arms denied John Shakespeare in his son's childhood was conferred, probably at William's instigation, in 1596.

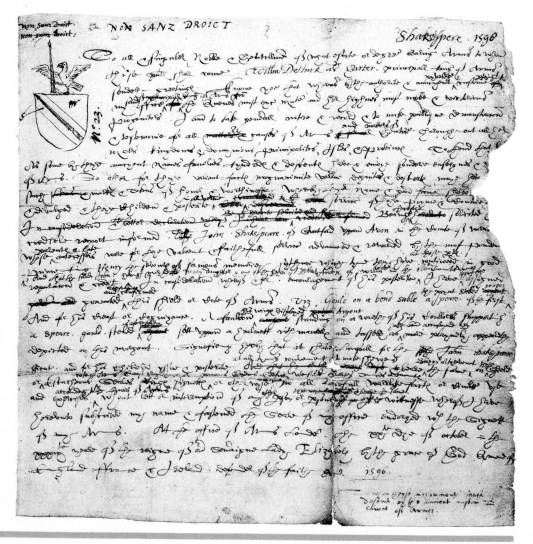

Susanna Shakespeare married the physician John Hall in 1607. They bought Hall's Croft, and Shakespeare's granddaughter was born there.

the London stage, with the first royal company. But in Stratford he had his own calamities. His only son, the twin Hamnet, was buried, as the register of Holy Trinity records, on 11 August 1596, aged 11 years. His father, John, died in September 1601.

In 1613 he bought the Blackfriars Gatehouse, close to the Blackfriars Theater. However, this seems to have been more for investment than for convenience, and he seems to have been content to return to his native town, describing himself as 'William Shakespeare of Stratford-upon-Avon in the county of Warwick, gentleman'.

MUSE OF FIRE

For the Lord Chamberlain's Men, and for the King's Men, he wrote for performances at court as well as for the big public theaters: including *Twelfth Night*, for Queen Elizabeth's Christmas revel, if intelligent speculation mixed with good scholarship is to be credited. Many of his Jacobean plays appear in the records of court performances. Severe outbreaks of plague closed the public

playhouses in 1603.

Before that, his interests had moved away from the romantic comedies that he had made his own, crowned with the achievements of *Much Ado About Nothing*, *As You Like It*, and *Twelfth Night*, and into darker areas: *Troilus and Cressida* for first performance to lawyers at the turn of the century, *Hamlet* itself at the same time: *All's Well that Ends Well* and *Measure for Measure* offering darker views of sexual love. After those comes that run of great tragedies which transcend all expectation – *Othello*, *King Lear*, *Macbeth*, *Antony and Cleopatra*, and *Coriolanus*. He struck a puzzlingly somber note with *Timon of Athens*.

In 1608, the King's Men were able to move into the upstairs, indoors, smaller Blackfriars Theater, already owned by James Burbage, but leased elsewhere until then. Here they learned to play a new style of romantic drama for more fashionable, expensive, and elite audiences. Shakespeare bought a house near to that theater, not far from St Paul's, but moved back to Stratford to live. His daughter Susanna married a highly-regarded local doctor, John Hall, on 5 June 1607. The Halls gave Shakespeare a granddaughter Elizabeth, christened on 21 February 1608 – their only child. His mother died in September 1609.

His last contributions to the London stage, after *The Tempest* of 1611/12, were joint efforts, collaborating with (almost certainly) John Fletcher for the pageant-play of *King Henry VIII* and *The Two Noble Kinsmen* in 1613. During a performance of *King Henry VIII*, at the Globe, on 29 June 1613, a cannon misfired and smoldering wadding landed on the roof-thatch. The theater burned down, but with no loss of life, and the second Globe, slightly bigger, on the same foundations, was opened by June 1614 – with a tiled roof. Said to be 'the fairest that ever was in England', it survived until 1644, when it was demolished during the Civil War.

SEE ALSO: Ch 3 70-2, 84-5, Ch 4 124-5, 130-5, 142-5, 148-55, 158-65, 176-7

THE FINAL YEARS

Throughout his London life, and in Stratford, Shakespeare had appeared in various legal transactions, which give, in the records, a tantalizing glimpse of him as litigant, or witness, or property conveyor. Few of the exhaustive modern accounts of these transactions cast light on the man, though the most celebrated, the Belott-Mountjoy suit, in which Shakespeare was involved as a bystander, does give us the first of his five extant signatures.

On 10 February 1616, his younger daughter Judith, aged 31, married Thomas Quiney, a vintner. On 25 March, Shakespeare signed his will, having brought in his lawyer to make some alterations. His health by now was failing, and on 23 April 1616 he died, aged 52. He was buried in the chancel of Holy Trinity, as a distinguished Stratford man, on 25 April 1616.

Shakespeare's will, though showing no anomalies to the expert, has always been a rich source of less salubrious speculation. His relatives and friends in London and Stratford are remembered generously. The executors are John Hall and Susanna, the latter receiving the bulk of the estate. His wife Anne gets only one mention, and that, it seems, an afterthought. In place of the care with which he arranges the succession of his estate through his daughter, he seems to give his widow only, and famously, 'my second best bed with the furniture'. Yet fanciful notions can be checked by the realization that a widow was automatically, and generously, accounted for, and their connubial bed over 34 years no doubt deserved its mention. The best bed would have been for visitors.

DESCENDANTS

His widow Anne survived him by seven years, dying on 1 August 1623. John Hall died in 1635 and Susanna in 1649. Judith Quiney lived until 1662, dying at the age of 77. Her children had all died young. With the death of Elizabeth Hall, who married twice, and had no children, there died the last of Shakespeare's direct descendants.

William Shakespeare's name survived in Stratford through New Place (until 1759) and other properties; but principally through his monument, a framed half-length bust on the north wall of the chancel of Holy Trinity, a few yards from his grave. It is not a very inspiring likeness. Downright off-putting is the motto on his gravestone, which forbids the movement of the occupant's bones: a malediction strong enough to prevent his widow being laid in the same grave (she lies alongside).

THE LEGACY

William Shakespeare's greatest monument, however, lies not in Holy Trinity, Stratford-upon-Avon, but in libraries,

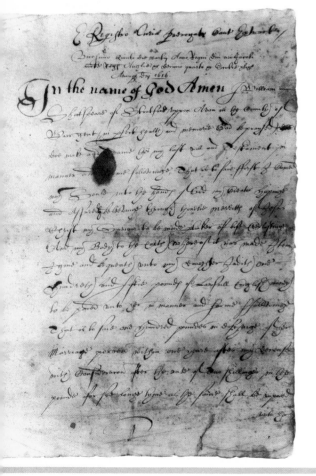

An early copy of Shakespeare's will. He revised and signed it shortly after his younger daughter's marriage and a month before his death.

Above *Shakespeare's tomb in the chancel of Holy Trinity, Stratford-upon-Avon.*
Right *The memorial window in Shakespeare's London parish church, St Helen's Bishopsgate.*

bookshops, and homes throughout the globe, in the collected edition of his works: and in theaters the world over, where he is performed with an attention such as no other dramatist has ever received.

The modern complete works are usually edited versions, divided into the three sections of Comedies, Histories, and Tragedies, of the monumental collection assembled by two of his fellow actors, in 1623. John Heminge and Henry Condell set out to collect, and see through the press, 36 of his plays. William Jaggard, though his printing shop was busy with other ventures, printed them in two columns in Folio size in the summer of 1623, produ-

Only one of Shakespeare's grandchildren, Elizabeth Hall, reached maturity. She is seen here with her first husband, Thomas Nash.

Shakespeare died. The flaws in this famous picture of the high-domed head are obvious, and do not make a very inspiring effect. Other portraits appear from time to time, with more or less likelihood of their being likenesses. The portrait in the first Folio is preceded and followed by verses of praise and dedication, and addresses to the reader. The most famous is the long encomium by Ben Jonson, who declares Shakespeare, rightly, to be *not of an age, but for all time.*

Gerard Jannsen's bust of Shakespeare on the north wall of the chancel of Holy Trinity Church, Stratford-upon-Avon.

cing a print-run of about 1,000 copies of the handsome volume, in size like a lectern Bible, later that year (200 have survived). This, the first Folio, is our principal text for the 36 plays.

The work of preparing copy for the printers, and the printing, has in recent times been the subject of great scholarly enquiry, most remarkably by Charlton Hinman of Virginia. 'F₁' as it is known, does not include *Pericles*, for the text of which we are dependent on a notoriously Bad Quarto. Nor does it include *The Two Noble Kinsmen*, which comes to us in a Quarto of 1634. Nor *Cardenio*, which has vanished, *The London Prodigal*, *The History of Thomas Lord Cromwell*, and five others, which all, ascribed to Shakespeare, appeared in the second impression of the third Folio of 1664. Modern scholarship, and taste, stops adding to the first Folio with *Pericles* and *The Two Noble Kinsmen*, though extending the Shakespeare apocrypha has always been a busy corner of the Shakespeare field.

The Folios also carry prefatory matter. There is the famous, and inept, engraving of Shakespeare by the young Dutchman Martin Droeshout, who was only 15 when

SEE ALSO: Ch 3 79-80, 86, Ch 4 168-9, 176-80

CHAPTER 3

ELIZABETHAN & JACOBEAN THEATER

The Globe – home of what was probably the most exciting, innovative, and successful acting company in the 16th and 17th centuries, the Chamberlain's Men.

There is a long-standing tradition of studying Shakespeare as a dramatic poet rather than as a playwright; that is to say his plays have been analyzed and discussed by critics as though they were primarily literary works to be read more often than to be seen. This approach gives a fundamentally false impression of his work. Shakespeare was essentially a man of the theater; that is how he made his living and he was successful at his job because he understood the craft and general business of the theater. Thus there was something more involved than an ability to write literary works of excellence; what was also required was an intimate knowledge of the whole heritage and tradition of drama and acting, of particular types of stages and acting places and their conventions for performance, of specific acting companies, their ways of working and the special talents of their various members, of audiences and their tastes.

THE DRAMATIC HERITAGE

It is important to dispel at once the notion that, in the pre-Elizabethan period, drama existed in a primitive state, awaiting the arrival of a genius like Shakespeare, who would turn raw, unsophisticated entertainment into 'art'. A rich tradition of theatrical entertainment, religious and secular, courtly and popular, professional and amateur, existed long before the year 1576, when the first Elizabethan public playhouse was constructed in London. There was also a considerable variety of outdoor and indoor playing spaces for different types of plays and entertainments.

Most people have a vague notion that some kind of religious drama was performed in towns during the Middle Ages, but it is not often realized that this was only one area of theatrical activity among many, and that the various forms of drama and their methods of presentation had a profound influence on the Elizabethan theater.

PUBLIC PERFORMANCES

The pageant wagon seems to have been the commonest stage for presenting the great religious cycle plays of the 15th and 16th centuries, usually referred to as mysteries or miracle plays (the term 'miracle' also includes plays based on the lives of the saints and the acts of the Apostles). These religious plays about the birth of Christ, the crucifixion, and the Day of Judgment were performed and produced by local guilds, who were paid in part for their labors. They were suppressed during the Reformation partly on religious grounds, as they were essentially Catholic dramas, and partly

Pageant-car of the Nativity (detail) by Denis van Alsloot commemorating the entry of the Archduchess Isabella into Brussels.

because the Tudor authorities were always anxious that if large numbers of people gathered to watch plays, they might, in fact, create civil disorder.

As for the performing of these plays, the pageant wagon, a stage on wheels, enabled the actors to travel easily to several different venues in a single town. The same principle of a mobile stage, though usually a more elaborate one, was used for civic and royal pageants, and a simpler version provided common traveling players with a means of transport for their costumes, props, and general baggage. Nomadic players could create an ideal stage by setting up a curtained booth area on barrels or trestles in suitable public places such as inn-yards, courtyards, and market-places.

A more permanent acting space was the so-called 'place-and-scaffold' theater where the set itself consisted of a number of scaffolds surrounding a central 'place' or 'platea'. Such a set-up was used for performance of the oldest surviving complete morality play *The Castle of Perseverance* (c. 1425). The simplest acting place of all was a public area such as a village green, a square, or a public street where traditional folk drama, such as plays about the adventures of Robin Hood, could be performed by local amateurs.

Frontispiece to the illustrated Terence des Ducs de Charles VI. *The miniature shows a scene from Le Théâtre Antique. Note the stereotypes and the actors wearing masks.*

PRIVATE PERFORMANCES AND COURT PERFORMANCES

It had long been customary to provide theatrical entertainments at court, both outdoors and in grand banqueting halls, during seasonal festivities or on special occasions such as receptions for foreign dignitaries. Pageants, royal processions, tilts, fights at barriers, masques, and interludes were particularly popular with the Tudor court, though records of such spectacles date back to at least the 11th century. Richard III, Henry VII, and Henry VIII all had their own small companies of players, called 'lusores', who were specifically required to perform interludes.

The word 'interlude' has been used in various contexts to describe most kinds of medieval play, though it usually refers to partially comic or farcical dramas for seasonal entertainment. However it is not always easy to distinguish interludes from morality plays, which had the serious function of imparting moral instruction, because morality plays often included scenes of knockabout farce. (Comic morality plays are often referred to as 'moral interludes'.) Similarly the word 'minstrel' is not especially precise and is used to describe a variety of theatrical performers from court poets and musicians, who recited or sang ballads about historical events and characters and romantic legends, to semivagrants who eked out a living on the road with their fire-eating, tumbling, conjuring, acrobatic, and juggling acts.

SEE ALSO: Ch 1 11, 20, Ch 4 87- 9

A PROFESSIONAL THEATER

With this broad range of dramatic activity, one might ask why the theater did not take off as a commercial activity before the Elizabethan period. The short answer is that, for commercial activity to be successful, there has to be a stable market, and this stability only became possible when the players were able to base themselves in London, by far the largest center of population. A substantial potential market was created by the huge population growth in London toward the end of the Tudor period (from 50,000 during Henry VIII's reign to between 160,000 and 180,000 by 1600). Furthermore, as long as the lifestyle of the players remained largely nomadic, their instability was exacerbated by laws introduced to control the problem of unemployment and consequent vagrancy. In 1572 the Act for the Punishment of Vagabonds was reinvoked. This was extremely threatening for traveling players because this legislation specifically classified them as vagabonds if they were unable to prove that they belonged to the household of an officially recognized patron or that they were licensed by local magistrates.

All and every person and persons being whole and mighty in body and able to labour, having not land or master, nor using any lawful merchandise, craft or mystery whereby he or she might get his or her living, and can give no reckoning how he or she doth lawfully get his or her living; and all fencers, bear-wards, common players in interludes and minstrels not belonging to any Baron of this realm or towards any other honourable personage of greater degree; all jugglers, pedlars, tinkers and petty chapmen; which said fencers, bear-wards, common players in interludes, minstrels, jugglers, pedlars, tinkers and petty chapmen, shall wander abroad and have not license of two justices of the peace at the least, whereof one to be of the quorum, when and in what shire they shall happen to wander . . . shall be taken, adjudged and deemed rogues, vagabonds and sturdy beggars.

The punishment for vagabonds ranged from a whipping to enforced slavery and

Traveling players. All stage properties, including musical instruments, had to be mobile and able to be loaded on carts and wagons.

even hanging: quite an incentive for actors to find themselves a patron and get on the right side of the law. It was not long after this that James Burbage, who was later to become the financial backer of Shakespeare's company, made a famous appeal to Robert Dudley, the Earl of Leicester, for continuation of his patronage:

We therefore, your humble servants and daily orators your players, for avoiding all inconvenience that may grow by reason of the said statute, are bold to trouble your lordship with this our suit, humbly desiring your honour that, as you have always been our good lord and master, you will now vouchsafe to retain us at this present as your household servants and daily waiters, not that we mean to crave any further stipend or benefit at your lordship's hands but our liveries as we have had, and also your honour's license to certify that we are your household servants when we shall have occasion to travel amongst our friends as we do usually once a year, and as other

noblemen's players do and have done in time past,
whereby we may enjoy our faculty in your
lordship's name as we have done heretofore.

PATRONAGE

As he was not obliged to pay his actors, Leicester's patronage did not guarantee them financial success, but it did prevent them from being treated like common criminals and hounded from parish to parish. Having an influential courtier as a patron must have been a considerable help in marketing terms, too, since it gave the company immediate credibility. Leicester no doubt had his own political reasons for helping a talented troupe of actors. There was a real advantage to the patron in terms of prestige and social status in being seen to support the actors and in providing entertainments for Queen Elizabeth's Christmas festivities. Burbage's company was granted a royal patent in 1574, and performed at court at Christmas that year and the following year.

The relationship between Leicester and Burbage's troupe of actors was typical of that between other patrons and performers. The day-to-day business aspects of their activities were the concern of the company and not the patron. The actors were responsible for the plays and costumes, and for their own wages and those of any extra actors and musicians they needed to hire. They performed for their patrons on special occasions but they were not obliged to remain permanently in residence at their masters' households. In fact their business demanded that they traveled and sought audiences wherever they could be found.

THE FIRST PLAYHOUSE

1576 was a crucial year: it was then that the enterprising actor James Burbage took a major gamble and scraped together the money to build the first London playhouse, just outside the city boundaries. He obviously judged that the time was right for a concerted effort to get established in the capital. The investment paid off and gave his company an advantage over his immediate rivals, Lord Pembroke's Men (1574-76), Lord Strange's Men (1576-77), and the Lord Admiral's Men (early 1570s to 1625). These

three companies did not have a secure London base and were more dependent upon touring for their living.

However Burbage did not have it all his own way. In 1583 one main acting company, called the Queen's Men, was formed by Sir Francis Walsingham, with the best available players from all other companies. With such personnel and patronage one might expect that they would have immediately dominated the theatrical scene, but they too were handicapped by not having their own London theater .

It has been suggested that this company was created to provide an official, respectable troupe of players, sanctioned by royalty and acceptable to the city authorities. An accident at a bear-baiting arena in 1583 had killed eight people and was said by some (who did not care to distinguish between

When the Act for the Punishment of Vagabonds was reinvoked in 1572 it presented groups of traveling players with a very serious problem. Unless they could prove that they belonged to an officially recognized patron or that they were licensed by local magistrates, they risked imprisonment, whipping, and even hanging. It is not surprising, therefore, that James Burbage should have made his famous appeal to the Earl of Leicester for the continuation of his patronage.

bear-baiting and acting) to illustrate God's wrath on the players. Whether or not the formation of the Queen's Men was a consequence of the disaster, the fact is that there was constant friction between the court and the London authorities over the whole business of acting, which placed the actors themselves in a rather vulnerable position. The city authorities were always liable to look for the slightest excuse to prevent players from performing in London, while senior courtiers obviously saw it as their natural right to encourage a traditional activity which provided royal entertainment and possible preferment for themselves.

THE CITY AND THE PLAYERS

There were several reasons for the London authorities to object strongly to actors taking the major step of building theaters and setting themselves up on a seemingly permanent basis in or around their area of

control. This new entertainments industry was a threat to the normal business activity of the city, which it was in their own interests to protect. Complaints were made that the attraction of plays discouraged apprentices from going to work and implanted seditious ideas in their heads. There was also a genuine health problem in that large gatherings of people attending plays were liable to spread plague.

But crowds were also viewed with considerable distrust by those who feared they might become riotous and damage private property. (Repressive societies tend to assume that congregations of people are always potentially subversive, and in repressive societies they are probably right.) Attacks on the plays and players were frequently made from a religious standpoint, as in this famous passage from Stubbes's *Anatomy of Abuses: Do they not maintain bawdry, insinuate foolery and renew*

COURT 'THEATERS'

The typical royal banqueting hall used for indoor performances was a large rectangular room with a screen and two or three doors for actors' entrances at one end, sometimes a gallery above the screen for musicians, seats along the sides, and a raised dais at the opposite end which provided the traditional vantage position for the most senior members of royalty in the audience. If required, a stage could be set up in front of the screen and the doorways hidden by some kind of curtain. A good example of this kind of acting space can still be seen in the banqueting hall at Hampton Court Palace.

The same basic arrangement was employed, though on a less grand scale, for theatrical performances in schools, the Inns of Court, and universities, where indoor performances of classical drama were common in the 16th century. This tradition directly influenced some of the more academic university graduate playwrights of the Elizabethan period. Shakespeare's early play *The Comedy of Errors* may have been written specifically for performance at the Inns of Court, with its particular tradition of staging classical plays in mind. The amateur but scholarly drama of the 16th century also helped to develop concepts of genre, of

tragedy as something entirely separate and distinct from comedy. Shakespeare did not take such distinctions too seriously; but for some of his contemporaries, like Ben Jonson, a self-consciously academic writer and classicist, these categories were matters of the greatest importance and provided criteria for judging art itself.

Middle Temple Hall; some scholars believe that Shakespeare wrote The Comedy of Errors *and* Twelfth Night *specifically for a private performance.*

remembrance of heathen idolatory? Do they not induce whoredom and uncleanness? Nay, are they not rather plain devourers of maidenly virginity and chastity? For proof whereof mark but the flocking and running to Theatres and Curtains, daily and hourly, night and day, time and tide, to see plays and interludes, where such wanton gestures, such bawdy speeches, such laughing and fleering, such clipping and culling, such winking and glancing of wanton eyes, and the like is used, as is wonderful to behold.

Such objections made against players on religious grounds may well have been sincere. However, it is easy to see how their moral language might have provided a suitable cover for influential magistrates who were more concerned with maintaining the status quo and preserving their own self-interest. Actors were attacked for put-ting on plays on the sabbath and during Lent, for creating false idols on the stage, for uttering obscenities, for wearing women's clothes, for being unnecessarily extravagant with their playhouse designs and costumes, and for profiting from an activity that was not considered to be a legitimate profession. (A parody of some of these charges can be found in the last act of Ben Jonson's play *Bartholomew Fair*.)

One must guard, though, against the rather simplistic notion that the main opposition to the actors was ideological, based in an extremist religion called purit-

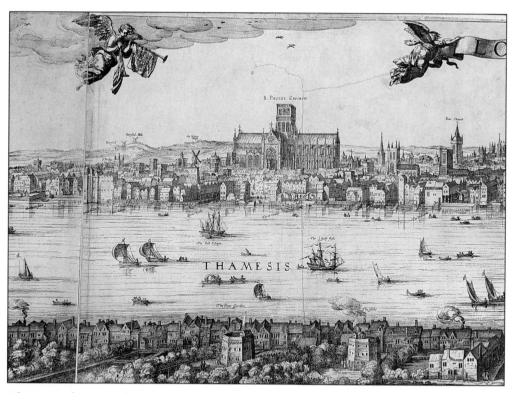

Above *Visscher's map of London showing the Bankside theaters, including the Globe. The Blackfriars can just be seen to the west.*
Below *The rapier and the cloak from Giacomo di Grassi* His Fine Art of Defence *(1594).*

anism. At best this is only a half-truth. Some puritans objected to theater; others supported it. The word 'puritanism' covered a wide range of religious and political thought, and its common usage to refer to a kind of joyless fanaticism is not helpful. For example, Leicester was a patron both of puritans and players, and Shakespeare's patron, the third Earl of Pembroke, was an eminent puritan in James I's government. Anyway, just how much notice the court took of these complaints must have depended upon the wider political context of its relations with the London authorities at any given time. Whether or not the players were defended by their royal patrons was liable to be a matter of political expediency.

The Queen's Men then were perhaps formed by the court as a kind of temporary concession to indicate to the city fathers that their authority was recognized and that some control was being kept over the players. This was the favored company at court after 1583 until the death of its famous clown, Richard Tarlton, in 1588. (The fact that its fortunes declined rapidly after Tarlton's death suggests that he was the company's major star. Certainly he was

COMPETING COMPANIES

During the 1560s and 1570s Leicester's company competed with various other troupes of actors for favor at court. There are contemporary records of plays being performed for Queen Elizabeth by Lord Rich's Men, Sir Robert Lane's Men, the Earl of Lincoln's Men, The Earl of Sussex's Men, the Earl of Warwick's Men, and Lord Howard's Men (later known as the Lord Admiral's Men). Other nobles, like the Earl of Oxford, patronized troupes of actors which might well have performed at court, though the records are incomplete. The personnel of these companies tended to change fairly rapidly, and players moved frequently from one patron to another. The need to travel constantly, in an age when traveling was an arduous business, obviously placed a great strain on the players.

It was only after 1576, when the acting companies began to establish themselves in London on a more permanent footing, that performing plays became more financially rewarding (for some) and more obviously a 'professional' activity. In the struggle to capture the London market three companies emerged as by far the most successful during the Elizabethan period, the Earl of Leicester's Men, the Lord Chamberlain's Men, and the Lord Admiral's Men.

THE ACTORS' COMPANIES

Out of this disruption emerged the most famous company of the period, the Chamberlain's Men (renamed the King's Men in 1603), to which Burbage now belonged and which Shakespeare soon joined. Where Shakespeare was working before he joined this company is not clear, but he may have been a member of Pembroke's Men since they were in possession of some of his early plays (on the other hand they may have been performing pirated editions). The Chamberlain's Men included a number of actors formerly performing for Strange's Men.

During the mid-1590s there were two main companies, the Chamberlain's Men and the Admiral's Men, both of which had their own playhouses, the Theatre and the Rose respectively (later the Globe and the Fortune), and these two dominated the London scene for almost 30 years, up to the death of James I. Their pre-eminence was affirmed by a Privy Council decree of 1598, which limited the companies allowed to play in London to these two only. This action resulted from the staging of *The Isle of Dogs* (by Nashe, Jonson and others), a play said to be 'containing very seditious and slanderous matter'. The Privy Council went so far as to order the destruction of all public playhouses, which must have mightily pleased the city authorities, though this drastic step was never taken.

In fact, only four years later, a third company, made up of Oxford's Men and Worcester's Men, was permitted to play in London, and one can only assume that local government objections to players were being constantly overruled by central royal authority. The entrepreneur Philip Henslowe was involved in this new outfit and his diary records that he lent the company money for playbooks and costumes, a favor no doubt calculated to put them considerably in his debt. For a short time after 1602 they performed at his old playhouse, the Rose, before establishing themselves at the Red Bull.

remembered well into the 17th century as one of the greatest comic actors of the age.) The Queen's Men were then succeeded by the Admiral's Men, a company greatly strengthened by the marriage of its leading actor, Edward Alleyn, to the step-daughter of Philip Henslowe, its financial backer. Sometime around 1590, the Admiral's Men amalgamated with Lord Strange's Men. This was about the time of Shakespeare's early writing career, and was a period of general instability and frequent changes of personnel between companies, exacerbated by the closure of London theaters from 1592 to 1594 as a result of plague.

SEE ALSO: Ch 2 43-7, Ch 3 61-6, 83-4, Ch 5 182-5

After the death of Elizabeth I, in 1603, the old move to bring the actors into direct royal control was revived when James I placed the companies under the patronage of various members of the royal family. The Chamberlain's Men became the King's Men, the Admiral's Men became Prince Henry's Men, and Worcester's Men Queen Anne's Men. The long-term effect of this was to transform the business of acting from a popular entertainment to an activity primarily intended for court enjoyment.

PUBLIC STAGES

The significance of the new playhouses built in or around London can hardly be over-stated, but they were not the only public venues in the capital for plays. While they were still trying to establish themselves in London the players exploited all the large public playing spaces available to them. Inns and possibly animal-baiting rings were adapted for performances, and a simple stage could always be improvised in the time-honored fashion by setting up a raised platform with a curtain in a convenient open area, like a market square. Where they performed for the general public was a matter of their own ingenuity.

Animal-baiting rings are known to have existed, from at least the 1560s, at Bank-side, an overcrowded and common haunt of the underworld on the south bank of the river Thames. These baiting houses were polygonal amphitheaters with galleries for the audience and a circular pit about 60 feet in diameter where unfortunate beasts were savaged to death. Although there is no conclusive evidence to show that these buildings were used regularly by players, it does seem to have been likely since public playhouses were so obviously influenced by their design. They were also ideal for accommodating large numbers of people who could not avoid payment.

THE PLAYHOUSES

There was no other venue, however, so magnificent and inviting as the public playhouses, with their imposing apron stages and vibrant audiences packed into pit and galleries. The sheer size of these grand

Two actors address the audience from a booth stage in the Netherlands. Others look out through the curtain which masks the tiring room.

Philip Henslowe's Diary scrupulously records 'box-office' receipts; here, those from Newington Butts between 18 July and 7 August 1594, mentioning 18 performances of nine plays.

arenas for public entertainment must have made a tremendous impression on the general population. When Sam Wanamaker's recreation of the Globe Theater is finally built, on its original site, it will be dwarfed by the surrounding high-rise office blocks in the city. In Shakespeare's day, it was the theaters and the churches that dominated the skyline. To own such a spectacular performing space was obviously the ideal of any Elizabethan company but there were inevitable obstacles. For one thing there was the old enemy, the city authorities, and for another the sheer cost.

The first problem could be avoided by building outside the city itself, which by today's standards covered a fairly small area, but close enough still to attract custom. The problem of finance was harder to overcome as actors were not generally rich or reliable enough to raise capital themselves. They were dependent upon the backing of entrepreneurial characters like James Burbage, who was both actor and businessman, to risk such an enterprise. Burbage might sometimes have regretted his historic decision to gamble on the actors' trade because he seems to have been involved in constant litigation as a result of the deal he made with his brother-in-law to raise funds for his first playhouse. As this was his risky investment, the actors who performed there were obliged to meet his

conditions of work. This made Burbage very powerful, especially as any actor who objected to his terms could easily be replaced.

Burbage's playhouse, called simply the Theatre, was built in 1576 in Shoreditch, an area just north of the city. As it turned out, this theater was not used exclusively by any single company. During its 22-year life most of the leading companies performed there and it was probably London's most desirable venue at the time. Shakespeare's plays were probably staged there until 1597. The Theatre was pulled down at the end of 1598 and reconstructed on the Bankside in 1599, where it was renamed the Globe. A second theater, the Curtain, was built in Shoreditch in 1577 but, of the two, the Theatre seems to have done the better business. Though little is known about it, a playhouse was in use at Newington Butts, south of the river, by 1580.

Burbage's great financial rival, Philip Henslowe, established the first of the Bankside playhouses, the Rose, in 1589. Henslowe's company, the Lord Admiral's Men, performed there until the end of the century and staged most of Christopher Marlowe's plays, as well as works by

INNS AND INN-YARDS

Local inns were a traditional and hospitable venue, and convenient for the players because they had some guarantee that their audiences would pay them for their labor. The inn-yards themselves were ideal for setting up a simple stage that could be seen from the yard and the surrounding galleries. It is probable that plays were also performed indoors at inns, making them attractive during the winter months. Playing in London inns was first recorded in 1557, at the Saracen's Head in Islington and the Boar's Head near Aldgate. Both these areas were outside the control of the city authorities who, in 1574, forbade performances in the city itself in 'great inns, having chambers and secret places ajoining to their open stages and galleries'. This order seems to have been successfully defied, as four inns within the city were used for playing for another 20 years or so, the Bel Savage, the Bull, the Bell, and the Cross Keys. Shakespeare's company, the Chamberlain's Men, is known to have used the Cross Keys as late as 1594.

However by 1596 the city authorities had their way, perhaps because the plague had been particularly bad in recent years, and playing structures within the city inns were demolished with the approval of the Privy Council. Outside the city boundaries two inns, the Boar's Head and the Red Bull, were converted into playhouses and continued to be used by acting companies well into the 17th century.

Chapman, Munday, Chettle, Dekker, Drayton, Greene, Kyd, and Lodge. The Swan Theater, owned by a successful and shady London goldsmith called Francis Langley, followed at Bankside in 1595. This turned out to be a disastrous enterprise for it was here that the Earl of Pembroke's Men staged *The Isle of Dogs* which provoked the full wrath of the authorities and restricted the companies allowed to perform around London to two.

A description of the Swan by the Dutchman, Johannes de Witt, who visited London in 1596, has survived: *There are four amphitheatres in London of notable beauty, which from their diverse signs bear divers names. In each of them a different play is daily exhibited to the populace. The two more magnificent of these are situated to the southward beyond the Thames, and from the signs suspended before them are called the Rose and the Swan . . . Of all the theatres however the largest and most magnificent is that of which the sign is a swan, called in the vernacular the 'Swan Theatre'; for it accommodates in its seats three thousand persons, and is built of a mass of flint stones (of which there is a prodigious supply in Britain), and supported by wooden columns painted in such excellent imitation of marble that it is able to deceive even the most cunning. Since its form resembles that of a Roman work, I have made a sketch of it.* De Witt's drawing provides one of the most important pieces of evidence for the internal design of the public playhouses.

THE GLOBE

The most famous of all the playhouses at this time, the Globe, was built then in an area which had already been developed for theater entertainment by Henslowe and Langley. The contractual arrangements for this enterprise illustrate a marked increase in the power and influence of some of the actors in the Chamberlain's Men company. A 31-year lease was taken out on this new property and the cost shared, half between James Burbage's two sons, Richard and Cuthbert (by this time James Burbage was dead), and half between five members of the company, William Shakespeare, Augustine

Phillips, Thomas Pope, John Heminge, and William Kempe. Now that he was a shareholder, Shakespeare must have been able to exert considerable control over matters of company policy and choice of plays. He would also have received a greater share of the profits.

Twenty-nine plays are known to have been written for this company between 1599 and 1608, and most were probably performed at the Globe. Of these, Shakespeare himself contributed more than half (the 16 plays from *As You Like It* to *Pericles*). There were also frequent revivals of old plays which had proved successful.

The Globe did not outlive Shakespeare; it was destroyed in 1613 when a cannon set the thatched roof alight during a performance of one of his last plays, *King Henry VIII*. A second Globe, with a more fireproof tiled roof, was built on the same site and continued to be used by the King's Men until it was demolished in 1644.

THE FORTUNE

In 1600, the great rivals of Shakespeare's company, the Admiral's Men, managed by Philip Henslowe and Edward Alleyn, transferred their business from the Rose on Bankside to a new theater called the Fortune, situated to the north of the city in the district of Finsbury. This move was probably made in direct response to the building of the Globe on Bankside which must have taken business away from the older Rose playhouse. The builder of the Fortune, Peter Streete, was instructed to follow 'the manner and fashion of the said house called the Globe', which he had also built, except that the Fortune was to be square rather than polygonal.

By 1610, Edward Alleyn had followed the example of the King's Men once more and introduced a shareholding system for ten members of the company. These were not the only similarities; in 1621 the Fortune suffered the same fate as had the Globe eight years earlier: *On Sunday night there was a great fire at the Fortune in Golden-Lane, the fairest playhouse in this town. It was quite burnt down, and all their apparel and playbooks lost, whereby those poor companions are quite undone.*

The Admiral's Men (renamed Prince Henry's Men in 1603 and Palsgrave's Men in 1612) never really recovered from this disaster, even though they built a second Fortune playhouse. Theaters had to close in mourning for King James's death in 1625, and this setback was followed by a serious outbreak of plague, which was ruinous for all companies but the King's Men.

THE HOPE

One other public playhouse existed; the Hope was built in 1614. This was another Henslowe/Alleyn scheme and possibly an attempt to re-establish themselves on Bankside after the burning of the Globe. This multipurpose playhouse-and-gamehouse probably revived an old tradition of provid-

Edward Alleyn was one of the leading actors of his age. With the Admiral's Men, he created all Christopher Marlowe's tragic heroes.

ing both plays and animal-baiting at one venue. The two activities did not work well together, and after Alleyn's death in 1626 the playhouse seems to have become exclusively an animal-baiting arena. It is doubtful that actors and baiting promoters could ever have got on for long as partners, though financial pressures forced them to work together from time to time.

SEE ALSO: Ch 2 47, Ch 3 78-80, Ch 5 182-5

Besides acting and writing plays, Shakespeare was a 'sharer' in the Globe, and he derived his main (and not inconsiderable) income from this.

THEATER DESIGN

The Globe, the Fortune and the Red Bull were the most successful playhouses of the period and provided long-term residences for the three major companies. An examination of what is known about Shakespeare's Globe gives a good idea of all the playhouses. Scholars are generally agreed that there were no major differences between the basic structure and design of these buildings, though it does seem probable that some minor improvements and changes would continually have been made.

Contemporary artists' impressions of the theater in its Bankside surroundings show a polygonal building with a thatched roof. From the surviving contract drawn up for the building of the Fortune playhouse we can deduce that there were exterior staircases; the height of the playhouse was 33 feet, and the diameter about 100 feet. (It should be noted that the Fortune was different in one major respect, being square rather than polygonal.) As for the interior, our main sources of information are provided by the famous De Witt sketch of the Swan, discovered in Amsterdam in 1880, and the surviving contracts for the Fortune and the Hope playhouses. De Witt's sketch of the Swan, made in 1596, was later copied by his friend Arend Van Buchell, and it is Buchell's copy which survives, so our impression is unfortunately third hand. Beyond this evidence we are left to make logical deductions about the stage and auditorium on the basis of the explicit and implied stage directions of the plays known to have been performed at the Globe.

THE ACTING SPACE

The superstructure which extended over the stage protected the actors from the elements and housed the mechanical devices necessary for various descents and ascents called for in plays. Somewhere beneath this and above the tiring-house was an upper-level acting area. The space above the stage may have been reserved for prestigious members of the audience, in which case a 'lord's room over the stage' (mentioned by Ben Jonson in *Every Man Out of His Humour*) could have been used by the actors when required.

A special musician's gallery does not seem to have been a feature of the Globe. Seven plays written for performance at the Globe mention music 'from within' and Marston's *The Malcontent*, performed at the Globe around 1603-4, refers to the 'not received custom of music in our theatre'.

The notion of an inner stage has been discredited as a fiction thought up by 19th-century scholars trapped in a proscenium arch mentality who, confronted with the expansive apron of Shakespeare's stage, felt obliged to add a small proscenium area upstage. Any action in such an area would not have been visible to a large section of the audience, and the existence of an inner stage is highly improbable. Where 'discoveries' are required, and this is fairly infrequent, some kind of curtained-off area within, or in front of, the tiring house wall might have been used.

SIZE AND STRUCTURE

Some further idea of the Globe's structure and dimensions can be inferred from the surviving contracts for the Fortune and the Hope. The contract for the building of the Fortune was drawn up between the Henslowe/Alleyn partnership and Peter Streete, a carpenter, in 1599. The playhouse was constructed of timber clad with plaster, and was a square building, 80 feet outside and 55 feet inside. The stage was 43 feet wide and extended half way into the yard (i.e. 27½ feet), it had three stories for galleries 12 feet, 11 feet, and 9 feet in height, and there were four separately divided gentlemen's rooms. It is generally assumed that the Globe's structure was very similar.

The Hope contract drawn up in 1613 is similar in content and adds an interesting detail; the superstructural 'heavens' area was to be built all over the stage and to be carried without any posts set on the stage itself (probably an innovatory idea). Also it stipulated that only two boxes at stage level should be made available for gentlemen. Inevitably the playhouses were different in some details but the similarities must have been far more striking.

THE DE WITT SKETCH

The sketch of the Swan reveals a tiring-house façade (the front of the dressing-room area) with two doors leading to the stage. Above the tiring house frontage, several people are looking out on to the large thrust stage, on which three actors are involved in a performance or rehearsal. Above is a tiled superstructure supported by two pillars, which are a fixed part of the stage itself, and above this is a hut with a trumpeter and flag. There are also three tiers of galleries for the audience, with entrances from the yard area around the stage (we know that the cheapest and probably most crowded place for the audience was in the yard itself).

The sketch is helpful but also frustrating in some crucial areas. It is not clear, for example, whether the people above the tiring-house are actors or audience and, if they are audience, there is no clear playing area shown above the stage, despite the fact that many plays require action 'above' or 'aloft' or 'on the walls'. Nor does the sketch show the whereabouts of a music-room, if one existed, or any kind of recessed discovery space (once thought of as an inner stage), required in some plays. Still, De Witt was not to know, when he made a casual drawing of the Swan, that his sketch would later be at the center of academic debates.

THE BOYS' COMPANIES

So far we have only discussed the public theaters, but plays were also performed at so-called 'private' theaters. To give some idea of these, it is useful to begin with a brief history of the Elizabethan and Jacobean boys' companies, which dominated the private theater scene during most of Shakespeare's career. The professional adult companies competed at various times with two principal companies of boys, the Children of the Chapel Royal and the Boys of St Paul's Cathedral choir school. The boys were originally selected for their singing talents but, as the theatrical activities of these two companies increased, so the acting abilities of the boys must have influenced recruitment. Traditionally they had performed plays only occasionally and for special events such as the Queen's Christmas festivities. However after 1576 (when the Theatre was built) the skills of the Chapel Children were turned into a profiteering venture by their manager, Richard Farrant. He organized performances of plays by these boys in an indoor theater within the area Blackfriars. This was located inside the city boundaries but, because of a technicality, was not subject to the control of the city authorities.

The Blackfriars enterprise with the Chapel Children was relatively short-lived. After Farrant died in 1580, there was some kind of amalgamation with the Paul's boys but legal wranglings over lease arrangements soon led to the closing of the Blackfriars Theater. The Paul's boys, however, continued playing through the 1580s. The main contributor of plays to their company was John Lyly, who appears to have found their acting suitable for his witty and highly mannered style of writing, with its frequent use of alliteration and verbal patternings (a style later satirized by Shakespeare in *Love's Labour's Lost*). The company survived until 1590 when it was suppressed after becoming involved in the Marprelate controversy, a mud-slinging match between puritans and bishops.

THE WAR OF THE THEATERS

These two companies reappeared at the turn of the century with new boys, of course, and new managers. By this time Shakespeare's career was well-established and, in *Hamlet* he refers to a group of *little eyases* (i.e. boy players) who were allegedly dominating the theatrical scene. This is probably an exaggeration, although there was clearly fierce competition between the boy and adult players. The revived boys' companies began by performing some of their old plays but soon began to specialize in satirical dramas, and included in their subject-matter for satire the adult companies themselves, their playwrights, and style of performance.

This issue of differing performance styles is a contentious one. Probably the boys were trained in the art of rhetoric which emphasized pronunciation and gesture. The adult players did not have this training, and a distinction is sometimes made between the 'acting' skills of the boys and the inferior 'playing' of the adults. Nonetheless the adult companies put on plays originally written for the boys and the boys performed plays written for the adults. In fact there is evidence that they stole each other's plays. The playwrights themselves did not necessarily write exclusively for either adults or boys.

It is difficult to believe therefore that styles of performance were always so clearly distinguishable. Perhaps when the boys ridiculed the stamping and ranting tragedians of the public stages they were satirizing a style of acting which was more appropriate in the large public playhouses. It has also been suggested that the adults' acting was more declamatory in the 1580s and 1590s. In his famous advice to the players on acting, Hamlet warns them against 'out-heroding Herod' (i.e. stamping the stage boards and raging), a fashion which had presumably become outdated.

SATIRE AND THE KING

Thomas Middleton was the main playwright for the Paul's Company and his comedies about swindling and corruption in the City of London seem to have been particularly popular. John Marston wrote some plays for this company but soon worked for the rival Chapel Children, who were given the distinguished title of The Children of the Queen's Revels in 1603. He was manager of the company for a short time and made his name by writing satirical tragedies, critical of the court. It was surely no coincidence that these plays followed the accession of James I in 1603. The extravagance and corruption for which he was soon notorious made him an obvious target for the playwrights, though direct attacks on the monarch himself were usually disguised by transparent devices like setting plays in foreign courts. *Troilus and Cressida*, one of Shakespeare's most cynical plays about authority and power, was written around this time and conveniently set in the mythical past. The Paul's Boys ceased performing around 1607, for no known reason, while the Chapel Children continued until 1613.

The Chapel Children's story during the 13-year period from 1600 to 1613 is extraordinary in that their satirical comedies and tragedies invoked the wrath of the authorities on several occasions (clearly the disguises did not fool anybody), resulting in playwrights, managers and possibly even boys spending time in prison. Yet they persisted with this kind of drama and managed to survive despite their stormy relationship with the King, even performing at court at Christmas 1608.

BOYS AND MEN

The sharp distinction that existed between boys' and adult companies around 1600 must have altered considerably within a matter of only a few years. The Children of the Queen's Revels would have looked a lot less like children when they moved to a new theater at Whitefriars in 1609, after the King's Men took over at Blackfriars. They were in fact amalgamated with an adult company, Lady Elizabeth's Men, in 1613. The company included two particularly famous actors, Salomon Pavey, noted for his portrayals of old men, and Nathan Field, who later acted with the King's Men and became a playwright himself.

There were also boys who performed in adult companies, usually playing women's parts, for which their unbroken voices were obviously suited. To judge by some of the

Unusually, Nathan Field graduated from a boys' company into an adult acting company.

female parts written during this period, like Shakespeare's Cleopatra and Lady Macbeth, some of these boys must have been particularly skillful performers.

As acting was a new profession boy actors did not have any traditional apprenticeship, such as existed in the various professional guilds. Their position would no doubt have been financially precarious but they did learn a trade and some of them went on to become shareholders in adult companies. Of the two most famous performers of the time, Richard Burbage is said to have been acting at the age of 13 and Edward Alleyn was already an attraction by the time he was 16. Generally, however, boys rarely graduated from the boys' companies to adult companies. Most of them, whose handling by their managers we would probably today call exploitation, disappeared into obscurity once their age made them ineligible for playing.

SEE ALSO: Ch 2 47, Ch 3 70-2, 78-80, 83, Ch 4 148-9, 158-9

THE BLACKFRIARS THEATER

The domination of the private theaters by the boys' companies did not then continue long into the Jacobean period. Shakespeare's company was to break into this specialist market when it began performing at the Blackfriars Theater around 1609, though it had attempted to stage plays there as early as 1596, when James Burbage first purchased the building. At that time the company met with opposition from the local inhabitants who had claimed that a theater in the Blackfriars was:

. . . a general inconvenience to all the inhabitants of the same precinct, both by reason of the great resort and gathering together of all manner of vagrant and lewd persons that, under colour of resorting to the plays, will come thither and work all manner of mischief, and also to the great pestering and filling up of the same precinct, if it should please God to send any visitation of sickness as heretofore hath been, for that the same precinct is already grown very populous; and besides, that the same playhouse is so near the Church that the noise of the drums and trumpets will greatly disturb and hinder both the ministers and parishioners in time of divine service and sermons . . .

One suspects a mixture of genuine and specious complaints here but evidently the case of the plaintiffs was upheld. James Burbage died in 1597 and the property passed to his sons Richard and Cuthbert. In 1600 the theater was leased by Richard Evans who, despite the complaints, succeeded in running it for his boys' company. Perhaps the local residents and city authorities thought the boys' theater would attract a more desirable clientele.

Burbage's sons and the Chamberlain's Men were soon occupied with the transference of the Theatre to the Bankside, but they were wise enough to retain the ownership of the more favorably positioned Blackfriars. By whatever means (persuasion, bribery or plain good fortune perhaps), they were able to establish this as their second

John Fletcher (left) and Francis Beaumont (right) collaborated on many romances and tragicomedies which appealed to the elite audiences of the Blackfriars Theater.

home by 1609, even though the Blackfriars liberty passed into the jurisdiction of the city authorities in 1608. Provided the adults did not imitate the boys and constantly offend authority, this new theater was always likely to be a commercial success. It differed greatly from the Globe, being centrally located, indoors instead of outdoors, and much more intimate. The minimum entry fee was sixpence for a seat (instead of a penny for a standing place at the Globe), and it was for this reason that the Blackfriars was referred to as a 'private' theater (i.e. it was more exclusive).

As it was indoors, it was protected from the unpredictable and often inclement English weather, which always threatened to deter audiences and reduce takings at the outdoor public playhouses. It appears that, after 1608, the King's Men continued to use the Globe during the summer months, when the more prosperous Blackfriars audience of landed gentry and Inns of Court students would have been out of town. Clearly the company was now performing

the necessary flying machinery used in plays performed there. By examining the plays we can also deduce that there were three doorways for the actors to make entrances, two trapdoors on stage, and a balcony for musicians, players and spectators. Entrance fees were higher than in the public play-houses, such as the Globe: sixpence for the galleries, a further shilling for a bench in the pit, two shillings to sit on the stage, and half a crown for a box.

If the assumption about the location of the tiring-house is correct, the actual play-ing space must have been severely re-stricted. The width would have been re-duced by nearly half to accommodate the side boxes, galleries and necessary access. Furthermore, there were certain vain gal-lants who considered it fashionable to sit on the stage itself, thus further impeding the actors and causing a general nuisance.

NEW AUDIENCES
Although the King's Men performed the same plays at both their public and private theaters, some difference in acting styles must have been required simply because the Blackfriars was a far more intimate, and perhaps more intimidating, playing space than the Globe. The expansive gestures and movements that would have been necessary in the public playhouses would probably have appeared excessive and comic in a cramped and claustrophobic indoor theater (hence, perhaps the boy actors' satire on the style of the adult performers). Satirical drama was in vogue when the boy actors performed at the Blackfriars, but when the King's Men took over a new fashion for tragicomedies developed. Shakespeare seems to have written the late plays, *Pericles* (c. 1608), *Cymbeline* (c. 1609), *The Winter's Tale* (c. 1610), and *The Tempest* (1611) with this new genre very much in mind. The most famous writers of tragicomedies though were Beaumont and Fletcher. In his preface to *The Faithful Shepherdess* (1608), Fletcher attempted a definition of this kind of play: *A tragi-comedy is not so called in respect of mirth and killing, but in respect it wants deaths, which is enough to make it no tragedy, yet it brings some near it, which is enough to make it no comedy . . .*

for two different audiences, but this can be overstated and it would be wrong to imagine that a simple or precise distinction can be made between a plebeian rabble at the Globe and a sophisticated aristocratic clientele at the Blackfriars Theater. Any-body who went to the indoor private theaters was as likely to go to the outdoor public playhouses as well.

SEATING AND ACTING SPACE
Our knowledge of what this theater actually looked like is unfortunately fairly limlited. Burbage most probably converted into an acting area seven rooms on the first floor of what had formerly been the Parliament Chamber or Great Hall of the Blackfriars monastery. The resulting space for actors and audience is estimated to have measured about 66 feet by 46 feet, much smaller than at the Globe. There was a paved auditor-ium, a pit and galleries with benches and boxes probably placed along the sides of the chamber and the stage itself. There is no certainty about the exact location of the stage area, though it does seem likely that some kind of tiring-house arrangement was set up against one of the shorter walls. A 'room over the stage' is known to have existed, which would have served well for

ADVICE TO THE AUDIENCE

Dekker's *The Gull's Hornbook* gives us a humorous insight into the effect of the practice of allowing the audience on the stage, in a chapter entitled 'How a Gallant should behave himself in a Playhouse':

Present not yourself on the stage (especially at a new play) until the quaking prologue hath (by rubbing) got colour into his cheeks, and is ready to give the trumpets their cue, that he's upon point to enter: for then it is time, as though you were one of the properties, or that you dropped out of the hangings, to creep from behind the arras, with your tripos or three-footed stool in one hand, and a teston mounted between a forefinger and a thumb in the other . . . It shall crown you with rich commendation, to laugh aloud in the midst of the most serious and saddest scene of the terriblest tragedy: and let that clapper (your tongue) be tossed so high, that all the house may ring of it . . .

Complicated plots and improbable events are characteristic of these plays, which are allegorical rather than realistic and tend to conclude with an idealistic picture of social harmony, presented from an obviously aristocratic standpoint.

Increased use of musical and spectacular effects, such as Prospero's masque in *The Tempest,* are characteristic of Blackfriars' plays. It is known that the audience at Blackfriars was often entertained with concerts of up to an hour before plays began. Act and scene divisions were also marked with musical pieces, and music was commonly incorporated into the structure of the plays put on there. Atmosphere could be further enhanced by lighting, as the stage was illuminated by candles, and this must have created some interesting chiaroscuro effects in the darkened indoor acting space. That the King's Men saw this new and exciting venue as their main home for the future is perhaps suggested by the fact that in 1613 Shakespeare established his London base within the Blackfriars area.

SEE ALSO: Ch 2 49, Ch 3 61-5, 84-5, Ch 4 166-75, Ch 5 182-5

MASQUES AND SPECTACLE

Favored acting companies were invited to perform at court. The traditional time for royal entertainments was the Christmas period, which concluded with a Twelfth Night play or a masque. The masque was essentially a sensuous and spectacular entertainment, which combined music and poetry with scenery and elaborate costumes. Originally the masque had been a relatively simple piece of theater featuring a procession of guests, usually in disguise, bearing gifts to a king or nobleman. During the reigns of James I and Charles I, the visual effects were dramatically increased and the scenic designer Inigo Jones introduced perspective scenery. For a time Inigo Jones worked with Ben Jonson, who introduced the anti-masque, an opening sequence of verse and dances which provided a violent contrast between initial disorder and chaos and a concluding order and harmony. Enormous sums of money were spent on this royal pastime, in which members of the audience often participated in the action.

The usual venue for court performances was a great banqueting hall, and some of these magnificent rooms were specially built for theatrical entertainments. A first Whitehall Banqueting House was built in 1572 and a second in 1581. The Queen's last suitor, the Duc d'Alençon, saw a number of performances by the two boys' companies at the second Banqueting House between November 1581 and February 1582, and the building itself was no doubt intended to impress him. The first Jacobean court masque, *The Masque of Blackness*, was also performed here. It required a stage about 40 feet square, with a temporary proscenium arch as wide as the hall, with Serlian wings and painted cloths behind it.

Of these purpose-built banqueting halls, the most spectacular and lavish was that ordered to be built by James I and called The first Jacobean Banqueting Hall at Whitehall. This was opened in 1608 with Jonson's *Masque of Beauty* and continued to be used primarily for the elaborate

Henry VIII's cockpit was converted into a theater by Prince Henry in 1611. It was later replaced by the Cockpit-in-Court, designed by Inigo Jones.

and costly Jacobean masques. The chaplain to the Venetian embassy, Orazio Busino, produced a fascinating description of the building and audience, after seeing Jonson's masque *Pleasure Reconciled to Virtue* in 1618.

. . . In the king's court . . . after Christmas day there begins a series of sumptuous banquets, well-acted comedies, and most graceful masques of knights and ladies. Of the masques, the most famous of all is performed on the morrow of the feast of the three Wise Men according to an ancient custom of the palace here. A large hall is fitted up like a theatre, with well secured boxes all round. The stage is at one end and his Majesty's chair in front under an ample canopy. Near him are stools for the foreign ambassadors. On the 16th of the current month of January, his Excellency was invited to see a representation and masque, which had been prepared with extraordinary pains, the chief performer being the king's own son and heir, the prince of Wales . . . Whilst waiting for the king we amused ourselves by admiring the decorations and beauty of the house with its two orders of columns, one above the other, their distance from the wall equalling the breadth of the passage, that of the second row being upheld by Doric pillars, while above these rise Ionic columns supporting the roof. The whole is of wood, including even the shafts, which are carved and gilt with much skill. From the roof of these hang festoons and angels in relief with two rows of lights. Then such a concourse as there was, for although they profess only to admit the favoured ones who are invited, yet every box was filled notably with most noble and richly arrayed ladies, in number some 600 and more according to the general estimate; the dresses being of such variety in cut and colour as to be indescribable; the most delicate plumes over their heads, springing from their foreheads or in their hands serving as fans; strings of jewels on their necks and bosoms and in their girdles and apparel in such quantity that they looked like so many queens, so that at the beginning, with but little

light, such as that of the dawn or of the evening twilight, the splendour of their diamonds and other jewels was so brilliant that they looked like so many stars. During the two hours of waiting we had leisure to examine them . . .

Only a few months after this eventful night the building was destroyed by fire and a second Jacobean Banqueting Hall was completed by Inigo Jones, in 1622, at a staggering cost of £9,850. As well as the banqueting halls, royal entertainments were often held at the Cockpit, a theater built at the time of Henry VIII for cockfighting and converted into an acting space by James I's son Prince Henry, in 1611. The Cockpit was later replaced by another Inigo Jones building, The Cockpit-in-Court.

Masques were extremely elaborate, and expensive, in their staging and costumes. This design for Oceania is by Inigo Jones.

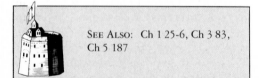

SEE ALSO: Ch 1 25-6, Ch 3 83, Ch 5 187

ELIZABETHAN STAGING

When the companies staged their plays in the commoner venues of public and private playhouses, they had to finance their own productions (the expensive and elaborate scenic devices and costumes employed in masques were paid for by royalty). Staging is a very conjectural area of investigation which began in earnest towards the end of the 19th century. At that time scholars were inclined to exaggerate the lack of stage scenery in Elizabethan and Jacobean plays. This was understandable because they were partly reacting to the elaborate and scenically detailed productions of their own age, but it is now recognized that an over-insistence on Shakespeare's 'bare stage' is inaccurate. That movable scenery was available is indicated by two important sources, firstly Philip Henslowe's diary, which lists his company's properties, and secondly the plays themselves. Henslowe's list includes many items of movable scenery, such as a 'tomb of Dido', a 'hell mouth', a 'bedstead', a 'bay tree', a 'tree of golden apples', a 'little altar', a 'moss bank', a 'great horse with his legs', and a 'cauldron for the Jew' (which must have been large enough for Barabas to fall into at the end of Marlowe's *Jew of Malta*).

SCENERY

The plays themselves make occasional demands for special scenic devices. For example, in Kyd's *The Spanish Tragedy* there is a bower scene in which two lovers, Horatio and Bel-Imperia, meet for a secret assignation. There they are surprised by Bel-Imperia's brother and accomplices, who hang Horatio on some kind of bower construction. In Act V of Middleton's *A Chaste Maid in Cheapside* there is a stage direction calling for a bed to be 'thrust out on stage'. Shakespeare's *Antony and Cleopatra* has the stage direction 'Enter Cleopatra, and her maids aloft, with Charmian, and Iras', which suggests that some kind of raised platform was used. Later the dying Antony is rather ignominiously hauled up

on to this construction, which was large enough to accommodate several persons and probably needed stagehands to move it on and off stage. In act V of *King Richard III*, Richard has the line: *Here pitch our tent, even here in Bosworth field* (neatly informing the audience of the location), and several lines later Richmond enters and some soldiers put up his tent. The two tents probably covered separate halves of the entire stage area; a considerable amount of action takes place within them and it seems unlikely that this would have been played out in small restrictive spaces with poor sightlines for the audience. Some theater historians have argued that stools, benches and other small items of furniture might have been left scattered about the stage during entire performances. This may have been so, but major obstacles like trees, beds, and caves would have had to be moved on and off stage, presumably by stagehands or actors playing minor roles.

Most entrances on stage must have been made through one of the upstage doors but more dramatic entrances and exits were possible. Ben Jonson referred contemptuously to a 'creaking throne' which descended from the heavens, and Henslowe is known to have paid the relatively large sum of £7 2s for such a device, which is required in several plays, notably Marlowe's *Dr Faustus*. Shakespeare made use of a similar entry in *Cymbeline* with the descent of Jupiter, indicated by the dramatic stage direction: 'Jupiter descends in thunder and

Releasing smoke from under the stage created the impression of fog as required in Arden of Faversham. *This could be a very risky practice.*

lightning, sitting upon an eagle. He throws a thunderbolt.'

Such devices were part of the stock-in-trade of the players, many of them inherited from the medieval theater. It was as much part of a playwright's craft to employ them to create suitable stage imagery as it was to use verbal imagery. It should be stressed that the companies would have been inclined to keep their properties and items of scenery relatively simple because they did not only perform in the playhouses where these objects could be easily accommodated. It was no use writing a play that could not be toured because the technical requirements were too complicated. Most of Shakespeare's plays avoid stage furnishings and clutter. In fact, about 80 per cent of his scenes could be performed on an entirely bare stage, so while we should be aware of scenic devices, their importance should not be overstated.

COSTUMES

Though the actors kept their scenery simple, they made up for this by spending lavishly on their costumes, and the tireman, or wardrobe master, was an important member of any company. Sometimes wealthy patrons passed on expensive costumes from their own wardrobes, but in this fashion-conscious age companies were prepared to pay vast sums for their costumes. Alleyn records a payment of £20 10s 6d. for a 'black velvet cloak with sleeves embroidered all with silver and gold' (£30 was the likely annual income for a company). Henslowe and Alleyn provided a complete inventory of their wardrobe, divided into 'Cloaks', 'Gowns', 'Antic suits', 'Jerkins and doublets', 'Frenchose', and 'Venetians', with detailed entries such as: 'a scarlet cloak with two broad gold laces, with two buttons of the same down the sides', 'a short velvet cap cloak embroidered with gold and gold spangles', 'one black velvet (gown) laced and drawn out with white sarsenet'.

In their use of costume, the players seem to have been more concerned to present visual splendor and luxuriance, wherever it was appropriate, than historical accuracy. A famous contemporary sketch of *Titus Andronicus*, a play set in ancient Rome, shows an anachronistic mixture of Roman and Renaissance dress. In Shakespeare's *The Tempest* most characters could have been costumed with the basic garments in the wardrobe but something special might have been made or purchased for Prospero's magic cloak and the costumes of Ariel and Caliban. Similarly in *King Lear*

Costumes formed a major item in any company's budget. Main characters, like Tamburlaine, were often elaborately dressed.

an especially extravagant costume would have been appropriate for Lear when he divides his kingdom, in a scene of ritualistic pomp and ceremony. Popular theatrical devices like dumb shows, processions, and masques in plays would have all been opportunities for the players to show off their expensive and colorful costumes. Costume colors were also used to signify class, occupation and even mood. Scarlet was used to indicate nobility or church figures like cardinals; blue represented merchants or serving-men and so forth.

SPECIAL EFFECTS

Lacking detailed 'realistic' scenery and often using symbolic or emblematic dramatic devices, the public and private stages were essentially nonillusionistic. There was generally no attempt made to conceal the fact that the actors were indeed actors playing characters other than themselves (though sometimes they 'played' themselves as well as their characters, as in the induction to Marston's *The Malcontent* where the players joke about the parts they are about to perform in the play proper). Shakespeare often made it very clear that what he was presenting was a fiction, and not life itself, as in the prologue at the opening of *King Henry V*.

This was no place for naturalism, our commonest acting style today, but this does not mean that the actors avoided realistic effects altogether. For woundings and killings, blood was released from bladders and sponges concealed in costumes. To judge from the plays, companies must have had their stock of realistic looking heads and skulls as well as other bits of human anatomy, like hands and fingers, which were sometimes required. The impression of fog could be created by releasing smoke from under the stage, and some such effect might have been used in original performances of *Arden of Faversham* (a dangerous practice one would imagine). Thunder was simulated by drums or the rolling of a bullet on a sheet of metal, and lightning was created by primitive fireworks. Drums were regularly used to provide the kind of martial music suitable for battle scenes when the appearance of a few actors in battle dress presenting their 'colors' would be enough to signify an army. Night scenes were created by the simple device of bringing actors on stage with flaming torches. There is no evidence to suggest that these kinds of effects differed greatly at public and private playhouses, though private theaters like the Blackfriars did have more resources for music and would not have needed the same volume for sound effects such as cannon fire (apparently replaced by a pistol shot in the Blackfriars).

VERSATILITY

Sound effects could be created by imaginative use of musical instruments. The Admiral's Men had three trumpets, a drum, a treble and bass viol, a bandore, a sackbut, three timbrels, and a chime of bells. Hautboys (oboes), lutes, citherns, and pipes were also available. A number of performers were particularly noted for their musical talents, Robert Armin and Augustine Phillips in particular. A playwright working closely with a company (as many did) would know just what musical resources were available and would write his plays with these in mind. Today it is not unusual to find writers working in relative isolation from the day-to-day activity of the theater and, once a play has been commissioned, the author may have little or no involvement in its rehearsal and production process. In Shakespeare's day playwrights were usually involved at every level of production, possibly even acting in their own plays. Division of labor was not so clearly demarcated as it now tends to be in our larger theaters, and the idea of having separate and specialist tasks like directing, construction and maintenance of scenery, acting, administration etc. would have seemed strange to Elizabethan companies.

For most of his career Shakespeare was a playwright, an actor and a financial speculator for one company. The idea that he was only valued as a writer and took no part in the staging of his plays is inconceivable. A successful company was clearly made up of people who were versatile, adaptable, and knew every aspect of their trade. Obviously there were those who had particular skills and, when it came to acting, would have been suited to certain roles, but the general set-up would have been such that everybody worked closely together and playwrights would have had confidence in their company's ability to mount a new play quickly and efficiently. The task of directing did not exist for the simple reason that it was superfluous. Actors would have been expected to know what was generally required, and playwrights expected to use the talent and workshop resources available.

Special effects could be dangerous. 'Chambers discharged' during a performance of King Henry VIII *set fire to the Globe.*

> *San.* Yes, if I make my play:
> Heer's to your Ladifhip, and pledge it Madam:
> For 'tis to fuch a thing.
> *An.B.* You cannot fhew me.
>   *Drum and Trumpet, Chambers difchargd.*
> *San.* I told your Grace, they would talke anon.
> *Card.* What's that?
> *Cham.* Looke out there, fome of ye.
> *Card.* What warlike voyce,
> And to what end is this? Nay, Ladies, feare not;
> By all the lawes of Warre y'are priuiledg'd.

THE ACTORS

In 1597 when the companies permitted to play in London were restricted to two, the Chamberlain's Men and the Admiral's Men, Shakespeare was 33 years old, a middle-aged man by Elizabethan standards, and some ten years into his career as a playwright, so quite experienced at his trade. We know a little about the other personnel in his company at this time. The eight leading members were Thomas Pope, Augustine Phillips, William Kempe, John Heminge, Richard Burbage, William Shakespeare, William Sly, and Henry Condell and, of these, all but Sly and Condell were shareholders. A further four people, not known by name, are thought to have been permanent company members along with about four boy apprentices. For plays with large casts, and there were plenty of these (Shakespeare's *King Richard III* has a cast list of well over 40, allowing for doubling-up of lords, messengers, soldiers, etc.), actors would have played several roles and it was common practice to hire extra performers and musicians as necessary.

The hierarchy is apparent, with the financial backers, who might or might not be actual performers, at the top, and the casual hirelings and boy apprentices at the bottom. The fact that Shakespeare's company stayed together for so long and continued playing well after his death is an indication of the stability that was created by this hierarchy. Without such a secure working structure it is doubtful that Shakespeare would have been able regularly to write about two plays a year.

RICHARD BURBAGE

The most famous actor of the Chamberlain's Men was Richard Burbage, tragedian, painter, and major shareholder in the company. Baker's chronicle, written in 1674 and some 55 years after his death, described him and Edward Alleyn as 'two such actors as no age must ever look to see the like'. Burbage was not so financially successful as Alleyn, but he is said to have amassed £300 value in land by the time of his death, which was a handsome sum in

Arguably the greatest tragedian of his age, Richard Burbage created many of the major roles in Shakespeare's greatest plays, including Richard III, Hamlet, Othello, and Lear.

those days. As he was involved in both the Blackfriars and Globe projects, we might assume that he was adept as a businessman.

He is known to have played the parts of Richard III, Hamlet, King Lear, Othello, and Ferdinand in John Webster's play *The Duchess of Malfi*. A contemporary's tribute to his acting described him as: *a delightful Proteus, so wholly transforming himself into his parts, and putting off himself with his clothes, as he never (not so much as in the tiring-house) assumed himself again until the play was done.*

KEMPE AND ARMIN

William Kempe joined the company in 1594 and left only a few years later in 1599. He was a specialist in comic roles and is known to have played the parts of Dogberry in *Much Ado About Nothing* and Peter in *Romeo and Juliet*. After he left the company he performed a morris dance from London to Norwich, known as the 'nine days wonder', and later made a name for himself in Europe by dancing across the Alps. An eccentric he may have been, but his dancing skills would have made him very employable for a time, when jigs were a main attraction at the playhouses and were often performed at the end of an afternoon's entertainment. Comic skills of the kind possessed by Kempe seem to have been less valued towards the turn of the century when the popularity of the clown began to be replaced by that of the serious tragedian. Perhaps Kempe fell out with Shakespeare's company because they sensed a decline in the clown's fortunes. It has even been suggested that he was inclined to indulge in disruptive improvisations during performances and was the real butt of Hamlet's remarks to the players who come to perform at Elsinore:

And let those that play your clowns speak no more than is set down for them; for there be of them that will themselves laugh, to set on some quantity of barren spectators to laugh too, though in the meantime some necessary question of the play be then to be considered. That's villainous, and shows a most pitiful ambition in the fool that uses it. (*Hamlet* III ii 36-43)

Kempe was succeeded by Robert Armin, a playwright and singer as well as a performer of comic roles, who performed the more subtle and demanding parts of Feste and the Fool in *King Lear*.

OTHER ACTORS

As for Shakespeare himself, little is known about his acting or even whether, when he became a shareholder in the company in 1594, he was valued more for his skills as a writer or a performer. Tradition holds that he played Adam in *As You Like It* and the ghost of Hamlet's father. Of the other actors, we unfortunately know very little. Heminge and Condell earned themselves an eternal reputation by collecting Shakespeare's plays and publishing them in the first Folio edition of 1623. That Shakespeare failed to undertake this task himself suggests that he was not especially concerned that future generations should perform his plays, nor was publishing a major source of income for him. He made his money as a shareholder in his company, which was normal practice for playwrights who had contracts with a single company. Other writers, like Ben Jonson, who took great pains over the publishing of his own plays, worked on a freelance basis, but this would seem to have been a rather precarious financial arrangement, and a good actor could have expected to make more money than a freelance writer.

William Kemp's 'Nine Daies Wonder', when he danced a morris through England.

RICHARD TARLTON

Both Kempe and Armin claimed to be descended from the most famous clown of the Elizabethan period, Richard Tarlton, who had performed with the Queen's Men during the 1580s. This was probably no more than an advertising gimmick but it was nonetheless quite a tribute to Tarlton, a clown, playwright, tumbler, drummer, acrobat, and fencer, who was said by Henry Peacham in 1638 to have the unique ability to make an audience laugh merely by walking on stage:

> Tarlton when his head was onely seen,
> The tire-house door and tapestry between,
> Set all the multitude in such a laughter,
> They could not hold for scarce an hour after.

A Playwright's Contract

Precise details of Shakespeare's contractual arrangements as a writer are not known, but a contract drawn up between Richard Brome and Queen Henrietta's Men in 1635 gives some idea of what was expected of a playwright and is probably fairly typical. In return for a weekly wage and one day's takings from the box office, Brome was required to write exclusively for this company, to produce three plays a year, to write prologues, epilogues, introductions, and inductions for plays as necessary, and to add new scenes for revivals of old plays. Furthermore his plays were the property of the company for which he wrote. The fact that the King's Men owned the plays Shakespeare wrote before he joined them in 1594, suggests that, in his early years, he was not closely attached to any company.

There was generally a reluctance to publish plays because this helped rival actors to steal them or produce pirate versions. But pirating went on with or without printed texts to refer to, and several of Shakespeare's plays, notably *King Henry VI,* (2 and 3) and *King Henry V,* appear to have been reproduced by faulty memory.

Copyright as we understand it today did not exist. Printers and publishers were theoretically protected by the Stationer's Register, but the companies and writers had no such protection. Marston's play *The Malcontent,* written for the boy actors, was stolen by the King's Men in retaliation for the plagiarizing of *The Spanish Tragedy.* Stolen and often inaccurate versions of plays gave rise to so-called 'bad' Quarto texts, which were often followed by corrective 'good' ones, brought out by the company to whom the play originally belonged.

Robert Armin succeeded Will Kempe and created the more subtle 'clown' roles, such as Feste.

PLAYS AND PLAYWRIGHTS

To be a financially successful playwright it was obviously necessary to be commercially minded and, in this respect, Shakespeare's background probably gave him an advantage over some of his fellow playwrights. At the start of his career he was competing with university-educated writers like Robert Greene, Thomas Lodge, Christopher Marlowe, John Lyly, Thomas Nashe, and George Peele. These playwrights, known collectively as the 'university wits', prided themselves on their classical learning and some of them saw themselves very much as the superiors of the common players.

Greene snootily referred to Shakespeare as an 'upstart crow', who, in his view, was no more than a hack writer and had no business aspiring to the status of playwright and poet. In a famous pamphlet entitled *The Groatsworth of Wit* (1592), Greene attacked the players for being insolent and haughty and one might guess that he was more than a little envious of their success. His view was that the learned 'poets' who had studied the classical masters ought to be the respected purveyors of art, though, ironically, he often exploited more popular native styles of writing, as is the case in his two most famous plays, *The Honourable History of Friar Bacon and Friar Bungay* (c. 1589), and *James IV of Scotland* (c. 1591). It is possible that he had a hand in Shakespeare's *King Henry VI* plays and Kyd's *The Spanish Tragedy*. He was equally famous as a writer of pamphlets and prose romances, and one of the latter, *Pandosto*, was a major influence on *The Winter's Tale*.

CHRISTOPHER MARLOWE

Vilified as an atheist, a homosexual, and a tavern brawler, Christopher Marlowe has often been associated with the darker side of Elizabethan life. He probably worked as a spy for Queen Elizabeth's secret service and his death in 1593, resulting from a fight in a tavern near London, may have been associated with his espionage work. One

rather implausible, not to say ludicrous, theory claims that he was not actually killed but instead was concealed and later came back to write plays under Shakespeare's name. He was only 28 when he died and though much sensational rumor surrounds his brief life, reliable biographical information is extremely scant. Unlike Greene, he worked closely with actors, mainly with the Admiral's Men. Between 1587 and 1593 he wrote seven plays, some of which continued to be peformed at the popular citizen playhouses until the closing of the theaters in 1642, at the outbreak of the civil war.

His first work, *Tamburlaine the Great*, was performed at the Rose where Edward Alleyn apparently excelled in the leading role of a humble Scythian shepherd who rises to conquer most of Europe, Africa, and Asia. This drama of a man who is magnificently eloquent, invincible, and brutal captures the Renaissance admiration of individual strength and will but, at the same time, presents a critique of absolute power and authority. A sequel to this, *Tamburlaine the Great* (2) followed a year later, which suggests that part 1 was an

The Tragical History of Dr Faustus *remains* Christopher Marlowe's *most popular play.*

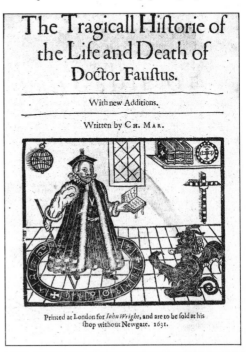

immediate box office success.

Marlowe's most often read and performed play today is *The Tragical History of Dr Faustus* (*c.* 1589). Based on a German medieval legend and borrowing heavily in its dramatic structure from the earlier morality tradition, it tells the story of the conflict between Dr Faustus's quest for knowledge and the limitations placed upon this quest by God (and the establishment perhaps, depending on one's reading of the play). The dubious quality of the text, first printed in 1604, has led scholars to argue that several farcical scenes were added by a later writer. However, Marlowe was writing for a popular audience which would not have been concerned with the niceties of distinction between tragedy and comedy, and he might well have included knockabout farcical scenes in his tragedy. Besides, it has been convincingly argued that the comic scenes are integrally related to the meaning of the whole play.

His other plays were *Dido Queen of Carthage* (*c.* 1587), possibly a collaboration with Thomas Nashe, *The Jew of Malta* (*c.* 1589), still being performed by Queen Henrietta's Men at the Cockpit as late as 1632, the history play *Edward II* (*c.* 1592), and a play about political struggles in 16th-century France, *The Massacre at Paris* (*c.* 1593).

THOMAS KYD

Marlowe was closely associated with the playwright Thomas Kyd. Both were involved in charges of atheism, and Kyd apparently saved his skin by implicating Marlowe when incriminating tracts were discovered in their shared lodgings. His major contribution to the drama of this period was *The Spanish Tragedy* (*c.* 1585-89), played by Strange's Men at the Rose and later by the Admiral's Men at the Fortune. This was an exceptionally popular play and was constantly revived and revised. Kyd's exploration of the ethics of personal revenge in an unjust world became a prototype for a series of revenge dramas, including Shakespeare's *Hamlet*, Cyril Tourneur's *The Revenger's Tragedy*, and John Webster's *The Duchess of Malfi* and *The White Devil*. The presentation of madness,

Thomas Middleton wrote a series of satirical comedies and, later, romantic comedies.

philosophical soliloquies, spectacles of horror, and an array of deaths in a concluding masque were characteristics of these plays, which offered audiences a vicarious insight into corruption and intrigue in court circles. Kyd is thought to have written another play, now lost, which influenced Shakespeare's *Hamlet*, often referred to as the *Ur-Hamlet*.

JOHN LYLY

In 1576, the year in which the first public playhouse was built, John Lyly came to London from Oxford. However, he was far more concerned with making a name for himself at court than working for the common players. His first plays *Campaspe* and *Sapho and Phao* were written for boy actors to perform at the Queen's Christmas festivities in 1583-84. In the late 1580s and early 1590s he wrote six plays for the Paul's boys, intended for both public and court performance. These plays are notable for their unique rhetorical style, which gave rise to the expression 'euphuism' (after his prose narrative *Euphues, The Anatomy of Wit*). Clearly he had high hopes for himself, for he sought the post of Master of the Revels, which would have given him control over both court and public entertainments. Unfortuntely for him, he lost favor at court and ended his days embittered and financially ruined.

GEORGE PEELE

Experimenting with various types of plays and entertainments, George Peele, like Greene, helped bridge the gap between classical and popular dramatic traditions. His earliest work, *The Arraignment of Paris* (*c.* 1581), a futile attempt to flatter Queen Elizabeth, was the first English play to describe itself as a 'pastoral'. *David and Bethsabe* (*c.* 1587) was one of the last biblical dramas of the age, *Edward I* (*c.* 1591), was an historical play, and *The Old Wife's Tale* (*c.* 1590) was a fantastical comedy. He also wrote civic pageants and occasional pieces for royal tournaments.

THOMAS MIDDLETON

A less sentimental view of London life was presented in the plays of Thomas Middleton, who wrote a series of satirical comedies for both boy and adult performers; *A Mad World My Masters* and *Michaelmas Term* in 1604, *A Trick to Catch the Old One* in 1606, *The Roaring Girl* in 1608, and *A Chaste Maid in Cheapside* in 1613. *The Roaring Girl* is remarkable for its time in its creation of a female transvestite (based on a real character), Moll Cutpurse, who exposes injustice and articulates the play's central attack on men's abuse of women. Middleton pursued this subject in his two famous tragedies of the 1620s, *The Changeling* and *Women Beware Women*.

BEN JONSON

One of the most learned writers of the age was Ben Jonson, though he was not actually a university graduate. Like some of the 'university wits', he had problems writing for a public which did not always share his idea of what the purpose of his art should be. He was a self-conscious imitator of the language and form of classical authors, in contrast to Shakespeare whose style was altogether more popular and eclectic. Jonson had a strong conviction that the playwright should be a moral educator and was perhaps too concerned with what

Ben Jonson was one of the most learned writers of the age and a self-conscious classicist.

audiences ought to like; Shakespeare, on the other hand, was the more uninhibited storyteller who had a shrewd appreciation of the various tastes of his audiences and knew what they did like. When audiences failed to respond positively to his plays, Jonson was inclined to take umbrage and blame their ignorance, as in this extract from *Everyman Out of His Humour:*

> *Come leave the loathed stage,*
> *And the more loathsome age: . . .*
> *Say, that thou pour'st them wheat,*
> *And they will acorns eat:*
> *'Twere simple fury, still, thyself to waste*
> *On such as have no taste!*

He joined the London players at about the same time as Shakespeare and is recorded as having performed the part of Hieronimo, the leading role in *The Spanish Tragedy*. By all accounts he was a quarrelsome and arrogant man and his volatile personality soon landed him in trouble. After killing a fellow actor, Gabriel Spencer, in a brawl, he only managed to save his own life by reciting his neck-verse in prison (an old custom by which one could be exempted from sentence by quoting Latin verse, usually Psalm 51).

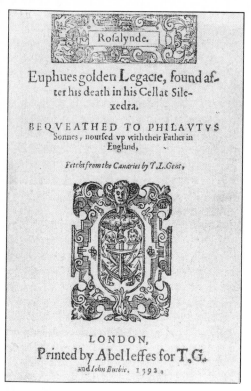

Rosalynde *was deeply influenced by John Lyly,
and was a direct source for* As You Like It.

His part in the now lost play *The Isle of
Dogs* (*c.* 1597), which precipitated wide
suppression of acting in London, also resulted in his imprisonment. He was active

UNIVERSITY PLAYWRIGHTS

Thomas Lodge and Thomas Nashe are better
known today for their vitriolic pamphlets
than their plays, though these had an
influence on the satirical comedies and
tragedies that became popular during the
Jacobean period. For most of the university
playwrights, who aspired to the status of
'poets', responding to the commercial
demands of the London theaters seems to
have been a disillusioning experience, as their
view of themselves as men of vision and
special talent does not seem to have been
shared by the players or the general public.
Their chief successors in comedy, Thomas
Dekker and Thomas Heywood, were both
more sympathetic to the popular taste for
festive and adventurous dramas which
celebrated the honest virtues of the London
citizen class.

in the so-called 'war of the theaters' between
adult and boys' companies, and attacked,
among others, the playwrights John Marston and Thomas Dekker in *Cynthia's Revels*
(*c.* 1600) and *The Poetaster* (*c.* 1601), both of
which were written for the Children of the
Chapel at Blackfriars. However, differences
with Marston cannot have been too serious,
as four years later they worked together
with George Chapman on a satirical comedy
about London life, *Eastward Ho!* (*c.* 1605), a
play which made fun of King James. This
resulted in yet another period of imprisonment for Jonson.

His career is remarkable for the fre-
quency with which he fell in and out of
favor with royalty, reflected in his writing
of both court masques and satirical dramas,
like *Sejanus* (*c.* 1603) and *Catiline* (*c.* 1611),
about court corruption. To gain a general
picture of Jonson's range as a writer, his
more famous comedies have to be set
alongside his tragedies, his masques, and
his critical work *Timber* (one of the first
important pieces of English dramatic criticism). Though he wrote a few plays in the
1590s, his career proper began in 1598 with
the comedy *Every Man in his Humour*.
Between then and 1616 he produced his
most famous comic works, *Volpone* (1605),
Epicœne (1609-10), *The Alchemist* (1610),
Bartholomew Fair (1614), and *The Devil is an
Ass* (1616). Between 1605 and 1612 he also
wrote eight masques for royal entertainment, but he fell out of favor in the later
years of James's reign and had little success
with the Caroline court. His later plays, *The
Staple of News* (1625), *The New Inn* (1629),
The Magnetic Lady (1632), and *The Tale of a
Tub* (1633), are generally considered to be
lesser works. He published his own work in
a folio collection in 1616, which set a
precedent for the publishing of the complete works of Shakespeare and the plays of
Beaumont and Fletcher.

BEAUMONT AND FLETCHER

Francis Beaumont and John Fletcher were
the great collaborators of the age, though
their dependence upon each other has
sometimes been overstated. This is no
doubt the case in John Aubrey's brief and
amusing biographical note on their lives:

THE REPERTORY

Writing in collaboration was evidently quite common, as many as four or five authors sometimes working together on a single play. This obviously helped to turn plays out quickly, in response to a continual demand for new work. Some authors were staggeringly prolific and make Shakespeare's 37 plays, in about 24 years, seem quite a modest achievement by comparison. Thomas Heywood, who wrote for the rumbustious Red Bull audience, claimed to have 'either an entire hand, or at least a main finger' in 220 plays and, over a period of 30 years, Philip Massinger wrote or co-wrote some 53 plays.

Most of the plays written during this period are now either lost or unavailable in modern editions. Consequently, reading or seeing Shakespeare's plays and the occasional work by his contemporaries is liable to give a rather partial impression of the range of theatrical entertainment available at this time. Looking back we tend to see Shakespeare as the pre-eminent dramatist of the age, but this is not how he would have appeared to his contemporaries.

They lived together on the Bankside, not far from the playhouse, both bachelors; lay together; had one wench in the house between them, which they did so admire; the same clothes and cloak etc. between them. They wrote some 15 plays together between 1608 and 1613, after which Beaumont retired. Fletcher continued to write by himself and in collaboration with other authors, including Shakespeare with whom he wrote *King Henry VIII.* They were both closely associated with the King's Men and developed the new genre of tragicomedy, written very much with the wealthier aristocratic audiences that would have visited the Blackfriars Theater in mind. During the Restoration period, in the 17th century, Beaumont and Fletcher were considered to be the best playwrights of the Jacobean period by established literary opinion.

SEE ALSO: Ch 2 44, Ch 3 70-3, Ch 4 87-9, 108-11, 172-3, 176-7, Ch 5 182-5

SHAKESPEARE'S AUDIENCE

Lastly we need to know something about the social make-up of the people who paid to see the plays of Shakespeare and his fellow playwrights. After all drama cannot take place without audiences. Thomas Platter, a German traveler, attended a performance at the Curtain, in 1599, and made some observations: *Thus daily at two in the afternoon, London has two, sometimes three plays running in different places, competing with each other, and those which play best obtain most spectators. The playhouses are so constructed that they play on a raised platform, so that everyone has a good view. There are different galleries and places, however, where the seating is better and more comfortable and therefore more expensive. For whoever cares to stand below only pays one English penny, but if he wishes to sit he enters by another door, and pays another penny, while if he desires to sit in the most comfortable seats which are cushioned, where he not only sees everything well, but can also be seen, then he pays yet another English penny at another door.*

Though Platter omits to mention the lords' rooms, where the entry fee was sixpence, his description gives us a picture of a theater which caters for a variety of social classes, with the exception of the very poor and unemployed, who must have made up a sizeable part of the population. Estimates for audience figures based on Philip Henslowe's diary suggest that about 15,000 people per week attended plays in 1595, and 21,000 per week attended in 1605 (audience figures were always highest for new plays and performances during holidays). Given that the population of London was somewhere between 150,000 and 200,000, this suggests that something like 10 per cent of the population regularly attended plays.

THE GROUNDLINGS

It is often assumed that the poorer members of the audience who stood in the yard area around the stage were unruly and ignorant. The 'groundlings' who paid the cheapest entry fee of one penny, so the argument

Even the more select audiences of private theaters were inclined to comment on the plays, chatter, and sometimes throw missiles at the players.

goes, were inclined to interrupt plays they disapproved of by jeering, cracking nuts, hurling fruit at the stage, and generally upstaging the players with their boorish behavior. These 'stinkards', as they are sometimes referred to, apparently passed their afternoons being bored and confused by the greater part of the plays they watched, waiting for some 'comic business', 'light relief' or horror effect to amuse them. This view seems to be based mainly on snobbery about the 'lower orders' backed up by a few comments from the plays of the period taken out of context. Thus Hamlet's famous complaint about the groundlings who are *capable of nothing but inexplicable dumb shows and noise* is sometimes cited to prove that much of the audience was rather moronic. I do not wish to give the impression that the audience was necessarily reverent or particularly 'well-behaved' in the way that we might describe a quiet and respectful bourgeois audience at the theater today. However it does seem extremely unlikely that people would regularly pay a substantial amount of their income to see plays which they found incomprehensible.

It is true that frequent complaints were made about riotous behavior at the playhouses by the city fathers, but then they had their particular reasons to exaggerate. It seems unlikely that audiences were as disorderly as they claimed, though disturbances certainly did sometimes occur, and not always of the audience's own making. Apprentice gangs occasionally ran riot on festive days, sometimes attacking brothels or playhouses. A contemporary account describes a violent attack on an indoor playhouse in 1617.

The prentices on Shrove Tuesday last, to the number of 3 or 4,000 committed extreme insolencies . . . part, making for Drury Lane, where lately a new playhouse is erected, they beset the house round, broke in, wounded divers of the players, broke open their trunks, and what apparrel, books or other things they found, they burnt; and not content herewith, got on the top of the house, and untiled it, and had not the Justices of Peace and Sheriff levied an aid, and hindered their purpose, they would have laid that house . . . even with the ground. In this skirmish one prentice was slain, being shot through the head with a pistol, and many other of their fellows were sore hurt, and such of them as are taken his Majesty hath commanded shall be executed for example sake.

The playwrights themselves sometimes complained about the ignorance of their audiences but we might guess that this was often a case of sour grapes. When plays are received badly it is tempting to blame the audience's lack of intelligence for failing to understand them. Shakespeare was not one to complain about his audiences, but then he usually had no need to; he was an extremely shrewd judge of his market.

The last word ought to go to Jonson,

. . . Soul of the age!
The applause! delight! the wonder of our
   stage!
My Shakespeare, rise; I will not lodge thee by
Chaucer, or Spenser, or bid Beaumont lie
A little further, to make thee a room:
Thou art a monument, without a tomb,
And art alive still, while thy book doth live,
And we have wits to read, and praise to give.

CHAPTER 4

THE PLAYS

Raphael Holinshed's Chronicles of England, Scotland
and Ireland: *Macbeth and Banquo meet the witches.*

The story behind a play by Shakespeare is usually borrowed from
another author. All except two (*A
Midsummer Night's Dream* and *The Tempest*) of
the 38 or 39 plays which Shakespeare is
known to have written or thought to have
collaborated on take their major story lines
from other published material. Even in
these two cases, numerous individual incidents and sections have their source or
analogues. The enchanted island, the magician who by the help of spirits seeks to settle
old quarrels and arrange marriages, and the
shipwreck all have counterparts in various
commedia dell'arte scenari as well as in the
emblems of alchemical literature, while
several accounts, both published and private, concerning a wreck in the Bermudas
in 1609 furnished details for the shipwreck
and for the fertile island.

Similarly, although there is no one
source for the main story of *A Midsummer
Night's Dream*, the theme of two men in love
with one girl can be found in Chaucer's 'The
Knight's Tale' (the undisputed source of *The
Two Noble Kinsmen*), which also gives details
of a marriage feast for Theseus and Hippolyta. The Pyramus and Thisbe story is in
Ovid's *Metamorphoses*, the man transformed
into an ass who has a dream vision of a moon
goddess comes from Apuleius' *The Golden
Ass* (translated by William Addlington in
1566), Puck is a creature of English folk
tale, while the appallingly wet summer of
1594 provides a topical allusion.

None of this, however, really accounts
for the play. It is the *synthesis* of English and
Greek, historical and mythical, comical-
pastoral-tragical which creates out of this
no-time and no-where, a dream vision of a
sometime-somewhere psychological truth
offered as an experience to the audience.
This process shapes even those plays which
follow their source material most closely.

HISTORY AND DRAMA
The imaginative combination of unrelated
times, events, and places into one psychological and emotional dramatic unity also
accounts for the supposed anachronisms in

the history plays. Shakespeare's historical information for *King Richard III*, for example (as indeed for most of the history plays including *Macbeth*, *King Lear*, and *Cymbeline*), comes largely from the second edition of Raphael Holinshed's *Chronicles of England, Scotland and Ireland* (1587). In the manner of medieval scholarship however, Holinshed tends to follow older authorities closely. His account of Richard III is taken verbatim from Edward Halle's chronicle *The Union of the Two Noble and Illustrious Families of Lancaster and York* (1548), which in turn comes from Sir Thomas More's *The Life of Richard III* (1513) and Polydore Vergil's *Historia Anglia* (1534).

Thus Shakespeare knew that the historical Queen Margaret had been dead for 20 years by the time of the events of his play. He brings her back from the grave so that her cursing reminiscence of past murders, chiming with the laments of the younger queens, creates a sense of a dreadful ritual of answering death culminating when Richard's victims, ghosts indeed, curse Richard in his dream before heaping blessings on the head of Richmond. This is not an historical truth, any more than More's portrayal of Richard as hunchbacked is historically true. Like More's distortion, it has the effect of casting Richmond – the future Henry VII and founder of the Tudor dynasty – in the role of God-given savior of his country despite his rather tenuous claim to the throne. The personal grief of the queens and the age-range of the characters from very young to very old express the historical events dramatically from the perspective from which most people normally view them – that of the family.

The political context is also the philosopher's stone whereby Shakespeare transforms the sordid dross of Giraldo Cinthio's story of domestic tragedy in *Gli Hecatommithi* into the tragedy of *Othello*. The historical background of the wars with Turkey lends both immediacy and universality to the love story. Desdemona's decision to accompany her husband becomes an act of genuine courage and a desire to be his equal in their marriage partnership, while Iago's jealous machinations against Cassio and Othello not only subvert the promise of that marriage but threaten the very safety of a garrison town in time of war. The audience, briefly cast in the role of citizens of Cypress during the Herald's speech, is invited to share in the double celebrations for Othello's marriage and the sinking of the Turkish fleet, and is thus caught up in the public implications of this particular private relationship. Just as with the theme of civil war in the history plays, so here the fear of Turkish expansion in Europe was a real one for a British audience. Most of them in 1604 would have been aware that Cyprus had in fact fallen to the Turks after a long and bitter seige in 1571. Shakespeare plays on his audience's knowledge of a recent political situation.

Of course the only evidence we can now have for Shakespeare's sources is the printed word, but we have no knowledge of the books which he actually possessed. Apart from those cases in which material is quoted wholesale, our knowledge of what he had read must be based on picking up verbal echoes contained in the plays, with the

Thomas North's translation of Plutarch's Lives *was a primary source of the Roman Plays. Shakespeare also drew on it for other plays.*

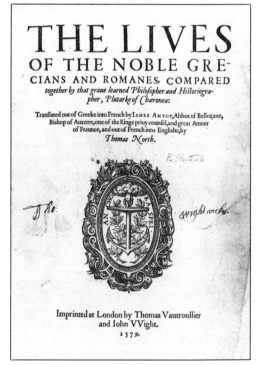

recognition that in some cases these might be coincidental.

Just as important as specific texts, is the general cultural milieu in which he lived, the universal wisdom contained in books of proverbs and collections of emblems which themselves often had a scholarly provenance back to the Bible or some classical text, but which formed both the basis and the means of expression of contemporary morals.

SHAPING CONVENTION

The conventional expression of conventional wisdom can, did, and does result in a lot of bad poetry; but the conventional use of images and ideas is itself a language, which like the language of words, can be used, re-formed and wrenched into new and exciting patterns. Perhaps the reason that Shakespeare took so much of North's translation of Plutarch's *The Life of Mark Antony* on a word-for-word basis in the writing of *Antony and Cleopatra* is because he found in it a ready-made structure of the sort that he had had to invent for *King John* or *Othello*.

The story had already excited many writers' imaginations. Spenser in the *Faerie Queene* cites the lovers as types of luxury and riotousness, but Chaucer includes Cleopatra in his *Legend of Good Women*. The ambivalence is an essential part of the story. Plutarch grudgingly recognizes that one of the reasons why Antony commanded such loyalty from his troops was because of his ability to mix freely with them, although the corollary to this is that his house in Rome became the resort of dancers, jugglers, and other undesirables. He disapproves of Cleopatra but cannot help acknowledging her power and fascination. Sir Thomas North falls upon the story with gusto. As has always been remarked, the language of his translation is exceptionally rich, and in some specific cases Shakespeare did little more than render North's prose in verse. However, as with the changes that he made to his own plays in the course of writing them, his alterations are usually more instructive than his borrowings. The development of Plutarch's lines: *she was layed under a pavilion of cloth of gold of tissue, apparelled and attired like the goddess Venus, commonly drawn in picture;* turns into:

Pyramus and Thisbe from Ovid's Metamorphoses, *source of the mechanicals' play in* A Midsummer Night's Dream.

> *She did lie*
> *In her pavilion, cloth-of-gold, of tissue,*
> *O'erpicturing that Venus where we see*
> *The fancy out-work nature.*

(II ii 202-5)

The clown who brings on the asps however, like Feste (*Twelfth Night*), and Touchstone (*As You Like It*), owes many of his jokes to reformation concepts of Christian salvation rather than to classical mythology. This, added to Cleopatra's later description of Antony as beyond imagination, create for an audience a sense of immortality and of the transcendence of love beyond the petty squabbles of the world. Shakespeare's wholehearted expression of both sides of the story throws the moral question back to the audience, ensuring that, like Cleopatra, custom cannot stale its infinite variety.

SEE ALSO: Ch 2 33-6, Ch 4 102-3, 106-25, 132-5, 142-3, 160-1, 174-7

THE EARLY PLAYS

If there had been professional theater reviewers in Elizabethan England, they would surely have been amazed, charmed, exasperated and at times even baffled by the extraordinary range of work flowing from the pen of the young William Shakespeare. This author's willingness to experiment in all available genres and to try out every possible combination of dramatic materials and moods must have been exhilarating for the theater-going public and potentially alarming for rival playwrights.

In this group of seven early plays there are two tragedies (perhaps the earliest and the latest plays in the group) and five comedies. The tragedies could hardly be more different from each other: *Titus Andronicus* is a bloody tale of mutilation, rape, death and revenge, while *Romeo and Juliet* is a romantic tragedy which has become one of the archetypes of our culture. Among the comedies we find a tightly constructed neoclassical play (*The Comedy of Errors*), a knockabout marital farce (*The Taming of the Shrew*), and three examples of romantic comedy (*The Two Gentlemen of Verona, Love's Labour's Lost* and *A Midsummer Night's Dream*). And we should not forget that during these same early years Shakespeare was engaged in writing sonnets, narrative poems, and the most ambitious sequence of historical plays yet to be presented on the English stage. It was indeed an impressive and varied output.

DATING THE PLAYS

There is, in fact, some debate among scholars about exactly how 'early' these plays are. There is very little hard evidence for the dating of most of them, but the conventional assumption that Shakespeare began writing around 1590 has led to all of them being placed in the 1590-96 period. Noting that this would make Shakespeare far more prolific at the beginning of his career than he was to be later, several recent editors have pushed the dates back somewhat, moving the starting point from 1590

Engraving of Love's Labour's Lost *used as a frontispiece to Nicholas Rowe's edition of 1709.*

to 1587 or 1586.

At all events, in everything he did at the beginning of his career, Shakespeare surpassed his models. The early plays are not tentative imitations of other men's work but rather bold and extravagant, marked by an astonishing degree of wit and invention at all levels. *Titus Andronicus* self-consciously goes one better than Ovid in its use of the Philomel myth (several characters comment on how Lavinia's situation is worse than Philomel's), and *The Comedy of Errors* doubles the confusions of its classical source by having not one but two pairs of identical twins wandering around Ephesus. *The Taming of the Shrew*, with its double plot and framing action, is the most sophisticated example of a dramatic structure composed from interwoven narratives of its time, while in the later comedies, *Love's Labour's Lost* and *A Midsummer Night's Dream*, there is very little narrative in the

structure and the plays are organized instead around overlapping series of themes, encounters and conversations.

SOURCES AND STYLE

Shakespeare was able to draw upon a rich variety of traditions and sources in writing these plays. On the one hand, he uses nonliterary materials from folklore and native tradition for the framing action and the main plot of *The Taming of the Shrew* and for the fairies in *A Midsummer Night's Dream*. On the other, he uses classical authors: Seneca for *Titus Andronicus*, Plautus for *The Comedy of Errors* and for the subplot of *The Taming of the Shrew*, Plutarch for the framing action of *A Midsummer Night's Dream*. He is influenced by his contemporary dramatists, Kyd and Marlowe in tragedy, Lyly, Peele and Greene in comedy, and he also makes use of romantic narratives in prose and verse. His favorite poets, Ovid and Chaucer, turn up everywhere.

If Shakespeare is often daring and original in the way he combines and juxtaposes different materials, seeing no objection to mixing English folklore with classical comedy in *The Taming of the Shrew* or medieval romance with classical history in *A Midsummer Night's Dream*, he is equally

'Romeo! O pale! Who else? What, Paris too?'
Romeo and Juliet, *Lyceum Theater, 1882.*

bold in essaying a range of tones and styles within any single play. He writes comic scenes for both his early tragedies and he enlivens the rather conventional world of romantic comedy both by the inclusion of parody and satire and by allowing space for reflection on the cruelty of love.

He experiments with 'high' and 'low' styles, using a relatively plain blank verse in *The Comedy of Errors* and *The Taming of the Shrew*, but a much more elaborate and rhetorical form in *Titus Andronicus*, *Romeo and Juliet* and parts of *Love's Labour's Lost*. Sometimes the colloquial prose speech of servants is contrasted with the more literary verse speech of their masters, but one has only to listen to Grumio in *The Taming of the Shrew*, Launce in *The Two Gentlemen of Verona* and Bottom in *A Midsummer Night's Dream* to realize that complex effects can be achieved in either medium.

SEE ALSO: Ch 2 44-6, Ch 4 87-9, 92-107, Ch 6 214-8

TITUS ANDRONICUS

CAST OF CHARACTERS

SATURNINUS, *son to the late Emperor of Rome,*
   aftwards Emperor
BASSIANUS, *brother to Saturninus*
TITUS ANDRONICUS, *a noble Roman*
MARCUS ANDRONICUS, *Tribune of the People,*
   and brother to Titus
LUCIUS,
QUINTUS,
MARTIUS,   } *sons to Titus Andronicus*
MUTIUS,
YOUNG LUCIUS, *a boy, son to Lucius*
PUBLIUS, *son to Marcus Andronicus*
SEMPRONIUS,
CAIUS,   } *kinsmen to Titus*
VALENTINE,

ÆMILIUS, *a noble Roman*
ALARBUS,
DEMETRIUS,   } *sons to Tamora*
CHIRON,
AARON, *a Moor, beloved by Tamora*
A Captain
A Messenger
A Clown
TAMORA, *Queen of the Goths*
LAVINIA, *daughter to Titus Andronicus*
A Nurse, *and a black* Child
Romans *and* Goths,
   Senators, Tribunes,
   Officers, Soldiers,
   and Attendants

Titus Andronicus is generally classified as one of Shakespeare's Roman plays, like *Julius Cæsar, Antony and Cleopatra* and *Coriolanus*, but it is startlingly different from the later plays, both in subject-matter and style. Set in the late Empire rather than in the early Republic, it displays tyranny, barbarity, corruption and depravity with the fascination of Juvenal or Tacitus. It excels in appalling horrors: Lavinia's entry in II iv with 'her hands cut off, and her tongue cut out, and ravish'd' is only the beginning of a series of ingenious mutilations and tortures. At one point the hero, Titus, has his hand cut off (Lavinia picks it up in her teeth). Later he kills the two men who have raped Lavinia and with her help cooks them and serves them up in a pie to their mother Tamora, Queen of the Goths.

Partly because of the excessive and apparently tasteless catalog of horrors it contains, it was formerly claimed that *Titus Andronicus* was not by Shakespeare at all, or that it was a collaborative play, partly written by Peele (though Greene, Kyd and Marlowe were also contenders). Today, however, most scholars believe that it is entirely Shakespeare's work and that it is his first tragedy, perhaps his first play. Like most of the early plays, it is difficult to date precisely and estimates range from 1586 to 1594. Favoring the view that Shakespeare's writing career began in the late 1580s

rather than around 1590, I would support a date at the earlier end of this spectrum. A sketch survives of Elizabethan actors performing the opening scene of *Titus Andronicus* which is of unique importance in depicting a Shakespearean play on stage. It was probably done by Henry Peacham around 1594-95 and is particularly interesting for showing the actors using a mixture of contemporary Elizabethan dress and classical costumes.

AUDIENCE REACTION

To the distress of Ben Jonson, who comments on the matter in the Induction to his play *Bartholomew Fair* (1614), *Titus Andronicus* was, with Thomas Kyd's *Spanish Tragedy*, one of the most popular plays of the Elizabethan and Jacobean stage; but its subsequent stage history has been limited. There was, however, a famous revival by the Royal Shakespeare Company at Stratford-upon-Avon in 1955, when Peter Brook directed Laurence Olivier as Titus with Vivien Leigh as Lavinia, Maxine Audley as Tamora and Anthony Quayle as Aaron, Tamora's black lover and accomplice. This was the first production to underline the 'modernity' of the play's obsession with violence and cruelty.

Nevertheless, Shakespeare may well seem, to the modern reader or playgoer, to be more 'of an age' than 'for all time' in

Anthony Quayle as Aaron the Moor in Peter Brook's famous revival of Titus Andronicus *at Stratford-upon-Avon in 1955.*

Titus Andronicus. It strikes us as a particularly Elizabethan play in its tone and in its literary antecedents. It is imbued with the influence of Seneca, whose gory tragedy of *Thyestes* provides an analogue for the cannibal banquet and was one of the *Tenne Tragedies* published in English translation in 1581. In its use of revenge as a dominant motif, the hero's assumption (perhaps not entirely a pretence) of madness and the elaborate and public *performance* of the climax it looks back to the *Spanish Tragedy* (as well as forward to *Hamlet*), while the role of Aaron as the ambitious and amoral outsider-villain recalls the Marlowe of *Tamburlaine the Great* and *The Jew of Malta*. In concentrating on the more sensational aspects of Roman history, Shakespeare's *Titus Andronicus* has more in common with

the later Roman plays written by other dramatists of this period than it seems to have with his own subsequent Roman plays.

THE INFLUENCE OF OVID

While the precise source of the Titus story is still uncertain (though it is generally assumed that Shakespeare used a lost prose history), there can be no doubt that Ovid's account of the rape and revenge of Philomel (told in the sixth book of the *Metamorphoses* and known to Shakespeare both in the Latin original and in Arthur Golding's 1567 translation) was used for the story of Lavinia. It is mentioned several times in the play, and the book actually appears on stage in IV i when Lavinia finally reveals what has happened to her by pointing out this analogue to the other characters.

The influence of Ovid, pervasive in all of Shakespeare's work in this period, seems to have affected the peculiar quality of the play's language which at times combines the narrative with the dramatic mode. The leisurely descriptions of horrific circumstances and events (for example, the 45-line speech delivered by Marcus when he first encounters the raped and mutilated Lavinia) are emblematic and stylized, more like Shakespeare's technique in his narrative poems, *Venus and Adonis* and *The Rape of Lucrece*, than his usual dramatic technique. There is in fact a curiously static air about the play, which proceeds by way of a series of tableau-like set-pieces enacted against symbolic settings: the imperial palace, the forest, the family tomb of the Andronici.

While *Titus Andronicus* is in some ways an extravagant, outrageous, even precocious piece of work, it looks forward most interestingly to some of Shakespeare's later plays. The pattern of revenge and madness is similar in *Hamlet*, while the patriarch who precipitates his own downfall and the degeneration of his society recurs in *King Lear*. The Philomel story is re-used in *Cymbeline* at the end of Shakespeare's career.

SEE ALSO: Ch 2 44, 45, 46, Ch 3 76, 81-5, Ch 4 138-45, 158-9, 162-3, 170-1, 176-7, Ch 5 183, Ch 6 209, 214-6

THE COMEDY OF ERRORS

CAST OF CHARACTERS

SOLINUS, *Duke of Ephesus*
ÆGON, *a merchant of Syracuse*
ANTIPHOLUS of Ephesus, ⎱ *twin brothers, and sons to*
ANTIPHOLUS of Syracuse, ⎰ *Ægon and Æmilia*
DROMIO of Ephesus, ⎱ *twin brothers, and attendants*
DROMIO of Syracuse, ⎰ *on the two Antipholuses*
BALTHAZAR, *a merchant*

Angelo, *a goldsmith*
First Merchant, *friend to Antipholus of Syracuse*
Second Merchant, *to whom Angelo is a debtor*
PINCH, *a schoolmaster*
ÆMILIA, *wife to Ægon; an abbess at Ephesus*
ADRIANA, *wife to Antipholus of Ephesus*
LUCIANA, *her sister*
LUCE, *servant to Adriana*
A Courtezan
Gaoler, Officers,
   Attendants

If this was Shakespeare's first comedy, it is as ambitious and complex as his first tragedy. Exploiting classical New Comedy in the same spirit of gleeful excess with which he exploits Senecan tragedy in *Titus Andronicus*, Shakespeare here involves two sets of identical twins in a fast and furious farce of mistaken identity. As in most such farces, the comedy revolves around sex, money and violence. Timing is of the essence and the action is carefully planned to take place on a single day. It also takes place in a single location (the Mediterranean port of Ephesus), so the play constitutes a rare example of Shakespeare observing the classical Unities of time and place.

DATING

There is in fact no external evidence for supposing that *The Comedy of Errors* was written before *The Taming of the Shrew* or *The Two Gentlemen of Verona*. However, it has seemed logical to scholars to put this, which is Shakespeare's most 'academic' comedy (in the sense of being directly derived from classical models, in this case two comedies by Plautus, the *Menaechmi* and the *Amphitruo*) first, at the beginning of his career, and to assume that he moved away from such influences, via *The Taming of the Shrew* (which uses the same incident from the *Amphitruo*), towards the more fluid and less plot-bound form of romantic comedy which he was to develop from *The Two Gentlemen of Verona* to *Twelfth Night*.

It is possible that this play was performed at Gray's Inn on 28 December 1594 as part of the Christmas festivities; certainly the revelers were entertained on that night with 'a comedy of errors (like Plautus his *Menaechmus*)', but unfortunately the account we have does not name the author. Some people have gone so far as to claim that it was actually written for this occasion, while others point out that it would have been very unusual for Shakespeare to accept a private commission of this kind and that, in any case, the style of the play makes it look more like 1589-90 than like 1594.

There are several links with *The Taming of the Shrew*, not just in the use of the source, though it is striking that both plays contain an arbitrary law against foreign merchants (*Errors* I i, *Shrew* IV ii) as well as a comic scene in which a man is turned away from a house (either his own or his son's) because someone else who has apparently usurped his identity is already inside (*Errors* III i, *Shrew* V i). While the ultimate source of the latter incident is indeed the *Amphitruo* (in which the imposter is no less than the god Jupiter), both elements occur together in George Gascoigne's play *Supposes* (1566), a prose version of Ariosto's *I Suppositi* (1509).

While the differences between *The Comedy of Errors* and *The Taming of the Shrew* are perhaps more striking than their similarities, both plays contain two contrasted heroines, a pair of sisters of whom one is a shrew, and both are set in a thoroughly

mercantile Mediterranean world, as compared with the more romantic Mediterranean of *The Two Gentlemen of Verona* and Shakespeare's later comedies. Ephesus was indeed famous as a center of witchcraft as well as being the city to which St Paul wrote of the principles of Christian marriage, while Padua, the main location of *The Taming of the Shrew*, was supposed to be a stronghold of rationality.

THE FRAMING ACTION

Like *The Taming of the Shrew, The Comedy of Errors* makes use of a framing action, though in this case it is more directly associated with the main narrative than in the Induction in *The Taming of the Shrew*. The play begins with Ægeon, a middle-aged merchant sentenced to death because of the state of hostility that exists between Ephesus and his home city of Syracuse. In a long speech describing his situation, he tells how 23 years previously his wife gave birth to twin sons in Epidamnum, and how he bought from a poor woman another pair of twin boys born in the same hour to be servants to his sons. However, on the voyage home to Syracuse, the ship was wrecked and the family separated, leaving Ægeon with one son and one servant but ignorant of the fate of his wife and the other two babies. Eighteen years later his son and servant set out to search for their brothers and in their turn disappeared. Now, after

The director Komisarjevsky gave due weight to the nightmarish aspects of the dual confusion of identity and the seriousness of the framing action.

another five years searching, Ægeon has given up hope of finding any of his family.

As any alert audience can immediately predict, the bulk of the play is going to be taken up by the adventures of the four young men who are wandering around Ephesus unaware of each others' existence. They are of course relentlessly and hilariously mistaken for each other in a crescendo of confusions until at the climax not only do the two pairs of brothers sort out their identities, but Ægeon is recognized and saved from execution and, as an added and unpredictable bonus, the Abbess, under whose roof the climax is enacted, turns out to be Ægeon's lost wife. The framing story of Ægeon is modeled on the story of Apollonius of Tyre which Shakespeare probably read in John Gower's *Confessio Amantis* and which he was to use again in *Pericles*.

While mistaken identity can be extremely funny, it is also potentially very frightening and Shakespeare gives due weight to these nightmarish aspects.

 SEE ALSO: Ch 2 95, Ch 3 58-9, Ch 4 87-9, 93-4, 96-9, 168-9, Ch 5 201, Ch 6 208, 209

THE TAMING OF THE SHREW

CAST OF CHARACTERS

A Lord,		
CHRISTOPHER SLY,		
a tinker,		
Hostess, Page,	*Persons in the Induction*	
Players,		
Huntsmen,		
Servants,		
BAPTISTA MINOLA, *a gentleman from Padua*		
VINCENTIO, *a merchant of Pisa*		
LUCENTIO, *son to Vincentio, in love with Bianca*		
PETRUCHIO, *a gentleman of Verona, a suitor to Katherina*		

GREMIO,	*suitors to Bianca*
HORTENSIO,	
TRANIO,	*servants to Lucentio*
BIONDELLO,	
GRUMIO,	*servants to Petruchio*
CURTIS,	
A Pedant	
KATHERINA, *the shrew,*	*daughters to Baptista*
BIANCA,	
A Widow	
Tailor, Haberdasher, *and* Servants *attending on Baptista and Petruchio*	

This play, in which Katherina the Shrew is married against her will to the fortune-hunter Petruchio who 'tames' her by frustrating her in every way and depriving her of food and sleep until she is prepared to behave like a proper subservient wife, has always been controversial. It is the only play by Shakespeare which provoked a theatrical 'reply' in his own lifetime in the form of John Fletcher's *The Woman's Prize or the Tamer Tamed*, written and performed around 1611, a sequel in which Petruchio, now a widower, marries again and is himself tamed by his second wife.

While *The Taming of the Shrew* has always been popular on stage, its appeal has been somewhat ambiguous with adapters, directors and performers playing up the misogyny and brutality of the proceedings on the one hand and apologizing for them on the other. Petruchio has regularly, at least since Garrick in 1754, carried a whip and threatened his wife with it, but at the same time actresses playing Katherina have 'softened' her role by indicating that she falls in love with Petruchio at first sight, by delivering her long final speech of submission in V ii ironically, or even by speaking an epilogue to distance themselves from the part.

It is unique among Shakespeare's plays in having an 'Induction' or completely separate 'frame' in which a hoax is perpetrated on Christopher Sly, a Warwickshire tinker, who, having been found drunk and asleep outside an alehouse, is cleaned up, removed to a grand house and convinced that he is really a nobleman who has been out of his mind for several years. The taming play is performed by traveling players for his entertainment. Although Inductions were popular around 1590 and Shakespeare achieves a similar effect in *The Comedy of Errors* (though that is not a true Induction because the frame is, in fact, part of the main fictional narrative), this one is remarkable for its use of his native Warwickshire as its setting and for the fact that it is incomplete in the text that we have: after the first three scenes we hear no more of Christopher Sly who is neither given an exit nor returned to his alehouse.

Modern productions often cope with this awkwardness by drawing on an anonymous play of the period known as *The Taming of a Shrew*, very closely related to Shakespeare's play, which does contain later references to Sly and a final scene in which he wakes up back in his original location.

THE TEXT

The relationship between *The Shrew* as we have it in Shakespeare's First Folio of 1623 and *A Shrew* as published in Quarto in 1594 has been at the root of most of the debates about the text, date and sources of the play. It was formerly thought that *A Shrew* was an independent work which preceded

Shakespeare's *The Shrew* and was the main source for it, but most scholars now believe that *The Shrew* came first and that *A Shrew* is some form of half-remembered, half-invented derivative version of it. Consequently the date has been pushed back: instead of placing it in 1593-94, modern opinion places it in 1588-90 and one recent editor argues that it is Shakespeare's first play of any kind.

THEMES

Assuming that *A Shrew* is not the source, Shakespeare has in *The Taming of the Shrew* cleverly interwoven a main plot taken from folklore with a subplot taken ultimately from classical comedy. The subplot is easy to trace because Shakespeare adapts the entire narrative, complete with some stock characters and some specific pieces of staging, from George Gascoigne's play *Supposes* (1566), a prose version of Ariosto's *I Suppositi* (1509), which is in turn a recycling of one of the standard plots of New Roman comedy as written by Plautus and Terence. (He uses some of the same material in *The Comedy of Errors*.) The main plot cannot be traced so specifically; there are all too many analogous wife-taming stories in classical, medieval and Renaissance literature, but none is closely similar

The Taming of the Shrew is unique among Shakespeare's plays in having an Induction.

---

and Shakespeare may have been relying more on folktale and oral tradition.

The three strands of the play are thematically linked by notions of disguise or transformation (Ovid's *Metamorphoses* is again a key influence): Sly is transformed into a nobleman, Katherina into an obedient wife, and the subplot centering on Katherina's sister Bianca is full of more literal disguises. Even Petruchio is playing a role, alerting the audience in advance about how he will perform towards Katherina in II i and again in IV i. Not surprisingly, the play is full of scenes in which various characters implicitly take over from Christopher Sly the role of on-stage audience. This emphasis on acting and role-playing has helped critics to come to terms with the play: it ends with a wager, and if we can contrive to see it as a game, we can soften the aggression which overtly dominates the play's sexual politics.

SEE ALSO: Ch 2 34, 42, 44, 45, Ch 3 84-5, Ch 4 94-5, 176-9, Ch 8 241, 252

THE TWO GENTLEMEN OF VERONA

CAST OF CHARACTERS

DUKE OF MILAN, *father to Silvia*
VALENTINE, ⎫
PROTEUS, ⎭ *the two gentlemen*
ANTONIO, *father to Proteus*
THURIO, *a foolish rival to Valentine*
EGLAMOUR, *agent for Silvia in her escape*
SPEED, *a clownish servant to Valentine*
LAUNCE, *the like to Proteus*

PANTHINO, *servant to Antonio*
Host, *where Julia lodges in Milan*
Outlaws, *with Valentine*
JULIA, *a lady of Verona, beloved of Proteus*
SILVIA, *the Duke's daughter, beloved of Valentine*
LUCETTA, *waiting woman to Julia*
Servants
Musicians

While *The Two Gentlemen of Verona* is less admired and less frequently performed than either of Shakespeare's other earliest comedies, *The Comedy of Errors* and *The Taming of the Shrew*, it is more easily seen as the direct forerunner of his later work in the genre. Where *The Comedy of Errors* and *The Taming of the Shrew* draw on classical models and folklore and create a primarily farcical atmosphere, *The Two Gentlemen of Verona* derives ultimately from medieval courtly romance and is, in fact, Shakespeare's first attempt at full-blown romantic comedy.

The starting point of the action is similar in all three plays: young men from one location travel to another. Their ostensible motives are varied, but an immediate effect of their arrival in the new location is romantic involvement with the women. This theme dominates *The Two Gentlemen of Verona* which begins by contrasting the situation of Proteus, who is in love with Julia and wishes to stay with her in Verona, with that of his friend Valentine who scoffs at love but falls for Silvia as soon as he arrives at her father's court in Milan. When Proteus' father decides to send him to Milan as well, Julia disguises herself as a page to follow him but discovers when she gets there that he has forgotten her and become Valentine's rival for the love of Silvia. After various adventures at court, Valentine, whose suit is not favored by Silvia's father, is banished and falls in with some outlaws in the nearby forest. Silvia, helped by a friendly Friar to escape an enforced marriage, runs away to join him, Proteus follows her and Julia follows Proteus. In a rather remarkable climax, Proteus attempts to rape Silvia, is prevented by Valentine, apologizes (to Valentine) and is forgiven by him. All this is very perfunctory and when Valentine adds that to prove the sincerity of his forgiveness he will give up Silvia to Proteus, Julia, still in disguise, faints and thereby precipitates a more sensible ending.

PROBLEMS WITH THE PLAY

From this brief synopsis it is apparent that *The Two Gentlemen of Verona* contains many elements that are to recur in later comedies like *A Midsummer Night's Dream, The Merchant of Venice, Much Ado About Nothing, As You Like It* and *Twelfth Night*. Its central focus is on the experience of romantic love which is shown to have the power to transform young men and women, causing them to defy their parents, forget their former lovers, betray their friends, and generally subordinate their whole lives to it. Julia, in disguising herself in male attire, looks forward to Portia, Rosalind and Viola, and the fidelity and dignity of both Julia and Silvia in the face of male infidelity and ludicrous excess is the beginning of a Shakespearean pattern of assuming female superiority in matters of love. Like the subsequent heroes and heroines, the two gentlemen have witty servants to comment on and parody their actions.

The Two Gentlemen of Verona *by William Holman Hunt (1851).*

Because of this apparent continuity with the later comedies, it has often been assumed that *The Two Gentlemen of Verona* must have been written after *The Comedy of Errors* and *The Taming of the Shrew*, but there is no external evidence for this; it is equally possible to argue on internal grounds that *The Two Gentlemen of Verona* might be the earliest of the three. It seems an uncertain and tentative piece of work technically: Shakespeare is awkward in handling some elements of the plotting, and has been accused of being inept with the ending, which would be surprising if he had already handled the complicated denouements of the other two plays more skillfully. The text bears evidence of incomplete revision: Shakespeare seems to have changed his mind about the locations of the play and the titles of his characters.

As for sources, Shakespeare is drawing here on a long tradition of medieval and Renaissance love-and-friendship literature. His immediate source for the story of Julia and Proteus was probably a translation of *Diana*, written in Portuguese by Montemayor around 1559, but he also uses Chaucer's *Knight's Tale*, which tells of the rival loves of Palamon and Arcite for Emily. At the end of his career he collaborated with John Fletcher to dramatize this story in *The Two Noble Kinsmen*, whose title recalls *The Two Gentlemen of Verona*.

One problem with this material for Shakespeare was that romantic love, as seen from the male viewpoint, was already a minefield of clichés and conventions. Valentine is immediately recognized in II i by Speed as the stereotype of the romantic lover and it is difficult, both for other characters and for the audience, to take such a stereotype seriously. Shakespeare was to explore many different ways of breathing new life into the old conventions, sometimes by concentrating on strong, active women, but the plot of *The Two Gentlemen of Verona* does not permit this.

SEE ALSO: Ch 2 44, Ch 3 84-5, Ch 4 94-7, 102-3, 128-35, 176-7, Ch 5 201, Ch 7 222

LOVE'S LABOUR'S LOST

CAST OF CHARACTERS

FERDINAND, *King of Navarre*
BEROWNE, \
LONGAVILLE, } *lords attending on the King*
DUMAIN, /
BOYET, \ *lords attending on the*
MARCADE, | *Princess of France*
DON ADRIANO DE ARMADO, *a fantastical*
   Spaniard
SIR NATHANIEL, *a curate*
HOLOFERNES, *a schoolmaster*

DULL, *a constable*
COSTARD, *a clown*
MOTH, *page to Armado*
A Forester
THE PRINCESS OF FRANCE
ROSALINE, \
MARIA, } *ladies attending on the Princess*
KATHARINE, /
JAQUENETTA, *a country wench*
Lords, Attendants, etc.

This play begins with the young King of Navarre and his three attendant lords taking a vow to 'war against their own affections' by spending three years in studying and fasting, not seeing any women the while. This last condition is immediately threatened by the arrival, on an official embassy, of the daughter of the King of France, accompanied coincidentally by her three attendant ladies. All looks set for a conventional courtship comedy with a happy ending, but one of the surprising features of *Love's Labour Lost* is that the women do *not* agree to marry the men at the end but rather insist on waiting a year to test the quality of their love.

Not only is the ending of this play unconventional, but in plot and structure it represents something of a new departure for Shakespeare, coming as it does after *The Comedy of Errors, The Taming of the Shrew* and *The Two Gentlemen of Verona*. For the first time he seems to be working without a strong narrative base. Not only is there no known source for *Love's Labour's Lost*, but Shakespeare has gone some way toward discarding the idea of a storyline altogether. Rather, the structure of the play consists of a carefully planned series of encounters, either between individual characters or between groups of characters, and the 'plot' evolves out of the conversational interplay of ideas which results. In this respect, it is comparable with *A Midsummer Night's Dream, As You Like It* and *The Tempest*, all of which favor thematic organization.

While *Love's Labour's Lost* was first published in 1598, it is generally assumed that it was written earlier, probably between 1592 and 1595, and moreover that it was revised before publication. The title page of the 1598 Quarto calls it 'newly corrected and augmented', and while such claims cannot invariably be trusted, it does seem likely that it is true in this case: in several places there are duplicate speeches and there are also several other obvious signs of revision.

THEMATIC ORGANIZATION

As in *A Midsummer Night's Dream* and *As You Like It*, encounters between the (would-be) romantic lovers in the central part of the play are interspersed with encounters with other groups who are differentiated by their social backgrounds from the lovers but related to them thematically or parodically. Here, Don Armado 'the braggart' with courtly pretensions unconsciously parodies the young lords and is both abetted and mocked by his witty young servant Moth. His love for the country wench Jaquenetta is seen as ludicrous (like Touchstone's for Audrey in *As You Like It*), while his rival for her affections, Costard, is a clown from much the same stable as Launce and Grumio. Scenes between the lords and ladies alternate with scenes between the lower-class characters much in the manner of Shakespeare's usual handling of plot and subplot.

At a surprisingly late stage (IV ii in

'Sweet hearts, we shall be rich ere we depart,
If fairings come thus plentifully in.
A lady wall'd about with diamonds!' (V i 1-3)

such a time to pair off with the young men, the ladies impose the year's trial period on their admirers.

ROMANTIC CONVENTION

While the delayed ending may seem unreasonable for a romantic comedy, one can sympathize with the women in their difficulty in knowing whether the men are sincere or not. Having broken the vows of abstinence they made in the opening scene they have turned immediately into highly conventional lovers, writing sonnets and swearing extravagant oaths according to the fashion. Their problem is to reject *taffeta phrases* and *silken terms* for *russet yeas and honest kersey noes* before their love can seem convincing. This concern with language itself pervades all levels of the play. Don Armado is characterized by his ridiculously inflated terminology, Moth delights in playing on words and even Costard can pun wittily. Holofernes and Nathaniel are pedantic language snobs; as Moth puts it; *They have been at a great feast of languages and stol'n the scraps* (V i 33-4). Some of this material, which would have been topical for an Elizabethan audience, constitutes a challenge for modern productions which are driven to using gestures, visual aids, and sometimes even blackboards to put the jokes across.

On the modern stage there has, in fact, been a tendency to emphasize the more lyrical, pastoral side of *Love's Labour's Lost*, to present it as a rather idyllic courtship game played by four young couples in a royal park, but the play has a strong satirical strain to balance its romance. Rosaline and Berowne, the principal pair of lovers, are an edgy couple, not as hostile as Petruchio and Katherina in *The Taming of the Shrew* or Benedick and Beatrice in *Much Ado About Nothing*, but sceptical and suspicious. The court ladies have a fairly realistic attitude toward love and sex, and Jaquenetta is pregnant by the end.

modern editions) an entirely new group of characters is introduced in the form of further villagers: Holofernes the schoolmaster, Sir Nathaniel the curate and Dull the constable. These interact mainly with the other noncourtly characters and eventually join with Armado, Costard and Moth to present a pageant of the 'Nine Worthies' to the lords and ladies. This entertainment, no more incompetent or ludicrous than the comparable performance of 'Pyramus and Thisbe' in *A Midsummer Night's Dream*, is unkindly received by the young men who scoff at the performers and insult them, despite the attempts of the Princess to be polite and encouraging. Shakespeare dissociates himself from their facile snobbery by giving Holofernes and Armado some dignified exit lines with which to rebuke the youths. Finally, the pageant is interrupted by a messenger bringing the Princess news of her father's death. Unwilling at

SEE ALSO: Ch 2 34, 39, 45, Ch 3 68, Ch 4 94-9, 102-3, 130-1, 132-3, 174-5, 178-80, Ch 6 207, 211, 213

A MIDSUMMER NIGHT'S DREAM

CAST OF CHARACTERS

THESEUS, *Duke of Athens*	OBERON, *King of the Fairies*
EGEUS, *father to Hermia*	TITANIA, *Queen of the Fairies*
LYSANDER, ⎱ *in love with Hermia*	PUCK, *or* ROBIN GOODFELLOW
DEMETRIUS, ⎰	PEASEBLOSSOM, ⎫
PHILOSTRATE, *Master of the Revels to Theseus*	COBWEB, ⎪
QUINCE, *a carpenter*	MOTH, ⎬ *fairies*
SNUG, *a joiner*	MUSTARDSEED, ⎭
BOTTOM, *a weaver*	PROLOGUE, ⎫ ⎧ QUINCE
FLUTE, *a bellows-mender*	PYRAMUS, ⎪ ⎪ BOTTOM
SNOUT, *a tinker*	THISBY, ⎬ *presented by* ⎨ FLUTE
STARVELING, *a tailor*	WALL, ⎪ ⎪ SNOUT
HIPPOLYTA, *Queen of the Amazons, betrothed to*	MOONSHINE, ⎪ ⎪ STARVELING
Theseus	LION, ⎭ ⎩ SNUG
HERMIA, *daughter to Egeus, in love with*	Other Fairies *attending their King and Queen*
Lysander	Attendants *on Theseus and Hippolyta*
HELENA, *in love with Demetrius*	

Like the earlier *Love's Labour's Lost* and the later *As You Like It*, *A Midsummer Night's Dream* depends for its structure less on linear narrative than on a careful counterpointing of themes and characters. In all three plays the bulk of the action takes place in a rural location, and the move out from the court or city (like the move into the forest at the end of *The Two Gentlemen of Verona*) allows conventions to be relaxed, relationships to change, and self-discoveries to take place.

It is also like *Love's Labour's Lost* in having no direct source for its main plot, though it draws on Chaucer's *Knight's Tale* and Plutarch's *Life of Theseus* for its framing narrative of Theseus and Hippolyta (this frame, being directly related to the main fiction, is more like that of *The Comedy of Errors* than like the Induction of *The Taming of the Shrew*), and uses Chaucer and Ovid for the story of Pyramus and Thisbe. Since Chaucer also employs the Theseus-Hippolyta story as the prologue to another tale of confusion and rivalry in love, it is arguable that he had an indirect influence on the whole of *A Midsummer Night's Dream*, not just on the opening and closing scenes.

Shakespeare was to dramatize the *Knight's Tale* directly in *The Two Noble Kinsmen* (written in collaboration with John Fletcher at the end of his career) and the contrast with *A Midsummer Night's Dream* is considerable. While both the *Knight's Tale* and *The Two Noble Kinsmen* are in the end rather somber narratives about the power of love to destroy friendship and the impossibility of a happy outcome when two men love the same woman, Shakespeare recasts this material in a comic vein in *A Midsummer Night's Dream* by the simple expedient of adding another woman: *Two of both kinds makes up four* (III ii 438). As Puck puts it when he is helping to organize the comic climax. In fact, the symmetry between the two pairs of lovers and the confusion of identity which results from Puck's mistaken application of the love-juice (he cannot tell the men apart) recalls *The Comedy of Errors*, while the tragicomic portrayal of male fickleness and female fidelity looks back to *The Two Gentlemen of Verona*.

LOOKING FORWARD

It is generally agreed that *A Midsummer Night's Dream* is later than all these plays (except, of course, *The Two Noble Kinsmen*), and it is usually dated around 1593-96 although there is no firm evidence. The culmination of the play in a triple wedding celebration has encouraged some scholars to suppose that it was actually written for a specific aristocratic wedding and no fewer than seven such occasions have been suggested, all inconclusively. Other scholars have rejected the whole idea on the grounds that multiple couplings are merely a convention of Shakespearean romantic comedy, but, while this may be true of later plays such as *As You Like It* and *Twelfth Night*, it was not a convention Shakespeare had established by the time he wrote *A Midsummer Night's Dream*, which is in fact his first comedy to have such an unequivocally festive climax.

While in many ways it recapitulates and surpasses the earlier comedies, it can more surprisingly be seen as looking forward to *Macbeth* in two of its more unusual features: its use of nighttime scenes and its use of supernatural characters. The lovers run away to the woods by night, which is fair enough. Less reasonably, the 'mechanicals', a group of Athenian workmen, decide to rehearse their production of 'Pyramus and Thisbe' *in the palace wood, a mile without the town, by moonlight*. Both groups come into contact with the fairies when Puck, on Oberon's orders, both interferes in the relationship between the lovers (initially making matters worse but eventually resolving them) and becomes an 'actor' in the mechanicals' rehearsal, precipitating Titania's passion for Bottom. The 'dream' that the mortals experience as a result of these maneuvers is finally dispersed by the morning and Theseus' hunting horns, yet for the audience the fairies are as real as the lovers and the nighttime world of the woods is as real as the daytime world of Athens.

A Midsummer Night's Dream does, in fact, take a rather self-conscious interest in the arts of poetry and drama. Theseus remarks to Hippolyta that

> *The lunatic, the lover, and the poet,*
> *Are of imagination all compact.*
>
> (V i 7-8)

dismissing the experiences of the lovers as mere fantasy, but later in the same scene he argues for the importance of generosity and imagination in the interpretation of illusion when he comments on the mechanicals' performance of 'Pyramus and Thisbe': *The best in this kind are but shadows; and the worst are no worse, if imagination amend them* (V i

'I pray thee, gentle mortal, sing again.
Mine ear is much enamoured of thy note;
So is mine eye enthralled to thy shape.' (III i 125-7)

209-11). Shakespeare seems to be musing on fiction itself in *A Midsummer Night's Dream*, as he was to do again toward the end of his life in *The Tempest*.

While *A Midsummer Night's Dream* is a popular play and frequently performed, it is one which has been radically reinterpreted in recent years. Having inherited from the 19th century a view of it as a pretty play about fairies, suitable for children and for adaptation as light opera or ballet, we have recently noticed (thanks partly to Peter Brook's brilliant and influential production for the Royal Shakespeare Company in 1970) that the dream comes close to nightmare at times when the women discover that eroticism can be cruel and vengeful as well as romantic and charming.

SEE ALSO: Ch 3 84-5, Ch 4 87-9, 176-7, Ch 5 199, 201, 202, 204, 205, 206, Ch 6 208, Ch 8 237, 240, 241, 250-1

ROMEO AND JULIET

CAST OF CHARACTERS

CHORUS
ESCALUS, *Prince of Verona*
PARIS, *a young nobleman, kinsman to the prince*
MONTAGUE, } *heads of two houses at*
CAPULET, } *variance with each other*
An Old Man, *of the Capulet family*
ROMEO, *son to Montague*
MERCUTIO, *kinsman to the Prince, and friend to Romeo*
BENVOLIO, *nephew to Montague, and friend to Romeo*
TYBALT, *nephew to Lady Capulet*
FRIAR LAWRENCE, } *Franciscans*
FRIAR JOHN, }
BALTHASAR, *servant to Romeo*

SAMPSON, } *Servants to Capulet*
GREGORY, }
PETER, *servant to Juliet's nurse*
ABRAHAM, *servant to Montague*
An Apothecary
Three Musicians
An Officer
LADY MONTAGUE, *wife to Montague*
LADY CAPULET, *wife to Capulet*
JULIET, *daughter to Capulet*
Nurse *to Juliet*
Citizens of Verona; Gentlemen and
  Gentlewomen of both houses; Maskers,
  Torchbearers, Pages, Guards, Watchmen,
  Servants, and Attendants

As Shakespeare's second tragedy, *Romeo and Juliet* seems at first an experiment in a completely different direction from *Titus Andronicus*. It is set in recent or contemporary Italy where *Titus Andronicus* was set in imperial Rome; it is a domestic tragedy rather than a political one; it is concerned with romance rather than with revenge. Yet it is in some ways more like *Titus Andronicus* than it is like Shakespeare's later tragedies. It is similar in being elaborate, formal, rhetorical – a self-consciously literary or 'poetic' piece of work which seems at times detached from reality. It even shares some structural features with *Titus Andronicus*: we find again the feuding families locked into a revenge spiral, the tit-for-tat killings which enhance the narrative and visual significance of what must have been an elaborate stage-property in both plays, the family tomb.

SOURCES AND TRADITION

The origins of the story are, however, very different from those of *Titus Andronicus*. As in his romantic comedies of this period, Shakespeare is here drawing on the medieval courtly love tradition. (*Romeo and Juliet* is usually dated 1594-96 and is thought to be roughly contemporary with *A Midsummer Night's Dream*, which contains a sort of parody of it in the 'Pyramus and Thisbe' play.) The story of Romeo and Juliet was fairly well known, but Shakespeare's im-

mediate source was clearly Arthur Brooke's narrative poem *The Tragical History of Romeus and Juliet* (1562, reprinted 1587) which in turn derives from Boiastuau's French version of 1559. Shakespeare also used what was for his generation the archetypal love tragedy in English (to be replaced by *Romeo and Juliet* itself), Chaucer's *Troilus and Criseyde*, taking at face value here a romance he was later to problematize in his own *Troilus and Cressida*.

For Shakespeare, the courtly love tradition had most recently flowered in the great Elizabethan sonnet sequences, and he was probably working on his own sequence at the same time as he wrote this play. *Romeo and Juliet* begins with a prologue in the form of a sonnet, and the moment when the two lovers first meet is ritualized by the way in which they speak a sonnet that ends in a kiss. More than this, the whole play can be seen as a dramatization of the world of the love-sonnet: an elevated and passionate but fragile state.

Like the heroes of some of the romantic comedies, Romeo begins the play as the stereotype of the unrequited lover, melancholy for Rosaline. His friend Mercutio seems equally stereotypical as the young man who mocks at love, but unlike most who play this role, he does not immediately fall in love himself; indeed his stance becomes embarrassing and unwelcome once Romeo has switched from the illusion of love to the reality, from Rosaline to Juliet. This development is, as in the comedies, difficult to express. Like the four young lords in *Love's Labour's Lost*, Romeo continues to talk and act like a conventional lover. But, as before, Shakespeare overcomes this problem by throwing the weight of the play onto the heroine: Juliet is no silent sonnet-mistress, the passive object of male desire, but, despite her youth, a forthright and passionate partner, at times putting Romeo to shame with her commitment and sincerity.

TRAGEDY OF FATE

However, despite its high profile as *the* love-tragedy everyone knows, *Romeo and Juliet* has seemed to many people stilted and artificial (like *Titus Andronicus*) in comparison with Shakespeare's later plays. It seems to need an undue amount of obvious manipulation or contrivance to make it work: the busybody role of the Friar (all right in a comedy like *The Two Gentlemen of Verona* or even *Measure for Measure*), the sleeping potion that makes Juliet appear to be dead (all right in a tragicomedy like *Cymbeline*), the accident whereby the letter telling Romeo what is going on does not reach him, the sheer bad luck of the timing at Juliet's tomb.

The death of Mercutio is central to the tragedy. Romeo's new-found love for Juliet prevents his pursuing the family feud, and Mercutio is killed almost by accident. Romeo is then forced to fight and kill Tybalt, making tragedy inevitable.

But this is tragedy of fate, not tragedy of character. The central and crucial death in the family feud is that of Mercutio, who dies by accident virtually when Romeo, because of his love for Juliet, refuses to fight the Capulets and tries to prevent others from doing so. Later the death of Paris is equally incidental. If there is something inevitable about the tragedy of Romeo and Juliet it is not in the nature of their characters but in the nature of their love. Even without the hostility of their families, it seems doomed from the outset by its absolute and uncompromising quality. It is compared with lightning and with gunpowder, and frequently associated with death, from Juliet's despairing cry

And death, not Romeo, take my maidenhead!

(III ii 137)

through her father's premature lament

Death is my son-in-law, Death is my heir;
My daughter he hath wedded;

(IV v 38-9)

to Romeo's final grim determination

Well, Juliet, I will lie with thee to-night.

(V i 34)

spoken as he prepares to visit the tomb, and Juliet's own last words as she stabs herself with Romeo's dagger affirming

O happy dagger!
This is thy sheath.

SEE ALSO: Ch 3 78, Ch 4 92-3, 98-9, 102-3, 152-3, 156-7, 170-1, Ch 5 193, Ch 6 208, 211, 217-8, Ch 7 220, Ch 8 242, 250

THE HISTORIES

Shakespeare's ten English history plays are normally grouped into two sets of four (tetralogies), with two standing apart chronologically and in subject-matter, as follows:

(a) FIRST TETRALOGY: *King Henry VI* Parts 1, 2 and 3 and *King Richard III*, written between about 1589 and 1591, dramatizing events from 1422 to 1485.

(b) SECOND TETRALOGY: *King Richard II* (1595), *King Henry IV* Parts 1 and 2 (1596-98), and *King Henry V* (1599), dramatizing events from 1398 to 1420.

(c) *King John* (written some time between 1590 and 1595), dramatizing events from 1199 to 1216.

(d) *King Henry VIII* (1613), dramatizing events from 1520 to 1533. This play was written in collaboration with John Fletcher, but I refer to 'Shakespeare' only, assuming that he took joint responsibility.

THE SOURCES

Shakespeare's main sources for all these plays, except *King John*, were the prose chronicles of Edward Hall (1548) and Raphael Holinshed (edition of 1587); a collection of didactic historical poems by various authors. A *Mirror for Magistrates* (1555, supplemented in 1559, 1563, 1574, 1578, and 1587) also provided much miscellaneous material. For *King Richard III* he relied mainly on Sir Thomas More's *History of King Richard III* (written 1513, first printed 1543, incorporated in Hall and Holinshed). It is widely accepted that the main source of *King John* is an anonymous two-part play *The Troublesome Reign of King John* (1591), but some scholars believe this derived from Shakespeare: hence the wide date-limits given above. Some leading ideas in the plays may come from the *Anglia Historia* (1534, supplemented 1555) of the Italian Polydore Vergil, who was a sort of historiographer royal to Henry VII. Discussion of many other possible minor sources will be found in the latest editions of individual plays.

HISTORY AS PROPAGANDA

An older generation of critics saw the two tetralogies as straightforward dramatizations of the so-called Tudor myth, first formulated by Polydore Vergil, which arranged history into a pattern whereby the sinful deposition of the Yorkist Richard II by the Lancastrian Bolingbroke (later Henry IV) in 1399 received its divine punishment in the civil unrest persisting, with a respite under Henry V, until the accession in 1485 of the first Tudor sovereign, Henry VII, whose marriage to Princess Elizabeth united the two royal houses.

This interpretation forces us to remember that history to the Elizabethans was not 'objective' but propagandist, factual accuracy being less important than the stimulating conveying of moral and ethical instruction. Nonetheless it oversimplifies. There were both Yorkist and Lancastrian 'myths' about the Wars of the Roses, and Shakespeare approached his sources not as a spokesman of government orthodoxy but as a creative artist whose business was to explore, not expound; he invented characters and episodes which make that exploration more complex; the role of Providence in the plays is deeply ambiguous; he shows a sophisticated awareness of history as ironical, baffling, and frequently unfair. His history plays are closer to his tragedies than to his comedies, except for *King Henry VIII* which belongs more with the last plays.

He employed native and foreign dramatic as well as nondramatic models. The Roman tragedies of Seneca, with their violent sensationalism and deep suspicion of attempts to find comforting morals in history, shaped the first tetralogy especially, and there and elsewhere we find many reminiscences of the English medieval Mystery plays with their cyclical view of history, and of the Morality plays with their interest in the processes of ethical choice. Romance, pastoral and folk drama all made their contribution. Uncertainties over chronology make it difficult to know whether anyone had written English history plays before Shakespeare – unquestionably his example was widely copied – but he adapted existing forms and conventions rather than inventing the genre entirely.

THE KING'S TWO BODIES

Why did he make the experiment at all? More's and Hall's habitual use of theatrical analogies and imagery may have been a powerful catalyst. Post-Armada patriotism, once the standard explanation, can be dismissed: all his principal sources appeared before 1588, so what motivated *them*? Contemporary history had to be handled circumspectly or not at all, but in the 1580s, when Elizabeth's hold on the throne was still far from secure, the civil wars of the preceding century offered a tempting – and safely remote – subject under cover of which the problems of Tudor government could be tactfully handled. Shakespeare may have been struck by the resemblance between the disintegration of rule following Henry V's death and the rivalry of factions during Henry VI's minority, and the situation during the minority of Edward VI, with Henry VII in the former case and Elizabeth in the latter as national saviors. This is not to suggest the plays are allegorical, but parallels were explicitly drawn, not least by the Queen herself, who raged at a revival of *King Richard II* pointedly sponsored by followers of the rebel Earl of Essex with 'I am Richard II, know ye not that?'

The history plays are successive investigations of the question 'What makes the ideal ruler?' One piece of 'technical' knowledge is required for a full understanding. Partly in order to explain away the paradox of the weak king, partly to encourage continuity of rule, medieval thinkers had evolved the Doctrine of the King's Two Bodies, according to which the monarch was both a private, mortal person and the current incarnation of an immortal office. His power was delegated to him by God, and his person was therefore inviolate: rebellion was a sin. Shakespeare nowhere *assents* to this doctrine, but he *uses* it repeatedly, playing off the vision of the ideal man-monarch against the often unimpressive or corrupt reality, and it influences not only the themes of the histories but also their structure. If they seem from this to be hopelessly mongrel in form, we should remember Dr Johnson's insight that they *are not in the strict sense either comedies or tragedies, but compositions of a distinct kind.*

SEE ALSO: Ch 1 17-20, Ch 2 44-5, Ch 4 87-9, 90-1, 108-25

Edmund Kean was famous for the sly courtesy with which he interpreted Richard III.

KING HENRY THE SIXTH

PART ONE
CAST OF CHARACTERS

KING HENRY THE SIXTH

DUKE OF GLOUCESTER, *uncle to the King, and*
Protector

DUKE OF BEDFORD, *uncle to the King, and*
Regent of France

THOMAS BEAUFORT, DUKE OF EXETER,
great-uncle to the King

HENRY BEAUFORT, *great-uncle to the King,*
BISHOP OF WINCHESTER, *and afterwards*
CARDINAL

JOHN BEAUFORT, EARL OF SOMERSET,
afterwards Duke

RICHARD PLANTAGENET, *son of Richard late*
Earl of Cambridge, *afterwards* DUKE OF YORK

EARL OF WARWICK

EARL OF SALISBURY

EARL OF SUFFOLK

LORD TALBOT, *afterwards* EARL OF SHREWSBURY

JOHN TALBOT, *his son*

EDMUND MORTIMER, EARL OF MARCH

SIR JOHN FASTOLFE

SIR WILLIAM LUCY

SIR WILLIAM GLANSDALE

SIR THOMAS GARGRAVE

Mayor of London

WOODVILLE, *Lieutenant of the Tower*

VERNON, *of the White Rose or York faction*

BASSET, *of the Red Rose or Lancaster faction*

A Lawyer

Gaolers, *to Mortimer*

CHARLES, *Dauphin, and afterwards King of France*

REIGNIER, DUKE OF ANJOU, *and titular King*
of Naples

DUKE OF BURGUNDY

DUKE OF ALENÇON

BASTARD OF ORLEANS

Governor of Paris

Master-Gunner of Orleans, *and his* Son

General of the French Forces *in Bordeaux*

A French Sergeant

A Porter

An old Shepherd, *father to Joan la Pucelle*

MARGARET, *daughter to Reignier, afterwards*
married to King Henry

COUNTESS OF AUVERGNE

JOAN LA PUCELLE, *commonly called* JOAN OF ARC

Lords, Warders of the Tower, Heralds,
Officers, Soldiers, Messengers, English
and French Attendants. Fiends *appearing to*
La Pucelle

PART TWO
CAST OF CHARACTERS

KING HENRY THE SIXTH

HUMPHREY, DUKE OF GLOUCESTER, *his*
uncle

CARDINAL BEAUFORT, BISHOP OF
WINCHESTER, *great-uncle to the King*

RICHARD PLANTAGENET, DUKE OF YORK

EDWARD *and* RICHARD, *his sons*

DUKE OF SOMERSET

DUKE OF SUFFOLK

DUKE OF BUCKINGHAM

LORD CLIFFORD

YOUNG CLIFFORD, *his son*

EARL OF SALISBURY

EARL OF WARWICK

LORD SCALES

LORD SAY

SIR HUMPHREY STAFFORD

WILLIAM STAFFORD, *his brother*

SIR JOHN STANLEY

VAUX

MATTHEW GOFFE

A Lieutenant, *a* Shipmaster, *a* Master's
Mate, *and* Walter Whitmore

Two Gentlemen, *prisoners with Suffolk*

JOHN HUME *and* JOHN SOUTHWELL, *two*
priests

ROGER BOLINGBROKE, *a conjuror*

A Spirit *raised by him*

THOMAS HORNER, *an armourer*

PETER, *his man*

Clerk of Chatham

Mayor of Saint Albans

SAUNDER SIMPCOX, *an imposter*

ALEXANDER IDEN, *a Kentish gentleman*

JACK CADE, *a rebel*

GEORGE BEVIS, JOHN HOLLAND, DICK, the
butcher, SMITH, the weaver, MICHAEL,
&c., followers of Cade

Two Murderers

MARGARET, *Queen to King Henry*

ELEANOR, DUCHESS OF GLOUCESTER

MARGERY JOURDAIN, *a witch*

Wife *to Simpcox*

Lords, Ladies, *and* Attendants;
Petitioners   Aldermen,
a Herald, *a* Beadle, *a* Sheriff,
Officers, Citizens,
Prentices, Falconers,
Guards, Soldiers,
Messengers, &c.

PART THREE

CAST OF CHARACTERS

KING HENRY THE SIXTH
EDWARD, PRINCE OF WALES, *his son*
LOUIS XI, *King of France*
DUKE OF SOMERSET
DUKE OF EXETER
EARL OF OXFORD
EARL OF NORTHUMBERLAND
EARL OF WESTMORELAND
LORD CLIFFORD
RICHARD PLANTAGENET, *Duke of York*
EDWARD, *Earl of March, afterwards*
    King Edward IV,
EDMUND, *Earl of Rutland,*
GEORGE, *afterwards Duke of*   } *his sons*
    Clarence,
RICHARD, *afterwards Duke of*
    Gloucester,
DUKE OF NORFOLK
MARQUIS OF MONTAGUE
EARL OF WARWICK
EARL OF PEMBROKE
LORD HASTINGS
LORD STAFFORD
SIR JOHN MORTIMER, | *uncles to the Duke of*
SIR HUGH MORTIMER, | *York*
HENRY, *Earl of Richmond, a youth*
LORD RIVERS, *brother to Lady Grey*
SIR WILLIAM STANLEY
SIR JOHN MONTGOMERY
SIR JOHN SOMERVILLE
Tutor, *to Rutland*
Mayor of York
Lieutenant of the Tower
A Nobleman
Two Keepers
A Huntsman
A Son *that has killed his father*
A Father *that has killed his son*
QUEEN MARGARET
LADY GREY, *afterwards Queen to Edward IV*
BONA, *sister to the French Queen*
Soldiers,
Attendants,
Messengers,
Watchmen, &c.

In this trilogy Shakespeare freely adapts his material, shaping it by historical retrospect and prophecy, patterns of imagery and parallelism of plot and character which substitute for a single hero a succession of temporarily dominant figures whose enmities create the impression of a country in a turmoil of uncertainty, deprived of stability under rival kings, both too weak to command the wavering loyalties of the nobility. This is the first appearance of a recurrent device in the histories, the splitting up of the ideal king (the perfect union of the Two Bodies, private and public) into two antagonistic characters. Henry V is frequently recalled as an embodiment of that now unattainable perfection, as he was to be in the later play bearing his name.

I am the son of Henry the Fifth,
Who made the Dauphin and the French to stoop,
And seized upon their towns and provinces.
               (Part 3 I i 107-9)

The Wars of the Roses snowball from a private dispute between individuals in *King Henry VI* Part 1 into a conflict which tears apart families, social classes, ultimately the nation itself in *King Henry VI* Part 3, in a sequence of actions demonstrating the principle of retributive revenge,

    Measure for measure must be answered
               (Part 3, II vi 55)

and

    . . . blows and revenge for me
               (Part 3 II i 86)

which overshadows all the histories up to *King Henry V*, and shows Shakespeare's early interest in the question of cause and effect. In this world

    Thy father slew my father; therefore die.
               (Part 3, I iii 47)

can justify infanticide, as individual lives are sacrificed to an abstract cause. The impression of a tragic ritual is intensified by stylized, emblematic staging and extensive use of formal rhetoric, yet the repeated interruptions of the ritual show anarchy never far below the surface.

THE TWO BODIES DOCTRINE

The political issues are crystallized in Part 3, Act I i, which recalls events later dramatized in *King Richard II*. Henry VI claims descent from Bolingbroke, who became Henry IV *by conquest*. York argues that Bolingbroke compelled Richard II to abdicate: Henry insists Richard did so voluntarily. Exeter objects that Richard

> . . . *could not so resign the crown*
> *But that the next heir should succeed and reign*

> (Part 3, I i 145-6)

a clear use of the Two Bodies doctrine. Moments later, with obvious parallelism, Henry entails the crown to York after his death, and when his own son protests

> *Father, you cannot disinherit me.*
> *If you be King, why should not I succeed?*

> (*ib* 226-7)

Henry replies that York and Warwick compelled him. He later attempts to abdicate in the joint favor of Warwick and Clarence. Meanwhile York is being persuaded by Edward that

> *But for a kingdom any oath may be broken:*

> (Part 3, I ii 16)

and by Richard that the oath was exacted

> 'No sooner was I crept out of my cradle
> But I was made a king, at nine months old.
> Was never subject long'd to be a king
> As I do long and wish to be a subject.'

illegally

> *An oath is of no moment, being not took*
> *Before a true and lawful magistrate*
> *That hath authority over him that swears.*

> (*ib* 22-4)

These pseudo-Machiavellian arguments usher in a new world of *Realpolitik* whose dangerous consequences are illustrated by the Prince of Wales's exclamation when York's heir, backed by Warwick, challenges Henry for the crown which he sees as his inheritance:

> *If that be right which Warwick says is right,*
> *There is no wrong, but everything is right.*

> (Part 3, II ii 131-2).

MORAL STANDPOINT AND CONTRASTING PERSPECTIVES

If the plays have a political moral it may be Joan of Arc's

> *Glory is like a circle in the water,*
> *Which never ceaseth to enlarge itself*
> *Till by broad spreading it disperse to nought.*
> *With Henry's death the English circle ends;*

> (Part 1, I ii 133-6)

Only too late does she realize that her remark equally applies to herself and France. The impartial distribution of ill-luck discounts a Providential reading of the trilogy, since all who put their trust in higher powers are cast down, the wicked (Joan, Beaufort, Suffolk, Cade, Warwick), the virtuous (Talbot, Gloucester, Henry), and the merely foolish (Eleanor). Warwick in lamenting

> *Why, what is pomp, rule, reign, but earth*
> *and dust?*

> (Part 3, V ii 27)

pronounces the epitaph of many besides himself. Shakespeare is not attempting to vindicate one side against the other (either politically or morally); he is showing the futility of taking sides.

The chronicle material is supplemented by episodes showing debts to popular romance and medieval drama, treating the same themes from contrasting perspectives in a first step towards the perfected double plot of *King Henry IV*. The Cade sequence in Part 2 examines in comic-horrific fashion the confusion attendant on rival claims for the crown which come down, in the end, to one person's word against another's: to

The trilogy begins with the ceremonial and dignified funeral of Henry V, and ends with the bestial and undignified death of Henry VI, reflecting the dramatic presentation of growing social disorder throughout the plays.

Stafford's *That's false* Cade can triumphantly retort

> *Ay, there's the question; but I say 'tis true.*
>
> (IV ii 135-6)

Cade's arrogance, distorted logic, crude idea of power, despotism, and contempt for his own followers ape the characteristics of his 'betters' and recall the Vice of the Moralities. Most terrifying is his demagogic hatred of knowledge: the clerk of Chatham's literacy condemns him, *Away with him, I say! Hang him with his pen and inkhorn about his neck.* Lord Say is vilified for promoting education and knowing Latin, and executed *because* he pleads *so well for his life.* In pitting Cade against the humanist Say, who holds that

> *. . . ignorance is the curse of God,*
> *Knowledge the wing wherewith we fly to Heaven,*
>
> (*ib* 69-70)

Shakespeare shows he knows the forces opposing the search for truth which constitutes historical enquiry.

Even Cade, however, has less impact than Richard of Gloucester, whose distinctive voice expounds in two soliloquies the cynical, amoral assumptions of a world with no room for the pious Henry VI. Richard's only beliefs are in his own right to the crown and his ability to gain it: he acknowledges, even relishes, his potentially tragic isolation from humanity:

> *Then, since the heavens have shap'd my*
> *   body so,*
> *Let hell make crook'd my mind to answer*
> *   it.*
> *I have no brother, I am like no brother;*
> *And this word 'love', which greybeards call*
> *   divine,*
> *Be resident in men like one another,*
> *And not in me! I am myself alone.*
>
> (Part 3, V vi 78-83)

The first trilogy is far from being apprentice-work, but in creating Richard, together with finding a new voice for expressing his individualism, Shakespeare grew up as a dramatist.

SEE ALSO: Ch 2 44, 45, Ch 3 80, Ch 5 182, Ch 6 209, 211, Ch 8 245-5

KING RICHARD THE THIRD

CAST OF CHARACTERS

KING EDWARD THE FOURTH

EDWARD, PRINCE OF WALES *afterwards* KING EDWARD V, RICHARD, DUKE OF YORK, *sons to the King*

GEORGE, DUKE OF CLARENCE, RICHARD, DUKE OF GLOUCESTER *afterwards* KING RICHARD III, *brothers to the King*

A Young Son of Clarence (*Edward, Earl of Warwick*)

HENRY, EARL OF RICHMOND, *afterwards* KING HENRY VII

CARDINAL BOURCHIER, ARCHBISHOP OF CANTERBURY

THOMAS ROTHERHAM, ARCHBISHOP OF YORK

JOHN MORTON, BISHOP OF ELY

DUKE OF BUCKINGHAM

DUKE OF NORFOLK

EARL OF SURREY, *his son*

EARL RIVERS, *brother to King Edward's Queen*

MARQUIS OF DORSET *and* LORD GREY *her sons*

EARL OF OXFORD

LORD HASTINGS

LORD STANLEY, *called also* EARL OF DERBY

LORD LOVEL

SIR THOMAS VAUGHAN

SIR RICHARD RATCLIFF

SIR WILLIAM CATESBY

SIR JAMES TYRREL

SIR JAMES BLOUNT

SIR WALTER HERBERT

SIR ROBERT BRAKENBURY, *Lieutenant of the Tower*

SIR WILLIAM BRANDON

CHRISTOPHER URSWICK, *a priest*

LORD MAYOR OF LONDON

Sheriff of Wiltshire

HASTINGS, *a pursuivant*

TRESSEL *and* BERKELEY, *gentlemen attending on the Lady Anne*

ELIZABETH, *Queen to Edward IV*

MARGARET, *widow of King Henry VI*

DUCHESS OF YORK, *mother to King Edward IV, Clarence, and Gloucester*

LADY ANNE, *widow of Edward Prince of Wales, son to King Henry VI; afterwards married to the Duke of Gloucester*

A Young Daughter of Clarence (*Margaret Plantagenet, Countess of Salisbury*)

Ghosts, *of Richard's victims*

Lords, Gentlemen, *and* attendants; Priest, Scrivener, Page, Bishops, Aldermen, Citizens, Soldier, Messengers, Murderers, Keeper

King *Richard III* was clearly in Shakespeare's mind during the composition of *King Henry VI* Part 3. However, the later play is an independent work with its own unity, stemming partly from concentration on Richard's career and partly from a complex structure relying on the balancing of contrasting elements. This play about an English king is full of echoes from Seneca and from medieval drama, and there is pervasive use of parallelism and contrast.

The most general contrast is between Richard's slow rise to power and his swift fall. He, like his victims, is *heav'd a-high to be hurl'd down below* in a *direful pageant* whose ironies demonstrate how the *course of justice* has *whirl'd about*. The action of *King Richard III* is indeed partly exemplary and set within an unambiguous moral framework. Richard is compared, by himself and others, to the Devil and the Vice of the Moralities (as a very different character, Falstaff, will be later), and he is denounced by Richmond as *A bloody tyrant and a homicide*, and *One that hath ever been God's enemy*. He is both the instrument and the victim of Divine justice: his reign is a punishment on the country for the Wars of the Roses, and his death a punishment for his reign; Richmond's victory, and his accession as the first Tudor monarch Henry VII, is a sign that God's wrath is assuaged. Richard, therefore, is no tragic hero. His one moment of pathos and self-knowledge:

> *Richard loves Richard; that is, I am I . . .*
> *I shall despair. There is no creature loves me;*
> *And if I die no soul will pity me;*

(V iii 183, 200-1)

is short-lived, and he is soon dismissing conscience as *a word that cowards use*.

If the play were no more than this it would be a crude cautionary tale. Shakespeare, however, characteristically complicates it by making us like, even trust, Richard, so that we feel the insidious *attractiveness* of evil. Up to Act IV i our moral outrage is neutralized or overridden by a reluctant fascination with Richard's exuberance, vitality, and invincibility. We alone are the confidants who know his hidden motives and appreciate his ironic jokes. Devoid of scruple himself, he persuades us temporarily to be so too. Because

Much of Richard III's success is due to his ability to act (a recurring theme in the play), and to exploit others' gullibility.

we come so close to identifying with Richard, we can (from Act IV ii onwards) see his faltering grip on events and increasing desperation as pitiable.

THE DEEP TRAGEDIAN

Much of Richard's success is due to his acting ability and his genius for exploiting the gullibility of others. He wins the crown through brilliant stage-managing of the Lord Mayor and citizens, aided by Buckingham who boasts that he too can *counterfeit the deep tragedian*. The play is full of theatrical imagery and openly conscious of its own nature as a tragedy, and also as a fiction. Richard's success at deception prompts the question 'What is truth?' which is discussed indirectly in Act III i 69-88. Prince Edward believes that, even without documentary evidence, *the truth should live from age to age*. He is too idealistic: in this play, truth is what Richard makes it.

The sense of history as a pattern, a process working itself inexorably out, is nonetheless strong. This is partly due to the artificially symmetrical arrangement of scenes. The wooing of Anne is balanced by that of Elizabeth, the reported dreams of Clarence and Stanley by the dramatized ones of Richard and Richmond; there are two scenes involving lamenting widows; the pretence of a military uprising materializes in the battles of Act V; Margaret's curses are fulfilled and recalled periodically as Richard's victims, and finally he himself, meet their doom. It will be noticed that these 'pairs' fall on either side of the pivotal Act IV i, thus binding the two sections of Richard's career together and encouraging us to see destiny at work. The rudimentary double plotting of the trilogy is abandoned in favor of a narrow focus in which the concentration on court intrigues, with the commoners very much the helpless victims, creates a claustrophobic tension. In no subsequent history play are Shakespeare's moral distinctions so clear-cut.

SEE ALSO: Ch 2 39, 44, 45, Ch 3 75, 78, Ch 4 108-11, 118-21, Ch 5 190, 196, Ch 5 202, 205, Ch 6 209, 211, Ch 8 244-5

KING JOHN

CAST OF CHARACTERS

KING JOHN
PRINCE HENRY, *his son*
ARTHUR, DUKE OF BRITAINE, *son of Geffrey,
    late Duke of Britaine, the elder brother of King
    John*
Earl of PEMBROKE
Earl of ESSEX
Earl of SALISBURY
Lord BIGOT
HUBERT DE BURGH
ROBERT FAULCONBRIDGE, *son to Sir Robert
    Faulconbridge*
PHILIP THE BASTARD, *his half-brother*
JAMES GURNEY, *servant to Lady Faulconbridge*
PETER OF POMFRET, *a prophet*
KING PHILIP OF FRANCE

LEWIS, *the Dauphin*
LYMOGES, *Duke of Austria*
CARDINAL PANDULPH, *the Pope's legate*
MELUN, *a French lord*
CHATILLON, *ambassador from France to King
    John*
QUEEN ELINOR, *widow of King Henry II and
    mother to King John*
CONSTANCE, *mother to Arthur*
BLANCH of Spain, *daughter to the King of
    Castile and niece to King John*
LADY FAULCONBRIDGE, *widow of Sir Robert
    Faulconbridge*
Lords, Citizens of Angiers, Sheriff, Heralds,
    Officers, Soldiers, Executioners,
    Messengers, Attendants

This puzzling play is indeterminate in date and uneven in quality, recalling sometimes the first trilogy and sometimes the second. In the contrast between weak king and powerful subject, *King John* reads like a first draft of *King Richard II* and was, perhaps, revised at the same time as that play was being written. In Act I John's resistance of a challenge to his title which his own mother admits is strong is pointedly juxtaposed with the Bastard's cheerful waiving of his claim to the Faulconbridge inheritance. Subsequently, as John becomes increasingly helpless, the Bastard becomes increasingly assured, until given *the ordering of this present time* by the exhausted king. Fortunately he is no rebel and promptly submits to the new king. Faced with the rival claims of John and Philip at Angiers, the First Citizen remains pragmatic:

> . . . but he that proves the King,
> To him will we prove loyal.

(II i 270-1)

John's plea

Doth not the crown of England prove the King?

is not accepted; the First Citizen insists that they *compound whose right is worthiest,* as both their claims seem of equal weight. The kings eventually patch up their quarrel by accepting the Citizen's suggestion that Blanche marry the Dauphin, a solution seen by the Bastard as yielding to *commodity* i.e. expediency and self-interest, which have replaced the old ideals of honor and truth. In this world he hopes to thrive:

> *Gain, be my lord, for I will worship thee.*

but his satirical soliloquies expose a political corruption which he is soon forced to take more seriously.

Although John seems to have consolidated his position, he is immediately presented with a second challenge when Pandulph accuses him of disloyalty to Rome and, following the extravagantly Protestant reply that the Pope's authority is *usurp'd* and that *we, under heaven are supreme head* of the Church, excommunicates him.

ARTHUR, JOHN, AND THE BASTARD

The episodes involving Arthur develop a number of major themes. John's employment of Hubert, reminiscent of Richard III's use of Tyrrel, is his first unequivocally wicked action, and it sets off a train of events foreseen by the Machiavellian Pandulph in his explanation of the political advantages to France of Arthur's death. As he predicts, England turns against John. The (false) report of Arthur's death precipitates the nobles, already disgusted by the *wasteful and ridiculous excess* and insult to *plain old form* represented by John's second coronation, to join France. Salisbury's reference to *the infection of the time* (V ii 20), which anticipates the imagery of *King Henry*

King John explores the problem of maintaining integrity in a world of power politics.

IV Part 2, is one among many suggesting widespread unease and discontent. John's personal disorder becomes the nation's. But again the insight into the ironies of history is more complex than this. Hubert spares Arthur, thus giving John the chance to repent, yet Arthur dies anyhow, accidentally killing himself with the words,

O me! my uncle's spirit is in these stones.

(IV iii 9)

It is as though some higher power than John were overseeing the action, yet to what end is obscure.

Arthur's death proves a turning-point in the maturing of the Bastard as in the deterioration of John. Unable to maintain his pose of ironical detachment (he has already been drawn into the war in John's service), he speaks with a new gravity:

I am amaz'd, methinks, and lose my way
Among the thorns and dangers of this world.

(IV iii 140-1)

Moved by horror to exclaim that

The life, the right, and truth of all this realm
Is fled to heaven;

(*ib* 144-5)

and to predict that *vast confusion* must follow such a hideous crime, he is ready for the responsibilities thrust on him by the King whose *royalty* he can claim *doth speak in me* (V ii 129). The world of the play becomes an inverted one in which an outsider, the Bastard, can effectively become king, while the real king is reduced to a *module*, a sham, writhing in the hell of his own nature, withering into *a scribbled form.* Yet order is restored, the Bastard giving way to the heir who is

. . . born
To set a form upon that indigest
Which he hath left so shapeless and so rude.

(V vii 25-7)

and delivering conventional moralizing comments on the transience of power, closing with

Nought shall make us rue,
If England to itself do rest but true.

(*ib* 117-8)

The optimism is, however, conditional.

SEE ALSO: Ch 4 112-3, 116-21, 178-80, Ch 5 199, Ch 6 211, 213

KING RICHARD
THE SECOND

CAST OF CHARACTERS

KING RICHARD THE SECOND
JOHN OF GAUNT,
  Duke of Lancaster,
EDMUND OF   } *uncles to the King*
  LANGLEY, *Duke*
  of York,
HENRY, *surnamed* BOLINGBROKE, *Duke of*
  Hereford, son of John of Gaunt, afterwards
  King Henry IV
DUKE OF AUMERLE, *son of the Duke of York*
THOMAS MOWBRAY, *Duke of Norfolk*
DUKE OF SURREY
EARL OF SALISBURY
EARL BERKELEY
BUSHY,
BAGOT,   } *favourites of King Richard*
GREEN,
EARL OF NORTHUMBERLAND

HENRY PERCY, *surnamed* HOTSPUR, *his son*
LORD ROSS
LORD WILLOUGHBY
LORD FITZWATER
BISHOP OF CARLISLE
ABBOT OF WESTMINSTER
LORD MARSHAL
SIR STEPHEN SCROOP
SIR PIERCE OF EXTON
Captain *of a band of Welshmen*
Two Gardeners
QUEEN *to King Richard*
DUCHESS OF YORK
DUCHESS OF GLOUCESTER, *widow of Thomas*
  of Woodstock, Duke of Gloucester
Lady *attending on the Queen*
Lords, Heralds, Officers, Soldiers, Keeper,
  Messenger, Groom *and other* Attendants

Richard II, like King John, emerged from the chronicle sources as an enigmatic figure, and this is reflected in the play. The initially impressive monarch presiding as *God's substitute* over a trial to determine the truth of rival claims subsequently forestalls its discovery ostensibly to prevent civil war, but in fact out of jealousy of Bolingbroke's popularity. The elusiveness of 'truth' is thus established from the outset. Richard, *basely led by flatterers*, is in the view of Gaunt, whom he treats with brutal contempt, *possess'd now to depose thyself*, and is warned by York that denial of Bolingbroke's right to his inheritance will leave him vulnerable,

> —*For how art thou a king*
> *But by fair sequence and succession?*
>   (II i 198-9)

As with John and the Bastard, the fates of Richard and Bolingbroke are closely intertwined, and conflicts of loyalty are prominent, for instance in Gaunt's dilemma as parent and counsellor, or in York's hesitation to which of his kinsmen to be loyal. The major split is, however, within Richard himself, who is both a hallowed king and a weak, ineffectual man.

He seems unaware of this split. He agrees with Carlisle that God will protect him while ignoring the warning that he must also act for himself. Taking refuge in his status as *the deputy elected by the Lord*, he meets setbacks with rhetoric, helplessness, or self-pity. His deeds cannot match his words in splendor. His vivid imagining of the threat to his crown turns his ironical anticipation of deposition in Act III iii into reality in Act IV i, where he yields with *willing soul* to Bolingbroke in a *pageant* publicly staged as a propaganda coup. He and Bolingbroke hold the crown between them, in an act symbolic of divided and weakened monarchy as Richard ceremoniously transfers his power, thus making himself *a traitor with the rest* since the power is not his to give away.

CONTRASTS AND PARALLELS

As Richard falls in our estimation, Bolingbroke rises – another resemblance to *King John*. The image of the two buckets (IV i 184-9) – memorably expresses both the nature of their relationship and the structure of the play as a whole. By the end of Act III iii Bolingbroke has been established as a superior candidate for the throne by his cautious yet courteous reception of Northumberland's flattery, his realism and firmness, and the moderation with which he pursues his rightful inheritance.

However, he is shown, by Shakespeare's favorite device of parallel scenes, to be no more likely to succeed than Richard, as Richard indeed foretells. The parallels suggest that Richard had the right, but not the strength of will, to be a true king, whereas Bolingbroke has the strength but not the right. For instance, in Act IV i the play seems to be starting all over again in a *new world*, as Bolingboke presides over a quarrel between Bagot and Aumerle which recalls that between himself and Mowbray in Act I i and iii. Again the disputants accuse each other of treason, again the king is implicated, again he tries in vain to make the peace, again he defers the issue. Bolingbroke's uncharacteristically impetuous attempt to occupy the throne is criticized by Carlisle, who takes over Gaunt's function as spokesman for the old order, even to the point of prophesying a dire future for the country. Again, compare Bolingbroke's handling of Aumerle's treachery with Richard's handling of Bolingbroke's, to which the Aumerle episode is an explicitly comic counterpart. Bolingbroke pardons Aumerle *to win thy after-love*, and tells York, as Richard told Gaunt, that his personal qualities have in some measure atoned for his son's defects. Yet York has warned that royal pity may prove *a serpent*, and Bolingbroke ought to have drawn this moral from his own present position.

Richard attains new self-knowledge in Act V. He recognizes his former posturing, admits that, deprived of his crown, he is nothing, recognizes that his misrule was essentially no better than anarchy, and sees his fate as ironically just:

I wasted time, and now doth time waste me.

(V v 49)

Those who cannot command history become its victims. Richard welcomes his death at Exton's hands with the final and most moving 'seesaw' image of the play:

Mount, mount, my soul! thy seat is up on high;
Whilst my gross flesh sinks downward, here to
*   die.*   (V v 111-2)

What is needed for the ideal king, as in *King John*, is an amalgam of position and

Richard, the weak but rightful king, is counterbalanced by the strong usurper Bolingbroke.

character which neither claimant can achieve on his own. The emblematic Act III iv presents statecraft parabolically as the prudent maintenance of the balance of power, and locates Richard's mismanagement of the *sea-walled garden, the whole land* in the *waste of idle hours* which allows rebellion to foment and Bolingbroke's power to tip the scales. Yet the future is bleak for Bolingbroke too, cursed with an *unthrifty son* who frequents taverns with *unrestrained loose companions*, and seems likely to replay the tragedy of Richard II.

History in this play is a dark process whose workings are inscrutable, as is suggested by the crucial 'perspective' speech (II ii 16-20). The dramatized events, if *rightly gaz'd upon*, will *show nothing but confusion*: only if they are *ey'd awry*, with an awareness of the pattern denied to those immersed in the events themselves, will the spectator *distinguish form*.

SEE ALSO: Ch 2 39, 45, Ch 4 87-9, 114-5, 118-21, Ch 5 183, Ch 6 208, Ch 7 219

KING HENRY THE FOURTH

PART ONE
CAST OF CHARACTERS

KING HENRY THE FOURTH
HENRY, PRINCE OF WALES,
PRINCE JOHN OF LANCASTER, *sons of Henry IV*
EARL OF WESTMORELAND,
SIR WALTER BLUNT, *friends of the King*
THOMAS PERCY, EARL OF WORCESTER
HENRY PERCY, EARL OF NORTHUMBERLAND
HENRY PERCY, *surnamed* HOTSPUR, *his son*
EDMUND MORTIMER, EARL OF MARCH
ARCHIBALD, EARL OF DOUGLAS
SCROOP, ARCHBISHOP OF YORK
SIR MICHAEL, *friend of the Archbishop*
OWEN GLENDOWER

SIR RICHARD VERNON
SIR JOHN FALSTAFF,
POINS,
BARDOLPH, *irregular humorists*
PETO,
GADSHILL,
LADY PERCY, *wife of Hotspur and sister of Mortimer*
LADY MORTIMER, *wife of Mortimer and daughter of Glendower*
HOSTESS QUICKLY, *of the Boar's Head, Eastcheap*
Lords, Officers, Attendants, Sheriff, Vintner, Chamberlain, Drawers, Carriers, Travellers

PART TWO
CAST OF CHARACTERS

RUMOUR, *the Presenter*
KING HENRY THE FOURTH
HENRY, PRINCE OF WALES, *afterwards Henry V,*
PRINCE JOHN OF LANCASTER,
PRINCE HUMPHREY OF GLOUCESTER,
THOMAS, DUKE OF CLARENCE, *Sons of Henry IV*
EARL OF NORTHUMBERLAND,
SCROOP, ARCHBISHOP OF YORK,
LORD MOWBRAY,
LORD HASTINGS, *opposites against King Henry IV*
LORD BARDOLPH,
SIR JOHN COLVILLE,
TRAVERS, *retainers of*
MORTON, *Northumberland*
EARL OF WARWICK,
EARL OF WESTMORELAND,
EARL OF SURREY,
EARL OF KENT, *of the King's party*
GOWER,
HARCOURT,
BLUNT,

LORD CHIEF JUSTICE
Servant, *to Lord Chief Justice*
SIR JOHN FALSTAFF,
EDWARD POINS,
BARDOLPH, *irregular Humourists*
PISTOL,
PETO,
Page, *to Falstaff,*
ROBERT SHALLOW,
SILENCE, *country Justices*
DAVY, *servant to Shallow*
FANG,
SNARE, *Sheriff's officers*
RALPH MOULDY,
SIMON SHADOW,
THOMAS WART, *country soldiers*
FRANCIS FEEBLE,
PETER BULLCALF,
FRANCIS, *a drawer*
LADY NORTHUMBERLAND
LADY PERCY, *Percy's widow*
HOSTESS QUICKLY, *of the Boar's Head Eastcheap*
DOLL TEARSHEET
Lords, Attendants, Porter, Drawers, Beadles Grooms, Servants

All the preceding history plays had been but a preparation for the writing of these two great masterpieces, which incorporate every strand of their predecessors into a structure of extraordinary formal beauty. They contain more invented material than ever before, yet no other plays transmit such a vivid sense of what it was like to live in specific historical circumstances, or such profound insights into the nature of time. The limitless possibilities of comedy and the restrictions of historical drama are combined in unparalleled richness.

The two-part division, whether premeditated by Shakespeare or not, is functional: there are two plays, not one ten-act play as is sometimes suggested, and each play is both independent of and interdependent with the other. The mood of *King Henry IV* Part 1 is predominantly celebratory and festive, whereas the mood of *King Henry IV* Part 2 is predominantly troubled and melancholy; both plays treat the same themes now as chronicle tragedy, now as comedy with roots deep in romance and folklore, so that the complexity of life seems perfectly caught.

THREE WORLDS

Three major areas, court, tavern, and rebel camp, each with its own ruler(s), are systematically compared and contrasted, as is made clear by the schematic first Act of Part 1. All three converge in Hal, who is at once rebel, roisterer and heir-apparent, and whose internal conflicts, as he consciously educates himself for the role of ideal king (Part 1, I ii 190-212), are thus externalized. He needs Hotspur's noble idealism without his *defect of manners, want of government*, Falstaff's sanity and realism without his irresponsible self-indulgence, Henry IV's prudence without his burden of guilt, and the advantage of an inherited rather than a usurped title. By synthesizing these qualities he can appeal to all classes of society so that the danger of discontented rebellion vanishes. Henry IV's fear of Falstaffian misrule under *Harry the Fifth* is wrong, Warwick's belief that *the Prince but studies his*

'I know thee not, old man. Fall to thy prayers.' Hal's inevitable rejection of Falstaff at the end of Part 2 was presaged in Part 1 (Act II) in the play-within-the-play.

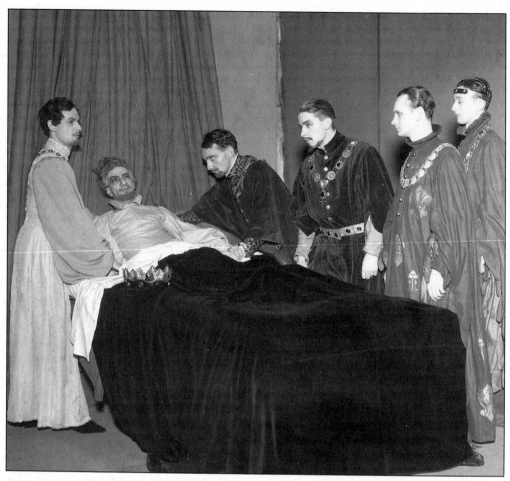

companions is right, and those who deplore Hal's turning to the Lord Chief Justice and rejecting Falstaff are over-sentimentalizing: Falstaff has known the score since Part 1, II iv 475, his reaction to the news of Hal's accession is both ugly and calculating, and he and his fellows are let off comparatively lightly. If we condemn Northumberland's *Let order die!* (Part 2, I i 154), we cannot forget that Falstaff is as great an anarch.

The three 'worlds' are also used to examine time itself. The rebels are obsessed with the past, and most of the historical recapitulations are presented through them, though two important ones are spoken by the King (Part 2, III i 57-79; IV v 183-212), and the Gloucestershire scenes with their display of *the old folk, Time's doting chronicles*, are dominated by a beautifully-realized sense of a past which is nonetheless irrecoverable and recollected in the shadow of death. The court, daily facing

'More would I, but my lungs are wasted so
That strength of speech is utterly denied me
How I came by the crown, O God, forgive me;
And grant it may with thee in true peace live!'

the pressure of unfolding events, and the tavern with its prevailing holiday mood and gratification of whim, instinct and appetite, are both dominated by the present. Hal alone, as the character who knows time is precious, able to be wasted or redeemed, is able to foresee and plan his and England's future. In this *wild* and *unquiet* age, where

Past and to come seems best; things present, worst

(Part 2, I iii 108)

men are *time's subjects*, playing the fool with time or profaning it, yet borne along on its stream, crowded and crushed by it, aware of its power to *shape* and the pressure of its inexorable *necessity*. The plays reflect on their own dramatic mode with unparalleled intensity.

'A king's son! If I do not beat thee out of thy kingdom with a dagger of lath, and drive all thy subjects afore thee like a flock of wild geese, I'll never wear hair on my face more.'

The nature of kingship is examined most tellingly in the play-within-a-play in Part 1, II iv. Falstaff plays the king, then, after he is 'deposed', Hal: Hal plays himself, then the King, i.e. his future self; thus Falstaff is always role-playing whereas Hal never is. Both playlets focus on their relationship, which Falstaff defends in both, and Hal denounces virulently in the second, using the Morality terminology common in these plays (lines 440-57). The first playlet, like *King Henry IV* Part 1, is full of good-humored fun, but in the second, as in *King Henry IV* Part 2, the mood darkens as Falstaff pleads earnestly for Hal's continued favor, which he is warned will be denied. As throughout, the comedy serves a serious purpose: the episode not only summarizes the course and meaning of the Falstaff-Hal relationship, it forces us to ponder Hal's obligations to his dual role; he has to be both a kingly man and a manly king. The same point emerges from the encounter between Douglas and Henry IV:

> *What art thou*
> *That counterfeit'st the person of a king?*
> (Part 1, V iv 26-7)

reminding us that Henry reigns by possession, not inheritance. Hotspur too, albeit *the king of honour*, is a counterfeit, and his and Hal's *double reign* unacceptable, while Falstaff sees himself in the same terms. Only Hal is the true prince.

SEE ALSO: Ch 2 41, 45, Ch 5 189, 196, Ch 6 208, 210, 211, 213, Ch 7 219-20, Ch 8 247

KING HENRY THE FIFTH

CAST OF CHARACTERS

CHORUS
KING HENRY THE FIFTH
DUKE OF GLOUCESTER, ⎫
DUKE OF BEDFORD, ⎬ *brothers to the King*
DUKE OF EXETER, *uncle to the King*
DUKE OF YORK, *cousin to the King*
EARL OF SALISBURY
EARL OF WESTMORELAND
EARL OF WARWICK
ARCHBISHOP OF CANTERBURY
BISHOP OF ELY
EARL OF
   CAMBRIDGE, ⎫ *conspirators against the*
LORD SCROOP, ⎬ *King*
SIR THOMAS GREY, ⎭
SIR THOMAS
   ERPINGHAM, ⎫
GOWER, ⎬ *officers in the King's army*
FLUELLEN, ⎪
MACMORRIS, ⎪
JAMY, ⎭
BATES, ⎫
COURT, ⎬ *soldiers in the King's army*
WILLIAMS, ⎭

NYM, ⎫
BARDOLPH, ⎬ *soldiers in the King's army*
PISTOL, ⎪
Boy ⎭
A Herald
CHARLES THE SIXTH, *King of France*
LEWIS, *the Dauphin*
DUKE OF BURGUNDY
DUKE OF ORLEANS
DUKE OF BRITAINE
DUKE OF BOURBON
The Constable of France
RAMBURES, ⎫ *French lords*
GRANDPRÉ, ⎭
Governor of Harfleur
MOUNTJOY, *a French herald*
Ambassadors to the King of England
ISABEL, *Queen of France*
KATHERINE, *daughter to Charles and Isabel*
ALICE, *a lady attending her*
HOSTESS *of the Boar's Head, Eastcheap;*
   formerly Mrs. Quickly, now married to Pistol
Lords, Ladies, Officers, Soldiers,
   Messengers, Attendants

King *Henry V* is advertised in the Epilogue to *King Henry IV* Part 2 as a forthcoming attraction starring Falstaff again, yet he is only referred to in the later play; we hear that *the King has kill'd his heart* (II i 86), and his death is described in a magnificent elegy. It is dangerous to read *King Henry IV* Part 2 retrospectively in the light of these references: Falstaff would have diverted attention from Henry, so he was dispatched as decently as possible.

This is the only Shakespearean history play to use a Chorus, an epic device to add dignity to the action and to atone for the inadequacies of Elizabethan staging. The picture of Henry presented by the choruses is unalloyedly admiring: he is *the mirror of all Christian kings*, a *royal captain* encouraging his men with *cheerful semblance and sweet majesty*, a *conqu'ring Cæsar, this star of England*. This accords with the impression of him given by the clerics as *a true lover of the holy Church* whose almost miraculous reformation of life and astonishing diversity of talents make him a paragon among men. The French king admits his *native mightiness* and even Pistol declares *I love the lovely bully*.

PLOT AND SUBPLOT

The play seems indeed so straightforwardly eulogistic of Henry that it has been thought boringly over-simplified, and certainly we miss Falstaff's sceptical enquiries about the reality beneath the ideals men profess. Yet the relationship between the main plot and the subplot is more complex than first appears: we occasionally see courage becoming rashness; friendliness, condescension; piety, humbug; diffidence, cloying coyness. Admittedly there is a telling contrast between the king's forces, unifying the entire British Isles in Gower, Fluellen, Macmorris, and Jamy, and the other ranks in Bates, Court, and Williams, and the disorganized fringe militia of Nym, Bardolph, and Pistol, unashamed profiteers turning tail at Harfleur, with Pistol the sole dejected survivor. These two groups seem

worlds apart: significantly, Henry and Pistol meet only once on-stage, and then Pistol cannot penetrate the king's disguise.

Henry sometimes comes closer to Pistol than this suggests, however. His rhetoric sometimes approaches Pistol's ranting; while his order that the prisoners' throats should be cut, however rationalized by Gower after the fact, again recalls the low characters. Further doubts are raised in Act IV i where the disguised Henry equivocally declares that *the King is but a man, as I am* and meets Williams's complaint that the king is responsible for his subjects' deaths in battle by arguing that the king does not intend the deaths, and affirming his trust in the king. Following Williams's scoffing at this, Henry picks a quarrel with him.

The strain of the personal equilibrium a king is called upon to maintain is emphasized by this and by the soliloquy in Act IV i (236-280) in which Henry reveals the worries beneath his outward confidence, decrying the *ceremony* which makes his life more careworn than that of the meanest subject. In contrast to Henry VI in *King Henry VI* Part 3 he does not idealize rustic life: indeed the references to the *wretch*, the *slave*, and the *peasant* with a *gross brain* do not fit easily with his public bonhomie.

Henry V personifies the doctrine of the king's two bodies, yet the strain of maintaining personal equilibrium is felt through the play.

Henry also voices his sense of his inheritance as a burden, imploring God to grant an English victory, not to punish him, by defeat, for Bolingbroke's rebellion.

The world of *King Henry V*, like that of *King Richard II*, must be viewed 'perspectively' (a word which is in this play too: V ii 315). It shows us a king who is both epic hero and fallible human, leading his country to a peace which is but the prelude to further war. With the victory at Agincourt the process of retribution, which has operated throughout the history plays, is suspended – but not ended, for despite the cementing of the English-French alliance in Henry's marriage to Katherine, the final chorus reminds us that the quarreling factions in Henry VI's minority

. . . lost France and made his England bleed,
Which oft our stage hath shown.

SEE ALSO: Ch 2 45, 47, Ch 3 76, 80, Ch 5 198, 205, Ch 8 242-3, 247

KING HENRY THE EIGHTH

CAST OF CHARACTERS

KING HENRY THE EIGHTH
CARDINAL WOLSEY
CARDINAL CAMPEIUS
CAPUCIUS, *Ambassador from the Emperor Charles V*
CRANMER, ARCHBISHOP OF CANTERBURY
DUKE OF NORFOLK
DUKE OF BUCKINGHAM
DUKE OF SUFFOLK
EARL OF SURREY
Lord Chamberlain
Lord Chancellor
GARDINER, BISHOP OF WINCHESTER
Bishop of Lincoln
LORD ABERGAVENNY
LORD SANDYS
SIR HENRY GUILDFORD
SIR THOMAS LOVELL
SIR ANTHONY DENNY
SIR NICHOLAS VAUX
Secretaries *to Wolsey*

CROMWELL, *servant to Wolsey*
GRIFFITH, *gentleman-usher to Queen Katharine*
Three Gentlemen
DR. BUTTS, *physician to the King*
Garter King-at-Arms
Surveyor *to the Duke of Buckingham*
BRANDON, *and a* Sergeant-at-Arms
Doorkeeper of the Council Chamber
Porter, *and his* Man
Page *to Gardiner*
A Crier
QUEEN KATHARINE, *wife to King Henry, afterwards divorced*
ANNE BULLEN, *her Maid of Honour, afterwards Queen*
An old Lady, *friend to Anne Bullen*
PATIENCE, *woman to Queen Katharine*
Lord Mayor, Aldermen, Lords *and* Ladies *in the Dumb Shows;* Women *attending upon the* Queen; Scribes, Officers, Guards, *and other* Attendants; Spirits

With the death of Elizabeth it became possible for dramatists to treat the history of her father's reign, and it is almost certainly to one such play, Samuel Rowley's *When You See Me You Know Me*, that Shakespeare refers disparagingly in the Prologue to *King Henry VIII*. As is implied there, the new play eschews subplot comedy (apart from the markedly unfunny V iii): it returns to the wave-like method of plotting used in the first trilogy. There is no single protagonist: instead we witness the rise and fall of Buckingham, Katharine and Wolsey, the pattern being broken by Cranmer who enjoys Henry's full backing. The subordination of character to plot allows Shakespeare to investigate the larger forces of history to which all men are subject. Theological controversy is also notably absent, Katharine's appeal to Henry being on personal grounds only, and sectarian disagreement playing a minor role in the nobles' opposition to Cranmer.

A clue to the play's method lies in its opening scene. Norfolk reports the Field of the Cloth of Gold in flamboyant terms: the

two kings are *suns of glory* by whose alliance
  . . . *pomp was single, but now married*
  To one above itself.

(I i 15-6)

the celebratory masque includes Frenchmen *all in gold* and pages *as cherubins, all gilt*, and is so spectacular

  . . . *that former fabulous story,*
  Being now seen possible enough, got credit

(*ib* 36-7)

Romance becomes reality. Buckingham's incredulity – *O, you go far!* – is followed, when he learns that Wolsey masterminded the ceremonies, by his condemnation of them as *fierce vanities*, extravagantly expensive yet yielding only *a most poor issue*. Political calculation is revealed beneath the attractive exterior, and to clinch the point this recreation of regal splendor is immediately followed by an exhibition of *device and practice* as Buckingham is arrested.

Wolsey's function is to subvert all ideals, to turn *princes into pages*, *men's honours* into *pitch*; Katharine objects that he and Campeius *turn me into nothing*. His base social origins spur him into triumphant

The danger of misrepresentation and the nature of 'truth' are keynotes in this play.

hostility towards his superiors, yet he joins them in eventual degradation, admitting his pride and rejecting the *vain pomp and glory of the world*. He falls from his high position but rises in the hierarchy of moral virtue. Katharine's memory of his corruption is countered by Griffith's praise of his meek resignation to his fate:

> *Men's evil manners live in brass: their virtues*
> *We write in water.*

(IV ii 45-6)

Katharine and Griffith, almost like ourselves as critics, debate the character of Wolsey, finding him, now a Machiavel, now a model of reformation; in their balancing the ideal against the actual they imitate on a small scale the structure of the whole play. Katharine's ensuing vision of *celestial harmony* and *eternal happiness*, which most strongly allies *King Henry VIII* with the other 'last plays', prepares us for the transfiguring prophecy of Cranmer.

ALL IS TRUE

As this suggests, and as befits its alternative title, *All is True*, the play is interested, sometimes ironically, in the discovery of historical and ethical truth. Many events are described rather than shown on stage in a technique forcing us to recognize the derivativeness and possible unreliability of much of our 'knowledge'.

But although *King Henry VIII* questions the existence of truth and the possibility of knowing it, philosophical scepticism is ultimately transformed into visionary romance with Cranmer's assertion of divinely-prompted truth and his prophecy of the glories of Elizabeth's reign and their phœnix-like resurrection in that of James. History now ceases to be a dark enigma and becomes a process of ripening and fulfilment. The symbol of the phœnix, a creature both mortal and immortal, had been used in the first trilogy, but assumes major importance here in resolving the paradoxes of the play's historical thought: like the phœnix, the persons in the drama of history fall only to rise again. The image of a life endlessly and inexhaustibly renewed is also, surely, an apt one for Shakespeare's history plays.

SEE ALSO: Ch 1 25-6, Ch 2 49, Ch 3 65, 77, 85, Ch 5 182, 197, 198, 199, 206, Ch 7 219, 220

THE COMEDIES

Master William Shakespeare's Comedies, Histories, and Tragedies the editors of the great Folio of 1623 called their book and, as Dr Johnson remarked, perhaps a little crossly, they *seem not to have distinguished the three kinds by any exact or definite ideas. An action which ended happily to the principal persons, however serious or distressful through its intermediate incidents, in their opinion constituted a comedy.* In spite of Johnson's grumble, the Folio's criterion is that accepted by the compilers of *Webster's New World Dictionary* who define *comedy* as 'any of various types of play or motion picture with . . . a nontragic ending.' At the most basic level, then, 'Shakespeare's comedies' are his 16 plays with happy endings, 14 of them so designated in the Folio, with the addition of *Pericles*, omitted altogether in 1623, and of *Cymbeline*, placed among the tragedies in the Folio.

CLASSIFICATION

What, then, beyond convenience of division for a volume such as this, gives the five plays of this section an integrity which separates them from the rest of the 16? The first answer, of course, derives from chronology; they all belong in a period of four or five years before and around the turn of the 16th century, after the early and varied experiments in comic form which culminate in the precise perfection of *A Midsummer Night's Dream* and at much the same time as Shakespeare is completing his dramatization of medieval English history. After *Twelfth Night*, and after Shakespeare, outside comedy, has turned from English to Roman history and in *Julius Cæsar* has made a great stride toward the tragedies, the comic directions change too, with the comedies of these later years reaching toward their happy endings through intermediate incidents serious and distressful (to use Johnson's terms) in quite a different sense and level of encounter with the human capacity for evil.

There is, though, more than chrono-logy to justify discussing these plays together. *In Tragedy*, wrote Evanthius in the 4th century A.D., *is expressed the idea that life is to be fled from; in comedy that it is to be grasped.* The assertion of vitality and community, of harmony and conviviality, fundamental to the energies of comedy, is at its most conspicuous and its most profound in this group of plays. All of them, to a greater or lesser extent, are wooing plays, wooings which achieve their balance and their capacity to entertain through the exploitation of a degree of sexual equality from which derives the prominence of their heroines. Wooings are designed, one supposes, to culminate in marriage or, rather, in marriages, for Shakespeare is rarely less than generous in this respect. In an earlier wooing comedy, Berowne had regretted that:

Our wooing doth not end like an old play:
Jack hath not Jill. These ladies' courtesy
Might well have made our sport a comedy.

(*Love's Labour's Lost* V ii 862-4)

But in this group of plays the courtesies *are* observed and the bridebeds attend as the plays conclude. Comedy endings are thus also beginnings, the comic form itself representative of the cyclical patterns of human existence, generation following generation, the ideal of harmony, symbolized in marriage, triumphing over the dangers and disruptions that have, during the course of the play, postponed its arrival. And among these dangers, almost always, if at first a little surprisingly in comedy, is the threat of death. Shylock's intentions for Antonio are very plain; Claudio believes Hero dead and does penance at her tomb; Rosalind flees to Arden to escape her uncle's threat of execution; Viola spends much of *Twelfth Night* grieving for a brother she believes drowned. Among these plays only *The Merry Wives of Windsor* lacks this dimension of encounter with death, and seems a somewhat lesser play because of it. For it is the assertion of life and community, of harmony and generation, beyond the threat of death, that gives to these comedies their resonance and something of their power.

It is requir'd
You do awake your faith.

Paulina demands at the end of *The Winter's*

Tale (V iii 94-5), and though the coming to life of a statue makes an extreme demand on our credulity in Shakespeare's creation of images of concord and joy in comedy endings, all of them require us to make this act of participatory faith in response to their symbolic harmonies.

Not that the symbolic harmonies displace all the realities. An earlier Elizabethan definition of comedy, by William Webbe in his *Discourse of English Poetry* (1586), described comedies as plays which *beginning doubtfully, drew to some trouble or turmoil, and by some lucky chance always ended to the joy and appeasement of all parties.* That doubtful or turbulent beginning is certainly characteristic of this quintet of plays, with the wistful, rather elegiac openings of *The Merchant of Venice* and *Twelfth Night*, the quarrelsomeness of *As You Like It* and *The Merry Wives of Windsor*, and the 'merry war' of Beatrice and Benedick in *Much Ado About Nothing*. The appeasement of *all* parties, however, is conspicuously not the formula for these plays, though it may be true for some of Shakespeare's earlier comedies.

Shylock, Don John, Jacques, Malvolio, Dr Caius are clearly unappeased, perhaps unappeasable, as their plays conclude, and all of them offer us an alternative to the idealized images of harmony and grace from which they withdraw, lone figures leaving the crowded stages on which Shakespeare's comedy conclusions are played. The dance of concord and of community, or the gruff assertion of solitariness and independence: the endings of these comedies are poised over the void that separates the two and derive some of their impressiveness from exploiting that precariousness of harmony and discord in balance, each one defining the other, sharpening its focus and also emphasizing its poignancy.

SEE ALSO: Ch 2 50-2, Ch 4 100-3, 128-37, 140-1, 168-73, 178-80

Sir Herbert Beerbohm Tree in his portrayal of Falstaff, with Ellen Terry and Mrs Kendall, in The Merry Wives of Windsor.

THE MERCHANT OF VENICE

CAST OF CHARACTERS

THE DUKE OF VENICE
THE PRINCE OF MOROCCO, } *suitors to Portia*
THE PRINCE OF ARRAGON,
ANTONIO, *a merchant of Venice*
BASSANIO, *his friend, suitor to Portia*
SOLANIO,
SALERIO, } *friends to Antonio and Bassanio*
GRATIANO,
LORENZO, *in love with Jessica*
SHYLOCK, *a rich Jew*
TUBAL, *a Jew, his friend*

LAUNCELOT GOBBO, *a clown, servant to Shylock*
OLD GOBBO, *father to Launcelot*
LEONARDO, *servant to Bassanio*
BALTHASAR,
STEPHANO, } *servants to Portia*
PORTIA, *a rich heiress*
NERISSA, *her waiting-maid*
JESSICA, *daughter to Shylock*
Magnificoes of Venice, Officers of the Court
of Justice, Gaoler, Servants, *and other*
Attendants

At the end of *A Midsummer Night's Dream* Shakespeare had presented a joyous pattern of interlocking harmonies on every level. The next comedy is an uneasier mixture of romantic and antiromantic elements. *The Merchant of Venice* probably dates from about 1596; it was entered in the Stationers' Register in 1598.

The story of the wager and the bond of human flesh may be traced in many forms before its first appearance in English in the late 13th century. The form closest to Shakespeare is the story of 'Gianetto and the Lady of Belmont' in Ser Giovanni's *Il Pecorone* (1558), which Shakespeare must have read in Italian or in an English version now lost. For the story of the three caskets he seems to have turned to one of the tales translated by Richard Robinson from the *Gesta Romanorum* and published in its second edition in 1595.

From such materials Shakespeare made *The Merchant of Venice*, but the play that resulted is peculiarly his own, and something of an oddity among his comedies. The clash of its disparate elements may be seen most vividly in the second scene of Act III. Shakespearean comedies, we know well enough, end in marriage, but here the marriages come in the middle of the play. Bassanio's choice of the leaden casket secures Portia as his wife and Nerissa as Gratiano's. Then comes Antonio's letter from Venice interpolating its emotional rawness between Bassanio's marriage to

Portia and its consummation, as she resignedly recognizes:

First go with me to church and call me wife,
And then away to Venice to your friend.

(III ii 305-6)

The Merchant of Venice is built upon contrasts, moving always between the harsh, legalistic, mercantile world of Shylock's Venice and the gracious unworldly beauty of Portia's Belmont. They are connected and contrasted in their use of riches. Bassanio's first mention of Portia is of her wealth. In the casket scene Gratiano reiterates one of the play's persistent ideas: *We are the Jasons, we have won the fleece.* (III ii 243). On hearing of Antonio's debt to Shylock, Portia is confident:

Pay him six thousand, and deface the bond;
Double six thousand, and then treble that.

(III ii 301-2)

Her view of wealth in the service of reciprocal human bonds, expansively expressed in eloquent verse, contrasts with Shylock's carefully husbanded prose, each syllable weighed, perceiving wealth in the service of itself, bonds as the means of individual power: *Three thousand ducats for three months, and Antonio bound.* (I iii 10).

COMMUNITY AND SOLITUDE

The roles of Antonio and Shylock, bound by their stories and by their mutual hatred, give the play its peculiar flavor. Comedy explores and celebrates society, presents us with images of harmony and community,

'Hath not a Jew hands, organs, dimensions, senses, affections, passions, fed with the same food, hurt with the same weapons, subject to the same diseases, healed by the same means, warmed and cooled by the same winter and summer, as a Christian is?' (III i 51-5)

but at the center of this comedy are two desperately solitary figures.

In sooth, I know not why I am so sad Antonio begins the play; we never discover the answer. Antonio remains alone, embarrassingly generous to his friend, ready to lose wealth and life for him. And he is present, the odd man in seven, at the play's conclusion, rewarded with news of his returning argosies, to make the final exit with three pairs of lovers – a final exit that needs to be very ingeniously staged if it is not to direct attention to his solitariness.

A couple of scenes earlier, there is no way of disguising the loneliness of Shylock's departure, defeated by Portia in the trial scene through the very letter of the law upon which he has so fiercely insisted, condemned to lose much of his wealth and to repudiate his religion. Not all Elizabethan notions transplant readily to the 20th century, and it is hard for modern audiences to mitigate their horror at the sentence on Shylock with the knowledge that he is thereby being offered the chance of salvation. *Hath not a Jew eyes?* he asks, in a speech that asserts the shared humanity of Jew and Gentile. But he ends by insisting on community in hatred and vengeance. *The quality of mercy is not strain'd*, implores Portia, pleading for community in forgiveness. But the social bonds prove inadequate in *The Merchant of Venice* to hold the disparate elements together. Upon a moonlit bank in Belmont, Lorenzo and Jessica find, through their love for each other, a harmony that seems momentarily to put them in touch with the music of the spheres, but even as they do so they remember the stories of tragic lovers divided by misunderstanding and by death.

The Merchant of Venice is the first of Shakespeare's comedies to present us with imperfectly realized final harmonies and it does so more extremely than any other. The yearnings of romantic comedy take us back to the grace of Belmont for the final scene, but there are many absences from this the least populous of any comedy conclusion.

SEE ALSO: Ch 2 39, Ch 4 87-9, 102-3, Ch 5 191, 196, 198, 200, Ch 6 211, 212, Ch 7 221, Ch 8 240

MUCH ADO
ABOUT NOTHING

CAST OF CHARACTERS

DON PEDRO, *Prince of Arragon*
DON JOHN, *his bastard brother*
CLAUDIO, *a young lord of Florence*
BENEDICK, *a young lord of Padua*
LEONATO, *Governor of Messina*
ANTONIO, *his brother*
BALTHASAR, *attendant on Don Pedro*
BORACHIO, }
CONRADE, } *followers of Don John*
FRIAR FRANCIS

DOGBERRY, *a constable*
VERGES, *a headborough*
A Sexton
A Boy
HERO, *daughter to Leonato*
BEATRICE, *niece to Leonato*
MARGARET, }
URSULA, } *gentlewomen attending on Hero*
Messengers, Watch, Attendants

Much Ado About Nothing is usually dated about 1598 and a Quarto was published in 1600. Its main narrative (though not its main interest), the story of Hero and Claudio, has been traced in various forms, that by Belleforest in the *Histoires Tragiques* of 1574, adapted from Bandello, being the closest to Shakespeare. But the principal source of the play's theatrical vitality and reputation, the courtship of Beatrice and Benedick, seems to be of Shakespeare's own invention. So too are the comic constable, Dogberry, and his watchmen, who manage to stumble on the truth about the duping of Claudio, but fail to reveal it before Shakespeare has moved the play onto a level of seriousness quite unpredictable from its origins and early episodes.

Much of the action of the play is motivated by misunderstanding, so that its title has been thought to contain a pun on *nothing* and 'noting' (observation). By failing to observe properly, Claudio first falls into the error that Don Pedro has deceived him and wooed Hero for himself, a misunderstanding preludial to his grosser error, at her bedroom window, when he allows himself to be tricked into supposing her unfaithful. Just as Claudio is duped about Hero, so Beatrice and Benedick are duped into believing that each is in love with the other. All this would be no more than entertaining theatrical trickery if essential truths were not in the process exposed. The doubts we feel about the fragility of Claudio's conventional relationship with

Hero are appropriately reflected in the ease with which the melodramatic villain Don John exposes the inadequacy of his love.

Similarly, the obsession with each other that we perceive from the first meeting of Beatrice and Benedick, expressing itself in the 'merry war' of their crypto-courtship, is satisfied by the speed and determination with which each of them responds to the reported love of the other. *I will be horribly in love with her* Benedick decides, and adds by way of excuse for himself, *When I said I would die a bachelor, I did not think I should live till I were married* (II iii 219-21). And Beatrice, with an almost pathetic vulnerability, thinks of marriage immediately:

If thou dost love, my kindness shall incite thee
To bind our loves up in a holy band.

(III i 113-4)

THE ANTICOMIC IMPULSE

The role Shakespeare uses to expose the inadequacy of Claudio's love and thus to test the love of Beatrice and Benedick in the resultant chaos, is Don John, that crucial anticomic voice to be found in all these comedies. He arrives with his half-brother Don Pedro and simultaneously they lay their plots in the two halves of the play, Don John to destroy love in the trick he plays on Claudio, Don Pedro to create it in the trick he plays on Benedick. Both, in the process, expose truths deeper than they are aware. In describing himself Don John offers a simple and striking account of the anticomic impulse: *I must be sad when I have*

cause, and smile at no man's jests; eat when I have stomach, and wait for no man's leisure . . . (I iii 10-12). Since comedy exists to celebrate human society, and its potential for concord, the presence of such a voice not only creates a plot to postpone the comic ending, but also makes it inevitable that the ending cannot be all-inclusive.

The plot that Don John creates results in Claudio's repudiation of Hero at the altar, and in her apparent death. After this impressive and painful scene, Beatrice and Benedick are left alone to contemplate the new situation and it is against its unhappy background, and partly because of it, that they overcome inhibition and manage to declare their love for each other in terms whose simplicity is impressive after all their earlier verbal fencing: *I do love nothing in the world so well as you; I love you with so much of my heart that none is left to protest* (IV i 266, 284). Then, to his expansive invitation *Come, bid me do anything for thee*, she replies, devastatingly, *Kill Claudio*. After recovering from his initial shock Benedick takes up the challenge, thus moving their relationship onto a level of seriousness and commitment that in performance should be moving and impressive: *Enough, I am engag'd; I will challenge him.*

The challenge is delivered but never taken up, for Dogberry's law finally manages to reveal the truth and the play moves

Benedick and Beatrice acknowledge their love in the painful aftermath of Hero's apparent death.

to a conclusion in reconciliation, marriage, and dance. But its arrival there, we may recall, has been more than a little fortuitous. At the end news is brought of the flight and capture of Don John. *Think not on him till to-morrow*, says Benedick to Don Pedro, *I'll devise thee brave punishments for him* (V iv 122-3). Don Pedro entered the play with two companions, Claudio and Benedick. Now they stand as bridegrooms, waiting to dance, while he stands alone and waits for tomorrow, and contemplates the need to punish his brother. As the dance begins we may perhaps remember that this group of well-meaning and sympathetic characters have been saved from the potentially disastrous consequences of their own capacity for misapprehension by the detective perspicacity of Dogberry and his colleagues: *What your wisdoms could not discover, these shallow fools have brought to light* (V i 221-3). Thus, precariously, does comedy arrive at its final celebration of joy, harmony and good fortune.

SEE ALSO: Ch 2 31, 45, 49, Ch 3 78, Ch 4 87-9, Ch 5 201, Ch 7 221, 222

AS YOU LIKE IT

CAST OF CHARACTERS

DUKE, *living in exile*
FREDERICK, *his brother, and usurper of his dominions*
AMIENS, } *lords attending on the banished*
JAQUES, } *Duke*
LE BEAU, *a courtier attending upon Frederick*
CHARLES, *wrestler to Frederick*
OLIVER,
JAQUES, } *sons of Sir Rowland de Boys*
ORLANDO,
ADAM,
DENNIS, } *servants to Oliver*

TOUCHSTONE, *the court jester*
SIR OLIVER MARTEXT, *a vicar*
CORIN,
SILVIUS, } *shepherds*
WILLIAM, *a country fellow, in love with Audrey*
A person representing HYMEN
ROSALIND, *daughter to the banished Duke*
CELIA, *daughter to Frederick*
PHEBE, *a shepherdess*
AUDREY, *a country wench*
Lords, Pages,
Foresters, and Attendants

As *You Like It* is Shakespeare's most thorough examination of the pastoral ideal to which he returned in many moods and at many stages of his career. The play is usually dated about 1599 or 1600, but was not printed until the Folio of 1623. Its principal source is the pastoral romance *Rosalynde* by Thomas Lodge, first published in 1590 and thrice reprinted before the end of the century. The narrative framework of Lodge's tale governs the shape of Shakespeare's play, but the overall tone of *As You Like It* is deeply affected by the two characters he chose to add to those he inherited from Lodge, Touchstone and Jaques. Once again, through these non-romantic additions, Shakespeare presents us with a play in which the romantic-comic and the realistic-satirical are in engaging and fruitful tension.

THE PASTORAL IDEAL

As You Like It is in some ways a rather static play. Once Shakespeare has moved the major characters to Arden, surprisingly little happens in terms of plot. Indeed much of the plot has occurred before the play even begins: the usurpation of Duke Senior's power by Frederick, and Senior's flight to Arden where *many young gentlemen flock to him every day, and fleet the time carelessly, as they did in the golden world* (I i 106-9). There is much violent and destructive action near the play's beginning – the argument and fight of the brothers Orlando and Oliver, re-enactment of that first of fraternal quar-rels; the wrestling match; the rage of Duke Frederick and the banishment of Rosalind – all part of that tendency for a play that will end in comic harmony to begin in discord and separation. When we reach Arden, however, action gives place to talk and time is fleeted as carelessly as one might wish.

From the enactment of hatred we move to the discussion of love.

Happy is your Grace,
That can translate the stubbornness of fortune
Into so quiet and so sweet a style.

(II i 18-20)

Thus Amiens responds to the exiled Duke's description of the contemplative value of the pastoral existence within moments of our first arrival in Arden. It is the ability to 'translate' experience imaginatively that the forest tests and explores. Rosalind sets off on her journey fearing thieves and ravishers; Orlando expects hardship and hunger. Both prove responsive to Arden's other possibilities, discovering, through the freedom it offers – a freedom from self through male disguise particularly important for Rosalind – a capacity for self-awareness, and a consequent ability to surrender the self in love, that would be impossible without the forest's liberation. Between the stylized literary pastoral love of Silvius and Phoebe and the reductive physicality of Touchstone and Audrey, Rosalind moves with a grace and wit, and a wry understanding of herself and her lover, which provide the foundation of our ability to believe in the play's multilayered happy ending, four pairs of lovers blessed by Hymen – or, as Jaques more disparagingly describes it, four *couples . . . coming to the ark.*

It is this insistence on the inescapable physicalities of human experience that gives the play its anchor and which is Shakespeare's deliberate importation into the more ethereal world of *Rosalynde*. Touchstone's legs, not his spirits, are exhausted as he arrives in Arden; he will outrhyme Orlando for eight years, provided his appetite for *dinners, and suppers, and sleeping-hours* is allowed for; and he arrives at the wedding to *press in . . . amongst the rest of the country copulatives.* Final, inexorable, physical truth is the state toward which time hurries the human body:

And then, from hour to hour, we rot and rot.

(II vii 27)

THE ANTICOMIC VOICE

Touchstone's remarks about our ultimate

'I could find in my heart to disgrace my man's apparel, and to cry like a woman; but I must comfort the weaker vessel, as doublet and hose ought to show itself courageous to petticoat.'

physical fate are reported, with much enthusiasm, by Jaques and glossed at length in his famous 'seven ages' speech, as he particularizes the stages of the ripening and rotting process. *I can suck melancholy out of a song, as a weasel sucks eggs* (II v 11-12), he remarks, in one of his earliest contributions to the dialogue – a precise, appropriate, and prophetic image of his ability to prey on life's potentialities and leave it empty.

Sans teeth, sans eyes, sans taste, sans everything

(II vii 166)

he triumphantly concludes his description of the last stage of the human progress, and then Orlando comes in carrying the toothless, 80-year-old Adam.

Welcome. Set down your venerable burden says the Duke; what he perceives, in the ancient loving loyalty of Adam, is venerability; what Jaques has described is senility. They differ only in the 'translation' of the beholder.

So four couples present themselves for marriage at the end and Hymen (supernatural presence, or old Corin the shepherd dressed up, or whatever the performers have decided) comes to bless them. And Jaques will have none of it:

I am for other than for dancing measures

(V iv 187)

he insists, with defiant independence, as the final dance of celebration begins. Off he goes to look for Duke Frederick, whose sudden conversion has been reported by the newly arrived Jaques de Boys, the missing brother of Orlando. As one Jaques walks in, with news of a happier ending than seems wholly credible, another walks out with a shrug of the shoulders at such romantic nonsense, to go in search of a wicked duke turned religious recluse – as though that were less incredible than four couples dancing in comedy's final idealization of concord. In drawing attention to the graceful artificiality of his conclusion by having Jaques depart from it, Shakespeare dares us to follow him.

SEE ALSO: Ch 2 30, 32, 34, 47, 49, Ch 3 65, 84, Ch 4 178-80 Ch 5 205, Ch 7 222, Ch 8 241

TWELFTH NIGHT

CAST OF CHARACTERS

ORSINO, *Duke of Illyria*
SEBASTIAN, *brother of Viola*
ANTONIO, *a sea captain, friend of Sebastian*
A Sea Captain, *friend to Viola*
VALENTINE, ⎫ *gentlemen attending on the*
CURIO, ⎭ *Duke*
SIR TOBY BELCH, *uncle of Olivia*
SIR ANDREW AGUECHEEK

MALVOLIO, *steward to Olivia*
FABIAN, ⎫
FESTE, *a clown,* ⎬ *servants to Olivia*
OLIVIA, *a rich countess*
VIOLA, *sister to Sebastian*
MARIA, *Olivia's waiting woman*
Lords, Priest, Sailors, Officers, Musicians,
and Attendants

In *Twelfth Night* the juxtaposition of the ideal romantic and the harshly unromantic reaches its furthest extreme in this group of comedies. The play, usually dated about 1600 or 1601, derives its main plot from one of the stories in Barnabe Rich's *Farewell to Military Profession* (1583). Shakespeare increases its romantic tone, removing that note of faintly salacious knowingness which is one of the less attractive features of Rich's style. To this central plot of love's problems resolved by the generous miracle of the arrival of a twin, Shakespeare adds the stories involving the characters of Olivia's household: Sir Toby, Sir Andrew, Maria, Feste, and Malvolio. And here the romantic mood is conspicuously absent; after the self-indulgent elegance of Orsino's opening remarks on music and the wistful pathos of Viola's arrival in Illyria, we confront a drunken Belch and a deluded Aguecheek.

Twelfth Night's tone of graceful, elegiac beauty derives from many sources, most clearly from Feste's songs, *Come Away Death*, *The Wind and the Rain*, and *O Mistress Mine*. Throughout the play he gives the impression of a fuller, sadder acquaintance with the poignant absurdities of human behavior than those around him – so much so that some directors try to suggest his recognition of Viola's disguise or are tempted to keep him on stage throughout the performance. His first song's two stanzas exquisitely distil the juxtaposed moods of the play. *Journeys end in lovers meeting*: there is the message of romantic comedy at its simplest and most confident; *Youth's a stuff will not endure*: there is its opposite, the melancholy, withering fact of mortality to set against the happy-ever-after vision.

In the buoyant grace of her hope and trust Viola epitomizes the romantic, verse half of the play.

> *O Time, thou must untangle this, not I,*
>
> (II ii 38)

she says as she realizes that Olivia has fallen under the spell of her male appearance. Her trusting willingness to submit to fate and time contrasts sharply with Orsino's determination to crush Olivia's opposition to his suit and Olivia's futile defiance of life's inexorable mutability in her cloistered mourning for her brother's death. But Viola's trust in time is not an oblivious fatalism: she experiences, movingly, the possibility that her brother is drowned, yet even in the moment of admitting it she draws back from despair:

> *I am all the daughters of my father's house,*
> *And all the brothers too – and yet I know not.*
>
> (II iv 119-20)

COMMUNITY AND SOLITUDE

In her relationship with Orsino and Olivia she brings them to an awareness of themselves and to the opportunity to escape from themselves; and she does so, appropriately, through disguise, through the temporary eradication of self. Her release from disguise, the end of the journey and the lovers' meeting for which she has prepared Orsino and Olivia, come through the gracious dispensation of comic providence, providing her with a twin when only a twin can free her from her predicament.

Viola dresses up self-effacingly to serve the master she loves; Malvolio dresses up self-assertively, in yellow stockings, to impress himself upon the mistress he assumes loves him. His imaginings of his

state as 'Count Malvolio' circle around the magnetic attraction of the first person pronoun and its attendant adjective (II v 45 ff.). *Go off; I discard you. Let me enjoy my private* (III iv 84-5) he insists later as his state of self-absorption reaches obsessive proportions. Malvolio's desire for dominance, for power and self-assertion, threatens all hope of community, and the community of Olivia's household unites to stop him. His imprisonment, however, takes the image of the trapped, isolated, incommunicable self into disturbing and painful territory. Even Sir Toby finds himself wishing that they were *well rid of this knavery*. Released Malvolio is, of course, to depart unreconciled and solitary from the play's conclusion: *I'll be reveng'd on the whole pack of you* – alone against community.

The final scene holds the opposing elements of the play in impressively contrasted tension. Around the central antiphonal litany of the reunion of Viola and Sebastian, the uncompromising resolutions of the subplot provide a harshly prosaic setting. The ritual of the recognition is pushed determinedly further than is necessary into the realm of high romance with the intoning of the recognition symbols:

My father had a mole upon his brow . . .

'By my life, this is my lady's hand; these be her very C's, her U's and her T's.' (II v 79-80)

And died that day when Viola from her birth Had numb'red thirteen years.

(V i 234, 236-7)

It is all, as Olivia observes with a kind of awe, *most wonderful*. For comedy is full of wonder in its fulfillment of our yearnings for restoration and reunion. Before this moment of perfection we have seen Sir Toby, bleeding from a head-wound, round on Sir Andrew and dismiss him from the play in all his pathetic vulnerability. After it we watch the failure to integrate Malvolio into the final resolution. In the midst of all this disintegration the lovers look forward to their *golden time*, so precariously, and wonderfully, granted, leaving Feste to sing to us of the wind and the rain, the rain that raineth every day. Against this hostile environment, comedy, with its images of idealized happiness, is the only refuge for the imagination.

SEE ALSO: Ch 2 49, Ch 5 185, 201, 202, 206, Ch 6 222-3, Ch 7 220

THE MERRY WIVES OF WINDSOR

CAST OF CHARACTERS

SIR JOHN FALSTAFF
FENTON, *a young gentleman*
SHALLOW, *a country justice*
SLENDER, *cousin to Shallow*
FORD, ⎱ *gentlemen of Windsor*
PAGE, ⎰
WILLIAM PAGE, *a boy, son to Page*
SIR HUGH EVANS, *a Welsh parson*
DOCTOR CAIUS, *a French physician*
Host *of the Garter Inn*

BARDOLPH, ⎫
PISTOL, ⎬ *followers of Falstaff*
NYM, ⎭
ROBIN, *page to Falstaff*
SIMPLE, *servant to Slender*
RUGBY, *servant to Doctor Caius*
MISTRESS FORD
MISTRESS PAGE
MISTRESS ANNE PAGE, *her daughter*
MISTRESS QUICKLY, *servant to Doctor Caius*
Servants *to Page, Ford &c.*

This section has so far followed an order that would probably be generally accepted as chronological. With *The Merry Wives of Windsor* we encounter a problem. Here is Shakespeare's only play set in contemporary England, and in continuous and specific detail in contemporary Windsor, with its final scene pausing in mid-career to make a long tribute to the Order of the Garter. In seeking to explain this, scholars have used the tradition, emerging at the beginning of the 18th century, that the play was written in two weeks at Queen Elizabeth's command, because she wanted to see Sir John Falstaff in love.

In 1597 the patron of Shakespeare's company, Lord Hunsdon, received his Garter knighthood. What more natural, it is suggested, than that the company playwright should compose a piece for the occasion; and since Lord Hunsdon's warning of the event seems to have been short, so too was Shakespeare's. This would imply, of course, that by 1597 Falstaff was sufficiently well known for Queen Elizabeth to want to see him in love, which puts a strain on the usual datings of *King Henry IV* (Parts 1 and 2). A few scholars thus remain inclined to date the play about 1601.

To accept the early date, however, helps explain something of the play's unusual quality. It is virtually sourceless: there are analogues in Italian stories for the episodes involving Falstaff's escapes from the jealous anger of Ford, but the inspiration for the play seems largely to derive from the Windsor setting which is most convincingly explained by its connection with the Garter celebration.

FALSTAFF

It is frequently, and rightly, observed that the Falstaff of this play is not the same as the Falstaff of *King Henry IV*. A comic, fictional character in a history play must always fight for his right to exist, protecting himself from exposure with brilliant verbal dexterity until he is finally silenced. A comic character in a comedy has no such problem and may be repeatedly humiliated yet still included in the final harmony.

The repeated humiliation of Falstaff, the ducking, the beating, and the burning (archetypal punishments for this apparent threat to middle-class morality), gives the play its satisfyingly structured pace, each stage building toward the final climax when all Windsor seems united in the duping of Falstaff. But as attention shifts to the subplot of Anne Page and her three wooers, we discover that while all Windsor has been deluding Falstaff, Anne and Fenton have tricked all Windsor. Shakespeare is still employing his usual comic formula of setting romantic plot alongside realistic.

PLOT AND SUBPLOT

This romantic plot may be more fragile than most, and Fenton may be thinly characterized and perhaps a little insignificant,

but he *smells April and May* and thus has a distinct advantage over pompous Dr Caius and foolish Master Slender, and his victory is the victory of love over materialism. Mistress Page has supported Dr Caius's suit for Anne because he is *well moneyed*; Page has favored Slender because he is *well landed*. They would, as Fenton points out,

   . . . have married her most shamefully,
   Where there was no proportion held in love.

                         (V v 208-9)

Queen Elizabeth is supposed to have asked to see Falstaff in love, but Shakespeare gave her no such thing. He merely showed Falstaff, as ever, short of funds and trying seduction as a way of solving financial problems. The irony of the final scene lies in the vehemence of the citizens' revenge on Falstaff for pursuing the same financial obsessions as they have themselves revealed. Their defeat provides the moment of understanding and community upon which all these comedy conclusions are based, even to the extent of showing an unassimilable element in Dr Caius, making his furious

Into provincial Windsor comes Falstaff, from another social sphere and another kind of play.

and vengeful exit to *raise all Windsor*, though here, as elsewhere in the play, confinement within a local habitation and a name seems to reduce the resonance, in comparison, for example, with the ominous generalization of Malvolio's departing cry.

The Merry Wives of Windsor is not the most profound of Shakespeare's comedies, but its vivid series of sharply defined roles for performers, and the pace and vigor of its plot, assure its vitality and theatrical resilience. And in its manipulation and juxtaposition of contrasted comic principles, of realism set against romance, it offers one more variation on the ideas that Shakespeare has so variously explored.

SEE ALSO: Ch 2 34, 45, 47, Ch 3 57, 78, Ch 4 118-21

THE ROMAN PLAYS

Julius Cæsar, Antony and Cleopatra, and Coriolanus present aspects of a disciplined, ordered society far removed from the primal passion and revenge ethic of Shakespeare's earlier 'Roman' play, Titus Andronicus. In these three plays, Shakespeare explores the social and political circumstances surrounding characters, whose names reverberate through the ages.

Although the plays were staged in 1972 in Stratford-upon-Avon as a sequence (Coriolanus, Julius Cæsar, and Antony and Cleopatra) depicting Roman society at different stages of development, there is not the continuity of the English history plays, and they will be considered here in the probable order of composition. All three plays have large casts requiring many actors to be employed as soldiers, tradesmen, citizens, or mob. As representatives of the ordinary people they provide a context in which we can perceive the public pressures which leaders ignore at their peril. A crowd may enlist the sympathy of the onlookers or their contempt, for in the theater we may be as fickle as any electorate.

Throughout the centuries theater-goers have generally preferred a strong plot and the vicarious experience gained from identifying with a central figure. The popularity of Julius Cæsar as a school text, with parts for the whole class, a multiple stabbing, and no rude bits may also have contributed to its dependability at the box office. However, it was long regarded as being successful only in parts and as having grave theatrical defects. Until comparatively recently both Antony and Cleopatra and Coriolanus had suffered from substantial adaptation or neglect. Dryden's All for Love which was first performed at Drury Lane in 1677 was a reworking of Antony and Cleopatra. The emphasis was shifted from the political conflict to a sentimental treatment of the lovers. It was subtitled The World Well Lost, and it held the stage in preference to Shakespeare's play. Though Dryden's play makes fewer demands of its audience, it is rarely performed today.

Nahum Tate's grotesque and gory

Of all the great love stories, only that of Romeo and Juliet rivals Antony and Cleopatra.

adaptation of *Coriolanus, The Ingratitude of a Commonwealth, or, The Fall of Caius Martius*, was produced in 1682 with the forlorn hope that it would 'turn to money what lay dead before'. In 1719 John Dennis also failed with his version, *The Invader of His Country*, in which Aufidius was killed by Caius Marcius. In recent years there has been a revival of interest in *Coriolanus* in performance prompted partly perhaps by the realization that it can be given contemporary significance as a political treatise.

DRAMATIC CONSTRUCTION

It is not so much the ethos and context of the Roman plays which have made them less approachable, as their construction. Audiences like to immerse themselves in the action and get emotionally involved. They enjoy the suspense and excitement of wondering what will happen next. Members of an audience will eagerly suppress their individual identities to share in the mood of the moment and empathize with the handsome hero or heroine. But the method of the Roman plays forbids this kind of response. They do not provide a steady focus of interest. The spectator is disconcerted and he finds it difficult to maintain a fixed attitude towards any of the characters for any appreciable length of time. There is no easy, straightforward identification. Being presented with a sequence of events rather than a plot causes a frequent, uneasy adjustment of the observer's attitude. By choosing stories too well known to be meddled with, Shakespeare accepted that his audience will expect to witness the inevitability of defeat and death. Freed from the dramatic imperative of determining what will happen next, he is able to examine how it happens.

In his notes to Weill's opera *Aufsteig und Fall der Stadt Mahagonny* Bertolt Brecht tabulated the contrasting emphases of epic and dramatic theater. Shakespeare's Roman plays offer narrative rather than plot, with eyes on the course rather than on the finish. Whereas dramatic theater involves the spectator and provides him with sensations, epic theater turns him into an observer and forces him to take decisions.

To describe the Roman plays as epic

The theme of alternative, conflicting forces of goodness runs through the Roman plays, demanding an intellectual response.

rather than dramatic is to affirm rather than deny their theatrical power. Each of the three plays has its moments of high drama, intense emotion, and eloquent expression, but these function within a critical debate. Public and private worlds are opposed: calculation is set against intuition, duty against loyalty. The use of choric figures who step outside the action and offer commentary complicates the audience's response. They interfere with a linear, organic progression, as does the juxtaposition of parallel scenes. The effect of such moments is to make the audience withdraw, think, contrast, analyze, and judge rather than simply share in the hero's emotional development. In the Roman plays good contends less with evil than with an alternative, incompatible force of goodness.

SEE ALSO: Ch 4 140-5, Ch 5 189, 203

JULIUS CÆSAR

CAST OF CHARACTERS

JULIUS CÆSAR
OCTAVIUS CÆSAR, ⎫ *Triumvirs after*
MARCUS ANTONIUS, ⎬ *the death of*
M. ÆMIL. LEPIDUS, ⎭ *Julius Cæsar*
CICERO, ⎫
PUBLIUS, ⎬ *senators*
POPILIUS LENA, ⎭
MARCUS BRUTUS, ⎫
CASSIUS,
CASCA,
TREBONIUS,
LIGARIUS, ⎬ *conspirators against Julius*
DECIUS BRUTUS, *Cæsar*
METELLUS
CIMBER,
CINNA, ⎭
FLAVIUS *and* MARULLUS, *tribunes*
ARTEMIDORUS, *a sophist of Cnidos*

A Soothsayer
CINNA, *a poet*
Another Poet
LUCILIUS, ⎫
TITINIUS,
MESSALA, ⎬ *friends to Brutus and*
YOUNG CATO, *Cassius*
VOLUMNIUS, ⎭
VARRO, ⎫
CLITUS,
CLAUDIUS, ⎬ *servants to Brutus*
STRATO,
LUCIUS,
DARDANIUS, ⎭
PINDARUS, *servant to Cassius*
CALPHURNIA, *wife to Cæsar*
PORTIA, *wife to Brutus*
Senators, Citizens, Guards, Attendants, &c.

The first record of a performance of *Julius Cæsar* is provided by Thomas Platter, a Swiss doctor from Basle, who saw what was probably Shakespeare's play at the Globe in the autumn of 1599. It is likely that Shakespeare wrote the play earlier that year. His main source was Plutarch's *Lives* in Thomas North's edition, first published in 1579 and reprinted in 1595. Working from the separate accounts of the lives of Marcus Brutus, Julius Cæsar, and Marcus Antonius, Shakespeare forged a unified, tightly structured play, condensing three years into a few days.

Julius Cæsar is dominated by a myth rather than a man. An audience comes to the play with the certainty of his greatness and is ready to share in the celebration of another victory. Amid the exuberance of a street party, it is not only the Cobbler who is jolted by the question, *Wherefore rejoice?* Though startled by the questioning of an assumed truth, an audience may just possibly subdue any doubts of Cæsar's achievement by identifying Flavius and Marullus as self-seeking subversives. Cæsar's first appearance shows a superstitious man accustomed to the exercise of authority, yet desperate for adulation.

The difficulty of relating to Cæsar in terms of words, actions, and reputation can contribute to an understanding of Brutus's behavior. His initial reluctance to share Cassius's antagonism is soon followed by a willingness to contemplate the *serpent's egg*, and our shifting perception of Cæsar can embrace both attitudes. Later we may be moved by Antony's Forum speech, yet recognize its political opportunism and adroit skill. The extent to which we can admire and empathize with a range of characters in conflict with each other takes the inquiry beyond the individual man.

The tension of the conspiracy is heightened by a sense of foreboding as character after character expresses feelings of fear and apprehension. The portents, petitions, and prophesies allow the characters to draw attention to the chronicle they are enacting. In the assassination scene the cries of *Liberty, freedom, and enfranchisement* echo hollowly. Brutus had sought to elevate the act by arguing *Let's be sacrificers, but not butchers*, but an audience may find it difficult to accept the staining with Cæsar's blood simply as emblematic ritual.

POLITICS AND MORALS

The emotional blood-letting clears the way for the debate of the issues in the Forum. The audience has its role defined.
1st Plebeian *I will hear Brutus speak.*

The audience's sympathy for the different characters and opinion of the moral and political influences constantly shift throughout the play.

2nd Plebeian *I will hear Cassius, and compare their reasons*

(III ii 8-9)

The friction and disagreements between Brutus and Cassius complicate the issue, denying a simple opposition.

Brutus's address is matter of fact and cogently argued. His reasoning is respected and, assured of the crowd's support, he leaves the stage to Antony. On the page we can be calmly appreciative of the irony of Antony's refrain of support for Brutus, but in performance theater and stage audience are drawn together. Antony has to work hard to sway the crowd but his technique demands admiration. The jolt is all the greater when we are denied a sustained sympathy by his dispassionate:

Now let it work. Mischief, thou art afoot,
Take thou what course thou wilt.

(III ii 261-2)

Brutus had looked no further than the assassination, but Antony here shows a callous disregard for the consequences of incitement. Antony is no heaven-sent avenger: he is human and as fallible as those around him. His emotive use of Cæsar's magnanimity in his will contrasts strongly with the plan *to cut off some charge in legacies.*

Brutus and Cassius are defeated less by Antony's rhetorical skill or the military support he receives than by the pervasive spirit of Cæsar. Their own Roman consciences prevent them from shrugging off the deed. Cæsar's presence in the second half of the play is only partly achieved by means of the *monstrous apparition*, since both Brutus and Cassius make frequent reference to him. Cassius dies with Cæsar's name on his lips, and Brutus's *Cæsar, now be still* suggests a laying to rest of the perturbed spirit that is both Cæsar's and his own.

Examination of character is set among a succession of scenes peopled by opposing forces, and it holds less interest in *Julius Cæsar* than the exploration of political and moral influences. The play offers a balance of conflicting merit and our sympathy and support repeatedly shift. We are not allowed the luxury or security of a still point.

SEE ALSO: Ch 2 38, 47, Ch 4 87-9, Ch 5 189, Ch 6 213, Ch 8 248-9

ANTONY AND CLEOPATRA

CAST OF CHARACTERS

MARK ANTONY,	}		VARRIUS,	
OCTAVIUS CÆSAR,	} *Triumvirs*		TAURUS, *Lieutenant-General to Cæsar*	
M. ÆMILIUS LEPIDUS,	}		CANIDIUS, *Lieutenant-General to Antony*	
SEXTUS POMPEIUS,			SILIUS, *an Officer in Ventidius's army*	
DOMITIUS ENOBARBUS,			EUPHRONIUS, *an ambassador from Antony to*	
VENTIDIUS,	}		*Cæsar*	
EROS,	}		ALEXAS,	}
SCARUS,	}		MARDIAN,	}
DERCETAS,	} *friends to Antony*		SELEUCUS,	} *attendants on Cleopatra*
DEMETRIUS,	}		DIOMEDES,	}
PHILO,	}		A Soothsayer	
MÆCENAS,	}		A Clown	
AGRIPPA,	}		CLEOPATRA, *Queen of Egypt*	
DOLABELLA,	}		OCTAVIA, *sister to Cæsar and wife to Antony*	
PROCULEIUS,	} *friends to Cæsar*		CHARMIAN,	} *ladies attending on*
THYREUS,	}		IRAS,	} *Cleopatra*
GALLUS,	}		Officers, Soldiers, Messengers, *and*	
MENAS,	}		Attendants	
MENACRATES,	} *friends to Pompey*			

*A*ntony and Cleopatra was written in 1606 or 1607. We have no record of an early performance but the play was registered in 1608. As his source Shakespeare again turned to the 'Life of Antonius' from North's Plutarch.

BEHOLD AND SEE

The opening scene establishes the structural pattern for the play. Our first sight of Antony and Cleopatra is framed by a Roman assessment of their relationship. We shall witness Antony's *dotage* upon his *strumpet*, but we may choose for ourselves whether or not to accept the unsympathetic Roman view. The stronger imperative is the instruction to 'look': *Take but good note*, and *Behold and see*. As there is an on-stage audience also watching, we are distanced from Antony and Cleopatra and we may sift another audience's reaction as we form our own. Antony's assertion *Here is my space* may be admirably triumphant, but we cannot escape an awareness that this is at the expense of his Roman responsibilities.

In the early scenes there is an intense focus upon Antony and Cleopatra. We witness the power and tensions of their

relationship and experience the impact of Cleopatra's shifts of mood, whether calculated or impulsive. We can endorse Antony's terse awareness of what he should do, and yet understand his difficulty. But no sooner do we begin to feel at home in Egypt than there is a dislocation. The play embraces the substance of Rome as we swing across the Mediterranean, and we see for ourselves the working of Roman ideas upon Antony. Antony and Cleopatra are not seen on stage together again until the middle of Act III.

Cæsar creates a proper seriousness for presenting the Roman view of Antony by prefacing his words with *This is the news* (I iv 4). When he asserts that

> *You shall find there*
> *A man who is the abstract of all faults*

we are qualified to set his judgment against our own impression of Antony. We may or may not agree with Cæsar's words, since much depends upon our own values. Almost immediately Shakespeare has Lepidus present an alternative assessment. A little later we are offered yet another perspective upon characters and events with Pompey's judgment of Antony, Cæsar, and

At first, Cleopatra is often condemned as a typical woman, but in Act V she transcends reality and achieves cosmic communion.

Lepidus. Pompey's view of Lepidus defines his role as mediator between Rome (Cæsar) and Egypt (as seen in its influence upon Antony). In a play which demands choice and decision, Lepidus's occupation of the middle ground is derided. Ultimately not only does he fail, but he is destroyed by the man he is attempting to serve.

Octavia attempts a similar role. Her function is 'to knit their hearts with an unslipping knot'. The rational justification for her mediation is set against the intensity of Antony and Cleopatra's relationship, and is destroyed by it.

In a play of fixity and flux Shakespeare ranges widely to offer a changing perspective. The conflict between passion and reason is dramatized with Cleopatra's intrusion on the battlefield. Whether Egyptian luxury and military necessity can be reconciled may be debated, but Enobarbus's prophecy reminds us of what we know must happen. Antony is taunted into taking the wrong decision to fight at sea.

Given Enobarbus's authoritative predic-

tion of the outcome, it is appropriate that he should report the inevitable massacre. His line is lyrical in its devastation:

Naught, naught, all naught! I can behold no longer.

(III x 1)

and the irony is that 'behold and see' has been a key instruction to the audience throughout the play. Again there is commentary by yet another newcomer, Scarus. We gain a fresh perspective untarnished by what has gone before, until

we have kiss'd away
Kingdoms and provinces

sets the echoes resounding once more. Antony's shame and dishonor sorely test Enobarbus's loyalty since his reason 'sits in the wind against him'. When we witness Enobarbus's suicide the scene is framed by anonymous Sentries who hear his self-accusation but believe him to be merely sleeping. He has oscillated, observed, commented, and having decided which side to take, regrets his decision – it was an impossible choice.

With the conviction that Cleopatra has betrayed him, Antony condemns her in Roman terms. She is now a *triple-turn'd whore*, a *false soul of Egypt*, *a right gypsy*, and *the witch shall die*. We have lived through too much to accept these words as a final judgment. What distinguishes this play is the characters' ability to rise above themselves. They have an awareness of their own destiny, so Antony can meditate on and exemplify man's precarious hold of his own existence:

Here I am Antony;
Yet cannot hold this visible shape.

(IV xiv 13-14)

It is not to undervalue the intellectual vigor of the play to recognize Antony and Cleopatra's triumph at the end. Their epitaph is given by Cæsar, and his phrase, *a pair so famous*, embodies an emotional truth which surpasses the cold political logic he has represented.

SEE ALSO: Ch 2 47, 49, Ch 3 74, Ch 4 87-9, Ch 5 189, 193, Ch 6 209, 212, Ch 7 220, 221, Ch 8 237, 252

CORIOLANUS

CAST OF CHARACTERS

CAIUS MARCIUS, *afterwards* CAIUS MARCIUS
   CORIOLANUS
TITUS LARTIUS, ⎫ *Generals against the*
COMINIUS, ⎭ *Volscians*
MENENIUS AGRIPPA, *friend to Coriolanus*
SICINIUS VELUTUS, ⎫ *Tribunes of the People*
JUNIUS BRUTUS, ⎭
YOUNG MARCIUS, *son to Coriolanus*
A Roman Herald
NICANOR, *a Roman*
TULLUS AUFIDIUS, *General of the Volscians*
Lieutenant *to Aufidius*

Conspirators *with Aufidius*
ADRIAN, *a Volscian*
A Citizen of Antium
Two Volscian Guards
VOLUMNIA, *mother to Coriolanus*
VIRGILIA, *wife to Coriolanus*
VALERIA, *friend to Virigilia*
Gentlewoman *attending on Virgilia*
Roman *and* Volscian Senators, Patricians,
   Ædiles, Lictors, Soldiers, Citizens,
   Messengers, Servants to *Aufidius, and other*
   Attendants

Conjectural evidence suggests that *Coriolanus* was written in 1607 or 1608. There is no record of an early performance and, as with *Julius Cæsar* and *Antony and Cleopatra*, it was first published seven years after Shakespeare's death in the first Folio. Plutarch's 'Life of Coriolanus' was Shakespeare's source.

The play begins noisily. An angry, hungry crowd demands attention. They have a general, grumbling grievance and it takes considerable skill from Menenius to calm them. There is a temptation to regard him as a genial, detached choric figure, since, as an elder statesman, he can afford to show a kindly tolerance. But he has a vested interest in maintaining the system, and it may well be that he is motivated principally by a delight in his own skill. Nevertheless, his success in subduing the crowd is soon undone by an arrogant Caius Marcius. He sets himself against the plebeians, scorning and despising them. His attitude is emotionally conceived, and we soon realize that Caius Marcius and the plebeians are similarly vulnerable to manipulation by those who are shrewder. As the stage clears, we are given a perspective upon their conflict and we also gain evidence of the political astuteness of Sicinius and Brutus.

PEOPLE AND POLITICS

The play is structured to offer us large public scenes and intimate private ones. It is soon established that the vehement disdain and grand manner of Caius Marcius can variously thrill and appal us, but we must wait and wonder before we see how he conforms to the more modest human dimension of a domestic scene with his wife. During the course of Act I we see Caius Marcius earning the addition of Coriolanus. He relishes the conflict, fighting bravely and impetuously, but he has no capacity to inspire loyalty. He enters Corioli alone and ‚unsupported, which highlights his personal valor but undermines his expertise as a military leader. His driving energy is expressed both in his personal courage and in his vehement condemnation of his troops. He cannot accept praise because of his false pride, and his innate sense of superiority will allow no tolerance nor respect for those he considers inferior and insignificant. He scorns the notion of an election not because he has any principled objection to dissembling, but from a derisive rejection of the notion that the plebeians should have influence or power.

The cold, ironic humor with which Coriolanus canvasses for votes draws attention to his role-playing, distances the audience, and invites an objective assessment of what he was being asked to do. His flippant contempt for the crowd is placed in juxtaposition with his real concern to know what Aufidius thinks of him. Earlier he has shown a boyish eagerness in chivalrous admiration for Aufidius:

> *And were I anything but what I am,*
> *I would wish me only he.*

(I i 228-9)

The admiration will later have its counterpart in an immature spite.

Coriolanus tries and fails to resist domination by his mother. Volumnia takes control of their scenes together, and it can be argued that she is responsible for his emotional immaturity. He can behave as a spoilt boy, torn by the conflict between obedience to his mother and his own natural defiance. Yet for all his fits of unattractive sulkiness, it is with his mother that he also shows the most amiable side of his nature.

The play is bound together with many parallel scenes and the principle of resembling contrast is repeatedly exploited to prompt the audience to make connections. Volumnia's manipulation of her son in III ii anticipates the moment when she will exert her influence to save Rome, but the theatrical imagery of the scene recalls the unhappiness and anger of Coriolanus when he was previously required to play a part. His defiant individualism does demand some sympathy: *There is a world elsewhere.*

We are not shown the process by which he decides to seek Aufidius and take his revenge on Rome. Our interest is focused upon the consequences of his decision, and in some ways the unexpected alliance between Aufidius and Coriolanus can be regarded as the climax to the play. There is emotional tension thereafter, but the remaining episodes are presented with a fluctuating rhythm which makes an easy involvement impossible. The alliance is furnished with a shrewd commentary from the servants. Although contempt for the ordinary people is almost taken for granted in the play, in scene after scene Shakespeare shows us plain citizens and soldiers speaking, more wisely than their tribunes and generals, of current events and policies.

When Coriolanus yields to his mother he 'holds her by the hand, silent' and the hand that has sworn and lived by the sword is now engaged in a private, intimate bond of loyalty and love in a moment that goes beyond words. He knows that his capitulation will seal his fate:

> O mother, mother!
> *What have you done?*

> (V iii 182-3)

and he accepts his destiny with resignation.

But let it come.

His death, like his life, is proud and violent. When he is condemned by Aufidius as a traitor, we are reminded of his banishment from Rome. We may feel a protective impulse towards him before the ignominy of his death, but the Second Lord's chilling assessment prompts us yet again to seek an objective perspective:

> *His own impatience*
> *Takes from Aufidius a great part of blame.*
> *Let's make the best of it.*

> (V vi 145-7)

Critics of *Coriolanus* in the theater have sometimes complained that the actor has not been sufficiently heroic, noble or grand, particularly in the early scenes. This is to wish it a different play. *Coriolanus* embraces political and human relationships and it is essentially a play which repeatedly challenges the audience to realign its sympathy.

Coriolanus has suffered in performance since Nahum Tate's grotesque adaptation in 1682. Interest in the play has recently revived.

THE PROBLEM PLAYS

Shakespeare's plays are all problem plays. In *Hamlet* and *Othello* the situation is evidently desperate and deadly and the questions are those of life and death, but in *As You Like It* and *King Henry IV* the actions performed by the characters equally ask an audience to consider some of the central ethical and historical problems of humanity. 'Problem play' is a modern critical concept, and it was invented as a way of explaining certain features of the four plays under consideration which critics, actors, and audience found difficult. The attempt was necessary because earlier generations, confident in their ethical assumptions about the nature of Shakespeare's other plays, tended to regard these plays as strange, deranged, and very disgusting.

All of these plays have had a troubled stage history. All of them have created difficulties for critics. 'Problem play' is a way of suggesting not only that the plays are about problems but that Shakespeare may have encountered dramatic problems in giving these ideas theatrical expression. The term may have its uses as a matter of critical convenience, but it would be a mistake to suppose that it provides any really useful analysis of the nature of these plays. Yet the critics who evolved the term were highly intelligent men and their efforts both define the difficulty and suggest a way of finding a more comprehensive and satisfactory explanation.

In 1875 Edward Dowden associated *Troilus and Cressida* with *All's Well that Ends Well* and *Measure for Measure*, and described the last as 'dark'. This gave rise to the term 'the dark comedies' which carries the implication that the plays are both obscure and also somehow pessimistic since they take a dark view of human actions and ethical intentions. In *Shakespeare and his Predecessors* (1896) F. S. Boas proposed the term 'problem play', saying that he was borrowing the term from the modern theater. The phrase, however, passed permanently into the currency of Shakespearean criticism with W. W. Lawrence's excellent, informative, and influential book *Shakespeare's Problem Comedies* (1931).

F. S. Boas had proposed to include *Hamlet* as a 'problem play'. Lawrence decided to exclude it. His reasons are illuminating and helpful. *Hamlet*, he said, was clearly a tragedy and 'when the problem play becomes a tragedy, it is, I think, best considered under that rubric'. This is a clear and exact demonstration of the problem about 'problem plays'. They are plays which critics and performers have found difficult to classify under the standard genres of comedy, history, and tragedy and therefore they have felt compelled to create a new classification or genre of their own.

Troilus and Cressida exists in two versions, one printed in Quarto in 1609, and the other printed in the first Folio of 1623 where Shakespeare's fellow actors, John Heminge and Henry Condell, gathered together his works for posterity. In the course of printing, the Quarto was provided with a Preface in the form of a letter to the reader which called *Troilus and Cressida, a new play, never staled with the stage, never clapper-clawed with the palms of the vulgar, and yet passing full of the palm comical,* which has been taken to mean that the anonymous writer thought he was describing a play designed for private performance which was both witty and satirical – in other words, a comedy. Heminge and Condell, however, proposed to place *Troilus and Cressida* in their volume immediately after *Romeo and Juliet*, and therefore clearly regarded it as a tragedy of love. As it turned out, professional complications made it impossible to print the plays in that sequence, and it makes its final appearance between *King Henry VIII* and *Coriolanus*, between history and tragedy.

William Shakespeare is entirely responsible for these problems because he came to mistrust the simple genres of comedy or tragedy. In *Hamlet* (II ii 392) he makes Polonius a genre critic complicating plays into *tragical-comical-historical-pastoral*. In his own practice he came consistently to blur such divisions. A man who writes *The Winter's Tale* with its central chorus defending the passage of 16 years on the stage, and then writes *The Tempest* where the whole action is carefully timed to take place between two and six o'clock is clearly aware of current critical theory, and is thinking most carefully about his business as a playwright. He had, however, always thought about it long, hard.

TEST TO DESTRUCTION

Somewhere around 1599 there is an evident and radical shift in Shakespeare's artistic endeavor. He stops writing the kind of comedy and the histories on which he had built his reputation and fortune. Instead he writes tragedy – but he has changed his mind about the way tragedy should be written for the stage. In *Titus Andronicus* and *Romeo and Juliet* he had already attempted formal tragedy, while *King Richard III* and *King Richard II* also carry the word 'tragedy' in their titles.

Hamlet and *Othello* are a completely different kind of play. They are not about men and women who merely fall from positions of power. They are not about people who have 'fatal flaws' or who are driven by inexorable fate. They are about men and women who are the bravest and most clearly intelligent people in their society and who, for that very reason, come to confusion and destruction. It is important to observe that bravery and intelligence shine as clearly in Ophelia and Desdemona as they do in Hamlet and Othello.

That this 'test to destruction' fascinated Shakespeare is surely shown by the way in which he explored every possible aspect of it through *King Lear, Macbeth, Antony and Cleopatra*, and *Coriolanus*. It also, however, affected all his other work. The 'problem plays' occur when the values of tragedy are applied to the problems of comedy. All four plays were written in different circumstances for different occasions. *Troilus and Cressida* and *Timon of Athens* have every appearance of having been written originally for private performance. *Measure for Measure* is clearly designed to appeal to the known interests of James VI and I. *All's Well that Ends Well* seems to be a normal public performance play.

What gives them their cutting edge and makes them such disturbing plays is

Actors and critics have concentrated on one set of problems to the exclusion of the others, thereby creating, by their own efforts, a 'problem' play.

that Shakespeare's successful dramatic resolution of the ethical and philosophical problems posed within the plot make them extremely difficult to classify within any comfortable moral or critical framework. Like the tragedies, they are deliberately designed to ask questions which range far beyond the walls of the theater. The 'problem plays' are plays in basically comic form which complement the tragedies and even allow Shakespeare to extend their scope and range. They are the intellectual instruments of a man exploring an enormously exciting technical, philosophical, and ethical discovery.

SEE ALSO: Ch 1 25-6, Ch 2 58-9, Ch 4 104-5, 132-3, 118-21, 124-5, 142-5, 148-55, 158-63, 178-80

TROILUS AND CRESSIDA

CAST OF CHARACTERS

PRIAM, *King of Troy*
HECTOR,
TROILUS,
PARIS, } *his sons*
DEIPHOBUS,
HELENUS,
MARGARELON, *a bastard son of Priam*
ÆNEAS,
ANTENOR, } *Trojan commanders*
CALCHAS, *a Trojan priest, taking part with the Greeks*
PANDARUS, *uncle to Cressida*
AGAMEMNON, *the Greek general*
MENELAUS, *his brother*
ACHILLES, *Greek commander*

AJAX,
ULYSSES,
NESTOR, } *Greek commanders*
DIOMEDES,
PATROCLUS,
THERSITES, *a deformed and scurrilous Greek*
ALEXANDER, *servant to Cressida*
Servant *to Troilus*
Servant *to Paris*
Servant *to Diomedes*
HELEN, *wife to Menelaus*
ANDROMACHE, *wife to Hector*
CASSANDRA, *daughter to Priam, a prophetess*
CRESSIDA, *daughter to Calchas*
Trojan *and* Greek soldiers, *and* Attendants

The problems of classification which the early printers and actors had with *Troilus and Cressida* were, I believe, a deliberate creation of the dramatist. The outlines of the story of Troy would be well known since there was a long European tradition of additions, adaptations, and commentary of all kinds on Homer's poems. The love story of Troilus and Cressida was not Homeric but had its origins in the late and rather dubious work of Dictys Cretensis (4th century A.D.), and Dares Phrygius (6th century A.D.). In *Troilus and Criseyde* Chaucer had treated both of them as reliable authorities, and Shakespeare had certainly read Chaucer.

There were, however, a number of other factors involved. At the beginning of the 17th century a great debate was in progress among courtiers, scholars, and writers about the nature of the classical world and the influence that it should have on the writing of English literature. Shakespeare had already made a conscious contribution in *Julius Cæsar*. Jonson would produce his classical tragedy *Sejanus* by 1603, while in 1604 he and Inigo Jones started an acrimonious but successful campaign for neoclassical art and architecture in England. One of the influential documents in this debate was George Chapman's translation of Homer, designed to educate his countrymen in the supremacy of this poet.

Shakespeare chose a traditional love story set in a recognizably Homeric context, which is then treated with scabrous disrespect, not merely in the cloacal invective of Thersites but in the fact that John Harrington had just used the name of Ajax, or a-jakes, as a witty euphemism for his newly designed water closet. This suggests that it was a contribution to such a debate, and that Shakespeare expected his audience to know the story and appreciate his subtle variations upon traditional themes.

THE PROBLEM

It would, however, be a major mistake to suppose that the play is simply a satire on heroism, chivalry, and romantic love, and is somehow vaguely antisin and antiwar. The chivalry, heroism, and love are real enough. Shakespeare simply follows his own practice in the tragedies of placing important historical statements of widely believed philosophical positions in the mouths of characters who, given their situation, cannot possibly fulfill them and whose belief in them is a major factor in their own destruction. *Troilus and Cressida* could be viewed as a vast expansion of the prayer scene in *Hamlet*. It opens with two scenes in which, while the lovers do not see each other, Pandarus is seen as working hard to bring about the consummation which they devoutly wish but are unwilling to talk about, even to each other, since words can clearly turn the course of their actions awry.

Everything is then shown awry in the scenes of council in the Greek and Trojan camps. Ulysses gives a magnificent account of order and degree, which he then proposes to Nestor they must subvert in order to bring Achilles back to battle. The Trojans debate returning Helen to her husband. Hector argues for this on every possible ethical, legal, and practical ground; he then subverts his argument by announcing his challenge to the Greeks. Hector and Troilus, who has also argued for 'honor' in keeping Helen, have thus subverted the love of Troilus and Cressida.

Cressida's entertainment in the Greek camp, where Ulysses proposes the kissing game and then calls Cressida a whore for winning it, is contrasted with the chivalrous entertainment of the perceived male enemy in the person of Hector. Love first revolts when Troilus watches Cressida dubiously entertaining Diomedes' dubious advances in a position in which he has been responsible for placing her. Then he allows himself the luxury of blaming her and Diomedes, and wishes to wash his hands, preferably in blood, of his own responsibility. Chivalry is bathed in blood by the death of friends and lovers.

It is therefore the more surprising that Shakespeare allows two characters to peep through the blanket of this dark. Thersites, who says that the whole war is about a whore and a cuckold and that there is nothing but wars and lechery, could hardly believe that important unless he could perceive a world where the words of honor and chivalry, which he so constantly and potently subverts, might have real meaning. The girl whom he describes as having a *mind turned whore* protests her commitment to the values of romantic love in a world where human actions, in love and war, deny the possibility of such values. Shakespeare's own enormous joke is that out of the true chaos of the Trojan war, Thersites emerges as the great romantic, and Cressida the true lover, because they are the only people who can conceive of a world elsewhere in which

Shakespeare's paradox is to turn Thersites into the great romantic, and Cressida, the whore of war, into the heroine of a possible peace.

the values they respect and live by could actually be realized.

If there is a problem about *Troilus and Cressida*, it is because Shakespeare panders to his audience with a tale of war and lechery, and then totally subverts them by asking them what they might mean by the terms hero, whore, or cuckold. The question of the tragedies is put in a form which seems satiric because it is hopelessly nearer the truth than the created pastoral world of the comedies.

SEE ALSO: Ch 2 49, Ch 3 69, 83-4, Ch 4 140-1, 158-9, 178-80, Ch 6 212-3

ALL'S WELL THAT ENDS WELL

CAST OF CHARACTERS

THE KING OF FRANCE
THE DUKE OF FLORENCE
BERTRAM, *Count of Rousillon*
LAFEU, *an old lord*
PAROLLES, *a follower of Bertram*
Two French Lords, *serving with Bertram*
Steward,
LAVACHE, *a clown,* } *servants to the Countess*
A Page, } *of Rousillon*

COUNTESS OF ROUSILLON, *mother to Bertram*
HELENA, *a gentlewoman, protected by the*
  Countess
A Widow of Florence
DIANA, *daughter to the Widow*
VIOLENTA, } *neighbours and friends to the*
MARIANA, } *Widow*
Lords, Officers, Soldiers, etc., French and
  Florentine

All's Well that Ends Well exists in only one early text, the Folio of 1623, and we have no certain knowledge of its date of composition or record of its first performance. The theme and style suggest the early years of the 17th century, while the use of the 'bed trick' – a loving wife substituting herself for a desired lover and offering her body in secret to the unmastered and unknowing importunity of her husband – provides an obvious if inconclusive link with *Measure for Measure* which was performed in 1604.

Shakespeare's ultimate source is the ninth story told on the third day of Boccaccio's *Decameron*. Shakespeare may have known this in its original version or he may have used the English version in William Painter's popular *Palace of Pleasure* (1566, 1567, 1575). Painter had also used a French version by Antoine le Maçon, and it is possible that Shakespeare had consulted that as well. The story in Boccaccio and later versions concentrates on how Giletta of Narbonne cured the King of France and received as her reward the hand of her childhood companion, Count Beltramo of Rossiglione. He is forced to accept her in marriage but refuses to consummate it, saying he would never return to her until she should show him the ring from his finger and a child conceived by him.

This extension of the psychological situation until it touches the limits of conventional comedy appalled some critics and has confused directors. Yet in *Much Ado about Nothing* Hero is presumed dead and

Claudio accepts marriage to her supposed cousin. In *The Merchant of Venice* Portia beguiles her own ring from her husband's finger and accuses him of infidelity. In *As You Like It* Orlando goes through a form of marriage with a 'boy'. These comic contortions may seem more acceptable because they are not sexually performed in a marriage bed with an unrecognized partner. Also death, though present and potent in all these visions of Arcadia, has advanced a step closer to the audience in *All's Well that Ends Well*. The situations are slightly more extreme, and the questions raised more specifically designed to upset ethical certainties based merely on comfortable supposition.

Shakespeare asks his audience to be interested in the situation of the King and the Countess, in Lafeu, and in the relations of an older generation to their successors and competitors. He creates Parolles to raise in acute form the questions of military and civil honor and their relationship to the union of the sexes. He complicates the matter further by the strong sister bond that, more than the promised dowry, induces the widow and Diana to help Helena. In surrounding his heroine with this multitude of questions, he also focuses attention on the depth of her passion.

Shakespeare's method is possibly most clearly revealed in his creation of Bertram. This young man appears to have extracted from the natural advantages of his social position and education almost every defect of character that it is possible for a human

being to possess. He is made exactly sufficiently horrible for an audience to wonder if he is in fact typical of his class, sex, and age-group. Shakespeare redresses the balance by asking us to believe that Helena sees in him qualities that are to us invisible, but it is her actions that put him on trial in order that the man may emerge from his potentially lethal set of prejudices.

BERTRAM AND HELENA

Precipitated into a marriage that was as unexpected as unwelcome, Bertram proceeds through the education of war to the discovery that words of honor may be merely 'paroles' in Florence as in France. The interrogation of Parolles is brilliant farce. The interrogation of Bertram about the death of Helena and his relations with Diana reveal his honor and dignity to be based on lies more miserable than fake military machismo. Parolles betrays his companions while failing to recover his drum, and has to accept, *Simply the thing I am*. Bertram's humiliation is more devastating, and he has to do more to recover from it. Helena's role, however, has been specifically designed to allow the actor playing Bertram to regain the sympathy of the audience. Helena has made Bertram exchange rings with her symbolically and

Shakespeare seized on elements of folk tale in his sources and then pushed the essence of the story to the edge of potentially sickening destruction.

sexually before he recovers her, and has slowly made him move inward towards her, since to acknowledge and accept his wife he had first to know himself. The man he discovers is the one she has loved.

This knowledge is available to the audience at an early stage of the play when the King points out that the noble ability to combine thought, action, and passion depends on character and intelligence rather than birth. The proposition is one that usually achieves universal acclaim, coupled with total practical neglect. It requires Helena to make Bertram capable of receiving what she has to give and return it. The bed trick is a powerful expression of sexual reality. Recognition and reorientation are as essential to modern psychotherapy as remorse and repentance were, or are, to the church. It is a great mistake to ignore their necessity in human affairs.

SEE ALSO: Ch 2 49, Ch 4 128-9, 132-3, 178-80, Ch 6 208

MEASURE FOR MEASURE

CAST OF CHARACTERS

VINCENTIO, *the Duke*
ANGELO, *the Deputy*
ESCALUS, *an ancient Lord*
CLAUDIO, *a young gentleman*
LUCIO, *a fantastic*
Two other like gentlemen
VARRIUS, *a gentleman, servant to the Duke*
PROVOST
THOMAS, } *two friars*
PETER, }
A JUSTICE
ELBOW, *a simple constable*

FROTH, *a foolish gentleman*
POMPEY, *a clown and servant to Mistress Overdone*
ABHORSON, *an executioner*
BARNARDINE, *a dissolute prisoner*
ISABELLA, *sister to Claudio*
MARIANA, *betrothed to Angelo*
JULIET, *beloved of Claudio*
FRANCISCA, *a nun*
MISTRESS OVERDONE, *a bawd*
Lords, Officers, Citizens, Boy, *and* Attendants

Measure *For Measure* may have grown from an imaginative intellectual proposition. Angelo believes his soul is being fished for by the devil,

> *O cunning enemy, that, to catch a saint,*
> *With saints dost bait thy hook!*
>
> (II ii 180-1)

Isabella, as a novice, could be described as saintlike, but for Angelo to describe himself as a saint is odd. On the other hand if Angelo is using saint in the sense used by the Protestant reformers – one who is saved and justified by his faith alone – then the proposition is: – what happens to the body politic of the state if its normal head of government is replaced by the rule of the saints? The play is certainly about the body politic – it has an elbow, a bum, and a change of head – and the new head feels forced to remove other human heads for performing what some of the characters regard as normal functions with the genitals. It is also a play written at a time of political change and religious difficulty.

Shakespeare's Vienna is thus temporarily governed by Angelo who turns out to have been created considerably lower than the angels, and the result is an immediate series of harsh repressive sexual measures which soon degenerate into compelled rape, tyranny and murder. Although the play was not printed until the Folio of 1623, a performance at court appears to have been recorded in the Revels accounts for 26 December 1604.

Shakespeare probably found the story in Giraldi Cinthio's *Hecatommithi* (1565), which also contains the story of Disdimona and the Moor. Cinthio also wrote a dramatized version published in 1583. George Whetstone produced a two part play called *Promos and Cassandra* (1578) based on the story, and in 1582 included a prose version of the story in his *Heptameron of Civil Discourses*. These versions differ in detail, and Shakespeare may have drawn on them all. He differs from them in one vital point: in all other versions the girl agrees to save her brother by enduring sexual intercourse with the judge. In Cinthio's original version, the judge sends her the head of her brother next morning; in the other versions he is saved. Only Shakespeare asks his heroine to stand on stage and speak the terrible words,

> *More than our brother is our chastity.*
>
> (II iv 185)

Such a decision inevitably again sharpens the religious and political issues to a point where they threaten to cut through the comic conventions. Politically the decision is realistic, since compromise with the kind of tyranny exercised by Angelo can hardly hope for a merciful outcome. Within the religion she professes Isabella's position seems secure, but the play, like the world, is filled with competing ethical systems which are not necessarily compatible, and

The play turns round a number of questions known to interest James I – the art of government and the legal force of marriage contracts.

Shakespeare evidently expected his audience to consider carefully the heavy ethical weight placed on her by this situation.

MERCY AND JUSTICE

The electric debate between Isabella and Angelo about mercy and justice occurs in the first half of the play until Angelo concludes it by actually proposing measure for measure to her – chastity or her brother's life. The ethical collapse of Angelo is due to causes other than his arguments about justice, and even Isabella's deployment of the full force of the Christian imagery of mercy cannot quite remove their cogency. It is the law, not the judge, that condemns Claudio, and if one takes the practical attitude that the law must function even if some jurors may themselves be guilty, then the mercy requested by Isabella could threaten anarchy rather than the rule of law.

The Duke as Friar, having watched the test to destruction of the rule of law, is now committed to the substitution for it of the law of grace, which Christians believed had replaced God's covenant with his chosen people by the salvation of the world through Christ. Grace, however, is forced to act in mysterious ways. The curious currents of Angelo's past life allow a bed trick which substitutes Mariana for Isabella, but such sexual psychological warfare proves insufficient to save Claudio. The substitution of Barnardine's head is proposed, but he refuses to be executed on theological grounds. The head of the dead Ragozine is then successfully substituted as a head trick.

These comic convolutions also carry a tragic edge. The Duke-Friar withholds from Isabella the knowledge that Claudio is alive until he has tested her quality of mercy to despair, and she has knelt alongside Mariana to ask pardon for the man she then believes to have killed her brother. In this way the shadow of Abhorson and Pompey falls even on the Duke. In a functioning body politic even the head is not exempt from the poisons working elsewhere.

SEE ALSO: Ch 2 39, 49, Ch 4 87-9, 160-1, 178-80, Ch 5 201, 206

TIMON OF ATHENS

CAST OF CHARACTERS

TIMON, *of Athens*
LUCIUS, ⎱
LUCULLUS, ⎰ *flattering lords*
SEMPRONIUS,
VENTIDIUS, *one of Timon's false friends*
ALCIBIADES, *an Athenian captain*
APEMANTUS, *a churlish philosopher*
FLAVIUS, *steward to Timon*
FLAMINIUS, ⎱
LUCILIUS, ⎰ *Timon's servants*
SERVILIUS,
CAPHIS, ⎱
PHILOTUS, ⎰ *servants to*
TITUS, *Timon's creditors*
HORTENSIUS,

Poet
Painter
Jeweller
Merchant
Mercer
An Old Athenian
Three Strangers
A Page
A Fool
PHRYNIA, ⎱
TIMANDRA, ⎰ *mistresses to Alcibiades*
CUPID, ⎱
AMAZONS, ⎰ *in the Mask*
Lords, Senators, Officers, Soldiers, Servants,
   Thieves, *and* Attendants

Timon of Athens* was first published in the 1623 Folio but the state of the text, and doubts about the nature of the play, have created formidable problems for editors and commentators. These are accompanied by a kind of general critical groundswell of disapproval indicating that the play was somehow rough, unfinished, or abandoned. It is true that there are textual difficulties but a great many of the problems that surround this play are possibly the self-inflicted wounds of criticism. A man who could change artistic direction in the middle of his professional career was capable of writing a great variety of plays, and *Timon* must be examined on its own merits rather than crushed into critical categories and then abandoned when it will not fit them.

Like *Troilus and Cressida*, it is a play on a Greek subject, which is perhaps why it was chosen to replace *Troilus* when that play had to be temporarily withdrawn from the printing process of the first Folio. It bears all the marks of being printed from an authorial draft, but what has puzzled commentators is that the characterization is left more at the level of role playing than psychological realization, and this is reflected in the speech prefixes which record Poet, Painter, or Steward rather than names. Since Shakespeare was a conscious artist interested in the theory and practice of

his craft, passages where art is discussed are always of particular interest. Painter and Poet discuss their respective offerings to Timon. The Poet praises the painter since his work *tutors nature*, and then describes his own allegorical work in which Timon is cast down by Fortune.

Timon then enters greeting his friends and his suitors, and it is immediately evident that these creative intelligences, as they see themselves, are but minor actors in this show and that as false friends of Timon they will enact their 'speaking pictures' more truly than they know. Their vision of themselves draws attention to the emblematic effect of the larger picture and reveals an equally serious flaw. Timon's generosity is only partial, since the art of princely liberality involved receiving and returning as well as giving. Only then was the true liberality of social behavior achieved. Timon is incapable of receiving gifts without returning them fourfold so that his friends are sycophants who give him presents as an investment, while Timon himself treads a primrose path where he has mistaken his indulgence of himself for true munificence. Since, in these circumstances, the object is to show the breakdown of a social process through neglect of the necessary psychological human rhythm, one must conclude that the absence of psychological characterization is precisely the point.

Locked into profligacy, Timon cannot profit from Apemantus or Alcibiades, who have both distanced themselves in different ways from the socially destructive round of Athenian society, or from his faithful steward who cannot conserve the means so deliriously dissipated. The banquet of hot water that Timon serves his guests before his exile is, like the Amazonian masque of the five senses, a false indulgence for which he must bear a heavy responsibility. Timon is shown to be a misanthrope, a hater of mankind, before he is forced to abandon human society.

TIMON AND SOCIETY

This is a rather different picture of Timon from the one found in Shakespeare's major classical source, Plutarch's *Life of Mark Antony*, and it also differs from the classical work which had made Timon's misanthropy famous, Lucian's dialogue *Timon or the Misanthrope* (2nd century A.D.). That Shakespeare is again using his information for his own purposes is shown by his use of the character of Alcibiades, whom Plutarch used as a comparable character to Coriolanus. His victories, the attempt to save his captain's life, his banishment and, in this play, his completely unhistorical capture of Athens emphasize that the pursuit of honor and the military virtues exist within a context of social duplicity that makes the capture of Athens the greatest victory of Athens' greatest soldier. To have given service, received banishment, and returned to conquer compares in sterility with the dishes of hot water.

The endeavor of Alcibiades has been fueled by the new creative life that Timon devised for himself in the woods. Having found gold, he waits like the Porter in *Macbeth* until all sorts and conditions of men find their way to his cave from which, by the gift of gold, he returns them to *the primrose way to th' everlasting bonfire*. Whores and bandits are supplied with money to destroy mankind, and Apemantus is delighted to spread the news and increase the work of destruction.

In these woods and in this pastoral landscape there is nothing to be learnt. Art

In this comedy, there is no return from the pastoral world refreshed to face society. Rather, Timon supplies the bandits and whores with gold in order to destroy society.

itself can have no place since the poet and the painter arrive to announce that, while they propose courtly promises, they intend to perform nothing. The paradox is again that their sterility, and Timon's, is contained within a work of art that is itself an attempt to avert the social breakdown that it so clearly depicts. The choice of a known classical Greek story, and an extremely free handling of it, suggest that *Timon of Athens* was intended for some private occasion where its grim message, and the truth-telling mirror it holds up to English society, might be laughed at but might also provoke thought and possible action.

The play is not a tragedy but a comedy of manners – very bad ones – but the creation of Timon's misanthropic tomb is an interesting monument to Shakespeare's social conscience.

SEE ALSO: Ch 2 49, Ch 4 87-9, 148-9, 164-5, 178-80

THE TRAGEDIES

Shakespeare's principal tragedies are *Hamlet, Othello, King Lear* and *Macbeth*. At least since A.C. Bradley's classic study *Shakespearean Tragedy* (1904) which dealt specifically with these four plays, others such as *Romeo and Juliet, King Richard II, Julius Cæsar, Antony and Cleopatra, Coriolanus* and *Timon of Athens* have for various reasons been excluded from the strictly 'tragic' part of the canon. The four great tragedies occupy a monolithic position in English and European literature: *Hamlet* is the first tragedy in the Western world since the magnificent masterpieces of 5th century classical Greece by Aeschylus, Sophocles and Euripides.

But it was not the great Hellenic drama which was to provide the matrix for English Renaissance tragedy, so much as the truncated Latin adaptations of the Greeks by Seneca, whose closet dramas on Greek themes were translated early in the Elizabethan period. Both *Hamlet* and *Macbeth*, for example, are heavily indebted to Senecan rhetoric and themes such as revenge and familial blood feuds.

FOR ALL TIME

Perhaps the most distinctive feature of Shakespeare's tragedies when compared to other great classics is the immediate accessibility of these masterpieces which, through their overwhelming humanity and imaginative range, have uniquely stood the test of time. Every generation has found or created its mirror-images in the Oedipal, political and existential *angst* of *Hamlet*, the sexual traumas of *Othello*, the radical pessimism of *King Lear* and the moral probings and haunted experience of guilt in *Macbeth*. Interpretations of these works since their first performances at the Globe Theater in Southwark between 1600 and 1607 to the present day provide unique insights into the cultural history of the last four centuries, as well as advancing our understanding of the plays themselves.

All four plays end in death. It is only in *Antony and Cleopatra*, Shakespeare's *Antigone*, that the prospect of a transcendence of death is at all contemplated in its uniquely 'split catastrophe', when Cleopatra is left behind to conjure up a vision of Antony *redivivus*. Hence the play is perceived rightly as bridging the gulf between Shakespearean tragedy and the romances of resurrection like *Pericles*, and *The Winter's Tale*.

Two of Shakespeare's tragedies, *Hamlet* and *King Lear*, feature royal protagonists and therefore engage with the Elizabethan political philosophy of kingship as it had been handed down by medieval theology. The tragic action of *Macbeth* evolves in tandem with the usurpation of a country through the murder of its legitimate king. *Othello* uniquely is a domestic tragedy in that its hero is a newly-married, middle-aged Moor of royal extraction, who is however portrayed during the play as a noble mercenary in the service of the naval and colonial power of Republican Venice.

TRAGEDY OF CHARACTER

Shakespeare's tragedies can neither be accommodated on the then prevailing neoclassical Aristotelian model nor to the medieval formula of tragedy as expounded and illustrated in Chaucer's *The Monk's Tale*. If Shakespeare's tragic protagonists partly rise and fall on the wheel of fortune, they do not thereby conform to the lapsarian pattern of Chaucer's monk's definition of tragedy as illustrating the fate of someone

> . . . that stood in greet prosperitee,
> And is yfallen out of heigh degree
> Into myserie, and endeth wrecchedly.

Blind fate never controls the destinies of Shakespeare's protagonists. Hamlet may repeatedly cast himself as a divinely appointed revenger, to set right a time which is *out of joint*, or proclaim an allegiance to a divinity that shapes our end and a providence that controls even the fall of a sparrow. But ultimately, and the ghost notwithstanding, Hamlet, like Macbeth, has to assume full responsibility for his choices and actions. In *King Lear* the king's folly and dotage which make him divide the realm may be construed as fate, but the two evil daughters' ingratitude is born from a calculated and acquisitive spirit of material

and political ambition. In *King Lear* Edmund's infamously Machiavellian and proleptically Darwinian creed, *Thou, Nature, art my goddess*, constellates the measure of the distance between medieval notions of ordained fate and the new spirit of a geo- and egocentric Renaissance world. Shakespeare's tragedies never break away totally from the formal and thematic mold of a medieval Christian past, but their proper imaginative sphere resides in the contemporary world of Montaignian scepticism and Galilean revolution, what Donne aptly termed a *new philosophy* [which] *calls all in doubt.*

In the tragedies, man's challenges to orthodoxy and his resilience and despair in the face of adversity have been intimately linked to each of Shakespeare's four tragic protagonists exhibiting a flaw, a fated character trait which overrides all other impulses and considerations: delay in *Hamlet,* ambition in *Macbeth*, ingratitude in *King Lear* and jealousy in *Othello*. Although such overly simplified readings of the plays are not now current, their prominence for so

Hamlet is undoubtedly Shakespeare's most famous and most frequently quoted play.

long highlights the extent to which 'character' rather than 'action' (as predicated in Aristotle's *Poetics*) is foregrounded in Shakespearean tragedy. Above all the four great tragedies in various ways and in infinitely complex and individualized guises present the spirit of man wrestling with the forces of evil both within and without.

Invariably 'man' loses, but during his doomed progress he discovers, and we with him, the innermost recesses and finest discriminations of the human soul. These stretch beyond the ken of abstract speculative philosophy. They can only be encompassed by a literary art which conjoins every human reflection with a set of specific interlocking dramatic situations.

SEE ALSO: Ch 4 104-5, 116-7, 140-5, 154-5, 160-5, 168-9, 172-3

HAMLET

CAST OF CHARACTERS

CLAUDIUS, *King of Denmark*
HAMLET, *son of the former and nephew to the present King*
POLONIUS, *Lord Chamberlain*
HORATIO, *friend to Hamlet*
LAERTES, *son to Polonius*
VOLTEMAND,
CORNELIUS,
ROSENCRANTZ, } *courtiers*
GUILDENSTERN,
OSCRIC,
A Gentleman
A Priest
MARCELLUS, } *officers*
BERNARDO,

FRANCISCO, *a soldier*
REYNALDO, *servant to Polonius*
Players
Two Clowns, *grave-diggers*
FORTINBRAS, *Prince of Norway*
A Norwegian Captain
English Ambassadors
GERTRUDE, *Queen of Denmark, and mother of Hamlet*
OPHELIA, *daughter to Polonius*
Ghost of Hamlet's Father
Lords, Ladies,
    Officers, Soldiers, Sailors,
    Messengers, *and* Attendants

Hamlet (1600) is Shakespeare's longest play. It remains the most famous work for the theater ever written, and has attracted more commentary than any other drama. Apart from the Bible, it is the most often quoted work in the English language and rhetorically the most cornucopian, not least for its maverick stylistic inventiveness. Its protagonist has encouraged a unique degree of projected identification. Coleridge's formulation 'I have a smack of Hamlet' is only the most famous statement of a nearly universal audience-reader response to Shakespeare's charismatic and deeply troubled prince of Denmark.

The scope of the play is dazzling. Its remarkable integration of themes from the Aeschylean *Oresteia* and Sophocles' Theban trilogy is compounded by its original adaptation of revenge motifs from earlier plays, notably Kyd's *Spanish Tragedy* and the lost *Ur-Hamlet*. The cannibalistic banquets and masque-like theatrical performances in revenge drama, in *Hamlet* become the vehicle for highly wrought symbolic statements about the human condition. The work's obsession with food imagery and its exploitation of the multiple ambiguities of the theatrical metaphor at the heart of the play, in Hamlet's discourse with the players and in his staging of the Mousetrap, intimates the degree of its transforming power in its use of traditional material.

The once prevalent view of Hamlet as a man who could not make up his mind because of an overly sensitive soul is no longer tenable. It does, however, focus attention on one of the central paradoxes of the play: that a young man in pursuit of an essentially immoral act of revenge killing, which may result in his eternal damnation, has long retained our enthusiastic admiration. When Hamlet's confidant and friend Horatio at the end of the play sums it up as a series of events

Of carnal, bloody, and unnatural acts;
Of accidental judgments, casual slaughters;
Of deaths put on by cunning and forc'd cause;
                                        (V ii 373-5)

the audience is jolted into an acute awareness of the double-take in the play: between us on the one hand who are privy to every one of Hamlet's moods, anxieties and moral dilemmas through his extended soliloquies and, on the other hand, the cast of characters who may understandably view Hamlet's disruptive antics and course of action with more alarm.

Admittedly, all three of Hamlet's direct killings are partly attenuated by circumstances: Laertes dies in the duel through his own faithless poisoning of the rapier's point, although Hamlet administers the blow; the killing of Claudius is a reflexive act immediately consequent on Laertes' dying warning to Hamlet that *the King's to blame* for the *point envenom'd*. The stabbing of Polonius through the arras poses far more ambiguous puzzles. Although there is no hint of premeditation in the killing, Hamlet bitterly remarks

Thou wretched, rash, intruding fool, farewell!
I took thee for thy better.

(III iv 31-2)

MODERN INTERPRETATIONS

The fate of Rosencrantz and Guildenstern deeply disturbs Horatio when he learns of Hamlet's sending them to England to their deaths. To his horrified

So Guildenstern and Rosencrantz go to't

Hamlet replies

Why, man, they did make love to this
employment;
They are not near my conscience;

(V ii 56, 57-8).

The 20th-century audience has increasingly felt that they should be, that Hamlet the supreme essentialist needs to be judged by his actions. Thus it has been noted that the monarchy of Denmark is elective, not hereditary and therefore not Hamlet's birthright. Furthermore Claudius' unmistakable love for Gertrude has been reappraised as well as his efficient squashing of the threatened Fortinbras invasion through diplomacy. He appears indulgent of Hamlet's naked and subsequently covert hostility up to the point of the politically explosive play-within-the-play, when no ruler could simply stand by any longer. In the middle of Act III Claudius is unrepentantly kneeling at prayer, when Hamlet, unaware of its futility enters unseen. He would happily have killed Claudius were it not that it might send his soul to heaven in a state of new-born grace. The temporary rehabilitation of Claudius has entailed a partial review of his court of sycophants, including Polonius, and the blame for Ophelia's madness has been squarely laid at Hamlet's door, as if she had never been used and abused by her brother and father to entrap Hamlet.

Tempting though it may be for the 20th century to create a villainous Hamlet in our own image and out of a sense of deep-rooted suspicion of any cult of the individual, the fact remains that the play's text unmistakably sets him apart from the others. As is often pointed out, the character derives part of his appeal from his

The text unmistakably sets Hamlet apart, yet of all Shakespeare's heroes he evokes the strongest degree of projected identification.

intellectual confronting of the multifaceted complexity of human experience, and in this is reminiscent of Brutus in *Julius Cæsar*, a play which is to good effect repeatedly recalled, not least in Polonius's tragically ironic *I did enact Julius Cæsar, I was kill'd i' th' Capitol, Brutus kill'd me* (III ii 100-101). Such disagreement as fruitfully informs readings of *Hamlet* above all acknowledges its rich multiplicity.

SEE ALSO: Ch 3 68, 78, 82, Ch 4 140-1, 176-80, Ch 5 183-205, Ch 6 207, 211, 214, Ch 7 219, 223, Ch 8 241, 243-4, 252, 254

OTHELLO

CAST OF CHARACTERS

DUKE OF VENICE
BRABANTIO, *a Senator, father to Desdemona*
Other Senators
GRATIANO, *brother to Brabantio,* ⎫ *two noble*
LODOVICO, *kinsman to Brabantio,* ⎭ *Venetians*
OTHELLO, *the Moor, in the service of Venice*
CASSIO, *his honourable Lieutenant*
IAGO, *his Ancient, a villain*
RODERIGO, *a gull'd Venetian gentleman*

MONTANO, *Governor of Cyprus, before Othello*
Clown, *servant to Othello*
DESDEMONA, *daughter to Brabantio, and wife to Othello*
EMILIA, *wife to Iago*
BIANCA, *a courtezan, in love with Cassio*
Gentlemen of Cyprus, Sailors, Officers, Messenger, Musicians, Herald, Attendants, &c.

The vastness of *Hamlet* is perfectly balanced by the suspense and sharp focus of *Othello*, written in late 1603 or early 1604. Of the four great tragedies, this play is unique in its sustained concentration on a domestic relationship, the unequal marriage between Othello and the young Venetian artistocrat Desdemona. Romantic stage tragedy did not exist before *Romeo and Juliet* (1595) and hardly extends beyond *Antony and Cleopatra* (1608), two texts with which *Othello*, though not strictly a 'romantic' tragedy, is often compared. But the mutuality which fuels the lovers' relationships in these two plays is starkly absent from *Othello*.

As a tragic protagonist Othello needs to be isolated from his kind. But he is rarely credited with being the peer of Hamlet, Lear and Macbeth. His intellect and moral imagination fall far short of their range, not least through the deflating influence of Iago's manipulating of the plot. Because of Iago, Othello is consistently shown in the course of the play to be more ignorant than the audience. He is therefore greatly diminished in our esteem, as we anxiously witness his tragically ironic and ritualistic progress towards the murder of Desdemona, in spite of all the rational and emotional evidence to the contrary. Othello's love for Desdemona is never truly questioned. Shortly before Iago's poison starts its work, Othello comments on Desdemona:

> *Excellent wretch! Perdition catch my soul*
> *But I do love thee; and when I love thee not*
> *Chaos is come again.*
>
> (III iii 91-3)

Professions of love like these, the Moor's commanding nobility and unshakable trust in his officers and his ingenuous sense of duty have traditionally impressed audiences in his favor.

PLEASURE AND ACTION

Many of Othello's apologists have excused or mitigated the Moor's violent jealousy by pointing an accusatory finger at Iago. Who, it is asked, could possibly have eluded the malicious and unsuspected schemings of Iago who, like Milton's Satan in *Paradise Lost*, could say *Evil be thou my good*? In Iago's Manichean world – he gleefully uses the phrase *Divinity of hell* – it does not suffice merely to subvert Michael Cassio's commission, the original cause of his feud with the Moor. Rather his deadly work of destruction is *pleasure and action*. Repeatedly he attempts to create a motive for his monstrous and meaningless plotting, unable perhaps intellectually to confront his own degeneracy. His thrice-professed suspicion of Emilia and Othello having cuckolded him rings hollow and is further undercut by his incisive wit and irony. Iago is dazzled by his puppeteering power.

The 'sentimental' school of thought on the play was dealt a fatal blow by F. R. Leavis in an essay called 'Diabolic Intellect and the Noble Hero' (*Scrutiny* 6,1937). Leavis dismissed as intellectually unjustified forgiving readings of the play. His literalist, novelistic and admirably uncompromising approach retains its validity in the history of *Othello* criticism to this day. In the wake of Leavis's essay, dissenting voices have concentrated on the magnificent rhetoric of the play, its scenic properties and use

*In the way he delights in his power and
sophistication, Iago resembles Richard III.*

of 'double time', its shrewd exploitation of
the symbolic riches afforded by two locations, and the presentation of other 'major'
and 'minor' characters such as Desdemona,
Emilia and Brabantio.

THE MOOR OF VENICE

More recently the imaginative force of color
in *Othello* has been closely studied. *Othello* is
a night-play, which begrudges its audience
the barest glimpse of daylight. The darkness of the setting accords with the bold
handling in the play of Othello's blackness.
The Elizabethan stereotyped view of the
black man is ruthlessly exploited by Iago
only to be discredited momentarily by the
play's presentation of Othello in his first
encounter with the Venetians and Brabantio
in particular. In the transforming power of
Desdemona's love the *sooty* Othello, whom
her father describes as such a thing that *she
fear'd to look on* becomes the man she marries
without parental consent because she *saw
Othello's visage in his mind.*

The alchemy of love is all the witchcraft
Othello seems to have used. But as the play
progresses the character of the Moor increasingly inhabits the type. In *Othello* III
iii, the central temptation scene, Othello's
swift transition from total devotion to the
savage *I'll tear her all to pieces* adumbrates the
resurgence of a primitive passion responding to a challenge which it fails to understand. When Othello threatens his wife
with the *magic in the web* of the handkerchief
woven by an Egyptian charmer as a talisman
of conjugal faith, he has regressed to a
Mandevillian world of

*The Anthropophagi, and men whose heads
Do grow beneath their shoulders.*

(I iii 143-4)

Othello's suicide concludes the play,
after he has pronounced his own epitaph,
Of one that lov'd not wisely, but too well.

(V ii 347)

SEE ALSO: Ch 3 78, Ch 4 104-5,
142-3, 158-9, Ch 5 186, 189, 196,
Ch 6 208, 210-1, Ch 7 222-3, Ch 8
240, 245, 246, 253-4

KING LEAR

CAST OF CHARACTERS

LEAR, *King of Britain*
KING OF FRANCE
DUKE OF BURGUNDY
DUKE OF CORNWALL
DUKE OF ALBANY
EARL OF KENT
EARL OF GLOUCESTER
EDGAR, *son to Gloucester*
EDMUND, *bastard son to Gloucester*
CURAN, *a courtier*
Old Man, *tenant to Gloucester*
Doctor

Fool
OSWALD, *steward to Goneril*
A Captain, *employed by Edmund*
Gentleman *attendant on Cordelia*
A Herald
Servants *to Cornwall*
GONERIL,
REGAN, } *daughters to Lear*
CORDELIA,
Knights *attending on Lear,*
   Officers, Messengers, Soldiers,
   and Attendants

The appeal of *King Lear* is of a wholly different order from the earlier tragedies. The play was written in 1605 and among Shakespeare's tragedies it occupies the lofty position of 'first among equals'. While the fortunes of other plays – *Hamlet* would be a case in point – have varied with the times, *King Lear* has never yielded its prominence, at least in the study. In the 17th century, Nahum Tate rewrote it for the theater (1681) so that, till 1843, this darkest of all plays ended on the stage like a happy romantic comedy in an apocryphal marriage of France and Cordelia. Dr Johnson approved of this mutilation in the 1765 Preface of his edition of Shakespeare's works, on the basis that the death of the innocent Cordelia offended against our innate sense of poetic justice – although, Johnson ruefully admitted, such a course of events only too truly reflects 'real' life.

It is precisely for this reason that *King Lear* has become the particular Shakespearean discovery of the 20th century. Its alleged negativity and existential void have captured the imagination of post World War II audiences, reared on a diet of Brecht, Beckett and Artaud. In a striking essay on the play included in *Shakespeare Our Contemporary* (1964) Jan Kott had staked a claim for the work's radical modernity, by analogy with Beckett's classic absurdist drama *Endgame* (1958).

The world of Shakespeare's play engages with early English history and evolves in the pitiless universe of a *deus absconditus*. From its fairy-tale opening – an old king and three daughters of whom two are evil and one, the youngest, is good – to its grim conclusion in an inverted image of the *pietà* when Lear enters with the dead Cordelia in his arms, the play relentlessly questions moral responsibility and pleads for compassion and understanding. The setting for Lear's 'passion' radically differs from the claustrophobic and incestuous chambers of Elsinore, the narrow alleys of Venice and island seclusion and candle-lit bedrooms of Cyprus, and the haunted castles of Scotland. *King Lear* provides Shakespeare's only royal tragic hero and is above all a public play. The elemental and apocalyptic power of Lear's mental and emotional turmoil is conveyed through his head-on collision with the unleashed forces of nature, because

This tempest will not give me leave to ponder
On things would hurt me more.

(III iv 24-5)

THIS CONTENTIOUS STORM

In his incipient madness Lear discovers in himself a nascent and radical understanding of the true meanings of kingship without political power. It is the *poor naked wretches* wherever they are who unfed and helpless have to bide the *pelting of this pitiless storm* whom Lear remembers in his anguished cry:

Take physic, pomp;
Expose thyself to feel what wretches feel,
That thou mayst shake the superflux to them,
And show the heavens more just.

(*ib* 33-6)

Lines like these, in conjunction with Lear's much-quoted address to Gloucester on *the great image of authority* and the dreadful inadequacies of manmade justice have at times been read as prophetically egalitarian and authorial statements on the human condition. In the context of the play's frenzied and abortive attempts at creating a language to articulate the horrors of experience, its focus on morally and economically extreme states of existence is almost a necessary condition. Even if the play's powerful dramatic probings encompass passionate pleas for charity and imaginative intelligence, it is always tough-minded. There is no scope for sentimentality or a passive and fatalist disowning of responsibility in *King Lear*, although both surface in the play's subplot.

THE SUBPLOT

The old king and the fool embody the fighting spirit in the play and are prepared to cross over from sanity to madness since authentic knowledge may only be found at the cost of that supreme sacrifice; old Gloucester on the other hand is the image of pliant conformism. His marriage and past adultery have produced two very different sons, the legitimate Edgar and the bastard Edmund. The latter is Shakespeare's most successful villain, descended in a direct line from Richard III and Iago. Edmund's splendid rejection of a fated and hierarchical world in his dismissal of his father's contemptible superstitions (*This is the excellent

'Thou think'st 'tis much that this contentious storm
Invades us to the skin; so 'tis to thee,
But where the greater malady is fixed,
The lesser is scarce felt.' (III iv 6-9)

foppery of the world . . .) is motivated by a devouring desire to supplant his brother. It contextualizes his ambitions, but does not become the vehicle for metaphysical speculations. In this respect Edmund's lines are characteristic of the play as a whole for, unlike *Hamlet, King Lear* remains firmly rooted in the human, material world of the living and dying.

King Lear provides no answers and no rewards. The good and the bad in it die alike and no tangible prospect is extended at the end of the play of a better future or of a Christian salvation beyond it. It is for precisely this reason that for centuries the play was deemed both unactable and morally unsound. The more fitting it is, therefore, that in the past ten years intensive textual research on the play has demonstrated its exciting dramatic viability and the extent to which theatrical considerations define the systematic differences between the two major source texts, the expansive 1608 Quarto and the clear-eyed Folio.

SEE ALSO: Ch 2 39, 47, 49, Ch 3 76, 78, Ch 4 108-13, 158-61, 178-80, Ch 5 189, 193, 203, Ch 6 213, 214, Ch 8 251-2, 255, 256-8

MACBETH

CAST OF CHARACTERS

DUNCAN, *King of Scotland*
MALCOLM, } *his sons*
DONALBAIN,
MACBETH, } *Generals in the King's army*
BANQUO,
MACDUFF, }
LENNOX,
ROSS,
MENTEITH, } *Noblemen of Scotland*
ANGUS,
CAITHNESS,
FLEANCE, *son to Banquo*
SIWARD, *Earl of Northumberland, General of the English forces*
YOUNG SIWARD, *his son*
SEYTON, *an officer attending on Macbeth*

BOY, *son to Macduff*
A Sergeant
A Porter
An Old Man
An English Doctor
A Scots Doctor
LADY MACBETH
LADY MACDUFF
Gentlewoman *attending on Lady Macbeth*
THE WEIRD SISTERS
HECATE
The Ghost *of Banquo*
Apparitions
Lords, Gentlemen, Officers, Soldiers,
    Murderers, Attendants,
    and Messengers

M*acbeth* (1606) is the last one of the great tragedies. It is also the shortest by far and in its sole extant text, the 1623 Folio, shows signs of contamination through suspected cuts and demonstrable accretions from Thomas Middleton's play *The Witch*. Although *Macbeth* is derived largely from a single source, Raphael Holinshed's *Chronicles* for the reigns of Duncan and Macbeth in 11th-century Scotland, it is also Shakespeare's most topical play. It alludes to the Gunpowder Plot of 1605 in the porter's scene and prophesies the destined reign of a future Stuart line in the show of eight kings descended from Banquo in Act IV. The play's concern with Scottish history may well have been initially inspired by the accession in 1603 of James VI and I.

VAULTING AMBITION

More to the point is the extent to which the Stuart accession regulated Shakespeare's imaginative treatment of the material of the play, as for example of Banquo who, in Holinshed, conspires with Macbeth to murder Duncan. Furthermore, in Shakespeare, but not in Holinshed, Macbeth is married to Lady Macbeth, and Holinshed's Duncan is young and ineffectual whereas Shakespeare's is venerably old, kind and of commanding presence. Although the play thematically owes much to the combined influences of *King Richard III, Hamlet* and Marlowe's *Dr Faustus, Macbeth* presents moral choices and the seductive lure of power with a new imaginative force. The vehicle for both is, paradoxically almost, the hardened thane of Glamis, *Bellona's bridegroom*, who without flinching unseams an enemy on the battlefield *from the nave to th' chaps*. Not only is Macbeth equipped with a uniquely discriminating and vivid poetic imagination, but he is a married man who dotes on his wife: It is the androgyny of this unholy couple which precipitates the murder of Duncan. In the course of the play Macbeth commits almost every conceivable crime: murdering his king, guest, kinsman and benefactor and framing two innocent grooms in their deaths, as well as killing his comrade-in-arms Banquo and, to compound it all, he becomes a slayer of women and an infanticide. During his short reign, Scotland is turned into a prison house in which every bond of fealty is violated.

That in spite of all this Macbeth retains much of our sympathy is a measure of the complexity of the character. His first words,

So foul and fair a day I have not seen

(I iii 38)

echo the witches' incantatory inversions of the natural order and intimate the extent to which he is subliminally possessed by the powers of darkness. When their prophecies are partly vindicated by Ross's greeting of

Macbeth as Cawdor, he wonders whether

> *Two truths are told*
> *As happy prologues to the swelling act*
> *Of the imperial theme.*
>
> (*ib* 127-9)

His momentary desire passively to submit to fate (lines 142-3) evinces signs of that same sensibility which forever teeters on the verge of the abyss.

THE USE OF SOLILOQUY

More so than *Hamlet*, *Macbeth* is a play whose imaginative bearings are defined by its asides, soliloquies and set pieces, such as the *To-morrow, and to-morrow* speech, or Lady Macbeth's death. But whereas Hamlet's soliloquies follow a formula barely developed from Richard III's public addresses and allow for a measure of disembodiment of speaker from discourse, Macbeth's tortured soliloquies home in relentlessly on the implications of his deeds for his soul, without giving any quarter to the audience. There is no provision in this play for the jaunty enjoyment of ill-doing of Richard III, or the enduring courtly sophistication and philosophical aphorisms of *Hamlet*. Macbeth's soliloquies are raw, sensory, visual and profoundly irrational. They constitute Shakespeare's supreme achievement in self-expression, and it is for this reason perhaps that *Macbeth* is the last of the plays to use soliloquy extensively. In the great 'see-saw' lines, commencing

> *If it were done when 'tis done, then 'twere well*
> *It were done quickly*
>
> (I vii 1-2)

uttered *in extremis* before the decision to murder Duncan is finally made irreversible, the turmoil of Macbeth's mind is perfectly established. What at first appears like a pragmatic proposition has within 28 lines been exposed as the heinous breach of nature that it is, not through ratiocination but by the impressive impact of images unconsciously arising from the outer reaches of Macbeth's better self. Nothing captures the *Macbeth*-music so well as the powerful similes and metaphors of virtue and pity in this soliloquy:

> *Besides, this Duncan*
> *Hath borne his faculties so meek, hath been*
> *So clear in his great office, that his virtues*

'Infirm of purpose!
Give me the daggers.'

> *Will plead like angels, trumpet-tongu'd,*
> *against*
> *The deep damnation of his taking-off;*
> *And pity, like a naked new-born babe,*
> *Striding the blast, or heaven's cherubin*
> *hors'd*
> *Upon the sightless couriers of the air,*
> *Shall blow the horrid deed in every eye,*
> *That tears shall drown the wind.*
>
> (*ib* 16-25)

It is ironic that Lady Macbeth should echo her husband's apocalyptic child imagery, when she protests her constancy through the perverted metaphor of the feeding baby plucked from her breast and brained by its mother. The powerfully mediated presence of youth and children underlines the extent to which the future and natural order elude the childless couple.

SEE ALSO: Ch 2 49, Ch 3 81-2, Ch 4 87-9, 112-3, 158-9, 178-80, Ch 5 189, 193, 197, 205, 211, 213, Ch 8 246, 247-8, 255, 256

THE ROMANCES

The last four complete plays that Shakespeare wrote, between 1608 and 1611, *Pericles, Cymbeline, The Winter's Tale*, and *The Tempest*, are neither tragedies, histories, nor Shakespearean romantic comedies, and they are all strikingly similar. They are sometimes spoken of as the Late Plays, or the Last Plays, but now they are usually called the Romances.

The Elizabethans and Jacobeans of Shakespeare's lifetime loved a romance, a sprawling story which could be enjoyed alike in popular novels or in highly-crafted verse epics like Spenser's *Faerie Queene*, and in drama all the way from the riproaring to the elegant and sophisticated. Such books tell ancient (often Greek) stories of love as an overwhelming experience, inspiring amazing quests and vivid, usually incredible, encounters, and plots, intrigues, dangers (particularly from the elements and wild beasts), coincidences, disguises, conflicts of loyalty, losses and recoveries, births and deaths, and the eventual reunion of lovers, and parents and children. The characters are preferably of royal or noble birth, and happily lack much psychological plausibility in their actions.

A 'NEW' DIRECTION

Shakespeare's four romances clearly fit the genre, if so loose a form can be dignified with such classification. What made him leave the high tragic experience which had almost completely occupied him for eight years is quite unknown. Speculation based on implied biography (he was exalted; he was bored; he was transformed by the birth of his granddaughter) is either sentimental or foolish. Slightly more impressive is the coincidence that in 1608 he and his company, the King's Men, were able to move into the Blackfriars Theater, making a second, smaller, house for them. Where the Globe held 3,000, this upstairs room, with some artificial lighting, held 300. It had already a wealthier clientele, prepared to indulge. Ben Jonson, who wanted to convert the London audiences to a love of astringent classical restraint, objected to the formlessness of dramatic romances and their cavalier way with serious matters like time and place: he called *Pericles* a 'mouldy tale'.

Shakespeare's romances were a new development for him and his company. But it is a mistake to imagine him changing course completely. Very many of the striking qualities of these four plays can be seen being developed earlier, if the right spectacles are worn. Twenty years before, *The Two Gentlemen of Verona* showed some romance characteristics, and *The Comedy of Errors* of the same period shares two main sources with *Pericles* (the story of Apollonius of Tyre, and Gower's version of it). *Twelfth Night*, halfway through his writing life, has many of those elements which later became full plays. This is simply to remark that Shakespeare's writing is all of a piece.

His four romances are very well made, for all the problems with the text of *Pericles*. The two halves of *The Winter's Tale* can be shown to be symmetrical in many ways. *The Tempest* works to precise limits of time,

Nicholas Rowe's frontispiece to Pericles, *showing the discovery of the Thaisa at Ephesus.*

The Storm, Antigonus pursued by the Bear
(*Joseph Wright of Derby*) – *probably the most
famous stage direction in English drama.*

---

place and action. *Cymbeline* and *The Winter's
Tale* are artfully constructed on numer-
ological bases. As long ago as 1817,
William Hazlitt noted, unfashionably, how
remarkably the last act of *Cymbeline* is
constructed: *the fate of almost every person in
the drama is made to depend on the solution of a
single circumstance – the answer of Iachimo to the
question of Imogen respecting the obtaining of the
ring from Posthumus.*

Romance stories invariably make much
of the wildness of the sea, which allows the
rather puppet-like characters to be out of
control of their own fates, so that even a
reasonably motivated quest (which few are)
can have the most unlikely consequences.
Although they may be royal or noble,
human beings appear to bob about as if seen
from some very lofty viewpoint, that of a
god or goddess perhaps. Shakespeare fully
enjoys the privilege, and makes spectacular
stage experiences (making the gods come
into the action, too) and extraordinary
reunions. He creates, as well, a new and
freer blank verse, which, although dense,
has lucid power. He experiments with
form, and with words – it has been noted
that a use of the word 'fierce,' for example,
is peculiar to these plays, and at the same
time difficult to pin down. He loves to
bring in music, and the songs and masques
of these four plays are memorable in
performance. One of the triumphs of 20th-
century theater has been the discovery of the
power of these plays on stage.

Central to all four is that bond which is
as old as humanity, that between parents
and children. In these plays, they have
separate, but interlocking, experiences, of
equal weight. All four plays dwell richly on
the special quality of love between a father
and a daughter, and the power of the
princess to restore to the king and his court
both truth and life. *All's Well That Ends
Well* of some years earlier had showed some
of that; but the ending was uncertain. In
these Shakespearean romances, in each case,
the ending is a triumph.

SEE ALSO: Ch 2 49, Ch 3 70-2, Ch
4 94-5, 98-9, 134-5, 150-1, 168-
75

PERICLES

CAST OF CHARACTERS

GOWER, *as Chorus*
ANTIOCHUS, *King of Antioch*
PERICLES, *Prince of Tyre*
HELICANUS, ⎫
ESCANES, ⎭ *two lords of Tyre*
SIMONIDES, *King of Pentapolis*
CLEON, *Governor of Tharsus*
LYSIMACHUS, *Governor of Mitylene*
CERIMON, *a lord of Ephesus*
THALIARD, *a lord of Antioch*
PHILEMON, *servant to Cerimon*
LEONINE, *servant to Dionyza*

Marshal
A Pander
BOULT, *his servant*
The Daughter of Antioch
DIONYZA, *wife to Cleon*
THAISA, *daughter to Simonides*
MARINA, *daughter to Pericles and Thaisa*
LYCHORIDA, *nurse to Marina*
A Bawd
DIANA
Lords, Ladies, Knights, Gentlemen, Sailors,
    Pirates, Fishermen, *and* Messengers

Pericles was a fine Jacobean high-romantic play. It was set in classical times, around the eastern Mediterranean, events being narrated and linked, with considerable artistry, by the late-medieval English poet, John Gower. The experiences of the central figures – Pericles, the brave, kingly hero, Thaisa his beloved wife, and Marina his lost and marvelous daughter, were no doubt compelling at the Blackfriars and Globe, and elsewhere. Sadly, the only version which has survived is a mangled text in a badly-printed Quarto; Heminge and Condell, for what reason we do not know, did not include it in the First Folio.

THE TEXT

This accident is unfortunate, but not quite fatal. Enough remains for admiration in the last three acts; and the great climactic moments of recognition ring with the right Shakespearean truth. The textual corruption is extensive, and scholars have attempted to clarify the principal difficulties. The original story, of Apollonius of Tyre, a popular Greek romance, was one of the best-known medieval and Renaissance tales. Our play partly comes from the retelling of the story in John Gower's *Confessio Amantis*, Book 8.

There are other sources, especially a prose version of the story by Laurence Twine: but an apparently insoluble problem concerns the relation of the play to a prose romance of the same year (1608) by a minor writer, George Wilkins, which tells the same story. Is this, *The Painful Adventures of Pericles, Prince of Tyre*, a prose report of a performance of the play, simply? – but 'simply' will not do for any of the textual enigmas in *Pericles*. The first two acts particularly, and many places elsewhere, give a text which cannot be by Shakespeare as it stands. Are such passages by Wilkins too? Or by someone else? If, so, who?

More certain is the form of the play as a kind of medieval miracle play – something like the Life of St Pericles in Five Episodes. He is controlled by pagan forces rather than by Christian Providence, but his unexceptionable virtue, his perceptiveness and his generosity make him a worthy hero, and we are glad when his fortunes eventually mend so dramatically. As the play is a romance, we do not expect such a hero to grow morally and spiritually toward an ultimate crisis, although the final experiences of the play make a strong dramatic climax. Rather, the episodes react symbolically upon each other. Thus, the unsavory solution to the riddle of Antioch in Act I – that the admired (and nameless) princess there is having an incestuous affair with her father, Antiochus, leading to their joint horrid end, divinely imposed (II iv 7-12) – contrasts with the wonderful discovery of Marina in Mytilene in Acts IV and V. There, her amazing virtue has both begun to change the seamy world she was imprisoned in, and dramatically restored her father Pericles to full life again: a tremendous theatrical moment further blest by the goddess Diana's appearance with

Admirable in his virtue and generosity, Pericles is a worthy hero and so we rejoice at the final, near-miraculous restoration of the royal family.

promise of more revelations. Birth, apparent death and restoration to life happen in a world of constant love and faithful marriage, however wide the shift of geographic settings and however incredible the events (Leonine, about to kill Marina early in Act IV at the command of his jealous mistress, becomes impatient:

> *I am sworn,*
> *And will dispatch.*
>> [Seizes her.
>> Enter Pirates.
> 1 Pirate. *Hold, villain!*
>> [Leonine runs away.
>> (IV i 92-3)

and so on).

POETRY AND IMAGERY

Poetry itself comes to life, too: not for nothing is the play presented by Gower, brought from the dead. The sea dominates, producing not only many strong – and symbolic – moments, but much of the

poetic value as well. So Pericles, committing his young wife's body to the waves, says:

> *nor have I time*
> *To give thee hallow'd to thy grave, but*
> *straight*
> *Must cast thee, scarcely coffin'd, in the*
> *ooze;*
> *Where, for a monument upon thy bones,*
> *And aye-remaining lamps, the belching*
> *whale*
> *And humming water must o'erwhelm*
> *thy corpse,*
> *Lying with simple shells.*

> (III i 58-64)

The Shakespearean imaginative vigor here energizes the moment with rich activity and beauty of phrase, to a culmination in Thaisa's body at rest. Such copious word-painting is characteristic of the play at its best. Such imagery, too, relates to the many visual effects, like Thaisa waking in the coffin, or Marina on the shore. Dumb-shows and stage-spectacles are managed by Gower, to insistent music at key moments. Gower's Shakespearean counterpart as Chorus, in *King Henry V*, is anxious to stir his audience to work to *piece out our imperfections with your thoughts* (Prologue, 23), in order to build a highly-charged imaginative model of the king and his actions – which is then usually at odds with what we see. Gower is a different intermediary. He appeals, certainly, for imaginative help; but he lets the narrative and the art of the actors and the stage pictures do the work without irony.

In the theater, the result can be an extraordinarily moving experience: invariably so in the presence of Marina, whether she is showing the jewel of her virgin beauty in the gross setting of the brothel, or in her near-miraculous reunion with her father. That final restoration of the royal family encapsulates the curiously ageless quality of this fundamentally Shakespearean romance.

SEE ALSO: Ch 3 65, 71, Ch 4 87-9, 122-3, 178-80

CYMBELINE

CAST OF CHARACTERS

CYMBELINE, *King of Britain*
CLOTEN, *son to the Queen by a former husband*
POSTHUMUS LEONATUS, *a gentleman, husband to Imogen*
BELARIUS, *a banished lord, disguised under the name of* MORGAN

GUIDERIUS, ⎱ *sons to Cymbeline, disguised under the names of* POLYDORE
ARVIRAGUS, ⎰ *and* CADWAL, *supposed sons to Belarius*

PHILARIO, *friend to Posthumus,*
IACHIMO, *friend to Philario,* ⎱ *Italians*
A French Gentleman, *friend to Philario*
CAIUS LUCIUS, *General of the Roman Forces*
A Roman Captain

Two British Captains
PISANIO, *servant to Posthumus*
CORNELIUS, *a physician*
Two Lords *of Cymbeline's court*
Two Gentlemen *of the same*
Two Gaolers
QUEEN, *wife to Cymbeline*
IMOGEN, *daughter to Cymbeline by a former queen*
HELEN, *a lady attending on Imogen*
Apparitions
Lords, Ladies, Roman Senators, Tribunes, a Soothsayer, a Dutch Gentleman, a Spanish Gentleman, Musicians, Officers, Captains, Soldiers, Messengers *and* Attendants

Critics but not playgoers have difficulty with *Cymbeline*. Dr Johnson in 1765 concluded his brief notes with: *This play has many just sentiments, some natural dialogues, and some pleasing scenes, but they are obtained at the expense of much incongruity. To remark the folly of the fiction, the absurdity of the conduct, the confusion of the names and manners of different times, and the impossibility of the events in any system of life, were to waste criticism upon unresisting imbecility, upon faults too evident for detection, and too gross for aggravation.*

Johnson's rather sterile Augustanism gave him no grounds for understanding romance. Nearly two centuries later, Shaw was so distressed by the Bard's incompetence in Act V that he had the play refinished by a better playwright – himself.

Even modern critics, welling over with good feelings about Shakespeare's last plays, find it hard to fit this play into a creative progression between *Pericles* and *The Winter's Tale*, where the customary dating (1609) would place it. *Cymbeline* stands as the very last play in First Folio, concluding the tragedies. Commentators find such confusion everywhere: this historical-pastoral-tragicomical-romance (to adapt Polonius in *Hamlet*) has a main plot about withheld tribute in Roman Britain, but kidnapped princes out of the tradition of Malory and Spenser, and a Renaissance Machiavellian plot engineered by a *slight*

thing of Italy (V iv 64). This Italian wager-plot seems to be out of Boccaccio, and the British history is a free fantasia on bits of Holinshed's *Chronicle*, with probable reference to an anonymous earlier play, *The Rare Triumphs of Love and Fortune* (performed 1582) and curious relation to Beaumont and Fletcher's first success, *Philaster* (1609).

Recent critics find it significant that *Cymbeline* is set at the time of the birth of Christ, and that it can be made to show flattery to the Stuart court. Shakespeare's interweaving of the story of an ancient British king and his daughter, an incredible tale of brothers in a pastoral arcadia, and elements of an older play, has a parallel in *King Lear*, no less: yet this is no towering tragedy, but to many critics an uneven hollow hodgepodge.

IN PERFORMANCE

Theater-goers feel otherwise. Problems of genre, and even of inconsistent characterization, disappear in the delight of enthralling spectacle, a succession of splendid surprises, and constant theatrical suspense: three hours of wonder. Iachimo, the sneak from Rome, emerging from the trunk in Imogen's bedroom to take note of the beauties of the room, including

> *On her left breast*
> *A mole cinque-spotted:*

(II ii 37-8)

'I draw the sword myself; take it, and hit
The innocent mansion of my love, my heart.
Fear not; 'tis empty of all things but grief;
Thy master is not there.' (III iv 65-8)

the strange older man living in a cave in Wales with two youngsters who do not know that they are royal princes, intruded upon first by a good-looking but starving young man who is really a princess and their sister (Imogen), and then by the villainous Queen's fool of a son (Cloten) who so lords it over one of the true princes that his head – *Cloten's clotpoll* (IV ii 184) – is shortly brought on; the beautiful boy (Fidele, i.e. Imogen) apparently dead, and then a princess come to life; the wicked stepmother Queen and her deceiving doctor, her poisons and dogs and cats; the entry to the hero, awaiting execution in jail, of the ghosts of his father, mother, and two brothers, and their 60 lines of elaborate verses before 'Jupiter descends in thunder and lightning, sitting upon an eagle. He throws a thunderbolt. The Ghosts fall on their knees.' (V iv 93) – these are only some

of the theatrical wonders in this extraordinary romance.

Cymbeline, empty as a mere speech-heading, has on stage a full royal presence of office. Posthumus, the separated-lover hero, who seems so waywardly underdeveloped on the page, comes in all his transformations to grow in performance to worthiness of reunion with his amazing young wife. She, Imogen, with the resourcefulness of Rosalind from *As You Like It*, the trenchancy of Beatrice from *Much Ado About Nothing*, the courage of Helena from *All's Well That Ends Well*, and a beauty all her own, can be seen to deserve even some of the adulation given her by sentimental Victorians. In performance, the play appears the work of a superb dramatic craftsman at the very height of his virtuosity.

The poetry is often in the new, dense, liberated blank verse of Jacobean Shakespeare, and is widely admired for its complex fluency: but it includes also such lyricism as the elegy *Fear no more the heat of the sun* and its pellucid recognition of a universal mortality:

Golden lads and girls all must,
As chimney-sweepers, come to dust
(IV ii 262-3)

and Posthumus' moment of reunion with his wife Imogen,

Hang there like fruit, my soul
Till the tree die
(V v 263-4)

called by the poet Tennyson the tenderest lines in Shakespeare.

Cymbeline is clearly an experiment: a fusion of tragicomedy and romance which, for example, includes the scalp-tingling oddness of the moment when the heroine in boy's clothes wakes outside a cave from a drugged sleep on a headless corpse dressed in her husband's clothes: or its extraordinary last scene, which can be seen to play with the idea of ending, to produce a dozen denouements, making a Shakespearean vision of the reality of achieved peace.

SEE ALSO: Ch 3 71, 75, Ch 4 87-9, 130-3, 150-1, 158-9, 168-73, Ch 5 185, Ch 6 213

THE WINTER'S TALE

CAST OF CHARACTERS

LEONTES, *King of Sicilia*
MAMILLIUS, *his son, the young Prince of Sicilia*
CAMILLO,
ANTIGONUS,
CLEOMENES, } *lords of Sicilia*
DION,
POLIXENES, *King of Bohemia*
FLORIZEL, *his son, Prince of Bohemia*
ARCHIDAMUS, *a lord of Bohemia*
Old Shepherd, *reputed father of Perdita*
Clown, *his son*
AUTOLYCUS, *a rogue*
A Mariner

A Gaoler
TIME, *as Chorus*
HERMIONE, *Queen to Leontes*
PERDITA, *daughter to Leontes and Hermione*
PAULINA, *wife to Antigonus*
EMILIA, *a lady attending on the Queen*
MOPSA,
DORCAS, } *shepherdesses*
Other Lords,
  Gentlemen, Ladies,
  Officers, Servants,
  Shepherds, Shepherdesses

A winter's tale is a fanciful, romantic story suitable for long dark nights. In 1610-11, Shakespeare made his play out of a paperback romance about royalty, sex, scandal, sudden violent feelings, death, lost children, confession, repentance, and young lovers who triumph. This fiction, *Pandosto. The Triumph of Time*, by Robert Greene, had first appeared in 1588.

SHAKESPEAREAN TRANSFORMATION

Shakespeare made significant changes. He wrote for the sophisticated audience of the small Blackfriars Theater, although we also have an account of a performance of *The Winter's Tale* at the main house, the Globe, on the afternoon of Wednesday 15 May 1611. The unusually small company must have been led in both places by Richard Burbage as King Leontes, whose instant, inexplicable jealousy so dominates the first, tragic, half. In the second half, however, the tone changes, and is controlled by the 16-year-old princess, Perdita, and the energetic rogue Autolycus. Shakespeare used other traditions as well, outside prose romance — there are traces of the older morality plays, where a man's soul is wrestled for by evil and good forces: and of the much newer fashion of writing with one eye on the Stuart court. The effect of time and the possibility of art — or even love — conquering death are notions which gripped Shakespeare long before: we need look no

further than *Love's Labour's Lost* (1595) and the Sonnets (probably 1598).

In Shakespeare's hands the story becomes a profound play with an extraordinary range of ideas and feelings and tones, a complete living world, rich with challenging, beautiful and varied verse and fine prose. The play has the attractive air of having been written by a great artist who knows exactly what he is doing; who can handle everything, from tiny effects to big emotions, with ease and skill.

In *Pandosto*, the princely young lover (who becomes Shakespeare's Florizel) is a cad, slipping away from Perdita when she is in difficulty. Florizel's steadfastness at Perdita's side takes her, and the audience, by surprise. In *Pandosto*, the accused Queen dies. Hermione does not die in *The Winter's Tale*, producing one of the greatest *coups de théâtre* in English theater. Shakespeare, for special purposes, reversed Greene's imaginary locations, putting winter in Sicilia and spring in Bohemia.

Above all, Shakespeare removes the suggestion of grounds for the jealousy: Shakespeare's King Leontes is suddenly struck, as by lightning out of a clear sky, by the certainty that his beloved wife is having an affair with his best friend, King Polixenes, and indeed bearing his child. The strong Renaissance interest in the clash between the claims of male friendship and heterosexual love is given here a terrible twist. Shakespeare's play is a study in

MR MUNDEN
as Autolicus in the Winter's Tale.
Engraved for the Theatrical Inquisitor.
Pub.d June 30, 1818 by Chapple Pall Mall.

Joseph Shepherd Munden as Autolycus, liar, thief, actor, and musician. Significantly, he is the first character we meet after Time moves the play forward.

obsession, with its manic need for instant proof — as in *Othello*, but now without the villain. Appalling consequences for everyone follow this royal madness and the conflict between two kings. Leontes' disintegration is terrible: at one point he reasons that he might be able to sleep again if he had his pregnant wife burnt alive:

> — *say that she were gone,*
> *Given to the fire, a moiety of my rest*
> *Might come to me again.*

(II iii 7-9)

It is remarkable that the audience is given no objective statement of Hermione's innocence: our certainty comes only from her public bearing and words, and from court comment. (Even Claudius in *Hamlet* is given direct-to-audience confession.) Yet that is enough. Confirmation of her integrity eventually comes from heaven; from a very off-stage Apollo, whose Delphic utterance gives unusually explicit information and instantly restores Leontes to sanity — but it was too late to rescue his son (Mamillius) and daughter (Perdita) as well as his wife from the destruction unleashed during the period of his obsession.

SICILY AND BOHEMIA

In 16 couplets, Time himself moves the play forward 16 years into a new pastoral world, a healing reality. The country scenes are not an idyll. Perdita is playing Flora, the goddess of flowers; Leontes' destructiveness has not razed life and beauty from the earth; she is forced to stop playing at princesses: yet she is a princess, all the time. The central scene, the very long IV iv (a quarter of the whole play), establishes without haste a new reality, a quite new way of thinking, apparently, rooted in country life and exploring the mutual dependence of Art and Nature.

In fact, an investigation of the Sicilian and Bohemian parts of the play shows much symmetry, which is particularly satisfying. The real bear in the storm in Bohemia which famously pursues and eats Antigonus is a sort of externalized version of the 'bear' which suddenly loomed out of the shadows of Leontes' mind and ate him, in the storm which drowned his Sicilian court. The first person we meet after Time is Autolycus, liar, thief, musician and actor. His invented bodily pains, at comic points in the scene, not only balance Leontes' earlier *I have tremor cordis on me . . .* and so on, but suggest that acting, making people mistake Art for Nature, so important in this second half, is second-best in a real world. So even Julio Romano's statue is transcended. Paulina's

> *It is requir'd*
> *You do awake your faith*

(V iii 94-5)

applies to the reality of the nature of forgiveness even more than it does to the spectacle of art.

SEE ALSO: Ch 2 39, Ch 3 70-2, 78, Ch 4 158-61, Ch 5 182, 183, 184, 193, 201-2, Ch 8 252

THE TEMPEST

CAST OF CHARACTERS

ALONSO, *King of Naples*
SEBASTIAN, *his brother*
PROSPERO, *the right Duke of Milan*
ANTONIO, *his brother, the usurping Duke of Milan*
FERDINAND, *son to the King of Naples*
GONZALO, *an honest old counsellor*
ADRIAN, } *lords*
FRANCISCO, }
CALIBAN, *a savage and deformed slave*
TRINCULO, *a jester*
STEPHANO, *a drunken butler*

Master of a Ship
Boatswain
Mariners
MIRANDA, *daughter to Prospero*
ARIEL, *an airy spirit*
IRIS,
CERES,
JUNO, } *spirits*
Nymphs
Reapers,
Other Spirits *attending on Prospero*

Full fathom five thy father lies;
 Of his bones are coral made;
Those are pearls that were his eyes;
 Nothing of him that doth fade
But doth suffer a sea-change
Into something rich and strange.

(I ii 396-401)

T*he Tempest* is itself 'something rich and strange', and, even within the group of romances, wholly unexpected. This short play, his last complete work, stands, rather oddly, first in Folio (and thus in almost everyone's complete Shakespeare).

It has no narrative source, though the influence of Virgil, Ovid, Montaigne, and contemporary accounts of shipwreck, can be clearly traced. It is Shakespeare's only bow in the direction of the neoclassical Unities, so influential in French, and later English, drama of the 17th century. Based on a misunderstanding of Aristotle, these supposed 'rules' for drama maintained that there had to be Unity of Time (the stage action to last a few hours, as long as the performance); Place (everything to happen in one location); and Action (no subplots). So the unified action of *The Tempest* on Prospero's island occupies one afternoon.

SOLEMN AND STRANGE MUSIC

This miraculous, dream-like play has been itself unusually fertile, and the inspiration of poems by Shelley, Browning, T.S. Eliot and W.H. Auden, as well as striking operas

and films. Theatrically very rich, it marks also a new development in Shakespeare's verse, now at the same time fluid, evocative and economical in structure. The play presents a full range of romance situations – exiled ruler and daughter, wild nature, young aristocratic lovers, someone magically *charmed from moving*, magic sleeps and invisibility. But all these are far extended, so that the father and daughter have been for 16 years alone, and thus the lost princess Miranda has never seen any other man than her father until she sees the young prince Ferdinand on the shore.

These matters are expressed with theatrical exuberance: a court masque, in which the goddesses Iris, Juno and Ceres appear and speak high-colored couplets before 'certain Reapers, properly habited . . . join with the Nymphs in a graceful dance': drunken servants mock the island's monster, the 'beast' Caliban, 'a savage and deformed slave', half fish, half man. An evil, aristocratic plot, to compound earlier usurpation of a throne with murder, is prevented by magic: and the central figure, the mysterious Prospero, is a magician, able, with the aid of Ariel, 'an airy spirit', to conjure up the terrible tempest with which the play opens.

The Tempest is much quoted, rarely performed, and, like a dream, quickly forgotten. Also like a dream, it shadows the mind with a sense that it is 'about' something just out of sight: if only that could be grasped, essential truths about existence in this sublunary world would become life-changingly clear for the reader or spectator. It is thus not surprising that it has attracted all kinds of speculation in varying degrees of wildness; some suggesting, for example, that the play is an allegory of Christian rebirth (which is in every way unlikely). Discussion in the play about the means of making a new society allows a legitimate debate about the primacy of Nature or Nurture – an elevated form of the modern discussion of the primary influence of heredity or environment. The shipwrecked sophisticated court party, on the way home from a royal wedding, contains a King, a (usurping) Duke – and corruption. Caliban, whose name suggests cannibal, speaks some of the most beautiful poetry in the play – indeed, in Shakespeare:

> *Be not afeard. The isle is full of noises,*
> *Sounds, and sweet airs, that give delight,*
>   *and hurt not.*

(III ii 130-1)

By Prospero's magic, before the final sailing-away in the magically-surviving ship, truths are made to appear: the plot whereby he had been exiled; the nature and power of forgiveness; the essence of married love; the responsibility of being a ruler. Important as these themes are to the development of the play, however, they all stand second to the exploration of the nature and function of art, and of theater itself.

It has been fashionable for a long time to see Prospero's

>   *I'll break my staff,*
> *Bury it certain fathoms in the earth,*
> *And deeper than did ever plummet sound*
> *I'll drown my book.*

(V i 54-7)

as 'Shakespeare's farewell to his art'. This is both sentimental and unconvincing. Parts of *The Two Noble Kinsmen* and *King Henry VIII* were yet to be written. More immediate is the sense that Shakespeare, with so much achieved, felt still a sense of new possibility in theater. A very great artist in his last works is often to be seen to be moving into new artistic areas. Shakespeare is exploring those worlds of magic, sleep, dream and imagination whereby perceptions are altered—*those are pearls that were his eyes:* and also their very evanescence:

Prospero's abjuring 'this rough magic' has been seen as Shakespeare's farewell, but it is always dangerous to try to make the plays yield biography.

> *The cloud-capp'd towers, the gorgeous palaces,*
> *The solemn temples, the great globe itself,*
> *Yea, all which it inherit, shall dissolve,*
> *And, like this insubstantial pageant faded,*
> *Leave not a rack behind.*

(IV i 152-6)

Imaginative insight has to be seized. The revelation may not be repeated. The *magus*, however, did not have a monopoly of such insight. Caliban could be given it as well:

>   *. . . in dreaming,*
> *The clouds methought would open and show riches*
> *Ready to drop upon me, that, when I wak'd,*
> *I cried to dream again.*

(III ii 135-8)

SEE ALSO: Ch 2 34, 49, Ch 3 71, 72-4, 76, Ch 4 124-5, 176-7, Ch 5 182, 189, 198, Ch 6 209, Ch 7 221, 222, Ch 8 252

COLLABORATION

The records of payments to authors found in Philip Henslowe's extensive financial papers show that collaboration was a common practice in the theater of his time. The reason for this was the economic pressure to produce large quantities of new work quickly.

It is generally accepted that Shakespeare collaborated with other playwrights on specific projects, but there is real difficulty in establishing the extent to which he did so. We know that he was already established in the London theater in the early 1590s because of an angry reference by Robert Greene in *Groatsworth of Wit* (1592): *there is an upstart crow, beautified with our feathers that with his tiger's heart wrapped in a player's hide supposes he is as well able to bombast out blank verse as the best of you and being an absolute* johannes factotum *is in his own conceit the only Shake-scene in a country*. The principal reference here is to Shakespeare the actor. The pamphlet is addressed to Greene's fellow playwrights, warning them not to trust actors.

The expression 'tiger's heart wrapped in a player's hide', however, seems to be a parody of *King Henry VI* (3, I iv 137). This has led some critics to claim that 'upstart crow, beautified with our feathers' refers not simply to Shakespeare the actor who struts about looking fine because he is speaking a well-written part, but to Shakespeare the dramatist who has plagiarized the work of Greene and his friends. This interpretation is then taken with other observations to prove that Shakespeare began his writing career by rewriting other men's plays. For example, a Quarto published in 1594 called *The Taming of a Shrew* is very close to Shakespeare's *The Taming of the Shrew*, but also contains lines borrowed from Marlowe. It has variously been considered as an early draft of Shakespeare's play, or as a source, but it is better explained as a pirated and faulty memorial reconstruction.

Theories of collaboration have long been used to explain away passages in a Shakespeare play that are thought to be not very good, and for this reason it has been proposed that large sections of the *Henry VI* plays are by Nashe and Greene. Similarly, the last act of *Macbeth* has been said to be too weak and the Porter's speech too crude to be by Shakespeare, while Hecate's rhyming couplets together with the witches' songs (which are undoubtedly borrowed from Middleton's *The Witch*) have given rise to a supposed revision by Middleton. However, octosyllabic rhyming couplets are a feature of the magic verse in *A Midsummer Night's Dream*, while the addition of an unoriginal song does not invalidate the scene in which it occurs. Many of Shakespeare's songs are second-hand, and no-one suggests that Shakespeare wrote parts of *The White Devil* because Cornelia, like Ophelia, enters to the traditional ballad 'How should I your true-love know'.

'NEW' WORKS

Conversely, scholars have a vested interest in discovering 'new' works by Shakespeare, such as Gary Taylor's recent championing of the poem *Shall I die*, and Eric Sams's of the play *Edmund Ironside*. Repeated claims have also been made for *Edward III*. Heminge and Condell, the compilers of the Folio state that their edition was prepared with the greatest care and represents the plays as Shakespeare would have wished to see them. They seem to have gone to some trouble acquiring copy, and it is perhaps significant that they did not include *Pericles* or *The Two Noble Kinsmen*. 'Perhaps' is of course the operative word since negative evidence is not conclusive.

Both arguments are applicable to *Pericles,* and also to the collaborative *Sir Thomas More* which was refused a license even after it was revised with an amusing insurrection scene attributed to Shakespeare. The right to print *Pericles* was registered in 1608 by Edward Blount but never acted upon. The following year a pirated text appeared which remains our sole evidence for Shakespeare's play. Arguments have been proposed for a collaboration with George Wilkins.

The case of *The Two Noble Kinsmen* is slightly different. The earliest published edition did not appear until 1634, and the title page ascribes the play to Fletcher and Shakespeare. This is not universally

The Two Noble Kinsmen *was first published in 1634 with both Shakespeare's and Fletcher's names on the title page.*

accepted and some critics consider that Massinger was Fletcher's co-author.

TEXTUAL ANALYSIS

External evidence for the authorship of these plays is simply not available. Critics must therefore attempt any analysis on purely stylistic grounds. Various tests have been proposed. The incidence of rhyme, adjectival participles, new coinage, and irregular lines of verse have all been adduced to prove authorial divisions within a given play, but none is conclusive; obvious stylistic features are easily imitated or borrowed.

Before making stylistic judgments, critics have to be absolutely certain that they have interpreted the bibliographical evidence correctly. *Timon of Athens*, a play which is a candidate for collaborative authorship because of its oddly emblematic style, is first and foremost a bibliographical problem. Probably printed from an author-ial draft which certainly contained some indecision and contradiction, it is likely that it was also difficult to read. Certain passages in V i given as verse in the Folio are, in more modern editions, traditionally and correctly emended to prose. Other scenes are left as verse and are accordingly disparaged as being inept or no more than notes for blank verse. However, these same lines rendered in prose suddenly become forceful and dramatic.

It may be that developments in computer applications will help in the study of this problem by facilitating the handling of the huge amount of data involved in studying basic language use. The habitual use of certain grammatical constructions which are normally too insignificant to be readily imitated may, for instance, be found to provide a kind of authorial fingerprint.

SEE ALSO: Ch 2 44, 49, Ch 3 63, 68-9, 81, 82, 83, Ch 4 87-9, 96-7, 108-11, 118-21, 164-5, 168-9

THE TEXT

Before we can even begin to talk about Shakespeare's plays as works of dramatic art, we first have to establish what the texts of these plays actually are. This is not as easy as it sounds. No manuscripts in his handwriting survive, except for disputed pages of the collaborative play *Sir Thomas More*, and editors have to turn to the earliest printed versions, which vary greatly both in the quality of their printing and the reliability of their manuscript copy.

THE QUARTOS

Twenty of the plays first appeared in individual Quarto format. Some of these were very popular and ran into several editions: six of *King Henry IV* (Part 1) and *King Richard III*, five of *King Richard II*. Chains of errors in each of these runs of texts show that each was reprinted from the preceding one, but that every time – as is only to be expected – additional errors of printing were introduced.

In a traditionally bound book, the pages are stitched together in groups or 'gatherings'. A Quarto volume is so called because each gathering consists of a single sheet of paper folded twice to give four leaves or eight pages. The manner of folding means that pages 1, 4, 5 and 8 are set up on one forme (frame of type) to be printed on one side of the paper, and that pages 2, 3, 6 and 7 are printed on the reverse.

The capacity for error when dealing with movable individual type is enormous. Letters can easily be 'turned' – inserted upside down, a 'u' for an 'n' – or they may be sorted after use into the wrong box, so that when they are reused, for instance an 'l' comes out instead of a 't'. The copying of any text, whether in handwriting or type, inevitably introduces error with words or even whole lines repeated, skipped or otherwise mistaken. Type was expensive and sometimes in short supply, and so could not be left locked up in position in formes while the book was sent back to the author for checking. The compositor himself would look over the first sheet pulled from the press for obvious errors, but painstaking proofreading against copy – comparing the printed version with the original – was probably not a normal practice. In these circumstances, and added to the fact that play texts were regarded as trivia printed to satisfy the fashion of a moment, it is a tribute to the skill of the printers that comparatively few purely typographical errors occur in most of the Quartos.

THE 1623 FOLIO

The other primary text that editors and serious readers of Shakespeare must consult is the first Folio of 1623. This is a large and carefully produced volume of 36 plays, excluding *Pericles* and *The Two Noble Kinsmen*, put together after Shakespeare's death by his friends and fellow actors John Heminge and Henry Condell. It is prefaced by a couple of enthusiastically laudatory poems by Ben Jonson.

The tone of Heminge's and Condell's address to the reader seems genuinely affectionate toward their dead colleague but this, added to the bibliographical clues contained in extant copies of the book, show that although it was a labor of love, it was also a labor of some difficulty.

. . . we pray you do not envie his Friends, the office of their care, and paine, to haue collected & publish'd them; and so to haue published them, as where (before) you were abus'd with diuerse stolne, and surreptitious copies, maimed, and deformed by the frauds and stealthes of iniurious imposters, that expos'd them: euen those, are now offer'd to your view cur'd, and perfect of their limbes; and all the rest, absolute in their numbers as he conceiued them.

A canceled sheet preserved in one of the copies in the Folger Library in Washington, D.C. shows one of their problems. The leaf prints the end of *Romeo and Juliet* on one side, numbered page 77, and the beginning of *Troilus and Cressida* on the other. Something probably to do with the ownership of the copyright to *Troilus and Cressida* caused the cancellation of the printing of the play at this point. The page of *Romeo and Juliet* was completely reset (the new sheet contains numerous spelling and punctuation changes and is misnumbered 79) and *Timon of Athens* was then begun on the reverse. *Troilus and Cressida* was later inserted, without page numbers, at the end of the histories section and with an idiosyncratic 'signature' (usually a code letter) to its gatherings.

UNAUTHORIZED PRINTING

At this period, copyright only existed as a legal instrument used by the government for the purposes of censorship. It did not rest with the author but with the stationer, publisher, or printer who registered the book's title with the Stationer's Company and gained the license to print it. Generally dramatists and the acting companies for which they wrote were loath to see their plays in print. A complete play script was a unique document (actors were given only their parts and cues, see *A Midsummer Night's Dream* I ii 58-9, III i 90) and represented a capital asset to a company for as long as it was popular with the theater-going public. Once published, it would generate money for the publisher or, worse, could be performed by a rival company, both resulting in a likely loss of revenue. The King's Men won an injunction in 1619 preventing the printing of their plays without permission, but even this was circumvented by the printer and bookseller William Jaggard and the publisher Thomas Pavier who were already halfway through production of a collection of nine Shakespearean and pseudo-Shakespearean reprints. They issued the five remaining titles, including *A Midsummer Night's Dream, The Merchant of Venice,* and *King Lear*, with title pages falsely dated 1600 and 1608.

A number of early Shakespeare Quartos therefore represent very erratic and inaccur-

---

SHAKESPEARE AND HIS TEXT

While there is little evidence to suggest that Shakespeare took much interest in getting his plays into print, the fact that he was also an actor and sharer in the King's Men, coupled with internal evidence such as Hamlet's advice to the players and a general fascination with the idea of 'playing' in much of his work, show that he was deeply involved with performance and the demands that it makes. This resulted in the many differences between the Folio and 'good' Quarto versions of three of his major plays, *Othello, King Lear* and *Hamlet* (Q₂ 1604). In each case the Quarto text represents the earlier version and the Folio the later revision for the theater. The changes range from several hundred individual substitutions of single words to the addition or excision of whole passages.

The major revisions in *Othello* consist mostly of additions (particularly to Emilia's part in the final act, enabling her to take over the strength of the female interest after Desdemona's death), but in both *King Lear* and *Hamlet* much more is cut than is added. The Folio *King Lear* omits the joint stool incident and paradoxically strengthens Albany's character by cutting his part to shreds. Hamlet, by the same token, loses his seventh soliloquy and can therefore no longer be accused of delay. The effect in both cases is substantially to alter the dramatic structure and perceived significance. Much existing Shakespeare criticism now needs to be

A CATALOGVE of the seuerall Comedies, Histories, and Tragedies contained in this Volume.

COMEDIES.		
The Tempest.	Folio 1.	
The two Gentlemen of Verona.	20	
The Merry Wiues of Windsor.	38	
Measure for Measure.	61	
The Comedy of Errours.	85	
Much adoo about Nothing.	101	
Loues Labour lost.	122	
Midsommer Nights Dreame.	145	
The Merchant of Venice.	163	
As you Like it.	185	
The Taming of the Shrew.	208	
All is well, that Ends well.	230	
Twelfe-Night, or what you will.	255	
The Winters Tale.	304	

HISTORIES.		
The Life and Death of King John.	Fol. 1.	
The Life & death of Richard the second.	23	

The First part of King Henry the fourth.	46
The Second part of K. Henry the fourth.	74
The Life of King Henry the Fift.	69
The First part of King Henry the Sixt.	96
The Second part of King Hen. the Sixt.	120
The Third part of King Henry the Sixt.	147
The Life & Death of Richard the Third.	173
The Life of King Henry the Eight.	205

TRAGEDIES.	
The Tragedy of Coriolanus.	Fol. 1.
Titus Andronicus.	31
Romeo and Juliet.	53
Timon of Athens.	80
The Life and death of Julius Cæsar.	109
The Tragedy of Macbeth.	131
The Tragedy of Hamlet.	152
King Lear.	283
Othello, the Moore of Venice.	310
Anthony and Cleopater.	346
Cymbeline King of Britaine.	369

reconsidered to account for these far-reaching changes in the text. The differences are also important for the ordinary playgoer who, for the first time in 350 years, has a chance to see not a conflated mish-mash of two incompatible texts cut to reasonable size by a modern director, but the play as shaped for the theater by Shakespeare himself.

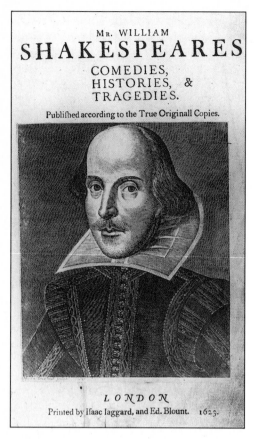

MR. WILLIAM
SHAKESPEARES
COMEDIES,
HISTORIES, &
TRAGEDIES.

Publiſhed according to the True Originall Copies.

LONDON
Printed by Iſaac Iaggard, and Ed. Blount. 1623.

The first Folio of 1623, compiled by Heminge and Condell, included 36 plays. It omitted Pericles *and* The Two Noble Kinsmen.

ate versions of the plays because their printing was unauthorized by either dramatist or company. These are now referred to as 'bad' Quartos, although Heminge's and Condell's description of them as 'stolne and surreptitious' is probably more precise. These unauthorized Quartos can be divided into two distinct categories. Firstly, there are plays which are essentially plagiarisms or imitations by other unknown writers cashing in on a popular title. Into this category come *The Taming of a Shrew* (1594) and *The Troublesome Reign of King John* (1591), although it must be said that the allocation is contentious and that both are sometimes regarded as the *sources* of their Shakespearean counterparts. Alternatively, *A Shrew* is sometimes placed in the second category of unauthorized Quartos: the reconstruction of the play from memory by one or two minor actors.

The first Quarto of *Hamlet* (1603), for instance, garbles speeches, rearranges whole scenes, and gives far less emphasis to the philosophical points of the play than the second Quarto or Folio versions. However the early scenes in which Marcellus appears are generally very close to the corresponding scenes in the other two texts, which has led to the almost universal agreement between commentators that the actor playing Marcellus was the culprit.

Minor slips and word reversions, particularly in the part of Buckingham, show that the Quarto of *King Richard III* (1597) is also memorial in origin, although other features in the text, taken with external evidence, suggest that its reconstruction took place in rather different circumstances. It seems that the company received a request for the play while on tour, and since the prompt copy was not in their baggage, corporately reassembled the text from memory. The resulting version is very close to that preserved in the Folio, but in this case the differences are instructive. Actors' memories, even corporately, may be faulty, but what they were trying to remember must be the play as it appeared in production. Any dramatist knows that there can be an enormous difference between the play in even its final draft, and that same play as it evolves through the period of rehearsal and initial performance.

It is also important to accept that even changes forced for the most basic of practical reasons, such as lack of money, can often result in artistic improvement because of the exercise of imagination required to overcome the difficulties. Thus a modern editor of *King Richard III*, while basing his text on the precise wording of the Folio (which probably represents Shakespeare's 'foul papers' or final draft) will need to incorporate from the Quarto certain features affecting the basic shape of many scenes, and which result in a simpler and more coherent dramatic structure.

SEE ALSO: Ch 2 45, 49, 51, Ch 3 79, 81, 83-4, Ch 4 96-7, 102-5, 112-23, 128-9, 148-9, 154-5, 162-3, 168-9, 176-7

SHAKESPEARE IN PERFORMANCE

We know rather little about the performance of Shakespeare's plays in the Elizabethan theater. Frustratingly, most of the documentary evidence that has survived relates to the work of acting companies other than the Chamberlain's Men, later the King's Men, to which Shakespeare was attached (so far as definite information goes) for most of his working life. We do not have incontrovertible evidence for the features of the stage for which he wrote – or rather the stages, for his plays were produced in public and private theaters, at court and in noblemen's houses, in the universities and Inns of Court, and on makeshift stages on tour. We know the names of some at least of his fellow actors, but we know little enough about their theatrical careers and almost nothing about the nature of their acting skills. Some documents exist that offer us a glimpse of costumes and properties, but the evidence is often difficult to interpret.

Scholars have devoted much labor to establishing what facts there are, and the results of their work are represented elsewhere in this volume. The work is important, for it cannot be too often emphasized that Shakespeare was a jobbing dramatist, crafting his plays for performance by actors known to him, in circumstances he could precisely envisage. Only the texts of his plays survive in a form that in the majority of cases must represent something quite close to the text he would have wished to hear spoken in the theaters of his own time.

Souvenir program of Sir Herbert Beerbohm Tree's 1902 production of Twelfth Night.

THE AGE OF SHAKESPEARE

It is an underlying assumption of this chapter that each succeeding age of theater will, and must, remake the plays in an idiom that speaks to its own time. There is no such thing as an authentic performance of a Shakespeare play, if by authentic we mean a duplicate of the performance Shakespeare imagined, or the performance (or performances) he saw. Even if such ideal or actual performances could be recovered and repeated – and they cannot – the outcome would not be theater but, rather, archeology.

At the same time, we cannot fully read Shakespeare's texts as theater-scripts (and there are several other legitimate ways of reading them) without attempting to recover as far as we can the original performances toward which they point. For Shakespeare wrote the words that survive as one element only of a composite experience that included physical presence and gesture, color and sound, and vocal inflection and pace. The scripts are working documents, framed in such a way that only particular action, in a particular space, and before a particular audience, can give them life.

THE DEMAND FOR NOVELTY

It should be remembered that Shakespeare's plays span a little more than 20 years, and that those years embrace a very rapid development in the subject matter and language of theater. The theater of *The Winter's Tale* and *The Tempest* around 1611, or of *Henry VIII* and *The Two Noble Kinsmen* a year or two later, would not have been felt by its patrons to be the same theater as that of *Titus Andronicus* or *Henry VI* (Part 1) around 1590. The fortunes of Thomas Kyd's *The Spanish Tragedy*, an enormously popular hit when first staged at the end of the 1580s, but a subject for rewriting within ten years, and for burlesque soon after, testify to the rapidly changing expectations of audiences.

Yet certain features appear to have remained relatively constant. The first of

Thomas Kyd's The Spanish Tragedy *was a tremendous success when it was first staged in the late 1580s, but, by the end of the century, it had become the subject of burlesque.*

these is the sheer voraciousness of the theater for scripts, an appetite comparable with that of television today. It has been calculated that something of the order of 2,000 plays were written between 1590 and the closing of the theaters in 1642, to satisfy the thirst for novelty. It was not the practice to allow a new play a continuous 'run' of performances, but to vary the program on a day-by-day basis. Peter Thomson's tabulation of performances at the Rose Theater in 1595 shows ten different plays in performance in two weeks.

Since companies were small, leading actors in particular must have been perpetually engaged in learning new roles. Thomson calculates that a leading actor of the Admiral's Men, the rival company to Shakespeare's, might have learned as many as 50 sizeable parts in the years between 1594 and 1597, and stored in his memory a further 20 parts for revivals of old plays in the same period. The situation for actors performing in Shakespearean roles cannot have been very differerent.

REHEARSALS

The obvious corollary is that rehearsal time must have been very restricted; it even seems possible that only complex scenes, such as court scenes, or banquets requiring elaborate 'blocking', were rehearsed at all, and the simpler two- or three-hander scene left to find its own shape in performance. The actor prepared his role, normally, not from a printed book that allowed him to grasp the overall shape of the play, but from a manuscript scroll containing his own part only, with one or two cue words written in.

The result of these features was, we might guess, that the first performance of a Shakespeare play was far less ordered than a modern first performance, much less a matter of a consistent directorial vision and more one of taut nerves, alert giving and taking of verbal cues, and almost improvised gesture and movement. In *Free Shakespeare*, John Russell Brown writes: *it was a theatre for discovery not for display, for happenings and unexpected conflagrations, also for lack of fire and inefficient confusion.*

REVIVALS

No doubt, performances would in the case of a popular play settle down with repeated revivals, though if any inference can be built on the 'bad' Quarto of *Hamlet*, apparently based on a remembered perform-

ance, texts remained subject to change and corruption. Performances were adapted, also, to different spaces and social settings; command performances at court may have been more finished artistic structures than those at the public theaters or on tour. Nevertheless, the earliest performances of, say, *Richard II* or *The Winter's Tale* are unlikely to have been the consciously crafted, word-perfect structures we look for today; equally, they were probably a good deal more energetic, risky, and exciting.

ACTORS AND ACTING

It is difficult to know the degree to which the actors' skills of gesture and voice complemented this atmosphere of risk. Two of the best-known illustrations of the Elizabethan stage may be thought to tend in this respect in different directions. The drawing for *Titus Andronicus* attributed to Henry Peacham (it is uncertain how directly it relates to performance) shows a relatively formal grouping of actors, several of them kneeling, and with a vividly-drawn Aaron gesturing ominously at his sword-point.

Some might interpret this drawing as evidence for a certain formality in acting-conventions, even for gestures based on those found in textbooks of oratory. Alan C. Dessen has shown conclusively how much there was in Elizabethan stage practice that we should today regard as primitive or stilted: torches to indicate night-scenes, or disheveled hair to indicate madness.

On the other side, the De Witt drawing of the Swan Theater shows a group of three

This unique sketch for Titus Andronicus *was probably done by Henry Peacham around 1594-95. It shows an interesting mixture of contemporary Elizabethan and classical costumes.*

actors, very vividly sketched, who interact gesturally in what appears a modified realistic fashion: the male actor, even if his posture is exaggerated, is patently addressing himself courteously toward the two ladies (played by boys), whose own posture and gesture indicate both shared feelings and a difference of rank.

The probability is that Shakespeare's theater employed expected conventions as a form of shorthand, along with more natural, and impromptu, gestures. Such a practice would accord well with what we have surmised were the conditions in which the plays were prepared: the conventional features would provide a certain stability, while more improvised moves would perhaps become possible as plays were established and revived.

THE VOICE

So far as vocal experiment and order are concerned, the evidence from the texts is surely conclusive that the Elizabethan theater was a place of marked flexibility, indeed of a sophisticated complexity in its employment of all the modes of vocal inflection, from the most stately and orotund to the most fluent and casual. Unlike Marlowe (who is not himself univocal), Shakespeare rarely uses the stately mode except for purposes of mockery; but all the subtle gradations of speech from solemn to frivolous are mimicked in the varying inflections

The De Witt sketch offers slightly different evidence of the actors' use of gesture.

of the actors' lines. A playwright who composed the words for Leontes in *The Winter's Tale* certainly *heard* the rhythms of his language as well as attended to its dictionary sense:

> *Too hot, too hot!*
> *To mingle friendship far, is mingling bloods.*
> *I have tremor cordis on me; my heart dances,*
> *But not for joy, not joy.*

> (I ii 108-11)

It is evident that this vocal sensitivity extended to hearing the consort of voices in a scene. Peter Thomson has remarked that *Twelfth Night* 'has contrasting vocal parts, whose observance in performance is almost compulsory', assigning Sir Toby and Malvolio to the bass/baritone register, Sir Andrew and Orsino as tenors, Olivia as graduating from contralto to 'her true soprano', and Viola as a mezzo-soprano. One might quarrel with these particular attributions, but the aural variety of the plays seems beyond question, deriving in part, perhaps, from Shakespeare's personal knowledge of his fellow actors.

SCENERY AND PROPERTIES

The initial performances of Shakespeare's plays seem to have made rather limited use of stage properties, and very restricted use of scenic effects. All of the plays require hand props; in some a letter or a ring may become a centrally important feature of the action. Chairs and tables are often required and sometimes larger properties, such as a bed, so the stage is not uniformly empty. In the later plays, a more ambitious scenic effect may be required, such as Jupiter's eagle in *Cymbeline*, descending from the heavens. It remains true nevertheless that the major visual feature in the earliest performances must have been the human figure of the actor vividly outlined against the unchanging façade of the tiring house.

COSTUME

Costume becomes therefore an especially important feature of the play-experience, and the evidence is that Shakespeare's company spent heavily on acquiring a wardrobe. Costume denoted rank, and the plays are very conscious of social distinctions. They frequently stress oddities of physical appearance, sometimes of dress (Malvolio in *Twelfth Night* is an obvious example), and sometimes of body (Falstaff and his companions for instance). The Roman plays may or may not have been consistent in providing ancient costume for all the characters; the probability is that the minor characters were anachronistically dressed. But the costume (and armor) must nevertheless have contributed vividly to the impression stage-performance conveyed.

ACTION

How far action confirmed and intensified this vividness is open to question. The scene of Antony's dying body being raised to the monument is exceptional, and must have been the occasion of rehearsal, requiring co-ordination of an unusual kind. Even an exceptional instance such as this may go some way toward corroborating the impression of a theater where the color and movement of the human figure dominate the play-experience, along with vocal subtlety and virtuosity.

It is simply not possible to reconstruct the earliest performances of a Shakespeare play. It is evident, however, that the experience they offered must have been exciting, vivid, and probably boisterous, in ways that are now somewhat unfamiliar; that the actors must have been widely skilled, alert, and accustomed to change of audience and physical circumstances; that the visual experience must have been colorful and energetic; and that the aural experience must have been wonderfully varied. It was a theater characterized by invention and daring.

SEE ALSO: Ch 3 56-86, Ch 4 92-3, 108-111, 118-21, 124-5, 134-5, 170-5, 176-80

THE AUDIENCE

The atmosphere during performance in the Elizabethan theater has sometimes been represented as verging on riot. This must be exaggeration, since a successful commercial enterprise, as this theater evidently was, could not flourish for long in such circumstances. Yet the sense of theater as an indecorous form of pastime, not much removed from the bear-baiting with which it sometimes shared premises, must have affected performance at least in the public playhouses. Moreover, the theater lived dangerously, both in relation to disapproving moralists and the city authorities, and to court censorship.

The audience may or may not have been drawn from a wide range of social classes; general Elizabethan indiscipline will have ensured that those attending, whatever their rank, will have tended toward high spirits. What this means is that the performers cannot have relied on social esteem, or expectations of decorous behavior, to hold their audiences. In a theater where the actor performed on a virtually bare stage, in intimate proximity to perhaps 3,000 spectators (when the house was full) and when many of these were standing, his style of playing must have been bold and dominating, and the tension of the occasion must have been strongly marked. It is an inseparable part of the early performances of Shakespeare's plays that many of them were given their first, or almost their first, performance in a theater that contrasted so sharply with our own, with its rather comfortable social and cultural associations.

The Age of Improvement

The years that followed the closing of the theaters in 1642 constitute the most clearly-defined watershed in the development of Shakespearean playing on the English stage. Playing did not cease entirely: there are records of a certain number of public performances, and rather more of performances in private houses. Nor is it wholly true that the 18 years up to 1660 systematically and thoroughly erased either established traditions of acting and staging, or customary expectations and behavior patterns among audiences. Memories within the acting profession, and among spectators, looked back to the 1630s to recall both individual practices and the attitudes and

Thomas Betterton, a leading actor in the Restoration theater, as Hamlet (c 1661). William Davenant claimed to have instructed him in 'every particle' of the role.

atmosphere of the earlier theater.

One of the leading figures in the new age, William Davenant, recollected when presenting *Hamlet* that he had seen 'Mr. Taylor of the Black-Fryers company act it, who being instructed by the author Mr. Shakespeare' provided a personal link back to the tragedy's earliest performances. No doubt Davenant was influenced by what he remembered when he came to instruct his own leading actor in the role, though we may be sceptical when we are informed that he 'taught Mr Betterton in every particle of it.' Betterton was too good an actor to offer simple mimicry of someone else's interpretation of so rich and diverse a role.

Betterton's Hamlet could not be Taylor's Hamlet, nor of course could it be the Hamlet envisaged by Shakespeare. With the gap of 18 years between the end of regular playing and the resumption of a reasonably full program at the Restoration, the English sensibility had decisively changed, and with it the English theater.

Actresses

To specify the changes in general sensibility to which the Shakespearean theater at this period was responding is a far from simple undertaking, given the elusiveness of identifying a common outlook at any moment in history. It is rather easier to enumerate the new circumstances and practices of playing. The introduction of actresses is perhaps the most obvious innovation.

The displacement of boys and young men in these parts did not take place uniformly or immediately, but a record exists of a woman playing the role of Desdemona in Shakespeare's *Othello* by late 1660, and thereafter women's roles began to be filled routinely by women players. By the end of the century, a range of actresses had established themselves as interpreters of important theatrical roles, including Shakespeare's. Such names as Anne Bracegirdle, Nell Gwyn, Katherine Corey, Mary S. Betterton, and Elizabeth Barry are as important as those of their male counterparts in the theater history of the last 30 or 40 years of the 17th century.

No doubt there were straightforward practical reasons for the change. The

WOMEN ON THE STAGE

The presence of actresses changed the play-experience in more obvious ways. The diaries of Samuel Pepys bear eloquent testimony to the erotic appeal of several actresses in Shakespearean as in other roles. While erotic response to Shakespeare's female roles must have been an element in their reception even while they were played by boys, there can be little doubt that the take-over of these roles by women quite significantly recast the relationship between the spectator and the fiction on stage.

In a perhaps more subtle way, it is evident that playing styles, and hence the nature of the play-experience, must have changed with the advent of actresses. For a boy, however practiced, to play a woman's role, is to introduce an element of distance into the performance. The move toward a more inward and emotional understanding of female roles in Shakespeare at this period is

no doubt connected with large changes in social *mores*. It stems also from the actress's more natural relation with her role.

apprenticeship system, for example, by which boys had been trained for the Elizabethan and later stages had disappeared during the Commonwealth, so that boys were not readily available for important or even lesser roles when playing resumed. But the social and aesthetic developments this change reflects are of much greater interest. Women had played on private stages, and particularly in court masques since early in the century. Their prominent place in the post-Restoration theater also owes something to court influence, since the years the court had spent in France during the Commonwealth had accustomed their eyes and ears to women's presence on the stage, and so sanctioned female players on public stages in England – even in the face of opposition from vocal survivors of Commonwealth opinions and prejudices. More particularly, the presence of women on stage reflected, and contributed to, the slow evolution of women's place in society.

It was urged initially that the presence of women would reduce the tendency of the stage toward ribald behavior, and improve the moral tone. Such hopes, if they were ever more than pious pretence, were soon thoroughly disappointed. The theater of the closing years of the century was a turbulent place, in part because of its traditional and perhaps unavoidable function as commentator on current politics, but also because of its need to assimilate new moral and social understandings.

A QUESTION OF TASTE

There were further changes of a practical nature that affected the performance and reception of Shakespeare's plays after 1660. Recent discussion of early 17th-century audiences has left to some extent unresolved their exact social composition, but there can be little doubt that in comparison with public-theater audiences of Shakespeare's day, the Restoration theater audience was more uniformly and self-consciously elite and fashionable. To some degree the plays had to be remade to fit such an audience's tastes and the consequences of this for the adaptation of texts is discussed below.

STAGING

Developments such as these carry forward elements already embedded in Elizabethan theatrical practice, and more especially in the work of the private theaters and at court. The masque elements in Shakespeare's plays, by no means confined to his last period, called on similar resources in the earlier theaters; but on the Restoration stage they assume a new prominence.

Music comes to play an increasing role, extending its function from the contribution it made to entertainment in the earlier period, and drawing nourishment from the development of English opera.

Stage settings confirm the trend toward the play as spectacle. While a forestage continues in existence, it is now a shallow area in front of representational scenery, consisiting of painted shutters mounted in grooves on the stage floor. Thus the performance takes place within a defined visual arena, rather than in the associative context of the unspecific Elizabethan stage. Even though the flats often represent a generalized setting – of an indoor or outside location – rather than a space particular to the play in hand, they nevertheless serve to further the process by which the play is coming to be construed as primarily a document in social rather than in more broadly philosophical relationships.

Taken together with other changes in theatrical practice, the result is to distance the audience from the actors on stage – as the proscenium arch isolates performers from watchers – while, paradoxically perhaps, intensifying interest in the shading of individual relationships.

Colley Cibber as Pistol in Henry IV *Part 2. This was performed in Drury Lane in 1729. He is principally remembered for the theatrical portraits in his autobiography* Apology for the life of Mr Colley Cibber, Comedian.

THE THEATERS

The intimacy that characterized the outdoor playhouses, and that was a feature of private playhouses and court performance, was retained in the theaters of the new age. The two theaters in Drury Lane and the theater in Dorset Garden were of moderate size, with the stage extending beyond the proscenium arch into the auditorium. Yet the changes introduced after 1660 were at least as significant as the continuities. Much emphasis came to be placed on competition between the two patented companies, the King's and the Duke's, for the more spectacular use of scenery and the more sophisticated employment of theatrical contrivances. The Dorset Garden theater in particular became an elegant house, expensively furnished with elaborate devices.

ADAPTING THE TEXT

In these circumstances, it became imperative that the texts of Shakespeare's plays should be adapted to the new social and theatrical world of the Restoration. Adaptation sometimes meant only staging the plays in a fashion that appealed to the taste of the new age. Thus the texts of plays such as *Henry IV* (Part 1), *Julius Cæsar*, *Hamlet*, and *Othello* were acted regularly without major changes. More characteristic, or certainly more notorious, were altered texts such as the operatic versions of *The Tempest* and *Macbeth*.

There were practical reasons for adaptation: in the absence of new plays in the first years after the Restoration, old plays had to be tailored to the theater's needs. The playwrights themselves on occasion regretted their work.

One major theater-piece arises from this group of adaptations. Dryden's *All for Love* transforms *Antony and Cleopatra* into a deeply serious moral fable, eloquent and high-minded. The rich ambivalences of Shakespeare's play, in language and theatrical design, are sacrificed for dignity and solemn expression.

Nahum Tate's *Lear* is perhaps the best-known of the adaptations. As a lesser playwright than Dryden, his work is altogether of less consequence theatrically, considered simply on its intrinsic merits. Yet it held the stage for a century and a half, with even Dr Johnson among its defenders, so that Tate's simplification of language, and his daring rewriting of the final act, plainly corresponded to something dear to the taste of his times, and useful to its theater practitioners.

Restoration theater valued in language and performance a decorum it considered 'classical'. If this preference had the effect of sapping the energy of some of Shakespeare's plays, it also in the best instances gave them an order and dignity that made for satisfying theatrical experience.

SEE ALSO: Ch 4 118-21, 140-3, 158-61, 164-5, 174-5, Ch 7 224-5

THE AGE OF THE ACTOR

The death of Betterton in 1710, according to Arthur Colby Sprague 'marks the end of a theatrical era almost as convincingly as the advent of Garrick in 1741 marks the begining of one.' The contrast of acting technique between the two men seemed to contemporaries more than a matter of training or temperament, and was taken rather as representing a wholly new understanding of Shakespeare's work, and its place in contemporary culture and thought.

DAVID GARRICK

In the view of Richard Cumberland, writing in 1746, Garrick's playing ushered in a

'Mr David Garrick as Benedict' (Benedick) in Much Ado About Nothing.

David Garrick rose to fame as a result of his 'natural' performance of Richard III. His interpretation offered a new acting style and a new inwardness in the understanding of Shakespearean characters.

new age. With the arrival on stage of this slight figure 'young and light and alive in every muscle and feature', *heaven, what a transition! – it seemed as if a whole century had been stept over in the transition of a single scene; old things were done away, and a new order at once brought forward, bright and luminous and clearly destined to dispel the barbarism and bigotry of a tasteless age too long attached to the prejudices of custom, and superstitiously devoted to the illusions of imposing declamation.* Cumberland writes with the exaggeration of youth – he was a sixth-former at Westminster School in 1746 – but his perception of the significance of Garrick's arrival merely overstates what his elder contemporaries also thought. He was commenting, it is true, on a non-Shakespearean piece, Nicholas Rowe's *The Fair Penitent*, yet the general tenor of his commentary applies just as much to the revolution in performance of Shakespeare's work that occurred in the

early years of the century.

Garrick's astonishing rise to fame took place in response to his performance as Richard III, a part in which Richard Burbage, in Shakespeare's own time, had achieved a special place in the public imagination. Garrick's acting seemed particularly in tune with the sensibility of the mid-18th century, just as Burbage's must have been with that of the late 16th century. According to observers, Garrick's *soliloquy in the tent scene discovered the inward man. Everything he described was almost reality; the spectator thought he heard the hum of either army from camp to camp. When he started from his dream, he was a spectacle of horror: He called out in a manly tone: 'Give me another horse;' He paused, and, with a countenance of dismay, advanced, crying out in a tone of distress, 'Bind up my wounds,' and then falling on his knees, said in a most piteous accent, 'Have mercy heaven.' In all this, the audience saw an exact imitation of nature.*

For writers in the 18th century, the word 'nature' denoted a profoundly approving sense of fitness. Here in particular, Garrick's acting seemed to draw together the text of Shakespeare's play and the 'natural' behavior of a man placed in Richard's extreme situation. There can be little doubt that an audience today would find Garrick's acting contrived and exaggerated; criteria of naturalness change as cultural perceptions change. But for contemporaries Garrick seemed the epitome of a new inwardness in the understanding of Shakespearean characters, offering a new stress on the significance of subtly-conceived emotional states, in contrast to the 'unnatural' rhetorical grandiloquence of earlier performances.

HAMLET

If Richard was initially Garrick's most celebrated role, his interpretation of other major characters in the tragedies, including Hamlet, Macbeth, and Lear, showed a similar development of acting style and interpretive understanding. Hamlet, for instance, had been one of Betterton's leading parts – one in which his interpretation was said to go back to Shakespeare himself. Betterton, we are told, imposed on his performance of the interview with the ghost a conscious control; he *opened with a pause of mute Amazement! then rising slowly to a solemn, trembling Voice, he made the Ghost equally terrible to the spectator, as to himself! and in the descriptive Part of the natural Emotions which the ghastly Vision gave him, the boldness of his Expostulation was still govern'd by Decency, manly but not braving; his voice never rising into that seeming Outrage or wild Defiance of what he naturally rever'd.*

Colley Cibber, in writing this passage, would no doubt have wished us to admire the accuracy with which Betterton represented the reality of Hamlet's situation; but he wished to commend nevertheless the actor's awareness of his responsibilities to conventions of decorum. The German traveler, Georg Christoph Lichtenberg, saw something different in *Garrick's* playing of the scene: *Suddenly, as Hamlet moves towards the back of the stage . . . Horatio starts, and saying; 'Look, my Lord, it comes', points to the right, where the ghost has already appeared and stands motionless, before anyone is aware of him. At these words Garrick turns sharply and at the same moment staggers back two or three paces with his knees giving way under him . . . His whole demeanour is so expressive of terror that it made my flesh creep even before he began to speak. The almost terror-struck silence of the audience, which preceded this appearance and filled one with a sense of insecurity, probably did much to enhance this effect. At last he speaks, not at the beginning, but at the end of a breath with a trembling voice: 'Angels and ministers of grace defend us!' words which supply anything this scene may lack and make it one of the greatest and most terrible which will ever be played on any stage.*

Lichtenberg notes that Garrick's playing involved 'no loss of dignity', a strain in his commentary that may remind us of Cibber. Yet the main emphasis falls on the fullness with which Garrick committed himself verbally and physically to acting out the emotions of the moment – and on the audience's willing participation in that emotional commitment. No doubt, objections could be made to contrasting the two performances in this way; no commentator ever conceives or conveys the full effect of a performance, and his expectations color

what he sees. Yet this is part of the point; what Cibber and Lichtenberg understood from Betterton's performance, and from Garrick's, represents a change in sensibility and in evaluation of Shakespeare's work that reflects, and did something to create, the threatrical world in the years leading to the mid-18th century.

CHARLES MACKLIN

Garrick was not alone in bringing the new world of performance into being. Only a few months before the arrival of his Richard III, Charles Macklin deeply impressed audiences with the naturalness of his interpretation of Shylock. The Jew was played as a villain, certainly, but not as the grotesquely comic figure he had become in traditional playing, especially in the performances of the adaptation, *The Jew of Venice* (1701).

The text Macklin played incorporated much of Shakespeare's original, and by his own self-account earned 'an uproar of applause' for 'the contrasted passions of joy for the merchant's losses, and grief for the

Charles Macklin as Shylock by Johann Zoffany (c. 1768). He shared with David Garrick a desire to transmit an imaginative understanding of character through vocal and physical skills.

elopement of Jessica' which he conveyed. His costume was modeled on that of Venetian Jews, and he took pains to study the manners of contemporary Jews in London. Lichtenberg remembered his attentiveness to vocal effect especially: *The first words he utters when he comes to the stage, are slowly and impressively spoken: 'Three thousand ducats.' The double 'th' and the two sibilants especially the second after the 't', which Macklin lisps as lickerishly as if he were savouring the ducats and all that they would buy, make so deep an impression in the man's favour that nothing can destroy it. Three such words uttered thus at the outset gave the keynote of his whole character.*

Macklin's achievement was a personal one, but his discovery of a method of performance acceptable to his contemporaries represents the putting into practice of advice that had for some years been voiced by practitioners and audiences. Aaron Hill, the dramatist, for example, had for some time been insisting on a method of acting that transmitted through vocal and physical skills an imaginative understanding of character and situation. He required, first, that 'The imagination must conceive a *strong idea* of the passion'; but 'that idea cannot *strongly* be conceived, without impressing its own

Audiences were increasingly drawn from a higher social sphere than in Shakespeare's day, but this did not necessarily result in quieter and more restrained behavior. This Rowlandson cartoon depicts Comedy Spectators.

form upon the muscles of the *face*'; nor '*can* the look be muscularly stamp'd, without communicating, instantly, the same impression to the muscles of the *body*'; so that 'the muscles of the body . . . must, in their natural, and not to be avoided consequence, by impelling or retarding the flow of animal spirits, transmit their own conceiv'd sensation, to the sound of the *voice*, and to the disposition of the *gesture*'. If the physiology of this is dated, the desire for a comprehensive physical expression of the 'passion' embedded in a theater-text corresponds to a view of theater that both Macklin and Garrick would accept as compelling.

POPULAR TASTE

As the reputation and commercial success of Shakespeare increased, so the capacity of the theaters grew. So also to a considerable extent did their social stratification. Allardyce Nicoll remarks that most of those attending the theater would probably be

best described as 'persons of quality', and contrasts the relative social narrowness of the audience with the broader spectrum of the Elizabethan theaters.

Yet the theater was also attended by rougher elements of the population, and theater-going could be a hazardous occupation, as when objects of some size (including on one occasion a keg) were tossed from the top gallery. Nor was the audience a passive one; noise was frequent, perhaps almost constant, whether from young men of fashion wishing to strike a figure or from amateur critics.

In such circumstances, it is not surprising if acting companies and their managers preferred to retain the more successful adaptations of Shakespeare's plays, where these provided strong theatrical effects, rather than return wholly to the originals. *King Lear* for example, continued largely in Tate's version, which satisfied public taste, though Garrick restored some original lines and (in 1768) Colman attempted (and failed in) a much more thorough restoration of the original text. But the Fool was not restored, even by Colman, because, he remarked, 'such a character in Tragedy would not be endured on the modern stage'.

Actors and managers tended to retain the most popular adaptations of Shakespeare's plays, among them Nahum Tate's now notorious version of King Lear. *David Garrick restored some lines, but did not reinstate the* Fool.

In a similar fashion Garrick retained Davenant's *Macbeth*, even while cutting about 200 of Davenant's lines, but nevertheless keeping music and songs, and dancing witches. The Porter was not reinstated, but Davenant's development of the Macduffs was cut. *Romeo and Juliet*, *The Winter's Tale*, *Hamlet*, and *Antony and Cleopatra* were all reworked, with the intent of avoiding situations which now seemed bizarre or crude to public taste, and chiefly, with providing strong moments that gave scope for visual and especially acting effects.

The playwright Oliver Goldsmith took a jaundiced view of the Shakespeare he saw: *What must be done? only sit down contented, cry up all that comes before us, and admire even the absurdities of Shakespeare . . . In fact, the revival of those pieces of forced humour, far fetch'd conceit, and unnatural hyperbole, which have been ascribed to Shakespeare, is rather gibbeting than raising a statue to his memory; it is rather a trick of the actor, who thinks it safest*

CULT STATUS

Garrick's contribution to the changing conception of Shakespeare's work went beyond the theater itself. One concomitant of the developing skill of actors was the tendency of performances to depend on just such a display of skill, and to draw audiences because of the fame of a leading actor. Garrick became a well-known public figure, and a man of some wealth. His commitment to Shakespeare's work, always genuine, led him toward the establishment of a Shakespeare cult in which his own fame played a significant part. The ambitious and ill-fated Shakespeare Jubilee at Stratford-upon-Avon in 1769, dogged by bad weather and financial loss, was largely Garrick's conception, and represented a public statement of the growing sense of Shakespeare's work as a source of national pride, almost a national institution.

The positive aspects of this sense of Shakespeare's place had made themeslves apparent since early in the century in, for example, the careful editing of Shakespeare's texts by scholars and men-of-letters such as Nicholas Rowe and Alexander Pope. (Rowe divided the plays into acts and scenes, and also supplied stage directions.) Editions of the plays became less expensive and more manageable in size than the bulky folios of the 17th century. For example, Rowe's ten-volume octavo edition, with illustrations, became in 1714 the even more popular and cheaper duodecimo set. Acting editions began to be published, and the study of Shakespeare became a vogue, even to the establishment by 'Ladies of Quality' of a 'Shakespeare's Club', which promoted revivals of the plays.

The negative effects of these developments remain to some extent with us: in the gradual establishment of an attitude of reverence towards Shakespeare's work which can be falsifying, in relation to a playwright who wrote largely for a popular and not an elitist theater.

acting in exaggerated characters, and who by out-stepping nature, chooses to exhibit the ridiculous outré of an harlequin under the sanction of his venerable name.

Goldsmith's view even in this strongly worded form pays tribute both to Shakespeare's reputation at this date, and in backhanded fashion, to the strong part played in it by his generation's leading actors. 'No matter what the play may be' he adds, a little sourly perhaps, 'it is the actor who gains an audience'.

SEE ALSO: Ch 4 104-5, 112-3, 128-9, 142-3, 158-9, 162-5, 172-3, Ch 7 225

THE ACTOR AND THE SPECTACLE

The theater of Garrick was one that continued in important ways in touch with the theater of Shakespeare. It is true that a proscenium arch had become a significant feature of stage design, and that actors had to play across footlights and an orchestra pit toward the audience. Yet the theater remained in essence an intimate space, with the actors playing downstage on the apron, only a few feet from the spectators.

Scenery was usually generic, rather than specific to the play's period or place, and costume could be widely anachronistic, with contemporary dress often doing duty for scattered times and places. Garrick remedied a number of the abuses that had threatened the centrality of the performers, clearing members of the audience from the stage, and insisting on discipline both on stage and in the house. Performance took place with the auditorium lit – another feature that recalls the theaters of Shakespeare's day – and actors had to be versatile in carrying in their memories a large number of roles. All this means that the essential conditions of theater had altered rather little, however widely sensibility had changed and acting styles altered.

CLASSIC STATUS

Garrick's championing of Shakespeare's work represents and was instrumental in the establishment of Shakespeare as a classic; and in that development lies the impetus for much that was new in Shakespearean performance during the 100 years after 1780. Classical status invited scholarship, and scholarship was applied in attentiveness to text and to vocal phrasing and nuance. It was also applied, in ways that may seem to us misdirected, toward the establishment of historical accuracy in the visual presentation of the plays.

Moreover, an author of classic stature had to be treated with full artistic seriousness. Writing in mid-century, J. W. Cole remarked that the taste of the age 'had

John Kemble and his sister, Mrs Sarah Siddons, in a scene from Macbeth. *Mrs Siddons was especially famous for the extraordinary force with which she played Lady Macbeth. John Kemble, renowned for his grace and dignity, interpreted his roles as full-blown studies of character.*

become eminently pictorial and exacting beyond all former precedent. The days had long passed when audiences could believe themselves transplanted from Italy to Athens by the power of poetical enchantment without the aid of scenic devices.'

As the century progressed, spectacle became more and more a requirement, and the success of productions became increasingly dependent on the lavishness of scenic effect. It is easy to mock at these developments, and certainly they mark a significant departure from the essential conditions of the Elizabethan stage. Yet sumptuous visual pleasure does not necessarily erase the human image, or subdue the vigor and effectiveness of speech and gesture. It does change the relationship between these elements of theater, and Shakespeare's plays become theatrical experiences of a different kind in a theater that devotes attention to spectacle.

JOHN PHILIP KEMBLE

The early years of the period are however characterized more by strongly individualized actors than by changes in design. John

Philip Kemble (1757-1823) was a good deal interested in the reform of stage setting, wishing to replace the 'architecture without selection or propriety' that he inherited from the stage of Garrick.

Yet his main contribution to the history of Shakespeare performance lay in his careful study and presentation of a number of leading roles, notably Hamlet, Coriolanus, and Hotspur. Kemble's voice was good (though he suffered in later years from asthma) and his deportment graceful. Contemporary and later critics have tended to admire particularly the composure of his playing, and a certain statuesque quality that they associate with the adoption of dignified stage-poses, and a slowness of delivery that became something of a mannerism.

Yet he could not have attracted and held the admiration of such as Hazlitt, Scott, and Byron who described him as 'the most supernatural of actors', had he not also enlivened his character-interpretations with something more than gracefulness. Russell Jackson is surely right to draw attention to *the impressive emotional range and responsiveness to the text* that emerge from contemporary critical comment. Kemble was a serious actor, interested in the detail of his roles, even securing Dr Johnson's approval for his inflection of the line to Horatio, 'Did *you* not speak to it?' – since Horatio as an educated man might be expected to address the ghost.

Kemble represents the temper of his age even in the care with which he interprets his roles; the Shakespearean acting-parts have become full-blown studies of character, interesting presentationally for themselves, rather than as elements in a dramatic whole. The distinction is not an absolute one, but the readiness to explore a leading role at the expense of a more complex view of dramatic action, develops a tendency already inherent in 18th-century theater, anticipates a marked element in Victorian theater, and accords with the interests of Romanticism current in Kemble's own day. The famous portrait by Sir Thomas Lawrence of Kemble as Hamlet, holding a skull and gazing soulfully aloft, serves virtually as an icon of early 19th-century sensibility.

EDMUND KEAN

The prominence of Edmund Kean (1790-1833) as Kemble's successor and rival serves as a convenient reminder that theatrical developments arise from individual talents and peculiarities, as much as from a pervasive 'spirit of the age'. Kean was in almost every way a contrasting figure to Kemble. Too small and unhandsome for sculptural effects, Kean made his mark through sheer energy of mind and body. The best-known description is Coleridge's: *Kean is original; but he copies from himself. His rapid descents from the hyper-tragic to the infra-colloquial, though sometimes productive of great effect, are often unreasonable. To see him act, is like reading Shakespeare by flashes of lightning.*

Kean's Shylock, which took London by storm in 1814, followed some years of hard-won success on the provincial stage. His performance of the Jew was full of variation and emotional detail, thoroughly incorporating the pride and the pain of Shakespeare's character – with the look, as one observer expressed it, 'of a man who asserts his claim to suffer as one of a race of sufferers'. His later characterizations betray something of the same emotional commitment, as in his famous interpretation of Richard III. There, the sly courtesy of his wooing of Anne was as remarkable as the savagery of his duel with Richmond. Hazlitt described how *he fights at last like one drunk with wounds; and the attitude in which he stands with his hands stretched out, after his sword is wrested from him, has a preternatural and terrific grandeur, as if his will could not be disarmed, and the very phantoms of his despair had power to kill.*

Theatrical energy of a similar kind was required to make plausible his Othello. For a man of such short stature as Kean's to have succeeded is remarkable, especially when his vocal range was poor and his voice unmusical. The kernel of the play became the scenes of suffering in the middle acts, when Kean found vocal and gestural equivalents for Othello the baited animal. Keats, it is reported, heard the 'very words stained and gory', as Kean uttered the resounding phrase *Blood, blood, blood.* What contemporaries admired about Kean's playing, even while they sometimes complained of its

Charles Kean's production of A Midsummer Night's Dream *at the Princess' Theater.*

extravagance (as well as about Kean's own unstable temperament), was this ability to convince them of the emotional intensity implicit in the written text.

SARAH SIDDONS

If Kemble and Kean form an instructive diptych of the Shakespearean playing of the period, perhaps the most gifted performer was neither of them, but rather Kemble's sister, Mrs Sarah Siddons (1755-1831). Mrs Siddons played Lady Macbeth with extraordinary force; in a well-known comment Sheridan Knowles asserts that so convincing was her personation that, 'Well, sir, I smelt blood! I swear that I smelt blood'. Her Katharine in *Henry VIII* was equally memorable for the authority with which she played the early scenes and the pathos of her character in decline, so that, like her brother, she exhibited an ability not simply to play strongly but with subtlety.

Perhaps most remarkable, Mrs Siddons seems to have been able to impose the strength of her stage personality even on productions that were becoming lavish in cast numbers and spectacle. Robert Speaight quotes an eyewitness account: *No fewer than two hundred and forty persons marched in stately procession across the stage. In this procession Mrs. Siddons had to walk . . . But at the time – as she so often did – she forgot her identity; she was no longer Sarah Siddons, tied down to the directions of the prompter's book: she broke through old traditions; she recollected that she was Volumnia, the proud mother of a proud son, the conquering hero . . . She towered above all around her, and yet became so true to nature, so picturesque and so descriptive, that pit and gallery sprang to their feet electrified by the transcendental execution of the conception.*

SPECTACLE

While spectacle had been an element of theater production over the centuries – in masques and courtly shows, and in the Restoration operatic adaptations for example – it became a central objective of theater during the period of Charles Kean, and especially in Kean's productions at the Princess' Theater from 1851. The pictorialization of theater, as Michael Booth has explained, derived from and mirrored Victorian habits of mind, aesthetic interests, and technological skills. Technical change and cheap labor made possible not only large numbers on stage, but also large numbers of stagehands manipulating elaborate machinery in the service of large-scale spectacular effects, often requiring cutting and reshaping of the text.

The concern with archeology was both a matter of increasing scholarship and of aesthetic preference, so that Shakespeare productions which meticulously reconstructed the era and place in which the play was set satisfied audiences both by their seriousness and by their visual appeal. Accumulation of detail became, as in painting and architecture, a necessary adjunct to worthwhile thinking and feeling.

The technical means were becoming available to make all this feasible, together with the economic means. Larger theaters with severely picture-frame stages provided the physical conditions for pictorialization, while steadily intensifying light sources exaggerated the distances between auditorium and stage. Longer runs justified the expenditure on sets and costumes. In these circumstances, Shakespeare productions added increasing pictorial information, including invented tableaux that extended and interrupted the action.

Kean's Princess' Theater productions are representative, and strongly develop the tradition inaugurated by Macready in the 1830s with productions of *The Tempest* and *Henry V*. The Princess' *Henry VIII*, for example introduced into Act V a panorama depicting the journey of the Lord Mayor and aldermen on the Thames, including representations of the Palace of Bridewell, Fleet Ditch, Blackfriars, St Paul's, London Bridge, and the Tower.

The work of Sir Henry Irving at the Lyceum was both outstanding and representative. Mindful more than most of the actor's place amid the scenery, it nevertheless promoted pictorial effect, sometimes under the hand of distinguished artists. Alma Tadema, to take one instance, designed for Irving between 1880 and 1901 a production of *Coriolanus* that seriously aspired to both scholarly research and creative art. Deciding to set the play in its historically correct Etruscan period, *in order to reconstruct the interior and exterior architecture of Etruscan public and domestic buildings, he studied Etruscan tomb carvings and Vitruvius on the Etruscan temple; for the scenes in Antium the Lycian tombs of Asia Minor.* The effect was a genuine piece of historical research but also a thing of some beauty, as the crowded life of ancient Rome was visually evoked on stage.

HERBERT BEERBOHM TREE

The tradition of pictorial Shakespeare, to which Kean, the Bancrofts, and Irving (among lesser figures), made notable contributions continued to the end of

---

THE BANCROFTS

Charles Kean was by no means alone in ambitious and visually exciting recreations of time and place. Productions of *The Merchant of Venice* tended to evoke special efforts of pictorial representation. The production by the Bancrofts at the Prince of Wales in 1875 for example was preceded by visits to Venice to secure accurate drawings of the various locations, and to provide detailed information for the reconstruction of the Sala della Bussola for the trial scene. The arches for the Doge's palace were accurately reproduced, and proved so bulky that part of the theater wall had to be cut away.

The Bancrofts' personal search was a mixture of enthusiasm, authenticity, and practical compromise: *Every hour seemed occupied in settling to what purpose we could best put it, and very carefully we chose picturesque* corners and places from the lovely city to make good pictures for our narrow frame. In the Palace of the Doges we saw at once that the Sala della Bussola, with its grim letter box, the Bocca de Leone, was the only one capable of realization within our limited space and this room we resolved should be accurately reproduced for the trial of Antonio . . . We also arranged to show different views of Venice in the form of curtains between the acts of the play. We bought many books, we made many drawings, we were satiated with Titian and Veronese, we bought many photographs.*

The atmospheric evocation of Venice was much admired, but Clement Scott for one had misgivings: *We are there. Every brick, every window . . . nothing could well be more lifelike and admirable . . . The finest passages in the play occur and fall dead upon the audience.* Scott's was, however, if not a lone voice, certainly not the preponderant one.

the century and beyond, culminating in the work of Herbert Beerbohm Tree at the Haymarket and His Majesty's, and during his annual Shakespeare Festivals. Tree's commercial success in sustaining lengthy runs for his flamboyant productions is remarkable (even *King John*, Tree said, reached 170,000 people in its 1899 production) and no-one can doubt that he succeeded in his aim of bringing Shakespeare to the people. His *A Midsummer Night's Dream* (1900), remembered for its use of live rabbits on stage and crowds of prettily-dressed children, drew *The Athenaeum*'s ultimate tribute: *The effects of twinkling lights and floating shapes were magical, and the whole, for the first time on record, merited its name, A Midsummer Night's Dream. High as is this eulogy, it is fully merited – stage illusion and stage splendour being capable of nothing further.*

Tree's most ambitious and successful production was *Henry VIII* (1910), the last in a series that included the magnificent 19th-century productions of Kemble (1811), Charles Kean (1855), and Irving (1892). Tree's intention was 'to give an absolute reproduction of the Renaissance' and his method 'the pageantry of realism'. Audiences found the performance over-

The colourful pageantry of Beerbohm Tree's Henry VIII (1910) was described by one newspaper as 'kaleidoscopic tableaux'.

whelming, partly because of its length (three-and-a-half hours, with considerable 'waits' while scenes were changed), but chiefly because of its dazling variety of movement and color.

The production made excellent profits and was seen in America as well as London, with the general reaction being represented by the critic of the *Daily Mail* (2 September 1910): *Never has any play of Shakespeare's been so sumptuously illustrated. The whole production is an edition de luxe of illustrated Shakespeare.* The comment is an apt one on the dominant tendency of Shakespeare production of the 19th century, with its concern for illustration, and the use of Shakespeare's texts as the occasion for lavish show – scholarly and serious as that show often was, if necessarily adapted to the exigencies of theater.

SEE ALSO: Ch 4 102-3, 114-5, 118-121, 122-5, 128-9, 144-5, 158-9, 160-1, 164-5, 174-5

THE ACTOR AND THE DIRECTOR

Concentration on the general effect of productions in the 19th century has tended to deflect attention from the work of the actor. Partly this is because the leading actors took on managerial as well as performance roles. While this was to some extent true of Garrick, it was centrally true of Charles Kean, Irving, and Tree. Neither the first nor the last of these was an actor of the first rank, but Irving undoubtedly was.

SIR HENRY IRVING

Taken at the age of 11 to see Irving's *Hamlet*, W. B. Yeats never forgot the intensity of Irving's playing, nor the way he made Hamlet 'strut' upon the stage. Even Max Beerbohm, not inclined to be laudatory, wrote of the extraordinary magnetism of Irving in performance. Such reactions were all the more surprising, given that Irving was not naturally well adapted to impress audiences: his bearing was poor, his walk clumsy, and his voice harsh. Yet by sheer personality as well as the hard work of detailed interpretation of a part, Irving dominated the great years of the Lyceum in the 1880s and 1890s.

Shaw could be scathing, and regularly attacked Irving from 1895 on, and Edward Fitzgerald regarded Irving's *Hamlet* as 'incomparably the worst I had ever witnessed'. But the general verdict was enthusiastic, especially in regard to Irving's major role of Shylock, where he played with the other outstanding actor of the Lyceum years, Ellen Terry. *The Merchant of Venice* ran for more than 200 consecutive nights, with the trial scene in which Terry's Portia and Irving's Shylock were wonderfully well matched, becoming a part of theatrical legend. Irving ensured that the impression of Shylock dominated, eventually cutting the last act so as not to dissipate its effect.

Sir Henry Irving as Iachimo and Ellen Terry as Imogen in Cymbeline *at the Lyceum (1896). Irving, and to a lesser extent, Terry, dominated the Lyceum Theater productions during the last two decades of the 19th century.*

Even so, the rather more gentle and sympathetic intelligence of Terry appealed to audiences very powerfully.

Terry's other major roles included Beatrice in *Much Ado About Nothing* and remarkably, Lady Macbeth, where she managed to find resources of power to balance what Henry James called her 'charm and a great deal of a certain amateurish, angular grace'.

WILLIAM POEL

Actors could, then, play an important role in the success of Shakespeare productions in these years. But even as the pictorial Shakespeare continued on its dominant way, the voices calling for a return to words and physical (as against pictorial) images, never quite stilled, began to be heard more strongly. The most distinctive, and perhaps eccentric of these was that of William Poel.

Where the vast Victorian theaters dwarfed the actor (Covent Garden seated 3,044, and Drury Lane 3,611; spectators could be 100 feet from the stage), Poel wanted a much more direct relationship between actor and audience. He also, as a scholar and a contributor to current work on the Elizabethan theater, wanted a return to the scenic structure (if not quite all the words) of Shakespeare's text, deploring the cutting and re-ordering which managers like Irving and Tree thought necessary to prepare the text for Victorian audiences.

Poel organized rehearsed readings of a number of plays, and then in 1894 founded the Elizabethan Stage Society 'with the object of reviving the masterpieces of the Elizabethan drama upon the stage for which they were written, so as to represent them as nearly as possible under the conditions existing at the time of their first production'. Even before this date he had mounted a production of the First (or 'Bad') Quarto of *Hamlet* to test theories about its viability as an acting version of the play.

A series of experiments followed: an open-air version of *The Two Gentlemen of Verona* in 1892, *Measure for Measure* in a reconstruction of the Fortune playhouse, *Twelfth Night* in the Hall of the Middle Temple (where the play was first performed in 1601 before Queen Elizabeth), and *The Comedy of Errors* in the Tudor Hall of Gray's

Inn. Commenting on the *Twelfth Night*, George Bernard Shaw remarked: *It is only by such performances that people can be convinced that Shakespeare's plays lose more than they gain by modern staging. I do not, like the E.S.S. {Elizabethan Stage Society}, affirm it as a principle that Shakespeare's plays should be accorded the build of stage for which he designed them. I simply affirm it as a fact, personally observed by myself, that the modern pictorial stage is not so favourable to Shakespearean acting and stage illusion as the platform stage.*

Shaw in particular approved the closeness of actor to audience, and he was untroubled by the Elizabethan costume and the fast delivery of the lines that Poel believed authentic. But he did castigate the 'bad acting, done by amateurs who were acutely conscious of themselves and of Shakespeare, and very feebly conscious, indeed, of the reality and humanity of the characters they represented'. Poel's productions continued to suffer from amateurishness, but their importance as a challenge to pictorial Shakespeare and in terms of a recovery of certain potentialities in Shakespeare's texts can scarcely be overstressed.

HARLEY GRANVILLE-BARKER

Poel's major 'discovery', according to Sprague, is that Shakespeare is to be trusted as a craftsman of practical theater. His Richard II in 1899 was Harley Granville-Barker, the director who more than any other showed through his writings as well as his productions that Shakespeare's craftsmanship is indeed worthy of trust. Barker respected but did not follow Poel's recreation of an Elizabethan stage, preferring to seek for 'Shakespeare's effects' without asking of the audience an impossible mental transfer to the times of Elizabeth I.

In his major Shakespeare productions at the Savoy, *The Winter's Tale* (1912), *Twelfth Night* (1912), and *A Midsummer Night's Dream* (1914), Barker sought these effects by bringing his actors well forward of the proscenium arch on to a specially-constructed forestage, and by finding in Norman Wilkinson a stage-designer who could interpret visually the spirit of the play. His 'dead-white set [for *The Winter's Tale*] with its white Graeco-Roman pillars on a white stage under under white light-ing' threw into relief Albert Rothenstein's extravagant costumes, of no single place or period. For *Twelfth Night,* Wilkinson's set favored pink, gold, and green with geomet-rically-shaped yew hedges and symmetrical-ly placed seats. In *A Midsummer Night's Dream* the design focus was on the fairies: *Barker dressed and painted them in shimmering gold from top to toe. Faces were gilt and eyebrows picked out in crimson. They wore masks, and quaint Indian head-dresses, with moustachios and wigs of ravelled rope and metallic curls. They came in all sizes, all but four fully grown. They did not skip and cavort, but stood in oriental poses and moved with a dignified, shuffling gait, making weird mechanical ges-tures.*

Such bold design had the effect of liberating the actor, as well as the audience, from the constraints of historical realism. The director could seek to interpret the play's essence, by paying attention to the cadences of the language and to the scenic architecture of the piece as a whole. Harold Child observed in *The Times* that *As soon as you see the thing, you know that Mendelssohn would never do. For our part, we should welcome Stravinsky.* The remark is illuminating, not only for the light it throws on Granville-Barker's astonishing liberation of the play from Victorian perceptions, but also for its prediction of directorial control, at once vital and possibly stultifying for the modern theater.

A Midsummer Night's Dream *was one of Harley Granville-Barker's revolutionary Shakespearean productions at the Savoy Theater.*

SEE ALSO: Ch 3 55, 56-9, Ch 4 94-5, 98-9, 102-3, 112-3, 130-1, 134-5, 152-3, 158-9, 172-3

FRANK BENSON

While Poel's work stimulated new lines of enquiry, work of a much less challenging kind, but invaluable to the development of the modern theater, was being undertaken by Frank Benson and his company, most importantly perhaps in the annual seasons they presented for 35 years from 1877, almost without interruption, at Stratford. Benson's productions were strongly-cast and unidiosyncratic, and made available a wide range of plays, a number of them previously neglected. His *Richard II*, for example, toured England extensively for a number of years, and drew favorable and complaining notice from both critics and such writers as W. B. Yeats.

THE MODERN STAGE: AN INFINITE VARIETY

If the difficulty of re-creating Shakespearean performance in the Elizabethan theater lies in the paucity of our information, the problem of describing Shakespeare on the 20th-century stage lies in the proliferation of both activity and comment. Partly this is a matter of the internationalization of Shakespeare's work through translation and adaptation. Distinguished work on Shakespearean performance took place in France, Germany, the United States, and elsewhere in the 19th century, and before, but the full tide of international Shakespeare performance has only flowed in the present century.

Any full account of Shakespeare in the theater since 1900 would have to pay tribute to directors such as Max Reinhardt in Germany, throughout Europe and in the United States, to Giorgio Strehler and Franco Zeffirelli in Italy and elsewhere in Europe, to Michel Saint-Denis and others in France and England, and to an array of American directors such as Joseph Papp, with his outdoor Shakespeare in Central Park, New York.

Such an account would need to deal with the remarkable efflorescence of the Royal Shakespeare Company, with its theaters in England and its international touring, and with its artistic directors including Trevor Nunn, Terry Hands, and John Barton. It would also have to refer to the dramatists such as Bertolt Brecht and Samuel Beckett who have adapted Shakespeare's plays, or incorporated his example and his writing into their own work for the stage.

The account of Shakespeare in the 20th century would also have to broaden into opera, musicals, and ballet, as well as film and television; the readiness to adapt Shakespeare's plays, going back to the theaters of the 17th century, has become in our time a major aspect of his presence in contemporary culture.

Yet even this account would be too narrow, for it neglects the contribution to Shakespeare performance not only of Russia, through directors such as Stanislavsky, and Komisarjevsky, and through major writers such as Chekhov, but also that of Eastern Europe, in the theaters of Poland, for example, under directors such as Jan Kott, and more recently in Japan and especially China. The transglobal performance of Shakespeare is an undeniable aspect of our present awareness of his work, not only through the interaction of theaters in various lands (directors, especially, travel routinely from one country to another, transferring their understanding of Shakespeare's work), but also in our cultural sense of the nature of the activity in which we are engaged when we attend a performance of a Shakespeare play.

The spectacular lighting and visual effects of Peter Hall's A Midsummer Night's Dream *(1959) exemplify a major aspect of 20th-century performance in the use of modern technology.*

MODERN TECHNOLOGY IN THE THEATER

If we try to summarize developments in 20th-century Shakespeare performance, two trends perhaps become apparent, both of them growing out of late Victorian experiment. One is the increasing sophistication of theatrical machinery, carrying on from the spectacular theater of the 19th century. Early in this century, in particular, and in the last decades of the 19th century, the rapid development of theater lighting made possible a range of emotional effects a good deal more subtle than the earlier Victorians could achieve, and the employment of electricity and modern technical devices allowed a variety of stage-configurations (and especially rapid set-changes) which were beyond previous capabilities.

Max Reinhardt's production of *A Midsummer Night's Dream*, revived and developed over a period of 34 years from 1905, and toured throughout Europe and into the United States, made use of a whole range of modern devices, including most memorably perhaps the revolving stage, an innovation first installed by Karl Lautenschläger at the Residenz Theater in Munich in 1896. The elaborate effects made possible

A production of King Lear *in 1936 by the innovative Soviet director Komisarjevsky whose formal choreography creates a stylized, almost balletic, feel in some scenes.*

by sophisticated stage machinery reached a kind of end-point, that was possibly also their nadir, with the installation of an infinitely-variable hydraulically-operated stage in Stratford-upon-Avon in 1972, a stage which has been only very sparingly used since then.

Spectacular lighting and visual effects have continued to flourish in, for example, Peter Hall's *A Midsummer Night's Dream* at Stratford-upon-Avon (1959-63), in John Hirsch's 'stroke of sheer theatrical magic' in the same play at Stratford, Ontario (1984), when 'the consecrated field-dew with which the fairies blessed the palace was reflected in shimmering light not only over the entire acting area but over the roof of the theater as well', and in the 1986-87 *Dream* in Stratford-upon-Avon, with its eye-pleasing designs by William Dudley, reminiscent of the strange and lovely story-book world of Arthur Rackham.

The *theatricalization* of Shakespeare performances has not receded since the days of the Victorians, but has in fact become more varied and more economical of means transferring the emphasis from sheer manpower to the speed and complexity of modern technology. There are clear signs that this approach to Shakespeare will not diminish in significance, and may even increase.

THE POLITICAL MIRROR

The second trend has been toward the employment of Shakespeare's work in support of various ideologies and aesthetic creeds. To some extent, this has been asssociated with the development of new theater-spaces, including studio theaters such as The Other Place in Stratford-upon-Avon, or the Cottesloe (National Theater), and the Pit (Royal Shakespeare Company) in London; but Shakespeare productions have embraced ideologies, commented on current issues, and taken up political stances in theaters of all kinds.

So far as spaces are concerned, the 20th-century tendency has developed Poel's instinct for direct audience-actor contact, both in large theaters such as the Tyrone Guthrie Theater in Minneapolis or the Stratford Festival Theater in Ontario, in both of which vast platforms extend deep into the auditorium, or in studio spaces such as The Other Place, where Trevor Nunn's powerful *Macbeth*, with Judy Dench and Ian McKellen, derived its impact in some measure from playing in the round in a very confined space with the very simplest of props.

The use of Shakespearean plays to underline or illustrate 'isms' of various kinds goes back at least to productions influenced by artistic creeds such as expressionism (Leopold Jessner's *Richard III*), 'futurism' (Granville-Barker's *A Midsummer Night's Dream*), and surrealism (Salvador Dali's designs for Visconti's *As You Like It*), and comes forward to those associated in one way or another with feminism (Buzz Goodbody's *Hamlet*). Such productions as these may be associated with the tendency this century to derive performances from directorial or design concepts, an early example of which would be Gordon Craig's problematic collaboration with Stanislavsky

on designs for *Hamlet* at the Moscow Art Theater (1912).

Political issues have often been addressed, most notably perhaps in performances of *Coriolanus*, where the 1932 production at the Comédie Française fell under right-wing attack for its democratic ideals, while Brecht's rewritten version for the Berliner Ensemble drew criticism from both right and left. The history plays, rather infrequently performed until this century, have provided opportunities for broadly political stances. *Henry V*, in particular, previously understood as a play of wide-ranging patriotic sentiment, has been reinterpreted as an antimonarchical, antiwar play, or one that simply emphasizes the weariness of the campaign in France, as in Adrian Noble's 1984 production for the Royal Shakespeare Company.

One of Salvador Dali's extraordinary surrealist designs ('Vaneur') for Visconti's production of As You Like It.

STAGING

The 20th century has certainly not shied away from experimentation in Shakespeare performance, to some extent loosening the stranglehold which bardolatry threatened to impose on Shakespeare the classic. For example, Terence Gray's productions at the Festival Theater, Cambridge (1926-33) used witty and shocking devices to jolt the audience out of complacency, such as the arrival of Sir Toby Belch and Sir Andrew Aguecheek on roller-skates in *Twelfth Night*, or the tossing of a property baby into the audience during Elizabeth's christening at the end of *Henry VIII*.

In a very different mode, Tyrone Guthrie spent a life-time of theater work devising appropriate styles for the plays he produced. Out of psychological understandings of the characters, he proceeded to discover ways of 'choreographing' the plays, so as to reveal their fluency of structure and the ritual occasions that punctuate it.

Barry Jackson, at the Birmingham Repertory Theater and at Stratford, offered Shakespeare in modern dress; his *Hamlet* (1925) used costumes that were contemporary formal or dress wear, and thus stimulated a series of revivals aimed at sharpening up the plays' topical meanings.

Peter Brook, though his Shakespeare productions are not numerous, found ways of revealing a new theatrical life in such plays as *Titus Andronicus*, *Measure for Measure* and, most famously, *A Midsummer Night's Dream*. Working always to make theater more theatrical, he has sought to transform it into *celebration*, rather than being a dutiful enactment of objects of a dead culture. *Our need in the post-Brecht theatre*, Brook has written *is to find our way forwards, back to Shakespeare*. It is a slogan which, *mutatis mutandis*, could well apply to a great deal of experiment that has taken place on the post-Victorian stage.

SEE ALSO: Ch 4 92-3, 94-5, 102-3, 112-3, 122-5, 132-5, 144-5, 152-3, 158-9, 162-6, Ch 7 233-6, Ch 8 237-58

Plays seldom performed before have been given new life in the contemporary theater. Many of these have been presented as ways of addressing modern political issues.

CHAPTER 6

POETRY

The verse of the later plays has a special music. The Tempest *is, indeed, 'rich and strange' in its language and imagery.*

Shakespeare the poet is first and fore-most Shakespeare the dramatic poet. His nondramatic verse, important though it is, makes up only a small portion of his total writing; 76 pages out of 1,344 in a standard edition of the collected works. In this chapter we shall look first at the poetry of the plays, then turn to the two narrative poems of the 1590s, *Venus and Adonis* and *The Rape of Lucrece*, then to two enigmatic later poems, *A Lover's Complaint* and *The Phœnix and the Turtle*, and conclude with the Sonnets; the great sequence published first in 1609.

DRAMATIC POETRY: VARIETY AND CONTRAST

The variety of Shakespeare's dramatic poetry is beyond measuring or charting. The range is between *Pray you undo this button* and *The multitudinous seas incarnadine*; between *He ploughed her and she cropped* and *The uncertain glory of an April day*; between *To pluck bright honour from the pale-faced moon* and *The rest is silence*. These are phrases only, which do no more than hint at the variety in the complex texture of whole speeches.

The richness of Shakespeare's poetry is not only in what he can do but in his power to vary what he can do. And variety is not only within the verse but in the contrast between verse and prose. Shakespeare's prose is a part of his poetry. The word poet meant a maker, as his age often insisted: a creative writer. A theater-poet (they did not have the word 'dramatist' in the 16th century) was one who made plays whether in verse or prose (or both).

Strong effects are created by the inter-change of verse and prose. Passion or heroism in verse is counterpointed by the realism, common-sense or cynicism of prose, as with Falstaff at the battle of Shrewsbury, or Iago introducing Roderigo to his philosophy of life, or Pandarus puncturing the lyrical enthusiasm of Troilus. But verse can represent order against disorder, as when at the end of the 'nunnery' scene during which Hamlet has ranted at her in distracted prose, Ophelia (so near distraction herself) laments in measured verse.

O, what a noble mind is here o'erthrown!

(*Hamlet* III i 150)

Shakespeare may have been completing his sonnets at the time he wrote Romeo and Juliet. *The play could almost be described as a dramatized version of the Elizabethan sonnet sequence.*

VERSE FORMS AND RHYTHM

There is interchange too in the forms of verse. Some plays have a good deal of rhymed verse, especially *The Comedy of Errors, Love's Labour's Lost, A Midsummer Night's Dream, Romeo and Juliet, King Richard II,* and *All's Well That Ends Well.* Mostly the rhyme is in the form of the heroic couplet, but it often takes more intricate forms. The dialogue of Romeo and Juliet at their first meeting forms a complete sonnet. There are quatrains (*abab*) in *Love's Labour's Lost,* and a complete sestet (*ababcc*) in one of the king's speeches in *King Richard II* (III ii 76-81). *A Midsummer Night's Dream* has the most lavish display of different forms, with blank verse, couplets, sestets, octosyllabic quatrains, and prose.

But the staple unit of Shakespeare's language in his plays is the standard blank-verse line in common use in the theater of his day, the unrhymed iambic pentameter of ten syllables with five stresses:

> *Uneásy liés the heád that weárs a crówn.*
>
> (*King Henry IV* (Part 2) III i 31)

This regular metronomic five-beat rising rhythm is not necessarily monotonous, as we can see from *Othello:*

> *Yet I'll not shed her blood,*
> *Nor scar that whiter skin or hers than snow,*
> *And smooth as monumental alabaster.*
>
> (V ii 3-5)

But beyond these straightforward examples the rhythm of the blank-verse line is metamorphosed into an infinite number of permutations. The reader or the actor who ponders on the rhythmic patterns of Shakespeare's verse soon begins to ask whether his extreme freedoms might not be partly explained on the principle that he alternates between the five-beat line and a four-beat line in which he gives himself an Anglo-Saxon liberty in placing the unaccented syllables.

> *Áge cannot wíther her, nor cústom stále*
> *Her ínfinite varíety. Óther women clóy*
> *The áppetites they feéd, but shé makes húngry*
> *Where móst she sátisfies;*
>
> (*Antony and Cleopatra* II ii 239-42)

Rhythm depends on the size and shape of words as well as their placing, and on the strength of the mid-line pause (cæsura) and the end-of-line pause. In the later years of his writing, Shakespeare's rhythms became less flowing and more abrupt, more jagged, with a heavy use of monosyllables and short phrases, as in Cominius's words:

> *His sword, death's stamp,*
> *Where it did mark, it took; from face to foot*
> *He was a thing of blood . . .*
>
> (*Coriolanus* II ii 105-7)

Or Ariel in *The Tempest*, also talking about swords:

> *Wound the loud winds, or with bemock'd-at*
> *stabs*
> *Kill the still-closing waters, . . .*
>
> (III iii 63-4)

The verse of the later plays has a special music of its own, and the adjectival recklessness of the last quotation is characteristic. It is often hard to follow, taking all sorts of liberties with grammar and word order. Antonio in *The Tempest* talks of an act that would disinherit Claribel:

> *She that is Queen of Tunis; she that dwells*
> *Ten leagues beyond man's life; she that from*
> *Naples*
> *Can have no note, unless the sun were post,*
> *The Man i'th' Moon's too slow, till new-born*
> *chins*
> *Be rough and razorable; she that from whom*
> *We all were sea-swallow'd, though some cast*
> *again,*
> *And by that destiny, to perform an act*
> *Whereof what's past is prologue, what to come*
> *In yours and my discharge.*
>
> (II i 237-45)

There is, however, an obvious and major question here. This is Shakespeare writing, but it is also Antonio speaking. The tortuous progression is an index of Antonio's mind as he goes about to corrupt

---

EARLY EXPERIMENTS

Looking at Shakespeare's earliest ventures in comedy, history, and tragedy, that is, *The Comedy of Errors*, the *Henry VI* plays, and *Titus Andronicus*, we could say that the young Shakespeare had shown extraordinary versatility in forging a distinct poetic style for each *kind* of play but that he had not created an individuality of speech for the characters. The verse of *The Comedy of Errors* is a triumph of simple and natural diction (*Where have you left the money that I gave you?*). It is a world away from the verse of *Titus Andronicus*, which is a perilous experiment in enameling horror with elaborate poetic ornament. The three *Henry VI* plays show a remarkable progress from the cumbrous and wooden speeches of the first play to the formal, stately oratory of the third.

But something else is happening besides the provision of a rhetoric for the private and public passions of historical figures. In Part 1, the only interest in the verse is the voice which Shakespeare found for the contemptuous iconoclasm of Joan of Arc. And at the end of Part 3, another individualist begins to speak with an even

more distinctive voice, the Duke of Gloucester, soon to become Richard III. With these two characters Shakespeare begins to fashion a speech for the person as well as for the play.

Sebastian. Shakespeare would not and could not have written thus in his early days but what we are listening to is not just 'late Shakespeare' but the mature dramatic language of the great ventriloquist producing a unique voice for person and situation. The emphatic rhythms given to Coriolanus in the following extract are very much in Shakespeare's late style.

> *He that trusts to you,*
> *Where he should find you lions, finds you*
> *hares;*
> *Where foxes, geese; you are no surer, no,*
> *Than is the coal of fire upon the ice*
> *Or hailstone in the sun.*

(I i 168-72)

But this is also the contemptuous language of an impetuous solder, and we have heard an early version of it in *King Henry IV* (Part I), when Hotspur talked about a courtier on the battlefield.

> *– for he made me mad*
> *To see him shine so brisk, and smell so sweet,*
> *And talk so like a waiting-gentlewoman*
> *Of guns, and drums, and wounds – God*
> *save the mark! –*

(I iii 53-6)

INDIVIDUAL VOICES

Shakespeare's verse style underwent great changes in the 24 years he was writing for the theater. But to chart those changes as though they marked the development of a single voice is to ignore the real triumph of his achievement, which is the provision of individual voices for his characters. It is not some achievement in the stakes of absolute beauty that makes the lines of Iago so great as (not now speaking prose) he contemplates the spread of his poisons. They operate

In The Merchant of Venice, *Portia's expansive, and lyrical verse contrasts strongly and significantly with the cold passion of Shylock's verse speeches and with his carefully husbanded prose.*

slowly at first:

> But, with a little act upon the blood,
> Burn like the mines of sulphur. I did say so.
> Look where he comes! Not poppy, nor
>   mandragora,
> Nor all the drowsy syrups of the world,
> Shall ever medicine thee to that sweet sleep
> Which thou owed'st yesterday.
>
> (*Othello* III iii 332-7)

This is a poetry of evil that Milton could not emulate. These lines are great because it is Iago who speaks them; and speaks them in the tone of voice of one who has labored to do what Iago has done, and exults in his own success, in the deviousness of his machinations, and in Othello's despair.

It is particularly interesting that it is the nonconforming individualists who seem to release Shakespeare's poetic energy and imagination, who begin to demand a voice of their own, each one his or her own distinctive voice. To say that his imagination conceived these bold characters and that then he had to find a language adequate to his conception is a crude way of putting it. You could equally well say that a new resourcefulness in his language helped him to discover these new characters. The two things grow together. His characters increase in interest in tandem with the developing power of his language to set them forth and give them life.

These characters are outsiders, such as Richard III and Shylock, or devil-may-care people such as Berowne in *Love's Labour's Lost* and the Bastard in *King John*. (And we could add one who at least stands outside the social class of the main characters, the Nurse in *Romeo and Juliet*.) As their dramatic function is to question the beliefs and assumptions which are the norms in their society, so the verse Shakespeare gives them separates them from their fellows. In *The Merchant of Venice* Portia's description of the quality of mercy is a mere poetic exercise beside the cold passion of Shylock.

> You call me misbeliever, cut-throat dog,
> And spit upon my Jewish gaberdine,
> And all for use of that which is mine own.
> Well then, it now appears you need my help;
> Go to, then; you come to me, and you say
> 'Shylock, we would have moneys'. You say
>   so —

> You that did void your rheum upon my beard
> And foot me as you spurn a stranger cur
> Over your threshold; moneys is your suit.
>
> (I iii 106-14)

SHAKESPEARE'S IMAGERY

The way in which every new character of stature frees a new dynamism of speech can be shown in considering what Shakespeare's dramatic verse is most famous for, the boldness of the figures of speech. He names objects and actions obliquely, by a similitude (metaphor), by singling out some part (synecdoche), by splitting into two (hendiadys), by combining two in one (pun). Macbeth's *Life's but a walking shadow* is a double metaphor by means of a pun, because a shadow was also a name for an actor. Hamlet's *slings and arrows of outrageous fortune* is complex. There is metaphor in speaking of fortune hurting us as sharp missiles do, metonymy in slings (for it is what is slung that hurts), and hendiadys in dividing the idea of speeding missiles into two nouns, slings and arrows.

Metaphors belong to characters.

> Even now, now, very now, an old black ram
> Is tupping your white ewe.
>
> (*Othello*, I i 89-90)

So Iago chooses his words in order to inflame Brabantio. Later in the play Othello is much less deliberate in speaking of Desdemona as his falcon.

> If I do prove her haggard,
> Though that her jesses were my dear heart-
>   strings,
> I'd whistle her off and let her down the wind
> To prey at fortune.
>
> (III iii 264-7)

Here Othello 'unconsciously' implies that his wife is a tamed bird only valuable to him so long as she is subservient. Metaphors are very often used in this way to suggest the underlying feelings or failings of characters. Here is Coriolanus speaking with his usual vehemence against giving political rights to the plebeians.

> — at once pluck out
> The multitudinous tongue; let them not lick
> The sweet which is their poison.
>
> (III i 155-7)

He compresses the confused babble of noise which is all he hears from the people into

In Hamlet, *Shakespeare explores the paradox of language intruding between the self and truth.*

the metonymy of a single tongue; and the disenfranchisement of the people is imaged in the violence of tearing that tongue out by the root. This image of the tongue immediately begets another, of the tongue of an animal ignorantly licking at some dangerous substance.

The way in which metaphors belong to characters can be seen by an exchange of an image in *Antony and Cleopatra*. In Antony's absence, Cleopatra lets her mind run over her past triumphs.

> *Broad-fronted Cæsar,*
> *When thou wast here above the ground, I was*
> *A morsel for a monarch.*
> (I v 29-31)

In a bitter moment later Antony says

> *I found you as a morsel cold upon*
> *Dead Cæsar's trencher.*
> (III xiii 116-7)

The tasty mouthful of Cleopatra's voluptuous self-portrait has become a half-masticated scrap on a dead man's plate.

Similitudes are the fiber of Shake-

spearean verse, and they come in every shape and form. The earlier plays are full of elaborate conceits, like Gratiano's in *The Merchant of Venice*, comparing the pursuit of love with a voyage.

> *How like a younker or a prodigal*
> *The scarfed bark puts from her native bay,*
> *Hugg'd and embraced by the strumpet wind;*
> *How like the prodigal doth she return,*
> *With over-weather'd ribs and ragged sails,*
> *Lean, rent, and beggar'd by the strumpet wind!*
> (II vi 14-19)

There is no need to undervalue similes like this because we admire the way the mature Shakespeare ambushes us with unannounced metaphors, such as *the native hue of resolution,*

> *man, proud man,*
> *Dressed in a little brief authority,*

or *the milk of human kindness.* The more formal developed comparison remains a constant and important feature of Shakespeare's verse, as in this sharply visual 'emblem' from *Troilus and Cressida*.

> *Time hath, my lord, a wallet at his back,*
> *Wherein he puts alms for oblivion,*
> *A great-sized monster of ingratitudes.*
> (III iii 145-7)

HIS OWN RIVAL POET

Many of the passages already quoted in this chapter show how direct, simple, and colloquial Shakespeare's dramatic verse can be. But dramatic verse is essentially artificial and it would be to accuse Shakespeare of a wasted life to praise him for reproducing natural speech. What is so outstanding about his verse is that he can incorporate the vigor and naturalness of ordinary speech into the artifice of patterned verse, or juxtapose the colloquial and the 'poetic'. We can always find what Shakespeare called in the Sonnets, speaking of the rival poet, *the proud full sail of his great verse*. What happens is that Shakespeare becomes his own rival poet. The huge range of registers available to him enabled him to make one style of speech challenge another. The conflict between ways of life becomes a conflict between ways of speaking.

In the funeral speeches in *Julius Cæsar*, the measured prose of Brutus, justifying himself for killing his friend, is followed by the brilliant *ad captandum* oratory of Mark Antony, working the mob into a frenzy. The voluble flattery of Goneril and Regan in the opening scene of *King Lear* is followed by Cordelia's brief responses: *Nothing, my lord.* The conflict of ideologies, expressed in a marked contrast in styles of speech, is often a matter of one character repudiating another's inflated and verbose style as a mark of insincerity and falsehood. One manner of poetry accuses another, as in Hotspur's speech in *King Henry IV* (Part 1).

> *I had rather be a kitten and cry mew*
> *Than one of these same metre ballad-mongers;*
> *I had rather hear a brazen canstick turn'd,*
> *Or a dry wheel grate on the axle-tree;*
> *And that would set my teeth nothing on edge,*
> *Nothing so much as mincing poetry.*
> *'Tis like the forc'd gait of a shuffling nag.*
>
> (III 1 129-35)

Another splendid example of one poet deriding another is the Bastard in *King John* reacting to the Citizen of Angiers, concluding with:

> *Zounds! I was never so bethump'd with words*
> *Since I first call'd my brother's father dad.*
>
> (II i 466-7)

But what is the style which truly speaks what the heart feels? It is easy enough for Berowne to announce that he is giving up

> *Taffeta phrases, silken terms precise,*
> *Three-pil'd hyperboles, spruce affectation,*
> *Figures pedantical—*
>
> (*Love's Labour's Lost* V ii 406-8)

HUMANIZING VILLAINS THROUGH METAPHOR

When we speak of the brilliance of Shakespeare's metaphors we are speaking of the brilliance by which he creates the psyche of imagined people through his metaphors. It is not only their failings that characters reveal in the metaphors Shakespeare gives them. One of the finest 'poems' in the plays is Iachimo's whispered monologue as he furtively tours the bedroom of the sleeping Imogen.

> *On her left breast*
> *A mole cinque-spotted, like the crimson drops*
> *I' th' bottom of a cowslip.*
>
> (*Cymbeline*, II ii 37-9)

Shakespeare's release of this extraordinary simile to his malign would-be seducer has a staggering effect. As with Macbeth's *pity like a naked new-born babe*, he humanizes his villains, uncomfortably humanizes them moreover, by reaching thus into the recesses of their imaginations.

but he finds it very difficult to attain *honest, plain words*. Gertrude demands of Polonius *More matter with less art*; he replies indignantly that he uses *no art at all* but at once falls into a *foolish figure* of speech. All the characters in *Hamlet* find language coming between them and essential 'matter'. *My words fly up, my thoughts remain below*, says Claudius. Hamlet himself constantly tries to suit the word to the action and the action to the word but is always let down as his language races ahead of him, even when he protests against the rant of Laertes. With *the rest is silence* he moves to the only condition in which words will not intervene between himself and the truth.

The rich variety of Shakespeare's dramatic verse is his tribute to the inexhaustible variety of human life, in which every individual strives to make language a means of reaching his or her objectives, of persuading others, of entering into communion with others, of truly identifying his or her own person and situation. But, whatever style is adopted, always there is to some extent a sense of failure, the sense of a gap between the tongue and the heart, between the word and the thing. This is true of the most magnificent of Shakespeare's verse, of Cleopatra hymning her adoration of Antony after his death or of Lear ecstatic in contemplation of life with Cordelia even in prison. At the end of *King Lear*, the old king is reduced to words so simple that they are almost gestures.

> *Thou'lt come no more,*
> *Never, never, never, never, never.*
> *Pray you undo this button. Thank you, sir.*
> *Do you see this? Look on her. Look, her lips!*
> *Look there, look there!* [He dies
> (V iii 307-11)

Although we do not know what it is that he is asking the bystanders to look at, in this breakdown of speech Lear is not necessarily further from the truth than he was in the sound and fury of his most articulate and majestic speeches.

SEE ALSO: Ch 4 92-5, 100-5, 108-11, 114-21, 128-9, 140-5, 148-51, 158-63, 170-1, 174-5

THE NARRATIVE POEMS

There are many brilliant set-pieces in Shakespeare's plays, such as Enobarbus's description of Cleopatra's barge or Clarence's description of his dream in *King Richard III*, which bear witness to his irrepressible delight in word-painting and story-telling. Such descriptive passages, which have to nudge their way into plays, are fully at home in the narrative poems of 1593 and 1594, *Venus and Adonis* and *The Rape of Lucrece*. The former is full of sensitive

This Shadowe is renowned Shakespear's Soule of th'age
The applause? delight? the wonder of the Stage.
Nature her selfe, was proud of his designes
And joy'd to weare the dressing of his lines,
The learned will Confess, his works are such,
As neither man, nor Muse, can praise to much
For ever live thy fame, the world to tell,
Thy like, no age, shall ever paralell.
W. M. sculpsit.

observations of birds, beasts, and flowers; of a timorous hare, an amorous horse, defeated hounds, and even a snail,

> *whose tender horns being hit,*
> *Shrinks backward in his shelly cave with pain.*
>
> (1033-4)

Venus and Adonis is acted out under open skies, but *The Rape of Lucrece* is claustrophobically an indoors poem. There Shakespeare reserves his descriptive virtuosity for a painting hanging on a wall, a painting of the siege of Troy to which he devotes 200 lines (1366-1568).

Shakespeare's non-dramatic verse represents only about six per cent of his published work. Even so, his narrative poems would stand alone as a major and important part of our literary heritage.

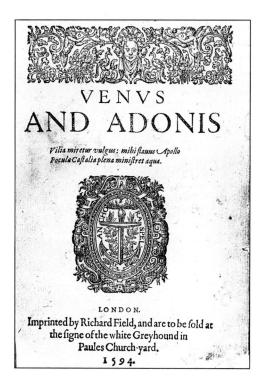

VENUS AND ADONIS

This poem begins as knockabout comedy and ends in tragic seriousness. The broad farce of an older woman trying literally to keep hold of an embarrassed boy anxious to escape is beautifully conveyed in a series of enchanting close-ups.

> *Upon this promise did he raise his chin,*
> *Like a dive-dapper peering through a wave.*
>
> (85-6)

Adonis will have nothing to do with her. He accuses her of not understanding love, of being driven by *sweating lust*. He breaks away to carry on hunting, but he is gored and killed by a boar. Venus laments over his body and vows that henceforth love will always be attended by unhappiness. This comic masterpiece with its sad and moving ending is a subversive Paradise Lost, with the future misery of mankind brought about not through a vain and disobedient woman but through the failure of a priggish youth to respond to sexual love.

THE RAPE OF LUCRECE

In *Venus and Adonis* creatures of myth are made very human; in *The Rape of Lucrece* human beings become statuesque and mythical. The poem is more a series of contemplations than a narrative; insofar as it is a story it is rather boring. The issues which Shakespeare raises in these contemplations reverberate throughout the rest of his work. The first is the irresistible urge to wickedness in a person of fully developed conscience. Tarquin knows what he is doing, hates what he is doing, cannot refrain from what he is doing.

> *Yet strive I to embrace my infamy.*
>
> (504)

The urge to possess is a kind of anti-creation, breaking the self in pieces,

> *Make something nothing by augmenting it.*
>
> (154)

The second issue is the vulnerability of an innocence that invites its own ruin just by existing; goodness generates iniquity.

> *What virtue breeds iniquity devours.*
> *We have no good that we can say is ours,*
> *But ill-annexed Opportunity*
> *Or kills his life, or else his quality.*
>
> (872-5)

The third issue is the question of what happens spiritually to Lucrece through her physical violation. Lucrece cannot believe that pollution is not pollution, that her 'untainted' mind clears 'her body's stain'. She thinks herself irremediably soiled by the defilement of the rape. She chooses to commit suicide in order to enact a metaphor; to let the tainted blood out of her body. Furthermore, suicide is demanded of her, she thinks, because if she lives the defilement of her body will spread to her soul, which must be released from the danger of contamination. This extraordinary idea, neither Roman nor Christian in origin, of committing suicide in order to save one's soul, has a sort of logic about it. If the body can be invaded and lose its innocence, so can the soul. The spread of evil in Shakespeare's tragedies can be more easily understood in the light of the strange relationships between good and bad implied in *The Rape of Lucrece*.

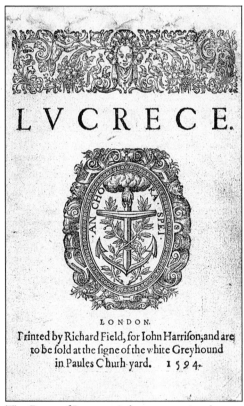

The Rape of Lucrece *is less a narrative than a series of contemplations. In the poem, Shakespeare explores themes he also developed in the plays.*

TWO ENIGMAS

A Lover's Complaint is a striking but odd poem, sophisticated, mannered, and precious, printed with the Sonnets in 1609. The speaker overhears a woman relating to a stranger the story of her seduction years before. The authenticity of the poem has been strongly urged in recent years but there is something foreign to Shakespeare in its thinking as well as in its style, and a question-mark remains over it.

    The Phœnix and the Turtle appeared without any title as an appendage to a straggling and inept poem by Robert Chester, *Love's Martyr*, in 1601. Jonson, Marston, and Chapman also contributed. Shakespeare's offering is a mystical meditation on true communion in love, a communion which does not depend on physical love. Venus is banished from this poem. Doves were sacred to Venus, but not the turtle-dove in this poem, who is a he, in love with a phœnix; now they are both dead, *leaving no posterity*. The anthem speaks in riddling terms of the unity of two persons in one being but proclaims that such love no longer exists on earth.

> *Love and constancy is dead;*
> *Phœnix and the turtle fled*
> *In a mutual flame from hence.* (22-4)

THE SONNETS

The search for a communion on earth and the failure of that search is the theme of the Sonnets. They tell of the relationship of three people, a handsome young aristocrat, an older poet of inferior social class, and a woman of dark complexion who is the poet's mistress and for a time the lover of the young aristocrat. There is also a rival poet. It is hard to think that these sonnets are not rooted in Shakespeare's own experiences but essentially they are autonomous dramatic meditations. They were published, probably without authority, in 1609, but many if not most of them must have been written many years earlier; no doubt the collection was added to and revised over a long period.

The power of the Sonnets is not so much in the individual poems as in their dialogue among themselves. They converse and argue with each other, and thus extend and amplify their significance. The real 'story' that they tell is of a poet's struggle to construct a meaning for his experiences and of his difficulty in making any meaning stick. As a critique of poetic feigning the Sonnets are astounding.

So all my best is dressing old words new,
Spending again what is already spent;

(76)

The love for the young man, his *better angel,* is defiantly proclaimed but it is always sliding out of his grasp as the human things break in: the social gap, the young man's philandering, the poet's jealousy. The suspicion becomes deeper that there is no such love as the poet searches for.

Lascivious grace, in whom all ill well shows,

(40)

The poet is aware that as he tries to defend his humanly-corrupt idol he is corrupting his own moral being.

And in the series of sonnets to the woman (printed at the end of the series to the youth), the poet has to grapple with his own infidelities. With a redoubtable talent for self-justification he tells himself (his first audience) many stories; that the woman is ugly, promiscuous, sexually insatiable, and

that he cannot keep away from her. He condemns himself as a mere rutting animal forced by his strong desire to enter *the bay where all men ride* (137) against all that his reason, conscience, and vows may say. He pictures himself in Byronic terms as the victim of lust – his own.

Savage, extreme, rude, cruel, not to trust;
Enjoy'd no sooner but despis'd straight;
Past reason hunted, and, no sooner had,
Past reason hated, as a swallowed bait,
On purpose laid to make the taker mad –

(129)

Well, he will give it all up and return to religion.

Buy terms divine in selling hours of dross.

(146)

But it cannot be.

My love is as a fever, longing still
For that which longer nurseth the disease.

(147)

All this is in a sense a poetic smoke-screen. The poet is constantly describing himself as betrayed: betrayed by the youth, betrayed by the woman, betrayed by his own libido. But these betrayals are portrayals, ways of putting things. Poetry is most certainly on trial in the Sonnets. The most decisive evidence of this is the way in which the comparisons keep crumbling. The poet is constantly seeking analogies to identify his situation or to prove his point. *Shall I compare thee to a summer's day?* But the comparisons constantly prove inadequate, with an alarming tendency to subvert the very proposition they are supposed to maintain. The tentativeness of the Sonnets, in putting up cases in such a way that their vulnerability is at once exposed, is the result of what the poet calls a *civil war* between love and hate for the one person (35).

Yet it might be argued that the great sonnets which conclude the series written to the young man move away from these unsettling hesitations and counter-statements. The poet speaks of long absence, of having tried new ways and new friends, and of returning to the youth in a condition of repentance and forgiveness.

Let me not to the marriage of true minds
Admit impediments. Love is not love
Which alters when it alteration finds.

(116)

Shakespeare's two major narrative poems were dedicated to the Earl of Southampton. When the Sonnets were published in 1608 the dedication was to 'Mr W.H.', and speculation about his identity and that of the 'fair youth' has been rife ever since. Perhaps the initials were reversed – W.H. standing for Henry Wriothesley, Earl of Southampton – but there is no way of knowing. It is unlikely that the 'fair youth' was intended to portray anyone in particular.

But this great affirmation of a love which survives time and mutability ends with a riddling couplet.

> *If this be error, and upon me prov'd,*
> *I never writ, nor no man ever lov'd.*

The suggestion is very strong that it is the existence of the writing that proves the reality of the love, and that *no man ever lov'd* in such fashion. The culmination of the love-quest is expressed in the optative mood: would that it were so!

> *And ruin'd love, when it is built anew,*
> *Grows fairer than at first, more strong, far*
> *   greater.*
>
> (119)

It grows in words. It is all a kind of dream.

> *Thus have I had thee, as a dream doth flatter:*
> *In sleep a king, but waking no such matter.*
>
> (87)

If Shakespeare shows his poet trying hard to get it right, and ruefully realizing that most of the time he has got it wrong,

he is also showing something magical happening as once again words fail to encompass one's deepest sense of the real. The sparks that fly off the anvil are perhaps the true fire of existence. Many times the poet promises the youth immortality.

> *Not marble nor the gilded monuments*
> *Of princes shall outlive this pow'rful rhyme;*
> *But you shall shine more bright in these contents*
> *Than unswept stone, besmear'd with sluttish*
> *   time.*
>
> (55)

What will be transmitted is not the lovely boy, whose name we do not even know, but the poet's dream about him, and his acknowledgment that it is only a dream.

SEE ALSO: Ch 2 34, 45, 46, Ch 4 90-1

CHAPTER 7

MUSIC & SONG

'If music be the food of love, play on,
Give me excess of it, that, surfeiting,
The appetite may sicken and so die.'

Like man in his seven ages, music in Shakespeare plays many parts. It rouses and lulls; seduces and subdues. It is magician and clown; it proclaims majesty and honors the dead. It is, perhaps above all, the great healer.

Its lowest form of life is probably its highest in the social scale. The King approaches and the trumpets sound. The 'flourish' and the 'sennet' march along with the stage directions in the history plays, as does the drum itself. When the King of Denmark has a banquet,

The kettle-drum and trumpet thus bray out
The triumph of his pledge.

(Hamlet I iv 11-12)

Kings are also the pipers' paymasters and they call the tunes. *Let's be merry:* (*King Henry VIII* I iv 104) orders Henry VIII, and *Let the music knock it* (*ib* 108). Music is an adornment to the court. 'Trumpets sound,'

as Lord Timon enters, 'addressing himself courteously to every suitor'; 'Hautboys playing loud music' accompany the great banquet; and at the Masque of Cupid and the Amazons, ladies 'with lutes in their hands' play and dance.

Kings, dukes and lords are also connoisseurs and critics. Richard II in Pomfret Castle listens from his dungeon:

Music do I hear?
Ha, ha! keep time. How sour sweet music is
When time is broke and no proportion kept!

(King Richard II V v 41-3)

He develops this as a morality-figure and reflects that *so it is in the music of men's lives.* Soon, with thoughts of *Bolingbroke's proud joy* and his own humiliation, Richard finds the faulty music intolerable:

This music mads me. Let it sound no more;

(ib 61).

When, later, Bolingbroke's own time comes and, as Henry IV, he lies mortally sick in the Jerusalem Chamber at Westminster, he wants no music:

> *Unless some dull and favourable hand*
> *Will whisper music to my weary spirit.*
>
> *(King Henry IV (2) IV v 2-3)*

So music plays discreetly in the next room, and Warwick calls out *Less noise, less noise!*

Katharine of Aragon also approaches her death with 'sad and solemn music'. She requests the musicians to play

> *that sad note*
> *I nam'd my knell,*
>
> *(King Henry VIII IV ii 78-9).*

SWEET MUSIC

More often in Shakespeare, music is *the food of love*. So Orsino names it, feasting his senses with an exquisitely languishing indulgence in the *dying fall* which

came o'er my ear like the sweet sound
That breathes upon a bank of violets,
Stealing and giving odour!

> *(Twelfth Night I i 5-6)*

Then, with his lover's restlessness, he finds its sweetness gone; and indeed, as Cleopatra, the supreme expert in love, says, it is a *moody food*:

> *Give me some music – music, moody food*
> *Of us that trade in love.*
>
> *(Antony and Cleopatra II v 1-2)*

If music goes with love, love itself is also a sort of music: Romeo says

How silver-sweet sound lovers' tongues by night,
Like softest music to attending ears!

> *(Romeo and Juliet II ii 166-7)*

And if night awakens love, then music goes with both. In the most musical scene of all (though most lies in the words) night and music combine to make enchantment for

Much Ado About Nothing, *like many of Shakespeare's romantic comedies, ends in harmony and accord, often with a dance as the wooing couples celebrate their forthcoming marriages.*

the lovers, Lorenzo and Jessica:

How sweet the moonlight sleeps upon this bank!
Here will we sit and let the sound of music
Creep in our ears; soft stillness and the night
Become the touches of sweet harmony.

(*The Merchant of Venice* V i 54-7).

MUSIC AS MORAL ARBITER

It is in this scene from *The Merchant of Venice* that something like a philosophy of music emerges. Music is part of the order of the universe. Those *patines of bright gold* that are the heavenly bodies sing in their motion, and this is the harmony of *immortal souls*. Consequently all things in nature respond when music touches their ears. Not to be moved by *the sweet power of music* goes against nature, and those human beings to whom music means nothing are themselves unnatural and associated with disorder:

'*Music in parts*' *is brought to Lord Pandarus of Troy* (Troilus and Cressida *III i 17*), *and the Duke Senior calls* '*Play, music,*' *to inaugurate rustic revelry* (As You Like It *V iv 171, 172*).

The man that hath no music in himself,
Nor is not mov'd with concord of sweet sounds,
Is fit for treasons, stratagems and spoils;
The motions of his spirit are dull as night,
And his affections dark as Erebus.

For the Shakespeare of *King Lear* the 'unnatural' is cognate with the 'unkind'. His villains affront nature, as they do the human conception of kindness; they also have no music in themselves. Iago certainly can let the canakin clink in song to serve his deadly purpose, but his real success lies in making discord, in untuning *the pegs that make this music*. In Richard III's ear there is indeed a voice that *sing'st sweet music* but it is that of James Tyrrell. As young Lorenzo says, concluding his indictment of the unmusical:

Let no such man be trusted.

(*The Merchant of Venice* V i 88)

The world, unfortunately, lies all too frequently at the mercy of such men. It is then, when conspiracy has had its day and the quick cross lightning has nimbly struck, that music heals and comforts. Marina *sings like one immortal* and the shipwrecked Pericles revives. King Lear awakes and music plays its part in aiding the restoration.

MUSIC AND DRAMA

The power of music is felt throughout Shakespeare's work. He also knows its effectiveness in the theater. *Music i' th' air* is heard, chillingly, in *Antony and Cleopatra* (IV iii 16-7) as

the god Hercules, whom Antony lov'd,
Now leaves him.

As Prospero abjures his rough magic, he invokes the greatest magician of all,

A solemn air, and the best comforter
To an unsettled fancy,

(*The Tempest* V i 58-9).

Here it leads Shakespeare to the conclusion of his own career, just as it had aptly and effectively concluded many of his plays. The magician works his spell.

Yet with all this reverence for the art of music, it is still one of the most characteristic of touches that puts an irreverent thought in Benedick's mind in *Much Ado About Nothing* as he cynically observes the effect of music on *Monsieur Love*, the listening Claudio:

Now divine air! now is his soul ravish'd.

Then in a nutshell the whole mystery of music, the crudeness of its physical means, the infinite subtlety of its spiritual ends, is bound up with a wry reflection before Balthasar begins to sing:

Is it not strange that sheeps' guts should hale souls
out of men's bodies?

(*Much Ado About Nothing* II iii 54-5)

SEE ALSO: Ch 4 104-5, 116-21, 124-5, 128-31, 134-5, 142-3, 158-9, 162-3, 168-9, 174-5

SHAKESPEARE AND SONG

While Benedick in *Much Ado About Nothing* cynically raises his eyebrow, Balthazar and his musicians perform the song *Sigh no more, ladies*. It is one of the 92 items listed in the Oxford Shakespeare's *Index of First Lines of Songs, etc.*, and is fairly representative. The lyric, with its varied length of line, its manageable verse-form, with a *Hey nonny nonny* refrain, invites setting to music and makes no bid to outdo the music with too dense or complicated a supply of poetic images. Its mood of comic realism (*Men were deceivers ever*) harmonizes well with the tone and subject-matter of the play, but has no essential role in the drama. Similarly, in *The Two Gentlemen of Verona*, the song *Who is Silvia?*, though addressed to a character in the play, is decorative rather than thematic or dramatically necessary.

SONGS AND THE NARRATIVE

In some plays the songs are more integral. It is hard to think of *As You Like It* without *Under the greenwood tree, Blow, blow, thou winter wind,* and *It was a lover and his lass*. The sophisticated pastoral needs such lyrics as a vital part of its relationship with the convention on which it makes urbane comment. Their special achievement is to preserve the charm and freshness, stripping away the artifice and substituting a more thoughtful realism. In this they are in keeping with the essential mode of the play.

In *The Tempest* Ariel's songs are part of the fabric. *Come unto these yellow sands*, with its strangely transposed courtliness, and the dreamlike random associations of watchdogs and *strutting chanticleer*, is the very stuff of the island's magic. *Full fathom five* does not merely make Ferdinand remember his supposedly drowned father; it is also unearthly music, waiting *upon some god o' th' island* on whom in turn awaits the time of judgment and renewal. *While you here do snoring lie*, the third song, plays a direct part in the plot, and *Where the bee sucks* is Ariel's delicately poetic counterpart of Caliban's drunken *No more dams I'll make for fish*.

Caliban, drunk in company with Trinculo and Stephano, sings the crude and deeply human 'Freedom, high-day! high-day, freedom!'

The tragedies have relatively few songs, but when they occur their effect is memorable. Most beautiful of all the lyrics, and probably most moving in its dramatic context, is the dirge *Fear no more the heat o' th' sun* in *Cymbeline* (not a tragedy in its outcome, yet hardly to be classed as tragicomedy either). In *Hamlet* Ophelia's madness betrays her into snatches of song, the pathos of which sometimes derives from their oblique reference to real events, and sometimes from the girl's innocence of their indelicacy and lewdness.

Desdemona's 'Willow Song' (*Othello* IV iii 39) is probably the most 'integral' of all the songs. Its setting is the scene in which Desdemona prepares for bed and chats with Emilia before bidding her goodnight and adding a prayer that bad may lead to better, not to worse. The song, she says, *will not go from my mind*; her mother's maid sang it when her own love affair took a tragic turn, and she died singing it. With the complete naturalness that characterizes this scene, the women talk casually about something else before Desdemona starts to sing. She breaks off to speak and at one point forgets the words (*Nay, that's not next*). Then, as with Ophelia, the song betrays her:

I call'd my love false love; but what said he then?
  Sing willow, willow, willow;
If I court moe women, you'll couch with moe men

This is another 'indecent' folk-song; Desdemona has probably hardly remembered or thought about it before, but now she stops and goes no further. It is of course too close to that concept of woman as whore which Desdemona knows nothing about, so that it 'abhors her' to say the word. The song leads naturally to a more serious turn in the conversation, and Desdemona asks whether Emilia believes

That there be women do abuse their husbands
In such gross kind?

The scene is wonderfully effective and dramatically enriching in the contrasts it provides. In this masculine play, here is the talk of women, and of a woman's point of view (*Oh, these men, these men!*). In a play of noise, here is quietness; in among the violence, peace. But the peace is disturbed.

Hark! who is't that knocks?

It is only the wind, but the reassurance has a desolate feeling about it. Desdemona's eyes itch, and that is said to *bode weeping*. Always there is unease lurking below the calm surface. As the girl's voice, without instrumental accompaniment and very softly as though singing to herself, takes up the old song, the melancholy loneliness of the sound intensifies our sense of what Othello calls *the pity of it*. The scene, like Ophelia's, goes well beyond anything we would normally refer to as 'dramatic effect'; yet it is still a masterly piece of 'theater', and the work of a dramatist who knew well how the power of the spoken word may be heightened by the power of music.

SEE ALSO: Ch 4 98-9, 130-3, 158-61, 170-1, 174-5

OPHELIA AND THE
ELIZABETHAN AUDIENCE

Many years ago, in a lecture at Cambridge, the Elizabethan scholar A.P. Rossiter developed an interesting line of thought on the effects of Ophelia's songs upon the various sections of Shakespeare's audience. A sensitive onlooker, then as now, must have found this *document in madness* pitiful and painful to watch. But there must also have been a part of the audience – that *quantity of barren spectators* who will laugh at anything – quite ready with a coarse word or a belly-laugh at the indecencies of the St Valentine's Day song. Shakespeare, practical man of the theater as he was, must have known what he risked, and must have weighed his gains, for the noisy coarseness of the insensitive only heightens the intensity of feeling in the minds of the more responsive and thoughtful. In the modern theater, of course, a reverent hush generally pervades the auditorium throughout the scene; but in Shakespeare's time the song would have provoked a whole complex of reactions, drawing the spectator towards the stage-as-reality (*a mirror to nature*) quite beyond the stylized rhetoric of theatrical madness.

SETTINGS FOR SONGS

In the 'Willow Song' Shakespeare almost certainly used, with some adaptations, an existing popular tune. It survives in several manuscript lute-books of the period and is often used in modern productions of the play. Roughly one third of the songs can be assigned to known Elizabethan melodies; in some instances (the traditional tune to *When that I was and a little tiny boy, Twelfth Night*, is an outstanding example) the original setting is so obviously right for the poem that words and music have become almost inseparable. Though countless composers have set *O mistress mine*, the tune found in Thomas Morley's Consort Lessons of 1599 has a simple charm and effectiveness in production because of its authenticity.

Robert Johnson (*c*.1583-1633) composed settings of songs in *The Tempest*, and John Wilson (1595-1674) wrote songs for Shakespeare and Fletcher's company, including a version of *Take, O, take those lips away* that is particularly attractive. But mostly the early tunes are anonymous, and not in the category of 'art song' but of folk music. Ophelia's *Bonny sweet Robin* goes to a melody found in the *Schole of Music* (1603), and a tune in the Fitzwilliam Virginal Book called *Hawken* fits Autolycus's *Jog on* in *The Winter's Tale*. Many of the incidental dances in the plays have similarly identifiable traditional melodies.

THEATRICAL COMPOSITION

The development of Shakespearean settings as an art form and indeed as a major industry for British composers dates from the Restoration. With the reopening of the theaters in 1660, appreciation of Shakespeare as the supreme genius of English drama finds increasing expression.

As they were revived the plays underwent adaptation, and the musicians were often involved in this supposedly civilizing process. The outstanding example is the production in 1674 of *The Tempest* at the new Duke's Theater in Dorset Garden by the Thames. Dryden, who had collaborated with Sir William Davenant in preparing the text of the play (which in his Preface he engagingly points out 'was originally Shakespeare's'), expresses the ambivalent attitude of the period in *Defence of the Epilogue*, 1672: *He is the very Janus of poets. He wears everywhere two faces, and you have scarce begun to admire the one ere you despise the other.* So it is a courtly, masque-like entertainment that emerges, with elaborate scenery and dramatic effects, and music to match. A large part of the music was entrusted to Matthew Locke (*c*.1630-77) whose highly imaginative 'Curtain Tune' includes what were then unusually explicit and dramatic directions such as 'lowder by degrees', 'violent', and 'soft and slow by degrees'. A specifically theatrical type of instrumental composition had come into being. The musical items include a *Masque of the Three Devils* and *Masque of Neptune*, both by Pelham Humfrey, and somewhere among all these proud pleasures of the new

'Where the bee sucks', among the best known Shakespearean songs sung by Ariel in The Tempest, *was a favorite with both Elisabeth Schumann and Elisabeth Schwarzkopf.*

age are the settings of Ariel's songs.

Pepys – who found *A Midsummer Night's Dream, the most insipid ridiculous play that I ever saw in my life* – had a great love of music, and among the pleasures he took in Shakespearean productions on stage were the *dancing and musique* in *Macbeth*! He also admired *To be or not to be* sufficiently to learn it by heart, and to suggest that a musical setting should be made in the recitative manner of the Italian opera just beginning to be known in London. It was to be a long time before Italian operatic composers were to take an interest in Shakespeare, but meanwhile, in the 18th century, the theaters of Covent Garden and Drury Lane came into being, and Shakespeare's fortunes flourished in both. Almost immediately the musicians became involved, Thomas Arne (1710-78) writing for productions of *As You Like It, Twelfth Night, The Merchant of Venice, The Tempest, Romeo and Juliet,* and *Cymbeline*, with William Boyce (1711-79) contributing to the last three.

THE JUBILEE

Boyce had also set to music an *Ode to the Memory of Shakespeare* published in 1756, by the actor William Harvard. This was to provide some ideas for another and grander ode by Garrick, to be delivered at Stratford-upon-Avon with music by Arne. *Dr. Arne works like a dragon at it*, wrote Garrick. *He is all fire and flame about it*. This was in 1769, the year of the Shakespeare Jubilee. Other composers were to benefit too, notably Charles Dibdin (1745-1814), whose tunes for the collection of Jubilee songs called *Shakespeare's Garland* became popular. The Ode itself was designed as the great climax of the birthday celebrations. Arne's florid overture prefaced Garrick's recitation accompanied by a repeated musical motif and leading into a triumphant chorus in praise of *the lov'd, rever'd, immortal name*.

Most admired of all was the soprano solo 'Thou soft-flowing Avon' sung by Sophia Baddeley, while the doors of the Rotunda were flung open to reveal the Avon. Now the music seems pleasant rather than suggestive of fire and flame. Handel had died ten years earlier, and there, surely, was a great work missed.

Charles Dibdin's collection of songs for Garrick's 1769 Jubilee – Shakespeare's Garland *– became very popular.*

LATER SETTINGS

Arne's settings of individual songs from the plays still have a place in the current repertory of most English singers. But when Shakespeare's songs occur in recital programs they are more often heard in the settings of composers from the time of Charles Stanford (1852-1924) and Hubert Parry (1848-1918) up to Gerald Finzi (1901-56) and Benjamin Britten (1913-76).

The Victorian age provided surprisingly little in this area; perhaps the most enduring has been the setting by Henry Bishop (1786-1855) of the four lines from *Venus and Adonis*, starting *Lo, here the gentle lark*. It is probable that few among the thousands who bought early phonograph records of this sung by Nellie Melba or Galli-Curci would have caught more than the opening words of the song, let alone realized that they were by Shakespeare. After Bishop's time, with the revival of the English song as an art-form, there came a great fondness for settings of Shakespeare's lyrics, not as Elizabethan pastiche but in the modern style and with well-developed piano accompaniments.

First in the line, and often forgotten in this respect, was Arthur Sullivan (1842-1900). His *Five Shakespeare Songs* (1863) included a delightful version of *O mistress mine*, and *Orpheus with his lute*, the most popular of the set, has a Schubertian grace about it, well brought out by Janet Baker among recent singers. Written only a few years later, Parry's *Shakespeare Songs* include some of the best-known lyrics such as (inevitably) *O mistress mine*, and *Blow, blow, thou winter wind*. The first is particularly deft and resourceful in its use of the piano, and the second, with more than a touch of Brahms in its ingredients, has the strength of a composer who is not afraid of a thoroughly committed melodic line and yet does not degenerate into obviousness. In *Where icicles hang by the wall*, Parry sustains a well-defined motif through a series of pleasantly impulsive developments.

These poems were set again and again by English composers over the years. One whose attractive, not too demanding idiom made his settings probably the most frequently performed of all was Roger Quilter (1877-1953): his *As You Like It* and *Twelfth*

Desdemona's 'Willow Song' (Othello IV iii), originally a folk-tune, has inspired several composers, and for years haunted Percy Grainger.

Night songs were to be found in the piano stools of most musical households in the earlier years of the century.

20TH-CENTURY SETTINGS

Others brought more toughness to the poems. *Under the greenwood tree* carries some recognition that *winter and rough weather* are realities to be reckoned with in the otherwise jaunty setting by Ivor Gurney (1890-1937). Peter Warlock (1894-1930) calls his *It was a lover and his lass, Pretty Ring Time*, and with some tricky touches in both the voice part and its accompaniment he puts it just beyond the easy reach of an amateur to whom Roger Quilter was manageable enough. Percy Grainger (1882-1961), a champion of the amateur musician, has a different kind of 'toughness' in his several settings of Desdemona's 'Willow Song' from *Othello*. An indefatigable collector of folk songs, he was haunted by the traditional tune, writing his first version of it at the age of 16, later adding strings and guitar, and exploring more sophisticated harmonic possibilities.

Finzi, among the younger generation, wrote one of the most satisfying of all collections of Shakespearean settings, *Let us garlands bring* published in 1942 in a version for voice and string orchestra. A pavane-like movement underlies *Come away, death*; *Who is Silvia?* has wonderful rhythmic flexibility; and loveliest of all is *Fear no more the heat o' th' sun*, with its consolation in the gentle curve of the melody and its movingly hushed exorcism at the end.

From Britten has come only a few individual settings, but his *Fancy* (*Tell me where is fancy bred*) is a miniature invention of genius, and his setting of Sonnet 43 (*When most I wink*) brings his *Nocturne* (1958) to a profound and magical conclusion. It also forms a link with Britten's major Shakespearean work, which appeared only two years later, the delightful opera *A Midsummer Night's Dream*.

SEE ALSO: Ch 3 61-6, Ch 4 100-3, 128-9, 132-5, 158-61, 164-5, 172-5, Ch 5 188, 194, Ch 6 214-5, 217-8

OPERA

Opera takes us to Europe. The bardolatry which in England had been sanctioned by the great Jubilee of 1769 spread to Europe around the turn of the century. By then operas had already been based on *Romeo and Juliet*, *The Merchant of Venice*, *As You Like It*, *Hamlet*, *The Merry Wives of Windsor*, *Macbeth*, *Antony and Cleopatra*, *Cymbeline*, and *The Tempest*. None of these has survived in the repertory, and for the most their composers are unremembered. It was with the Romantic movement that Shakespeare came to excite a new generation, particularly of French and Germans.

Some were attracted to the lyrics: Schubert's *An Silvia*, written to a German translation but fitting the English text perfectly, is probably still the most famous of all Shakespearean settings, closely followed by the Serenade *Horch, horch, die Lerch* from the song in *The Two Gentlemen of Verona*. The third of this set, incidentally, is the *Trinklied* (Drinking Song) *Come, thou monarch of the vine* from the barge-scene in *Antony and Cleopatra*. In the same year (1826) as Schubert wrote these songs in Vienna, the 17-year-old Berlioz was finishing his concert overture called *A Midsummer Night's Dream*, performed at Strettin in 1827. The incidental music, with its famous Scherzo and Nocturne, dates from 1843 in response to a royal commission for a performance of the play.

HECTOR BERLIOZ

If fashion was the word for 1843, for some choice spirits in 1827 it was passion. In *The Memoirs of Hector Berlioz* (trans. David Cairns. Gollancz 1969) the most passionately exultant and inventive musician of the age tells what the discovery of Shakespeare meant to him: *Shakespeare, coming upon me unawares, struck me like a thunderbolt. The lightning flash of that discovery revealed to me at a stroke the whole heaven of art, illuminating it to its remotest corners.*

The arrival in Paris of the English players in 1827 was, he said, 'the supreme drama of my life'. As might be suspected, more than art was involved, for he also fell in love with the actress who played Ophelia and Juliet, Harriet Smithson, and was later

Hector Berlioz's last major work, Béatrice et Bénédict, *was based on* Much Ado About Nothing. *Shakespeare had been a passion and source of inspiration to the composer for 35 years.*

to marry her. But the genius of
Shakespeare, bound by no rules and (as it
seemed to him) a pure flame of poetry and
personal impulse, inspired him, and already
the 'Dramatic Symphony', *Roméo et Juliette*
was occupying his thoughts. Produced in
1839, it was a work of astonishing original-
ity both in overall conception and in the
detail of execution. The orchestra is the
protagonist, with Friar Laurence as the only
character from the play heard as soloist
(though Mercutio's Queen Mab speech is
sung and later played as a scherzo). A chorus
narrates and participates as the warring
families, in the former role paying tribute
to the poetry: *Dont Shakespeare lui seul eut le
secret suprême et qu'il remporta dans le ciel.*

Shakespeare also inspired Berlioz's *King
Lear* Overture (1831), *Tristia* (1848), a
separate solo *La mort d'Ophélie* (based on
Gertrude's *There is a willow* speech in *Hamlet*
IV vii), and his opera *Béatrice et Bénédict*
(1862), an adaptation of *Much Ado About
Nothing*. The French title for Shakespeare's
play was *Beaucoup de bruit pour rien*, and
Berlioz had thought of writing an opera in
the Italian style 30 years previously. In the
event he simplified the play along the lines
which his title suggests. To replace Dogberry he substituted a character called

Somarone (meaning 'Great donkey'), a pompous professional musician who composes
an *Epithalane grotesque* – curiously, a quite
lovely piece of music. Otherwise the most
delightful things in the opera are the
nocturne for Hero and her maid, the solo for
Béatrice with its wide range of emotions as
she comes to acknowledge her love and its
consequences (*Adieu, ma frivole gaieté!*), and
the Overture with its rhythmic wit and
luminous orchestration. The opera was
Berlioz's last major work, and David Cairns
writes well of it: *In this unlooked-for epilogue
to his career Berlioz repays some of his life-long
debt to Shakespeare, reminds us that he is not
always a loud composer and can be a witty one,
and finds for a moment in art the felicity that life
denied him.*

GIUSEPPE VERDI

Still more than Berlioz, it is Verdi who
comes to mind when one thinks of
Shakespeare and opera. Not that he was the
first Italian of note to set a Shakespeare-
based libretto. Before his *Otello* (1887) came
Rossini's (1816), just as Berlioz's *Roméo et
Juliette* was preceded by several Italian
versions, notably *I Capuleti e i Montecchi*
(1830) by Bellini. For that opera the
librettist, Felice Romani, appears to have
drawn on Shakespeare's own source, the
novella of Matteo Bandello; and there are
other strands and episodes in the story
which come from neither.

MACBETH

Verdi's first Shakespearean opera was *Macbeth*. He had known Shakespeare (he said)
from earliest youth, and 'read and re-read
him continually'. (The Italian translation of
Shakespeare used by Verdi was by Carlo
Rusconi, published in 1838. Verdi would
then have been 25. His remark quoted here
was made in 1865 in angry reaction to
French critics who accused him of not
knowing Shakespeare.)

He had already considered *King Lear,
Hamlet,* and *The Tempest* as possible operatic
subjects when he decided upon *Macbeth* in
1846. His librettist was Francesco Piave,
who wrote the books for many of his most
successful operas including *Rigoletto, La
Traviata, La forza del destino,* and *Simone*

VERDI AND LADY MACBETH

In many respects Verdi's *Macbeth* defies convention. For one thing, the principal tenor is assigned merely the secondary role of Macduff, while Macbeth himself is a baritone. His main solos correspond to Shakespeare's *Two truths are told*, *Is this a dagger*, and *My way of life* speeches. It is Lady Macbeth who embodies the great creative drive of this opera, if not in its original version of 1847 then certainly in the revised edition of 1865 in which the opera is almost invariably heard nowadays. It is eminently a role for the *prima donna*, making formidable demands on the singer both technically and dramatically.

Yet it does not present the soprano in the manner to which she was then accustomed, and Verdi's objections to Eugenia Tadolini as a proposed Lady Macbeth are justly famous: *Tadolini has many qualities which are too fine for this role! She is beautiful and elegant, and I shall want to have a Lady Macbeth who is deformed and ugly. Tadolini sings perfectly and I want Lady Macbeth*
not to sing *at all. Tadolini has a superb, brilliant, clear and powerful voice, whereas I want for Lady Macbeth a voice that is hoarse, stifled and hollow.*

He took endless pains over the role and the whole opera. His first Lady Macbeth, Marianna Barbieri-Nin, recalled in her memoirs that he alienated many in the cast because, with more than 100 rehearsals, he was still not satisfied. The sleepwalking scene took three months' study, with Verdi insisting that it should be done with scarcely any lip-movement and with the face completely immobile. The duet following Duncan's murder had to be rehearsed 150 times to make it 'more speech than song'. In the Paris version of 1865 an additional solo (*La luce langue*) gave to Lady Macbeth the aria corresponding to Macbeth's *Light thickens* speech in Act III. With the sleepwalking scene and her impressively demonic first solo, it makes of Lady Macbeth one of the greatest and also most difficult roles in the dramatic soprano's repertoire.

Boccanegra. In approaching him with a sketch for *Macbeth* Verdi wrote: *this tragedy is one of the greatest creations of man. . . If we cannot make something great out of it, at least let us try to do something out of the ordinary.*

Something extraordinary was indeed made, and yet the first impression of an English-speaking listener who comes freshly to it is likely to be of a kind of banality. Familiarity breeds respect, but at first it seems impossible to take Verdi's witches and assassins seriously, while the very Italian jollity of Lady Macbeth's Brindisi is hard to accommodate. In some of the finest passages one still feels that Verdi is the prisoner of operatic conventions.

Curiously, it is a passage that arises out of these conventions which may be the point where the opera captures the unwilling Shakespearean. At the discovery of Duncan's murder comes one of those concerted pieces, with the whole stage one great sea of song and the music rising with a powerful surge of emotion, with which at least one of the acts in an Italian opera of that period was supposed to end. The prayer (*O gran Dio*) is followed by a lamentation, marked

Following Macbeth, *Verdi had long wanted to compose another Shakespearean opera, but it was nearly 40 years later when he began work on the masterpiece* Otello.

grandioso and irresistible in spite of (or perhaps because of) the fact that it is in compound time and almost like a waltz. The essence of Italian opera is in that, and to the newcomer it is likely to bring a genuine first intimation of the power of this strange art.

OTELLO

By 1884 when Verdi began work on what he called *il progetto di cioccolata* ('the chocolate venture') he had a lifetime of achievement behind him, and the best was yet to be. He had long wished to undertake an opera on another of the Shakespeare tragedies. He rejected a libretto on *Hamlet* on the grounds that it presented Hamlet himself as too conventional a hero-figure. *King Lear* was always in his mind, to the very end of his life, but he was awed by the subject and nothing came of it. *Othello* was suggested to him in 1879, when he also met the remarkable man who was to be his librettist, Arrigo Boito (1842-1918). He combined literary and musical talents, as the composer of *Mefistofele* (1868) and a writer and translator whose early work included a libretto on *Hamlet* (*Amleto*) for the composer and conductor, Franco Faccio.

His concept of the librettist's job was a high one, rejecting the very term 'libretto' as denoting 'conventional art' and substituting 'tragedy'. By this time the musical conventions had also given way to a more flexible form where the set-pieces became subsumed in a new dramatic realism. The masterpiece which *Otello* turned out to be was a product of the time and its conditions as well as the work of the writer and the great musician.

As a dramatist, Boito valued the dramatic Unities and saw that Shakespeare's play conformed very closely, with the exception of its first act, set in Venice. He was also a man of the theater and realized that the storm at sea would make a splendidly vigorous and dramatic opening to the opera. The first act in Shakespeare enables us to see Othello as the solid, reliable, self-controlled man that he appears to be; this comes to us in the opera through the massive phrases of the brief solo in which he announces the victory at sea. Boito also incorporated into the Love Duet of Act 1 some of the lines from Shakespeare's first act which tell of the strange courtship. The Italian translates almost literally into Shakespeare's

> *She lov'd me for the dangers I had pass'd,*
> *And I lov'd her that she did pity them.*
>
> (*Othello* I iii 167-8)

The Iago of the opera has a solo with no counterpart in Shakespeare, a 'Credo' in which he expounds his belief in innate evil and in the falsehood of any kind of eschatology. Verdi considered the interpolation 'truly Shakespearean', and he also welcomed the *Ave Maria* which follows Desdemona's 'Willow Song'. For the rest there is a remarkable fidelity to the play. The temptation scene follows Shakespeare closely; the arrival of the Venetian ambassador, Lodovico, is marvellously worked into the great ensemble of Act 3; and the scene of Otello's death proceeds with a

Like many before and after, Verdi and Boito were fascinated by Falstaff, around whom they created their most charming opera.

dignity and poignancy in which genuine tragedy is achieved. When the score was completed Verdi wrote to Boito: *It is finished! Salute to us (and to Him)*. Whether 'He' was Shakespeare or God is not certain.

FALSTAFF

The further and perhaps greater miracle of *Falstaff* followed. It took three years in the writing, and at times the old man told his friends that he doubted whether he would live to finish it. But in his 80th year it had its première at La Scala, Milan, and Verdi was there to rehearse.

The opera is essentially based on *The Merry Wives of Windsor*, but for Falstaff himself Boito also drew on the two parts of *King Henry IV*. The Honor monologue, delivered in the opera for the edification of Pistol and Bardolph, derives from the soliloquy in Part 1 (V i 127-140), the passage in praise of good wine at the start of Act 3 arises out of the *sherris-sack* speech in Part 2 (IV iii 85-122); and the famous miniature arietta *Quand'ero paggio* is suggested by Falstaff's remark to Hal that at his age he *could have crept into any alderman's thumb-ring* Part 1 (II iv 321). The incorporation of such material from the history plays has the effect of making the tun of man a fuller character than is presented in *The Merry Wives of Windsor*. The opera is not given its title for nothing.

OTHER 19TH-CENTURY OPERAS

Verdi and Berlioz are the masters among the composers of Shakespearean opera, certainly in the 19th century. But others survive, even some which had been confidently written-off in the period of reaction against all things 'Victorian'. The *Hamlet* of Ambroise Thomas (1811-96) was considered by Verdi to be so bad as to constitute an insult to Shakespeare. Certainly its ending has some surprises, as Hamlet dies at Ophelia's funeral; yet such a development is scarcely more outrageous than many of the alterations made in English acting versions of the 18th century. At any rate, Thomas' opera has star-parts for baritone-Hamlet and coloratura-soprano-Ophelia, and even without 'stars' to fill the roles it has been respectfully received at revivals.

Its première at Paris in 1868 had been preceded by that of Gounod's *Roméo et Juliette* in the previous year. This too had its detractors ('bourgeois' is the deadly term here), yet it still reappears from time to time, usually with grateful acknowledgment, even outside France where it has remained a favorite with singers and the public. Always in danger of turning into a love-duet with interludes, it nevertheless coheres dramatically and remembers Shakespeare in Mercutio's 'Queen Mab' solo, Roméo's perception of light from yonder window, and Juliette's *O Roméo, pourquoi ce nom est-il le tien?*

Sturdier than these French romantic tragedies, very probably, is the other well-known Falstaff opera, Otto Nicolai's *Die lustigen Weiber von Windsor* (1849). Nicolai was not the first in Germany to write on the subject. Karl Ditters von Dittersdorf (1739-99), a popular Austrian composer, called his opera *Die lustigen Weiber von Windsor und der dicke Hanns* (1796), and in 1799 Mozart's rival Antonio Salieri (1750-1825) had a great success with his Falstaff opera, given two alternative titles: *Le tre burle Falstaff*

Gounod's Roméo et Juliette *sometimes lacks drama, but has romantic coherence and is appropriately poetic.*

and *Der dreimal Gefoppte*.

Nicolai's merry wives share the center of the stage with Falstaff, and this is an opera primarily of situation rather than character. The libretto follows Shakespeare fairly closely, though the *dramatis personæ* are reduced from 20 to ten, and in Windsor Forest Anna and Fenton appear as Titania and Oberon. Musically, the promise of the famous Overture is fulfilled in the frequently enchanting score. Like Gounod, Nicolai also suffered criticism, the German equivalent of 'bourgeois' being 'Biedermeier'; it was not to trouble the composer unduly as he died, in his 39th year, only two months after the successful première.

THE 20TH CENTURY

The 20th century has also produced its share of Shakespearean operas, including two Falstaff operas from England. Gustav Holst (1874-1934) and Ralph Vaughan Williams (1872-1958) had so much in common that it is not surprising to find them drawn towards the same Shakespearean character – Falstaff. Their operas are complementary in the sense that Holst's *At The Boar's Head* (1924) draws on *King Henry IV* Part 1, and Vaughan Williams' *Sir John in Love* (1929) is another opera based on *The Merry Wives of Windsor*.

Holst described his work as 'a musical interlude in one act'. He wrote his own libretto, or, rather, selected Shakespeare's words, so that Falstaff's entrance is with *A plague of all cowards, I say* carrying on through the impersonation scene, neatly interpolating Hal's *I know you all*, and Sonnets 12 and 19. A soldiers' chorus tells of the *stirring times*, and Falstaff and Bardolph duly join up, taking tearful farewell of Doll Tearsheet and the Hostess. The opera ends delightfully as Bardolph returns and *in a hoarse whisper* tells the Hostess, *Bid Mistress Tearsheet come to my master*. The little opera is a subtle piece of work, with an interweaving of folk tunes among much that is strong and characteristic in invention: no 'Biedermeier' touch here.

SIR JOHN IN LOVE
About his Falstaff opera Vaughan Williams wrote: *My chief object in* Sir John in Love *has been to fit this wonderful comedy with, I trust, not unpleasant music.* What is notable about the music — apart from the fact that the composer's modest intentions are more than fulfilled — is that it contains so much that looks ahead to major and much later works, such as the Fifth Symphony and even occasionally the Sixth. It also captures a great deal that is Elizabethan and Shakespearean, as in the portly sail of *Falstaff will learn the honour of the age* or in *Go thy ways, old Jack*, embodying the very spirit of Windsor.

Vaughan Williams wrote his own libretto, and took the opportunity to interpolate some of his favorite Elizabethan lyrics, borrowing *When daisies pied* from *Love's Labour's Lost*, and *Sigh no more, ladies* from *Much Ado About Nothing*, with verses by Fletcher, Sidney, Jonson, Middleton and all: a posthumous reopening of the Mermaid tavern, with the *poets dead and gone* making their offering to Shakespeare, the master-spirit of the age.

Benjamin Britten's A Midsummer Night's Dream *is probably English opera's most enduring garland for Shakespeare.*

ANTONY AND CLEOPATRA

Samuel Barber's *Antony and Cleopatra* was commissioned for the opening of the new Metropolitan Opera House of New York in 1966, and is only just now resurfacing after being nearly drowned by the magnitude of the occasion. It resembles Walton's *Troilus and Cressida* (1954) (based on Chaucer's poem, not Shakespeare's play) in attempting to continue the grand line of 19th-century opera into the second half of the 20th. The libretto rearranges Shakespeare adroitly, though Enobarbus is never properly established, so that his death means less than it should, and it does not risk the Clown as the humble instrument of death. Musically, it is no match for Cleopatra's *infinite variety*; but it makes enough of this, the richest of all the plays, to make one wonder why it has not been a favorite among the many who have searched Shakespeare for operatic subjects.

BENJAMIN BRITTEN

If the succession of master-spirit were traced from poetry to music, and from Elizabethan to the present age, the election (in England) might well light upon Benjamin Britten. His two Shakespearean operas, *The Rape of Lucretia* (1946) and *A Midsummer Night's Dream* (1960), are 'Shakespearean' not only in subject but in integrity: like Shakespeare with his imagery, Britten with his motifs and unity of design makes a close-knit artistic creation, yielding more to the active listener on each encounter. *The Rape of Lucretia* has a libretto by Ronald Duncan, author of *The Way to the Tomb*. Its lines, frequently memorable, not infrequently embarrassing, are the writer's own and not from Shakespeare's poem.

For *A Midsummer Night's Dream*, Britten and Peter Pears made their own adaptation, involving some respectful surgery. In one sense the task was simplified, for, as Britten said, the play 'already has a strong verbal music of its own'. Getting it into manageable shape 'entailed simplifying and cutting an extremely complex story'. Accordingly the opera starts with *Over hill, over dale*, omits the Athens scene, and then reduces the lovers' dialogues so skilfully that one hardly notices what is happening. Resourceful as ever, Britten gives Puck his domi-

nance by making him a speaking-part for a boy-actor, while Oberon's more sinister other-worldliness is expressed in the distinctive tones of a powerful counter-tenor. The masterstroke is very probably the provision of musical comedy in the Pyramus and Thisbe performance, where parodies of Verdi and Schoenberg become a counterpart (or at least a suitable alternative) to Shakespeare's *very tragical mirth*.

LEAR

The opera that remains for immediate mention is one that takes Shakespeare into the 20th century in the way that theatrical producers of our age have done. Aribert Reimann's *Lear* (1978) has as well prepared a libretto as any since Boito, and the score, remarkably consistent in idiom, has a concentrated and powerful tragic depth. Edgar's disguise as mad Tom makes a chilling use of the falsetto voice, while the Fool (which conventionally tempted falsetto-treatment) is a speaking part.

His comments include a reference to Gloucester as *Des Königs Spiegelbild* ('a mirror-image of the King'), and there are other interpretative touches, less explicit but still telling, in the music: for instance when the King says *Hier bin ich, ein armer, alter Mann* ('Here I am, a poor, old man'), the music, by reference to the proud division-of-kingdom solo at the beginning of the opera, comments that he has brought this on himself. The part of Lear, written for Dietrich Fischer-Dieskau, loses something of the gentler elements without a solo corresponding to *poor naked wretches* in the storm, but tenderness enters with a fine lyrical solo for Cordelia amid the uneasily brooding peacefulness of Shakespeare's Act IV vii, and there is beauty and pathos in the duet for father and daughter that follows. Still more moving is the finale, as the earthly music of grief overlaps with an unearthly tingling sound that fades very slowly as the curtain falls.

SEE ALSO: Ch 4 98-9, 102-5, 118-21, 128-9, 130-3, 136-7, 142-3, 158-5, 170-1, 174-5

OTHER MUSICAL INTERPRETATIONS

Opera has done well by Shakespeare, and it is surprising that ballet has not done better than it has. Several Shakespeare-based ballets have been arranged, such as the *Hamlet* which Robert Helpmann choreographed to Tchaikovsky's concert-overture. The one full-length ballet of real note is Prokofiev's *Romeo and Juliet* which makes the most, as does Berlioz's dramatic symphony (and indeed the modernized version of the play in Leonard Bernstein's *West Side Story*), of the balletic character of the family feuds and street brawls. *West Side Story*, incidentally, provides a reminder of the many adaptations of Shakespeare for other stage purposes. *Kiss me, Kate*, the musical by Cole Porter (1948), is based on *The Taming of the Shrew*, with 'Brush up your Shakespeare' as one of its wittier numbers. Energetic rock-musicals such as *Catch my Soul* (*Othello*) and an all-black musical version of *The Two Gentlemen of Verona* have also enjoyed success.

INCIDENTAL MUSIC

Apart from the setting of individual songs already discussed, incidental music requires mention. Mendelssohn's *A Midsummer Night's Dream* gave the cue for many more, and, especially in the late 19th century, music was in demand to cover the elaborate scene-changes in their realistic productions. Edward German's scores for *King Henry VIII* and *King Richard III* are good examples of music in the English theater at the time. In modern productions there has been some imaginative writing such as Guy Woolfenden's for the Royal Shakespeare Theatre at Stratford-upon-Avon (well represented by a suite called *Sounds and Sweet Ayres* 1978).

Into this category come the film scores of William Walton. For Laurence Olivier's films of *Henry V* (1944), *Hamlet* (1948), and *Richard III* (1955) Walton provided music that survives in its own right while being wonderfully apt for its purposes. He had previously written for the film of *As You*

Leonard Bernstein's West Side Story, *a musical version of* Romeo and Juliet *set in modern America, was a box-office hit on both sides of the Atlantic and a successful film.*

Like It (1935) – his first Shakespearean film score – with Elisabeth Bergner as Rosalind, Olivier as Orlando: oddly, this seems not to be remembered or collected when these things appear on phonograph records. The film itself is only memorable for Walton's music and the presence of Olivier.

There is not much these days that fails to find a place in the record catalogues. They remind us, at most turns of the page, of the Shakespearean connection, and of much that cannot be covered in a single chapter. There are orchestral works such as Elgar's *Falstaff*, songs from improbable sources like Strauss, Sibelius and Stravinsky. A recent reissue of recordings by an Italian tenor of the 1920s has two solos from Wolf-Ferrari's strange opera, *Sly*, where Christopher lives a tragic life of his own, ending in suicide. The Choir of King's College, Cambridge, and a group of singers

called Swingle II have both recorded choral settings, delightful ones too, of Shakespeare songs by Vaughan Williams.

CODA

If one had to choose a single composition to represent Shakespeare and music in combination and interaction, it would be hard to improve on the *Serenade to Music* which Vaughan Williams wrote for Sir Henry Wood's Jubilee in 1938. The lovers' scene from the last act of *The Merchant of Venice* supplies the text. The moonlit serenity is disturbed by the trumpets which *wake Diana with a hymn*, and for the minor key of *the man that hath no music in himself*. But it opens and closes with *soft stillness and the night*, which *become the touches of sweet harmony*, and its spirit is imbued from first to last with a love of words and music: a spirit well-tuned to Shakespeare's own.

Laurence Olivier's Henry V, Hamlet *and* Richard III *are among the most memorable of Shakespearean films, and William Walton wrote all the scores. The wonderfully apt and atmospheric music also stands in its own right.*

SEE ALSO: Ch 4 96-9, 102-5, 112-3, 122-5, 128-9, 158-61, Ch 8 242-5

CHAPTER 8

SHAKESPEARE ON FILM

From the first public displays of motion pictures nearly a century ago, when film was a medium capable of recording only the visual scene, and with acting limited to the mimetic expression and movement of the performers, Shakespeare's more popularly presented plays were drawn upon, if only for short scenes extracted from the total action. These brief films involved the well-known characters and they were at times performed by star players from the theater. But the silent cinema, which was to last some 30 years until 1928, when sound-on-film became at last technically viable, scarcely served Shakespeare well, for the obvious reason that the theater is the place for the performed word.

THE ADVANTAGES OF FILM

However, there are certain important aspects of Shakespeare's work that have made it attractive to the cinema. Because the plays were largely written for presentation on the virtually bare stages of the public theaters of his time, Shakespeare was entirely free to create a continuity of action that was widely spaced out in place as well as time. In *Antony and Cleopatra*, to take an extreme case, the locations, with 42 changes of scene, involve settings in Alexandria, Rome, Messina, Misenum, Syria, Athens, and Actium, to say nothing of battles on land and sea. This could well be the scenario for a spectacular film. The audience, cued by a few words, knew where it was and imagined the rest.

Where the setting seemed magical, as in *A Midsummer Night's Dream* or *The Tempest*, the imagination of a responsive audience creates the best of all settings, inspired by the atmosphere of the play. But for the most part Shakespeare's plays have gained as a result of the better settings devised for them in the picture-stage theaters from the later 18th century onward,

and again, when appropriately designed, from the much more elaborate scenery devised for the Shakespearean cinema. Again, the sheer scale of Shakespeare's action only too often goes far beyond the bounds of even the most spectacular theatrical production, and Shakespeare initially felt the need to apologize for this:

> *On your imaginary forces work.*
> *Suppose within the girdle of these walls*
> *Are now confin'd two mighty*
> *   monarchies, . . .*
> *Into a thousand parts divide one man,*
> *And make imaginary puissance;*
> *Think, when we talk of horses, that*
> *   you see them. . . .*

But there are other matters of importance in the adaptation of the plays to the screen. Shakespeare wrote for a theater where many members of the audience were relatively mobile during the performance, especially in the pit; where many looked down closely on the action from the theater's gallery seats near the stage; while a few were often seated on the stage itself. Shakespeare's developing mastery of touch shows not only in a growing freedom of form in both verse and prose, but also in the increasing variety in scale. His range extended from a most delicate intimacy to the heights of stage rhetoric.

The cinema can offer varieties of visual and aural presentation from the close-up for soliloquies (presented perhaps with unmoving lips as spoken thought), to large-scale scenes with massed crowds or armies necessary as auditors for such public speechmaking, as occurs in *Julius Cæsar*, *Coriolanus*, or *King Henry V*. Sir Peter Hall once said that Shakespeare's dialogue is often heard to best advantage when spoken quietly, as in a room, rather than in a great auditorium, and that this variety of vocal distancing can readily be provided by the cinema.

In the best of the Shakespearean films

we are about to discuss, the aim has been to render as clear as possible to a modern audience what Shakespeare's dialogue, written almost four centuries ago, is intended to convey, and the continued closeness of the performer to his or her listener can assist this greatly.

Nevertheless, it has to be recognized that the nature of film is observation of human behavior in all its aspects, with speech as a natural part of this rather than an art in its own right. The film medium

The Warner Brothers film of Othello *(1965) starred Laurence Olivier and provides a record of the British National Theatre production.*

has therefore to be used with great restraint in Shakespearean adaptation in order to lay stress on the values of what is said as against the visual attractions of the action. It is the nature of this compromise in the service of Shakespeare that will reveal the imagination and skill of those who attempt to bring the plays to the screen.

SHAKESPEARE'S PLAYS ADAPTED AS SILENT FILMS

That Shakespeare's work should be continuously adapted during the period of the silent film (that is, from the 1890s to the late 1920s) might seem like some kind of contradiction in terms. Shakespeare's most celebrated characters were to appear over the span of a quarter century as interpreted by famous players – but deprived of the very speech that makes Shakespeare remain the supreme dramatist writing in the English language. The plays were mined for their familiar stories, and research has shown that approaching 500 adaptations of one kind or another were produced during the so-called silent period of the cinema's early history.

Shakespeare's plays carried no fees for film rights, and the film-makers felt secure in the knowledge that the key characters and basic stories were well enough known.

What may seem absurd is that the great majority of these early films attempted to present the action of the plays in a much abbreviated form.

Certain of these early, silent films have a basic historical value which should spare their being dismissed as mere curiosities in the development of Shakespearean presentation. Many starred notable players from the theater, whose style of performance reflects the manner and choreography, the gesture and 'body language' of the contemporary theater. The décor and costuming, too, come direct from the theater of the period, the cinema being used as a recording device rather than as an art in its own right. Though we may reject the great majority of those surviving prints of the many different contracted versions of popular plays, we do well to pay closer attention to certain valuable recordings of notable theatrical performances.

Among these is a glimpse of Sarah Bernhardt in her controversial, turn-of-the-century appearance as Hamlet (in the duel scene with Laertes recorded for the Paris Exposition of 1900 and accompanied at the time by sound effects), and another of the great actor, Mounet-Sully in the graveyard

Sir Frank Benson as Richard III, filmed at Stratford in 1911. Captions occupy about half the film.

scene from *Hamlet*, made around 1913.

More important are two British films, one of Sir Frank Benson and the other of Sir Johnston Forbes-Robertson from the period 1911-13, both of which survive intact in the British National Film Archive. The first shows a succession of tableaux-like scenes from Benson's production of *King Richard III* at Stratford-upon-Avon in 1911, 1,385 feet in length, with captions occupying some half of this footage. The film shows very clearly what his production looked like; it was shot at Stratford in sections during the span of a week, the company working on the film during the mornings, while appearing on the stage at night. Benson had been trained by Sir Henry Irving at the Lyceum during the later years of the 19th century, and believed in strong gesticulation.

In 1913, the same year as Forbes-Robertson's *Hamlet*, Harry Baur, the distinguished French actor, made his first film appearance as Shylock in a French version of *The Merchant of Venice*, two reels of which survive in the British National Film Archive. Similarly, two reels only survive of Matheson Lang as Shylock in a six-reel British version of *The Merchant of Venice* (1916); Lang's stage settings were transported from the theater to a glass-roofed studio outside London, and the film remained a straight recording of the play's action with no attempt at screen adaptation.

The 1920s added little prestige to the Shakespearean silent film, probably because the medium was by now well established in its own right and did not have to wear the borrowed plumage of Shakespeare. The more outstanding adaptations, of which two survive, were to be German: *Othello* (1922) directed by Dmitri Bukhovetsky, and starring Emil Jannings and Werner Krauss; *The Merchant of Venice* (1923), directed by Peter Paul Felner, greatly expanded from the original and retitled, *The Jew of Mestre*, with Krauss as Shylock (renamed Mordecai) and Henny Porten as Portia (renamed Beatrice); and *A Midsummer Night's Dream* (1925), directed by Hans Neumann.

FORBES-ROBERTSON'S HAMLET
Like Sir Frank Benson, Forbes-Robertson had been trained by Irving, but he was more restrained in movement. His refined voice, with its measured rhythms and clear articulation, has also been preserved for us in phonograph recordings completed late in life. In 1913, Cecil Hepworth, Britain's leading producer of the time, undertook a recording of this notable actor's long-established production of *Hamlet* as performed just before his retirement. Irving's stage designer, Hawes Craven, executed the sets in the style of the late-19th-century theater, but several scenes for the film were shot on outdoor locations, notably at Lulworth Cove in Dorset; here a set representing the castle at Elsinore was constructed, and Hamlet is seen confronting his ghostly father, a superimposed, see-through figure. The film runs one hour and 40 minutes at silent speed, and although the acting is in its measured style more suitable for the stage than the screen, it preserves what can be considered the best visual rendering of the play as it was presented about a century ago, a great deal of the footage being occupied by lines from the text presented, silent-film style, by means of full-frame captions. Forbes-Robertson's stance and movements are graceful and dignified, and quite free from any gross overacting.

THE SOUND FILM: ENGLISH LANGUAGE ADAPTATIONS

It is one of the curiosities of film history that Hollywood's most celebrated couple, Mary Pickford and Douglas Fairbanks Senior, their marriage soon to collapse, chose as their first sound film a lively adaptation of *The Taming of the Shrew* (1929), made 'with additional dialogue by Sam Taylor', who directed the film. The play was much cut and treated farcically, Katherina well able to handle Fairbanks' rough, but basically good-humored Petruchio, her final speech of capitulation delivered with a knowing wink to the other ladies at the feast.

The least distinctive of the earlier sound film adaptations was, unhappily, the only British one, the studio-bound *As You Like It* (1936), Paul Czinner's production with his wife, Elisabeth Bergner, as an infuriatingly arch and mannered Rosalind. Notable only

Above: The Taming of the Shrew *(1929) starring Mary Pickford and Douglas Fairbanks Senior was one of the first Shakespearean sound films. The text was much cut, but Laurence Irving's sets are notable.*

Below: *The casting of* A Midsummer Night's Dream *(1935) was intriguing. Mickey Rooney, aged 11, makes a lively Puck, and James Cagney a vigorous Bottom.*

was the presence of Laurence Olivier as Orlando, Henry Ainley as the Duke, and Leon Quartermaine as Jaques, while William Walton composed his first Shakespearean film score. More interesting were the two immediately preceding Shakespearean films, both made in America, *A Midsummer Night's Dream* (1935), directed by Max Reinhardt, the distinguished German emigré stage director and a fellow-refugee from Germany, William Dieterle, well established in Hollywood; and *Romeo and Juliet* (1936), directed by George Cukor, with Norma Shearer (aged 36) and Leslie Howard (aged 43) as the juvenile lovers, a richly caparisoned MGM production, with John Barrymore as Mercutio. Both films, though substantially cutting the text and developing as much visual action as possible, still remain enjoyable.

A Midsummer Night's Dream is treated as much like ballet as possible; the choreography for the fairies is like a magic dream in a Disney cartoon feature, with generous appropriation of Mendelssohn's romantic 19th-century score. The atmosphere of the play is developed in the manner associated with the late-19th-century theater, and carried forward with stage elaboration by Reinhardt in the early 20th century. Perhaps the virtue of these adaptations is that in both cases they were conceived as films in their own right; although the cutting of the text was wholesale, enough is left to make the films markedly Shakespearean. Victor Jory (with his stage experience) does well by what is left of Oberon's poetry.

LAURENCE OLIVIER: BALANCING THE INTERESTS OF SHAKESPEARE AND THE FILM:

Laurence Olivier has explained that he learnt some basic points of technique in the effective adaptation of Shakespeare to film from the productions of the 1930s. He maintains in particular that speeches requiring climactic delivery in big voice should always be filmed at a distance from the actor, pulling the camera away as vocal delivery grows louder, contrary to basic film technique, requiring climactic moment normally to be in close-shot. He also

realized that Shakespeare's many quieter, more intimate scenes could be pitched like true conversation in low-key tones with remarkable effect, including close observation of facial expression.

HENRY V (1944)

King Henry V is a chronicle play featuring in turn all ranks of English society – the King, his lords and advisers, the army, its common soldiers as well as its representative officers (English, Scottish, Welsh, Irish), and the London ragtag and bobtail (Bardolph, Nym, and Pistol) from the good old times when Henry V was the wayward Prince Hal, and Falstaff was living at the Boar's Head tavern in Eastcheap. In addition, there are the scenes of the decadent French court circle. To this, Olivier added a full-scale expanded action for the battle of Agincourt, prior to the scenes when the French and English court circles are seen together in postwar amity, and Henry woos the French princess in homely terms.

All this variety of background and action is bound together by the descriptive

Olivier's Richard III *was shot in color with stylized sets – a lengthy film full of fine touches.*

speeches of the Chorus, who acts as narrator, seeing the complex action in its broad historical perspective. Olivier cut about one third of the play's text, including words prejudicial, in modern eyes, to the heroic, chivalric stature of the King – such as his threats to the innocent citizens of Harfleur and his commands to his soldiers to kill their prisoners.

The memorable scenes in this warm, virile, patriotic film version of *King Henry V* are many, and must include the charge of the French knights at Agincourt, into whose ranks the English bowmen launch their whirring flights of arrows, and Henry's speeches to his men before battle, spoken with full-voiced vigor by Laurence Olivier. On a more intimate level are the lament by Mistress Quickly (Freda Jackson) for Falstaff, whose death she describes in simple, common speech, or the scene in the English camp at night, with the soldier speaking in a West Country accent about what the wars mean to the common re-cruits, followed by the King's own speech after his nighttime wanderings through the camp in disguise, testing the metal of his men. The idiomatic variety as well as the greatness of Shakespeare's writing is shown to highest advantage in this, the first outstanding version of a Shakespearean play to be filmed using the powers of the screen to enhance the human and dramatic values of the play.

HAMLET (1948)

Although it was to take five years of distribution before the production costs of *Henry V* were recovered, its instant success (it was released parallel to the liberation of France) led to the production of Olivier's *Hamlet* with the same designers (Carmen Dillon, Roger Furse) and composer (William Walton). The style of *Hamlet* was to be very different: after the color and panache of *Henry V*, *Hamlet* was filmed in stark black-and-white, with austerely conceived settings with minimal furnishings; the halls

THE FOUR PHASES OF *HENRY V*
Laurence Olivier adapted the play for the screen in successive phases, each with its own distinctive visual style:

(1) The opening and closing scenes (framing the film as a whole) are presented as if the play is being performed in an Elizabethan public theater, reconstructed realistically.

(2) The scene then abandons the theater for full-scale studio settings (with a more or less naturalistic appearance) for the tavern and the London streets.

(3) The scenes at the French court are characterized by more artificial settings, furnishings and costuming, with a decorative medieval appearance derived from the illustrations for the Duc de Berry's *Book of Hours* and for Froissart's *Chronicles*.

(4) For the Battle of Agincourt Olivier used the wholly naturalistic countryside locations on an estate near Dublin in neutral Eire, where men from the Eirean Home Guard stood in alike for Henry's English army and the French knights-at-arms. (The film was made, it must be remembered, when Britain was wholly occupied with preparations for D-Day.)

All these variants are bound together by the narrative speeches of Chorus, backed once the theater is left, by appropriate generalized scenes. The effect of the whole film, with its rich coloration, is enhanced by William Walton's finely heroic and cheerful score, perhaps his best composed for a Shakespearean film, and Robert Krasker's brilliant Technicolor camerawork.

stonewalled and lofty, columned like a cathedral, and the rooms permitted only some occasional, formal medieval décor. There are deep-focus vistas down arched corridors, emphasizing Hamlet's isolation and melancholy. The castle ramparts are like half-lit stairways and stone-flagged platforms set high in pitchblack darkness and floating mist, photographed in constant shadow by Desmond Dickinson. Walton's music is similarly austere and grand, with the occasional use of courtly period music.

Working on the text with his friend, the theater critic Alan Dent, Olivier cut *Hamlet* even more drastically than he had *King Henry V*. Patently, as in most theatrical productions, a great deal of the text had to go, but some of the omissions became especially controversial – the loss of such key characters as Fortinbras, Rosencrantz and Guildenstern (whose interchanges with Hamlet are so revealing of his character), the loss of two of Hamlet's soliloquies (*O, what a rogue and peasant slave am I!* and *How all occasions do inform against me*).

Some words in the text are modernized for clarity; for example, 'persist' for 'persever' and 'hinders' for 'lets'. Sections of the play are performed in mime – Hamlet's distracted visit to Ophelia is played with her description for Polonius in voice-over; Hamlet's adventures at sea are pictured, again with his account of them to Horatio in voice-over. The play scene is presented entirely in mime with pastiche music in medieval style. Hamlet's soliloquies are partially played voice-over as spoken thought – only breaking midway through into direct speech (*and yet within a month . . .; perchance to dream . . .*).

The film occasionally makes use of special effects: Hamlet's fearful reaction to his Father's ghost, with its skull-like, helmeted visage, makes the screen-image pulsate to the loud thud of his heartbeats; Yorick's skull bears the illusion of a living being in Hamlet's eyes. Olivier's performance turns to bravura whenever the moment warrants it, culminating in the ten minute duel with Laertes, and the final, 12-foot leap down on to Claudius, standing transfixed before Hamlet's flying sword plunges into his body. If the film has a technical

fault, it is the overuse of the mobile camera, so constantly tracking, panning, lifting skyward, or craning up to peer down on the grouped characters from on high. But the movements can be splendid, as in the wordless play scene, where the camera glides slowly back and forth behind the seated figures of the King and Queen, like a creeping spy.

RICHARD III (1955)

Richard III was made at the invitation of Sir Alexander Korda. Olivier's magnificent postwar stage performance for the National Theatre in Shakespeare's first great star role inspired the offer, and faced him with the problem, in his own words, of 'reducing the length, elucidating the plot, unraveling irrelevancies, and relating the result to the type of audience'. *Richard III* has 'an absolute delta of plot', with Richard as the spider (either as Gloucester or as King) in the center of the web; with drastic cutting, rearranging, and clarifying, the film still runs two and three quarter hours.

Olivier took the final scene of *King Henry VI* (Part 3) (V vii), the coronation of Edward IV (Cedric Hardwicke), attended by Gloucester and Clarence (John Gielgud) to prepare for Gloucester's six-minute soliloquy (*Now is the winter of our discontent . . .*) with some additional lines from *Henry VI*, all to show in a brilliantly conceived continuity Richard's cynical plot to weave his way through murder to the throne, all spoken with smiling self-approval straight off the screen to the audience, but culminating in a paranoiac outburst that reveals the pathological roots of his nature. Olivier's famous make-up, the leering, long-nosed face, the crooked back, the medieval costume with long, pointed shoes, make Gloucester a spider-like figure.

For this film, the technique derives much from television, emphasizing Richard's direct and knowingly humorous confidences with the audience; in the manner of television production at the time, the key sets (the Palace, the Westminster area, the Tower of London) are made physically contiguous, so that a few paces move the cast from one location to the other. Much of the initial plotting is made clear by turning

Orson Welles's Macbeth *is full of powerful images, sometimes to the point of melodrama. Welles's personality dominates the film.*

Richard into a narrator, prying around, spying through windows, observing this person, pointing out that. The complex situation is unwoven before our eyes as much as in our ears, a scene for Richard to 'bustle in'. Anne is as much hypnotized by this scheming monster as she is blackmailed into consenting to marry her late husband's murderer, his mood changing swiftly from malicious humor to sadism and back again. Once King, Richard turns on his closest aide, Buckingham (Ralph Richardson) and, all humor gone, becomes a ruthless tyrant. His final cornering is like a scene from Bedlam, the bearers of ill tidings rushing in with hand-held torches while Richard rages like a madman.

OTHELLO (1965)

Olivier's only other major Shakespearean appearance for the cinema was in a rendering in 1965 of the celebrated stage production of *Othello*, in which he gave a phenomenal performance of the Moor as a Negro. The film was directed by Stuart Burge and based directly on John Dexter's quatercentennial production for the British National Theatre, following the stage version closely, and running almost three hours. One is aware in long shot that the sets are stage sets reconstructed in the studio, with entrances and exits into the wings. Olivier does little to adjust the scale of this titanic performance, using big voice when close to the cameras, and film technique as such is employed only in the sense that the camera is placed at variant distances from the players. The film's value lies in its record of Olivier's work as a Shakespearean actor seen at its highest peak.

ORSON WELLES

Orson Welles brought to film-making an extensive if still youthful experience both in the theater and radio drama during the 1930s, making in his first film, *Citizen Kane* (1941) one of the established masterpieces of the cinema. His approach to Shakespeare was at once imaginative and unorthodox; this was made clear in his theater production of *Macbeth* with an all-black cast, set in Haiti with the witches practising voodoo, and also in his modern-dress of *Julius Cæsar*, in which he played Brutus.

MACBETH

Working on a very low budget, he made in 1948 a film version in 23 days of his recent theater production of *Macbeth*, in which his concept of the play's basic theme, pre-announced at the beginning of the film, was that it showed the 'agents of Chaos, priests of hell and magic' exploiting human ambition as a plot against 'Christian law and order'. To emphasize this he created a new character – that of a monk, opposed to the witches, giving him lines borrowed from such subsidiary characters as Ross, whom he suppressed in this much-cut, speeded up, but still strikingly conceived adaptation of the play.

The film is primarily set in a strange, primitive structure, a circle of rocky crags; the interiors are more like rock-hewn caverns than rooms in castles. Water drips from the ceilings. The composition of the images is often formalized – the men-at-arms are constantly grouped in stage-like patterns holding aloft tall, slender lances. As in *Citizen Kane*, deep-focus shots exploit foreground figures in massive close-up (especially Macbeth), seen as framing supporting characters sharp-focused but small and distant in the background. Macbeth's bloodied hands after the murder of Duncan (which occurs almost immediately after the King's arrival) are thrust forward like the hands of a giant to the camera; thunder rolls incessantly as one deed of violence follows sharply upon another. Macbeth shouts,

Methought I heard a voice cry, 'Sleep no more;'
not after Duncan's murder but later, as his wife urges him to bed, pleading,

You lack the season of all natures, sleep.
When Banquo's blood-boltered ghost haunts the regal feast, he is seen seated alone at the far end of the long table, all other guests having vanished in Macbeth's terror-stricken sight.

Although in scene after scene Welles overdoes his stylized, melodramatic effects, there is no doubt a powerful, if overwrought imagination is at work; witness the end of the sleepwalking scene, when Lady Macbeth, wakened by her husband's anxious kiss, runs screaming from him down an avenue of stone monoliths, leaping to her death from a cliff-edge. Welles himself called the film a 'violently sketched drawing of a great play'. It is a pity that the sound track is so poorly recorded, and that Welles, who towers physically over the whole production, seems to have indifferent command of the rhythms of Macbeth's speech, in spite of his magnificent voice and overriding personality. His Lady Macbeth, a radio actress, is no match for him, or for the demands of the part.

OTHELLO (1955)

The story of the making of *Othello* (the money always on the point of running out; work on the film constantly postponed, and spread over three years) is entertainingly told by Micheal MacLiammóir in his published diary of the production, *Put Money in Thy Purse*. MacLiammóir, who plays Iago, had first met Welles when, at the age of 16, he had worked for MacLiammóir at Dublin's Gate Theater. The locations in Italy and Morocco (for Cyprus) are striking, a prominent part of the film's visually dramatic quality. The architectural settings are varied and handsome, their beauty almost a drain on the film, which opens with morbid grandeur on the funeral cortège of Othello and Desdemona (Suzanne Cloutier) which proceeds while Iago, haltered, is thrust wild-eyed into a wooden cage and swung aloft over the crowds to witness the outcome of his fell deeds. Black-cowled monks process to a heavy-chorded dirge and the clangor of mourning bells. Welles's theatrical personality, always larger than life, dominates the film, though the sound-recording is again poor.

The cast, however, matches the master more effectively, especially MacLiammóir, whose Iago is an Elizabethan Machiavel, quiet-spoken and cerebrally evil. Fay Compton makes a strong Emilia, but Suzanne Cloutier, ever beautiful and playing for youthful inexperience, fades to insignificance in her scenes with Welles. When Othello strikes her in public, the blow comes as a major shock, the violence achieved by editing. One of the most successful scenes is when Iago murders Roderigo in a cloud of steam – Welles decided to set this scene in a Turkish bath because the hired costumes were not avail-

able, a brilliant example of improvisation. The final smothering of Desdemona takes place in near darkness.

CHIMES AT MIDNIGHT (1965)

Welles's third, most assured Shakespearean film, *Chimes at Midnight*, was created round the figure of Falstaff. It was shot mainly in Spain; Henry V is crowned in Cordova cathedral. Welles loved Falstaff, 'the most completely good old man in all drama,' he said of him, and he made him a magnificent and deeply moving figure, the most broadly humane and arguably the best Falstaff of our time. The film covers a continuity of action involving Falstaff as the principal character and taken primarily from *King Henry IV* (Parts 1 and 2), and *King Henry V*, the tragic climax coming with Hal's rejection and condemnation of Falstaff once he has become King, a bitter blow from which the old man never recovers.

This special Shakespearean continuity had originally been assembled by Welles for a stage production in Belfast in 1960, leaving in just sufficient of the historical background to clarify the situation of Falstaff, Prince Hal and his cold-natured father, King Henry IV, and the rebellion led by Henry Percy (Hotspur) with which he has to contend.

Polanski's Macbeth *(1971) was a violent, and controversial adaptation of the play.*

MACBETH: OTHER SCREEN ADAPTATIONS

Two other English-language adaptations of *Macbeth*, ten years apart, were to be made in Britain. The American George Shaefer's production (1960) with Maurice Evans and Judith Anderson is a cool and somewhat academic rendering both in visual style and performance, though many brilliant talents are involved. Ian Bannen stands out as a vigorous and enraged Macduff. In 1971, however, the Polish film-maker, Roman Polanski (working with Kenneth Tynan) produced a brilliant but controversial adaptation, with the youthful Jon Finch and Francesca Annis as the Macbeths.

Polanski's adaptation is violent and bloody — Cawdor's execution consists of flinging him from a castle height with an iron collar round his neck — except, strangely, for the playing of the two leading characters, their stature more that of a young suburban couple whose obsessive ambitions bring about their collapse, since the assassination of their King lies well beyond their joint strength. The greatness of Shakespeare's tragedy — the downfall of a valiant general at the height of his career, a

WE HAVE HEARD
THE CHIMES AT MIDNIGHT
Falstaff says these words to his senile old friend Shallow at the beginning of the film. Welles saw his adaptation as a 'dark comedy, the story of the betrayal of a friendship', and he concentrates his camera on his key characters – the King, deeply concerned about his wayward son (a chilling performance by John Gielgud), and the little community at the tavern where Falstaff reigns with a doting Mistress Quickly (Margaret Rutherford), Doll Tearsheet (Jeanne Moreau), and his devoted band of nondescript followers. After his rejection by Hal, now King, and banishment from London, Falstaff is left to wander the streets alone – *The King has killed his heart*, says Mistress Quickly. After his death, his coffin is manhandled to its grave on a common handcart. *Chimes at Midnight* is not only one of Welles's finest films, it is also one of the best Shakespearean adaptations for the screen.

man bound closely to a much-beloved wife, both lured into betrayal of their royal benefactor by their superstitious belief in the witches' prophecies – was not within the scope of these two relatively untried players.

Polanski makes the error of letting us see the Macbeths in bed together, and even of presenting Lady Macbeth in the nude in the sleepwalking scene. Jon Finch speaks his lines, often effectively presented as voice-over, at urgent speed, missing the dire, satanic poetry of Macbeth in his naturalistic delivery. Duncan, a middle-aged warrior king, joins in a festive dance with his hostess; one wonders how this alert and active man can let himself be murdered. And in this adaptation we witness the murder itself, which is surely against Shakespeare's dramatic intent. The scintillating image of Macbeth's *dagger of the mind* seems another error of judgment, lessening the hallucinatory impact.

There is, however, an interesting development of Ross as an Iago-like, sardonic messenger of ill; appearing as third murderer, he is witness to, if not actually participant in the killing of Banquo. He bears ill news in turn to both Lady Macduff and later to Macduff himself in England. An effective addition to the play is to make Donalbain jealous of his brother, and seen at the end of the film sneaking off to consult the witches once Malcolm is crowned king.

The concept of the witches seems somewhat alien to the play, where they are conceived as agents of evil; Polanski makes them slovenly members of some Scottish coven – one a bedraggled girl to be seen in the nude. However, the first view of them, foraging for trophies of battle in the wet sands and finding the severed limb of a soldier, is suitably horrifying.

JULIUS CÆSAR:
TWO ADAPTATIONS
Julius Cæsar depends on the casting and interpretation of Brutus; the true central figure of the play, the stoic and rational man, who desires to avoid violence, but who fears what his friend Cæsar may become if made absolute ruler of Rome. Once drawn into the conspiracy, he naturally dominates the conspirators.

MGM (1953)

Joseph L. Mankiewicz and his producer, John Houseman (former associate of Orson Welles) saw their film in black and white as full of contemporary reference to the recently fallen fascist dictatorships of Germany and Italy. (The film was later to be re-released by MGM tinted sepia to simulate color, to its obvious detriment.) In their casting and treatment they wanted to give a modern slant to the interpretation of key characters – James Mason (Brutus), Louis Calhern (Cæsar, played brusquely like a modern gangster boss), Edmond O'Brien (Casca, the cynic), and above all Marlon Brando (Antony), playing as the brutal and cunning demagogue. Brando shouted his lines in spurts of eloquence without regard to rhythm. But at the same time the more traditional Shakespearean style was allowed to be present in the masterly delivery of John Gielgud as Cassius.

The production, played on a plain but massive set, was well-rehearsed in advance of shooting, and then completed expeditiously in the order of the script, the massed crowds in the Forum receiving Antony's rousing orations with carefully rehearsed roars that sounded like 'Sieg Heil' and were specially recorded for Mankiewicz by a

Joseph Mankiewicz's treatment of Julius Cæsar *(1953) was vigorous and effective.*

baseball crowd. The text severely cut, the action was sustained by a heavily orchestrated score by Miklos Rozsa.

Apart from the assassination of Cæsar – all the conspirators but Brutus falling at the same time on their victim, who staggers toward his former friend only to receive Brutus's sword through his body – the two most powerful scenes are those between Cassius and Brutus, the first when Brutus is induced to consider joining the anti-Cæsar faction, and the later quarrel scene, Brutus pacing in anxiety at his friend's accusations.

BRITISH VERSION

Fifteen years after (1969) came the second screen version of the play, produced by the Canadian, Peter Snell, and directed by Stuart Burge, director of *Othello* with Laurence Olivier in 1965. Charlton Heston was anxious to play Antony, while John Gielgud played Cæsar. Heston gives a striking performance as Antony, a very different interpretation from Brando's: he is alert and volatile, claiming his ascendency over the crowds in the Forum by addressing, now one, now another member of the crowd individually until he wins the ears of the whole. Gielgud's natural authority inspires his traditional approach to the playing of Cæsar, and he insisted on restoring lines that had been cut in order to retain, as he asserted, the overall rhythm of the writing. (Excessive cutting can leave the verse truncated, its organic flow lost, appearing like bits and pieces of quotation rather than full-scale dialogue.) Cæsar's assassination is carried out by the conspirators individually, each in turn piercing Cæsar's body in ritual slaughter.

Jason Robards, an actor of powerful personality, was (after much debate) cast as Brutus. Inexperienced in Shakespearean performance, he played Brutus with a modern slant as a man opposed to political assassination and who misjudges the opportunism of Antony, in so doing betraying the coup d'état he has been induced to endorse. Robards speaks his lines naturalistically, portraying Brutus as a deeply worried man but without conveying the inborn greatness the character requires if he is to dominate the play as he should.

249

ROMEO AND JULIET: TWO ADAPTATIONS

As Shakespeare's most romantic tragedy, with its potentiality for continuous, colorful action and exploitation of beautiful Italian locations, *Romeo and Juliet* invites adaptation for the screen. Already staged by MGM with elaborate studio settings, the more modern, postwar approach to film-making on outdoor location led to two Anglo-Italian adaptations, the first (1954) directed by Renato Castellani, and the second (1968) by Franco Zeffirelli.

Laurence Harvey (aged 26) starred in the first with Susan Shentall (virtually unknown) as a beautiful but (in Shakespearean terms) inarticulate Juliet. An experienced actor such as Harvey was needed to carry the film, though he seemed miscast for so romantic a role. In the second film, both the leads were totally inexperienced in speaking Shakespeare – Leonard Whiting (aged 16) and Olivia Hussey (aged 15). The truth of Ellen Terry's remark was proven – 'An actress cannot play Juliet until she is too old to look like Juliet'.

Flora Robson, who played the Nurse in 1954, did her best to coach her Juliet, but Castellani himself cared little for the poetry and concentrated on the story, even scripting scenes himself, notably for Friar Lawrence (Mervyn Johns), a character he developed into a more prominent role. He worked throughout for speed and vividness of action, and many scenes of visual beauty were added – the marriage of the young lovers, for example. Castellani's aim was to achieve overall naturalism and, with Robert Krasker's brilliant Technicolor cinematography, to exploit to the full the beauty of Venice and Siena. John Gielgud spoke the Prologue, giving Shakespeare full flavor, while for Zeffirelli's adaptation, Laurence Olivier spoke both Prologue and Epilogue.

THE RSC AND FILM ADAPTATION

The Royal Shakespeare Company developed film versions of its successful stage productions through the subsidiary, Royal Shakespeare Enterprises, not only to get its work more widely seen internationally in cinemas, but also shown on television. The screen's potentialities for the intimate in

Zeffirelli's Romeo and Juliet *vigorously exploits the action and the Italian locations.*

the playing of Shakespeare had fascinated Peter Hall, who hated what he called the traditional 'vocal varnish' which the old actor-managers had tended to apply in rhetoricizing the lines on the stage. He felt most of Shakespeare was written to be spoken 'very tight to his audience', without 'excessive projection' except for the more obvious big voice speeches.

A MIDSUMMER NIGHT'S DREAM

Peter Hall's Stratford production of *A Midsummer Night's Dream* was adjusted to be re-enacted on location in the 17th-century house and grounds of Compton Verney in Warwickshire, Shakespeare's native county. The text was kept virtually intact, and played with great emphasis on quiet speaking in relative close-shot, the lines post-synchronized with indoor acoustic to achieve maximum clarity in enunciation. Peter Hall had trained his comparatively youthful company in the speaking of Shakespeare as he conceived it – 'thoughtful speech' was his term for it – with an underlying recognition of the iambic pentameter for rhythm (however free Shakespeare's use of it) and with emphasis on the meaning while never losing the overall poetic quality of the lines. In the film, the 'working class' comic players, whose dialogue is in prose, gave highly individualized, naturalistic performances.

The fact that Peter Hall conceived the play as a dark comedy with strong sexual undertones led to a very different interpretation from that of Reinhardt and Dieterle in the 1930s. The autumn when the film was shot was abnormally damp, but exactly suited to the director's purpose – the seasons are, after all, 'out of joint' because the fairies (conceived as woodland spirits) are quarreling. The fairies were given a dull green skin coloring and scanty clothing, while Puck is a mischievous, Halloween figure played with relish by Ian Holm. The magic of their movements is of the simplest – they appear and disappear in a trice with a sound like an arrow loosed from a bow.

The whole concept of the play, performed *on the dank and dirty ground*, divided the critics, though the present writer thought highly of the film which, like Olivier's *Othello*, received its first release on American television in 1969, and remains mostly appreciated by modern student audiences for its anti-romantic comedy. A device frequently used to good effect is the spreading of certain speeches through a variety of locations on the estate, sharp cutting from one place to the next as the speeches proceed. Guy Woolfenden, a frequent composer for the RSC, provided light, atmoshperic music.

KING LEAR (1970)

With the same producer, Lord Birkett, Peter Brook's celebrated production of *King Lear* for the RSC, starring Paul Scofield, which had toured internationally with acclaim, was now adapted for the screen with financial backing from Danish television. Locations in the wintry wastes of northern Jutland resembled the surface of the moon. Rough, timeless costuming and settings (largely constructed on the location) gave the production a primitive, pagan appearance belonging to the 'Dark Ages', a rough-hewn world of its own. As for the text (its full length playing some four and half hours), this had to be drastically cut; it was even considered at one stage dispensing with it altogether after the manner of Kurosawa's version of *Macbeth*,

and the poet, Ted Hughes, was invited to experiment with 'translating' it for modern audiences with new dialogue. Eventually, Peter Brook wrote an action treatment without dialogue into which Shakespeare's lines were later inserted.

In addition to Paul Scofield, many of the cast came from the original stage production – for example Irene Worth (Goneril), Alan Webb (Gloucester), and Tom Fleming (Kent). Other key members of the cast included Susan Engel (Regan), Anne-Lise Gabold (Cordelia), Patrick Magee (Cornwall), Cyril Cusack (Albany), Ian Hogg (Edmund), Robert Lloyd (Edgar), and Jack MacGowran (Fool).

Scofield's Lear, with his gruff, chesty voice with an occasional break of pitch revealing extreme old age, and introducing ominous pauses and silences, and a fight for words adequate to express his rage, is one of the great performances of our time, and its record on film is of major importance. After the experience of *A Midsummer Night's Dream*, close-ups are used more sparingly, but the special stylization favored by Brook – now a profile, now even the back of a head – all emphasize the disintegration of Lear's

Peter Hall's A Midsummer Night's Dream *gave due weight to the poetry of the play.*

innate power and the senility that collapses finally into madness.

The surreal truths about his condition spoken by his beloved Fool as they bump together over the roadless countryside in a primitive wagon, are uttered softly, intimately. Lear gains new measures of perception when abandoned in the elemental storm, floundering through the mists and the mud and the drowned rats in this naked, cruel landscape. Treatment of the famous storm speech is stylized, deeply moving, and extremely powerful.

In this film, the great problem of the play in stage production, how to deal with the intricacies of the counterplot, coming so late in the action and with the leading figure so long absent from the stage, is succinctly resolved after the wonderful, if lengthy scene between the mad king and the blinded Gloucester played on wide, empty sands by the ocean. The film was beautifully photographed in black-and-white by the Danish cameraman, Henning Kristiansen. This, like Peter Hall's *A Midsummer Night's Dream* remains one of the most effective of the film adaptations of a Shakespearean play.

OTHER ADAPTATIONS

Other notable adaptations include Zeffirelli's witty, vigorous near-burlesque version of *The Taming of the Shrew*, an American-Italian production with Richard Burton as a Rabelaisian Petruchio and Elizabeth Taylor a termagent Shrew. Burton and Taylor co-produced the film with Zeffirelli, and it contained an outstanding performance by Michael Hordern as the father of the Shrew, permanently on the verge of nervous breakdown at the sight of his daughter. The film seemed like a parallel to the Burton-Taylor film of *Who's Afraid of Virginia Woolf?*, released the same year (1966).

In contrast, Frank Dunlop's lengthy adaptation of *The Winter's Tale* (produced by Peter Snell) also made in 1966 was expanded from a production presented at the Edinburgh Festival and recorded in continuous close-up for the television market. Laurence Harvey played Leontes, but the acting in general seemed undistinguished.

HAMLET (1964, 1969)

A far more interesting experiment in filming a successful stage production was Tony Richardson's adaptation of *Hamlet* (1969) as presented at the Round House, with Nicol Williamson as the Prince.

Hamlet and Horatio are interpreted as university scholars of mature years, Nicol Williamson particularly playing the Prince as a kind of neurotic outsider, speaking in a quick, nervous, querulous voice, angry and emotionally distraught alike with his Mother and Ophelia (Marianne Faithful), who has a kind of knowing, almost sexual relationship with her somewhat lecherous brother, Laertes, and suggesting a more intimate relationship with Hamlet than is traditional.

In another dimension of value as a record is the Hamlet of Richard Burton (1964), a direct, from-the-stage recording, with an audience present, of this great actor's performance under the direction of John Gielgud in New York. This was undertaken experimentally and is somewhat indifferent for sound.

ANTONY AND CLEOPATRA (1972)

Peter Snell also produced Charlton Heston's internationally sponsored adaptation of *Antony and Cleopatra*. Heston himself is impressive as the aging Antony, but his Cleopatra (Hildegard Neil), though young and beautiful, is no match for him. Enobarbus is finely played by Eric Porter.

THE TEMPEST (1980)

Derek Jarman's camped-up version of *The Tempest*, backed by Elizabeth Welsh (as the Goddess) singing 'Stormy Weather' with a chorus of white-clad sailors, seemed at times some kind of burlesque of this deeply-felt play. Its setting in the empty and dilapidated Palladian Stoneleigh Abbey in Warwickshire seems deliberately bedraggled. It is interesting that the tempest is a nightmare dreamed by Prospero.

SEE ALSO: Ch 4 96-7, 102-5, 108-13, 118-23, 132-3, 140-3, 158-65, 172-5, Ch 7 235-6, Ch 8 256

THE SOUND FILM FOREIGN LANGUAGE SHAKESPEAREAN FILMS

Foreign language Shakespearean films have been made in a number of countries, notably Russia and Japan. Of these the most outstanding are those adapted by two anglophile Russian directors of the highest rank, Sergei Yutkevitch and Grigori Kozintsev, and by Akira Kurosawa, the distinguished Japanese director with a marked dynamic style of his own. Kozintsev was a Shakespearean scholar, and author of two books (both translated), *Shakespeare: Time and Conscience*, and *King Lear: the Space of Tragedy*. Yutkevitch, like Kurosawa, was also a painter and set designer.

THE RUSSIAN ADAPTATIONS

Yutkevitch's approach to *Othello* challenged that of Orson Welles. 'I start from life, Welles from death,' he said. His *Othello* was photographed in the softly tinted colors of the Sovcolor process, sensitive to half-lights. His Othello is the star actor, Sergei Bondarchuk, best known internationally for his later grand scale production of *War and Peace*, in which he played Pierre. Bondarchuk's Othello, a large, handsome, romantic figure, dark-faced in his flowing white robes, gave a splendidly positive start to Yutkevitch's film, the adventurous tales which won him Desdemona's love pictured in a montage sequence and followed by their secret marriage in warm Venetian settings (with Cassio as their close aide), soon to be followed by their removal to Cyprus.

Andrei Popov gives Iago a sinister appearance, his mouth twisted when smiling, and he picks up Desdemona's dropped handkerchief (an important motif much emphasized in the film) while they are still in Venice. Othello arrives in Cyprus, leaping up the succession of rampart steps, his huge red cloak wind-blown behind him, to

Grigori Kozintsev's King Lear *(1970) is an impressive adaptation, with a powerful clarity of purpose. That Kozintsev himself is a Shakespearean scholar is apparent in his treatment.*

clasp Desdemona (already there) in his arms. Breaking this lyrical, romantic atmosphere is Iago's distorted face; his evil, calculating jealousy is central to Yutkevitch's interpretation of the play. Othello's motif is less jealousy than the unquestioning trust he puts in Iago, for whom Yutkevitch uses spoken thought, his face at one time mirrored in well-water. In one symbolic scene, Iago subtly goads Othello as they walk by the sea among festoons of suspended fishing nets – as Othello's suspicions of Desdemona deepen, he seems ever more enmeshed in the hanging nets.

Filmed on location on the Crimean coast, the vast white structure used for the citadel, with its patios and porticos, provides wonderful pictorial backgrounds to Othello's successive scenes with Iago and Desdemona, culminating in the use of a great galleon anchored in the harbor, from which Othello is induced by Iago to spy on Desdemona's meeting with Cassio. The mobile camera is used fluently throughout, with numerous tracking shots and panoramic views, Othello's statuesque figure dominating the scene. The richly orchestrated score by Aram Khachaturian under-

Andrei Popov, a sinister Iago, contrasts with Sergei Bondarchuk's romantic Othello in Sergei Yutkevitch's exciting and fluent adaptation.

lines every emotional climax; organ music accompanies the smothering of Desdemona, a symbolic wind blowing out the candle by the bed; after the act, Othello's hair magically turns white, just as his eyes turn incandescent when the truth of Iago's deception is borne in upon him.

GRIGORI KOZINTSEV

Kozintsev's two Shakespearean adaptations, *Hamlet* and *King Lear*, each occupied some four years in the making. Far more austere in conception than Yutkevitch's *Othello*, they were filmed in black-and-white on bleak locations in Estonia along the Baltic coast, using non-Russian actors for the most part from that area. The translations were by Boris Pasternak, rendered into modern prose. The music for both films was by Dimitri Shostakovich.

Hamlet is conceived as a mature scholar dedicated to his work at the celebrated German university of Wittenberg; on his father's sudden death he is forced to return most unwillingly to Denmark, followed soon after by his Danish friend and fellow-scholar, Horatio. The poetry of the play (muted by Pasternak's prose) was to be established, in Kozintsev's view, by the visuals he devised and his use throughout the film of basic symbolisms.

Hamlet (Innokenti Smoktunovsky) is a grave man, mature and meditative, his soliloquies spoken thought as he wanders, an alien soul, among the crude and pleasure-loving courtiers of Claudius's court. Claudius (Michail Nazwanov) is a 'bloat' and powerful figure, an able if self-indulgent monarch, tough and scheming. The Ghost is a vast apparition, gliding along the ramparts, his long cloak flowing in the night wind; his eyes glow as he towers over Hamlet, while afterwards, like Olivier's Hamlet, Kozintsev's lies prone on the ground. Much is made of the King's spies, Rosencrantz and Guildenstern, giving a political touch to the drama, while Hamlet (after disposing of them on shipboard to England) returns to the earth of Denmark in simple worker's garb, a man of the people not a prince of the court. Ophelia, small and wraithlike in her pitiful madness, creeps through the ranks of

ACROSS CULTURES

Interesting adaptations of the Shakespearean story-line of *Macbeth* to accommodate Japanese tradition involve the treatment of the supernatural in Kurosawa's film. With no witches in Japanese culture, the supernatural is represented by an old woman of the woods, a traditional Japanese evil spirit, who enunciates the prophecies.

Washizu and Miki are initially lost on horseback in Cobweb forest on their return from the wars, and it is to this place of potential terror, confusing like a maze and accompanied by eerie chanting and the mocking laughter of the Evil One, that Washizu is drawn to solicit a further spur to his ambition. The castle he takes over is called the Castle of the Spider's Web, and is situated near the maze-like forest, seat of the evil spirit who betrays him. The film opens and closes with a dire, fatalistic chant, its theme, 'Ambition destroys', intoned as the camera passes over the wasteland where Cobweb Castle once stood.

Claudius's armored guards.

Kozintsev's *King Lear* is an equally impressive film, like his *Hamlet* one of the great screen versions of Shakespeare's plays. His Lear, Yuri Yarvet, an Estonian actor of relatively slight build and with a face like that of Voltaire, was unable to speak Russian and learned his lines phonetically. As with Peter Brook's adaptation, the complications of the subplot are far better clarified and resolved than can easily be achieved on the stage. The underlying theme is clear – the land and its people under Lear's tyranny and his daughters' misrule have been reduced to beggary and it is to this pass that Lear too must be reduced to learn the truth about himself. Thereafter the forces of 'right' have to take charge once Cordelia and Lear are dead. Kozintsev sees Albany as a scholar who realizes that he must rejoin the supporters of justice; he also allows the Fool – Lear's truthteller in the absence of Cordelia, whom Shakespeare abandons after Lear acquires, through the purgation of insanity, a new sense of social justice – to remain 'on stage' as a melancholy pipe-player accompanying Lear's awakening in Cordelia's tent. It is the Fool who closes the film, a solitary figure abandoned amid the ruins.

AKIRA KUROSAWA

Many Shakespeareans (including Peter Hall and Peter Brook) have stated they believe Kurosawa's adaptation of *Macbeth* to be the best of all Shakespearean films –though it involved total removal of the story to 16th-century Japan (when a period of inter-clan-like civil wars paralleled those of Macbeth's Scotland), and most drastic of all, an entire re-scripting of the dialogue in slightly stylized modern Japanese prose without a line taken from Shakespeare.

CASTLE OF THE SPIDER'S WEB (THRONE OF BLOOD) (1957)

Kurosawa created his own treatment of the story, making the film with minimal dialogue and a heavy stress on atmosphere and action. Filmed in black-and-white, using period Japanese architecture, armor and costume, the visual effect is continuously striking pictorially. The acting and make-up are stylized, influenced by Noh though not acted strictly in that tradition.

The maverick Japanese actor, Toshiro Mifune (now an international star) plays Washizu (Macbeth) in a fiercely intense manner, a man of few words but of sudden, violent action, a relatively youthful warrior-general in the service of his Lord, whom he murders in order to seize his place. Asaji (Lady Macbeth) is played with quiet, immobile authority by the distinguished stage actress, Isuzu Yamada, her face made up like a Noh mask.

Her influence over Washizu comes from her greater age; she at once controls and directs his impulsiveness in the few moments of dialogue they have together, she seated on the ground, he pacing furiously. The scene culminating in the off-screen murder of the Lord is carried out wordlessly, Washizu shaking with terror, and is followed by an outburst of violent action when Asaji's calculated cries rouse the castle. It is a supreme moment in the film, as indeed is the banquet at which Washizu, now lord of Cobweb Castle, sees the ghost of the murdered Miki (Banquo), and his later discovery, when Fate has turned against him, of Asaji washing her hands in feverish hallucination, and his final, prolonged death at the hands of his own warriors, transfixed by a festoon of slender arrows, one seen directly piercing his throat on screen. The music, used with great restraint throughout the film, has moments of quiet tunefulness, but is mostly instrumental phrasing and percussion effects in traditional Japanese style.

RAN (1985)

The final achievement of finance to make *Ran* ('Chaos', *King Lear*) fulfilled a long-held ambition for Kurosawa, then aged 74. Once again the story is adapted in Japanese terms; this is a 16th-century samurai King Lear (Hidetora, played by Tatsuya Nakadai). Three sons are substituted for Lear's three daughters, Taro, Jiro, and Saburo; two seek to betray their aged, senile father, the ruler who divests himself of power in their favor while banishing the youngest, Saburo, for opposing his will. Goneril and Regan are combined into a single, demonically-inspired woman, Lady Kaede (Mieko Harada), wife of the eldest son, Taro, and lover of Jiro.

Kurosawa's second great Shakespearean film – at $12 million the most expensive ever produced in Japan and co-sponsored by Buñuel's former French producer, Serge Silberman – abandons Shakespeare's verbal poetry entirely to recreate *King Lear* in terms of Kurosawa's own philosophy: the betrayal of the human species by those who seek power by wholly destructive means.

BORROWING FROM SHAKESPEARE

I have neither the space nor the intention to discuss the 'look-alike' films which have taken specific plays and produced parallels to them with either borrowed characters or borrowed plots. Outstanding among these have been André Cayatte's *Les Amants de Vérone* (1948, *Romeo and Juliet*), Ken Hughes's *Joe Macbeth* (1955), F.M. Wilcox's *Forbidden Planet* (1956, *The Tempest*), Peter Ustinov's *Romanoff and Juliet* (1960), Robert Wise's *West Side Story* (1961, *Romeo and Juliet*), Andrzej Wajda's *The Siberian Lady Macbeth* (1961), and Claude Chabrol's *Ophélia* (1962). Nor have I space to discuss Jiri Trnka's feature-length Czech puppet version of *A Midsummer Night's Dream* (1959), with its fine animation techniques.

NOTABLE TELEVISION PRODUCTIONS

BBC television productions of quality go back to the 1940s, from such individual presentations as George More O'Ferrall's *Hamlet* (1947), and Royston Morley's *King Lear* (1948) to the beginning of Shakespearean television repertory, with Peter Dews' BBC-TV *Age of Kings* (1961) in 15 one-hour parts, encompassing *King Richard II*, the two parts of *King Henry IV*, *King Henry V*, the three parts of *King Henry VI*, and *King Richard III*, followed by the BBC's *Spread of the Eagle* (1963), making nine one-hour performances out of the Roman plays. There was Christopher Plummer's notable *Hamlet*, directed by Philip Saville on location at Kronberg Castle in the quatercentennial year (1964), and Michael Barry's serialized production, 1964-65 of *King Henry VI* (Parts 1, 2 and 3) and *King Richard III*, known as *The Wars of the Roses*, adapted from the Peter Hall and John Barry productions for the RSC.

There was also a notable, light-hearted production in color of *The Tempest* for American television directed by George Schaefer in 1960 with a remarkable cast – Maurice Evans (Prospero), Richard Burton (Caliban), Roddy McDowall (Ariel), and Lee Remick (Miranda). More recently we have had Laurence Olivier in the Granada Television production of *King Lear* directed by Michael Elliott, and the ambitious undertaking by BBC-TV to produce all the Shakespeare canon in seasons of plays spread over several years, beginning in 1979.

The results vary, but the investment in money and resources in these ambitious television productions shows that Shakespeare remains the supreme 20th-century screenwriter as well as playwright.

Akira Kurosawa's Ran *is a tour de force in translating the poetry of* King Lear *into visual terms. It received great critical acclaim in the West.*

Shakespeare's Lear has laid waste the land through selfish tyranny, and handed over this wasteland to his daughters who continue to ravage it and its people in civil strife. Hidetora and his two elder sons reduce their world to a kind of existential chaos of destruction; brother wars against brother, and both against their father. The panoplied ranks of their soldiers in their distinctive, heraldic colorings have the beauty of angels – but angels of destruction, bright against the sky that turns from blue to grey over the blackened earth beneath, while fire destroys the fortresses of power. Kurosawa's fatalistic film is performed on an epic, timeless scale of its own, the battles sometimes waged in steely silence. Taking his full cue from Shakespeare, Kurosawa has created a new hell on earth, a hell conceived in visual splendor, but unlike Shakespeare he leaves no hint that power might pass to better men and the wasteland be restored. Kurosawa's god-like eye views man's self-destruction with a detached objectivity.

It would seem now that the grand period of Shakespearean adaptation for the

cinema (from Olivier's *Henry V* to Kurosawa's *Ran* – a 40 year span) may well be over, with ever-increasing costs balking potential producers. But this is not true of television, a good medium for the intimate, less spectacular aspects of the plays.

SEE ALSO: Ch 4 158-63, Ch 8 251- 2

READING LIST

Chapter 1 THE ELIZABETHAN WORLD

S. Adams (ed.) *Elizabeth I: Most Politick Princess*
P. Collinson *The Religion of Protestants*
S. G. Ellis *Tudor Ireland*
C. Haigh (ed.) *The Reign of Elizabeth*
D. M. Hirst *Authority and Conflict: England 1603-58*
P. Johnson *Elizabeth I: a study in power and intellect*
D. M. Palliser *The Age of Elizabeth*
D. B. Quinn & A. N. Ryan *England's Sea Empire, 1550-1642*
A. G. R. Smith *The Emergence of a Nation State*
R. Strong *The Cult of Elizabeth: Elizabethan Portraiture and Pageantry*
C. Wilson *Queen Elizabeth and the Revolt of the Netherlands*
K. Wrightson *English Society, 1580-1680*

Chapter 2 SHAKESPEARE'S LIFE

The judicious and scholarly books by S. Schoenbaum must head any list on Shakespeare's life. *William Shakespeare: A Documentary Life* (1975) has a revised compact edition 1987; see also *William Shakespeare: Records and Images*, and *Shakespeare's Lives*.
T. W. Baldwin *William Shakespere's Small Latine & Lesse Greeke* 2 vols.
G. E. Bentley *Shakespeare: A Biographical Handbook*
E. K. Chambers *William Shakespeare: A Study of Facts and Problems* 2 vols.
M. M. Reese *Shakespeare: His World and His Work*

Chapter 3 ELIZABETHAN & JACOBEAN THEATER

J. Arden 'On playwrights and playwriting' from *To Present the Pretence*
D. Bevington *From Mankind to Marlowe*
M. Bradbrook *The Rise of the Common Player*
A. Gurr *The Shakespearean Stage*
M. Hattaway *Elizabethan Popular Theatre*
C. Leech & T. W. Craik (eds.) *The Revels History of Drama in English*

vols 3 & 4
A. M. Nagler *Shakespeare's Stage*
P. Thomson *Shakespeare's Theatre*
G. Wickham *Shakespeare's Dramatic Heritage*

Chapter 4 THE PLAYS

SOURCES
Geoffrey Bullough (ed.) *Narrative and Dramatic Sources of Shakespeare* 8 vols
Emrys Jones *The Origins of Shakespeare*

THE EARLY PLAYS
Edward Berry *Shakespeare's Comic Rites*
M. C. Bradbrook *The Growth and Structure of Elizabethan Comedy*
M. C. Bradbrook *Themes and Conventions of Elizabethan Tragedy*
Nicholas Brooke *Shakespeare's Early Tragedies*
John Russell Brown & Bernard Harris (eds.) *Early Shakespeare*
Keir Elam *Shakespeare's Universe of Discourse*
A. C. Hamilton *The Early Shakespeare*
Leo Salingar *Shakespeare and the Traditions of Comedy*
Kristian Smidt *Unconformities in Shakespeare's Early Comedies*
Ann Thompson *Shakespeare's Chaucer*

THE HISTORIES
D. Bevington *Tudor Drama and Politics*
W. Clemen *A Commentary on Shakespeare's 'Richard III'*
D. L. Frey *The First Tetralogy: Shakespeare's Scrutiny of the Tudor Myth*
H. Jenkins *The Structural Problem in Shakespeare's 'Henry IV'*
E. Jones *The Origins of Shakespeare*
H. A. Kelly *Divine Providence in the England of Shakespeare's Histories*
M. Manheim *The Weak King Dilemma in the Shakespearean History Play*
R. B. Pierce *Shakespeare's History Plays: the Family and the State*
I. Ribner *The English History Play in the Age of Shakespeare*
D. Riggs *Shakespeare's Heroical Histories: 'Henry VI' and its Literary Tradition*
A. P. Rossiter *Angel with Horns*
P. Saccio *Shakespeare's English Kings: History, Chronicle and Drama*
E. M. W. Tillyard *Shakespeare's History Plays*
S. Wells (ed.) *Shakespeare Survey 38*
J. Dover Wilson *The Fortunes of Falstaff*

THE COMEDIES
Ralph Berry *Shakespeare's Comedies:*

Explorations in Form
John Russell Brown *Shakespeare and his Comedies*
Lawrence Danson *The Harmonies of 'The Merchant of Venice'*
Bertrand Evans *Shakespeare's Comedies*
Northrop Frye *A Natural Perspective: The Development of Shakespearean Comedy and Romance*
R. Chris Hassel *Faith and Folly in Shakespeare's Romantic Comedies*
J. Dennis Huston *Shakespeare's Comedies of Play*
Clifford Leech *'Twelfth Night' and Shakespearean Comedy*
Alexander Leggatt *Shakespeare's Comedy of Love*
J. R. Mulryne *Shakespeare 'Much Ado About Nothing'* (Studies in English Literature 16)
Ruth Nevo *Comic Transformations in Shakespeare*
Leo Salingar *Shakespeare and the Traditions of Comedy*

THE ROMAN PLAYS
Harley Granville Barker *Prefaces to Shakespeare* First Series
Ralph Berry 'The Metamorphoses of *Coriolanus*' *Shakespeare Quarterly* XXVI
Maurice Charney (ed.) *Discussions of Shakespeare's Roman Plays*
David Daniell *Coriolanus in Europe*
Emrys Jones *Scenic Form in Shakespeare*
G. Wilson Knight *The Imperial Theme*
Jan Kott *Shakespeare Our Contemporary*
Margaret Lamb *'Antony and Cleopatra' on the English Stage*
M. W. MacCallum *Shakespeare's Roman Plays and their Background*
Kenneth Muir (ed.) *Shakespeare the Dramatist*
John Palmer *Political Characters of Shakespeare*
Michael Scott *'Antony and Cleopatra': Text and Performance*
T. J. B. Spencer (ed.) *Shakespeare's Plutarch*
D. A. Traversi *The Roman Plays*

THE PROBLEM PLAYS
Nigel Alexander *Measure for Measure*
J. W. Bennett *Measure for Measure as Royal Entertainment*
M. C. Bradbrook *Shakespeare the Craftsman*
Reuben Brower *Hero and Saint*
Francelia Butler *The Strange Critical Fortunes of 'Timon of Athens'*
R. W. Chambers *Man's Unconquerable Mind*
Bertrand Evans *Shakespeare's Comedies*

E. A. J. Honigmann 'Timon of Athens' in *Shakespeare Quarterly* 12
W. W. Lawrence *Shakespeare's Problem Comedies*
A. D. Nuttall *'Measure for Measure: Quid Pro Quo' Shakespeare Studies* IV
J. G. Price *The Unfortunate Comedy*
I. A. Richards 'Troilus and Cressida and Plato' in *Speculative Instruments*
E. Schanzer 'The Marriage Contracts' in *Measure for Measure' Shakespeare Survey* 13
D. L. Stevenson *The Achievement of Shakespeare's 'Measure for Measure'*
Gary Taylor *Troilus and Cressida*
Ann Thompson *Shakespeare's Chaucer*
Patricia Thomson 'Rant and Cant in *Troilus and Cressida' Essays and Studies* 22

THE TRAGEDIES
A. C. Bradley *Shakespearean Tragedy*
H. B. Charlton *Shakespearean Tragedy*
Terry Eagleton *William Shakespeare*
Robert Heilman *This Great Stage*
Robert Heilman *Magic in the Web*
G. Wilson Knight *The Wheel of Fortune*
L. C. Knights *Some Shakespearean Themes*
Jan Kott *Shakespeare Our Contemporary*
R. Ornstein *The Moral Vision of Jacobean Tragedy*
Matthew N. Proser *The Heroic Image in Five Shakespearean Tragedies*
Caroline Spurgeon *Shakespeare's Imagery*

THE ROMANCES
Dennis Bartholomeusz *'The Winter's Tale' in Performance in England and America 1611-1976*
Howard Felperin *Shakespearean Romance*
Northrop Frye *A Natural Perspective*
Frank Kermode *The Last Plays*
G. Wilson Knight *The Crown of Life*
D. J. Palmer (ed.) *Shakespeare's Later Comedies*
E. C. Pettet *Shakespeare and the Romance Tradition*
Hallett Smith *Shakespeare's Romances*

COLLABORATION
Pollard *et al Shakespeare's Hand in The Play of Sir Thomas More*
Kenneth Muir *Shakespeare as Collaborator*
S. Schoenbaum *Internal Evidence and Elizabethan Dramatic Authorship*.

THE TEXT
The First Folio of Shakespeare – The Norton Facsimile (Charlton Hinman)
Shakespeare Quarto Facsimiles
P. Alexander *Shakespeare's Henry VI and Richard III*
F. Bowers *Bibliography and Textual Criticism*
W. W. Greg *The Editorial Problem in Shakespeare*
Charlton Hinman *The Printing and Proof Reading of the First Folio of Shakespeare*
Ernst Honigmann *The Stability of Shakespeare's Text*
A. W. Pollard *Shakespeare's Fight with the Pirates*
J. K. Walton *The Quarto Copy for the First Folio of Shakespeare*

Chapter 5 SHAKESPEARE IN PERFORMANCE
David Addenbrooke *The Royal Shakespeare Company: the Peter Hall Years*
John Barton *Playing Shakespeare*
Bernard Beckerman *Shakespeare at the Globe 1599-1609*
Ralph Berry *On Directing Shakespeare*
John Russell Brown *Free Shakespeare*
Richard David *Shakespeare in the Theatre*
Alan C. Dessen *Elizabethan Stage Conventions and Modern Interpreters*
Richard Foulkes (ed.) *Shakespeare and the Victorian Stage*
Andrew Gurr *The Shakespearean Stage 1574-1642*
Alan Hughes *Henry Irving, Shakespearean*
T. C. Kemp and J. C. Trewin *The Stratford Festival*
W. Moelwyn Merchant *Shakespeare and the Artist*
G. C. D. Odell *Shakespeare from Betterton to Irving* 2 vols
William Poel *Shakespeare in the Theatre*
Jocelyn Powell *Restoration Theatre Production*
Cecil Price *Theatre in the Age of Garrick*
Gámini Salgádo (ed.) *Eyewitnesses of Shakespeare*
Robert Speaight *Shakespeare on the Stage*
Arthur Colby Sprague *Shakespearian Players and Performers*
Peter Thomson *Shakespeare's Theatre*
J. C. Trewin *Benson and the Bensonians*
Stanley Wells *Royal Shakespeare*
William Winter *Shakespeare on the Stage* 3 vols

Chapter 6 POETRY
Ian Donaldson *The Rapes of Lucretia: A Myth and its Transformations*
P. Edwards, I-S Ewbank & G. K. Hunter (eds.) *Shakespeare's Styles: Essays in Honour of Kenneth Muir*
Keir Elam *Shakespeare's Universe of Discourse: Language Games in the Comedies*
Gerald Hammond *The Reader and Shakespeare's Young Man Sonnets*
G. R. Hibbard *The Making of Shakespeare's Dramatic Poetry*
R. A. Lanham *The Motives of Eloquence: Literary Rhetoric in the Renaissance*
J. W. Lever 'Shakespeare's Narrative Poems' in *A New Companion to Shakespeare Studies*
M. M. Mahood *Shakespeare's Wordplay*
George Rylands 'Shakespeare the Poet' in *A Companion to Shakespeare Studies*
Hallet Smith *Elizabethan Poetry: A Study in Convention, Meaning and Expression*
Ann & John O. Thompson *Shakespeare: Meaning and Metaphor*

Chapter 7 MUSIC & SONG
E. W. Naylor *Shakespeare and Music*
R. Noble *Shakespeare's Use of Song*
S. Northcote *Byrd to Britten: A Survey of English Song*
F. W. Sternfeld *Music in Shakespearian Tragedy*
D. Stevens *A History of Song*
J. Stevens *Music and Poetry in the Early Tudor Court*

Chapter 8 SHAKESPEARE ON FILM
Robert Hamilton Ball *Shakespeare on Silent Film*
Brenda Cross (ed.) *The Film Hamlet*
Alan Dent (ed.) *Hamlet: The Film and the Play*
Charles W. Eckert *Focus on Shakespeare Films*
Jack. J. Jorgens *Shakespeare on Film*
Grigori Kozintsev *Shakespeare: Time and Conscience*
Grigori Kozintsev *King Lear: the Space of Tragedy*
Michael MacLiammóir *Put Money in Thy Purse*
Roger Manvell *Shakespeare and the Film*
Roger Manvell *Theatre and Film*
Laurence Olivier *Confessions of an Actor: an Autobiography*
Laurence Olivier *On Acting*

INDEX

ACKNOWLEDGMENTS

Mobius International would like to thank the following for their assistance in the production of this book:

Managing editor: Linda Doeser
Art editor: Claire Legemah
Picture researcher: Caroline Lucas
Editorial director: Richard Dawes